Born in 1941 in Tokyo, **Hayao Miyazaki** is known as the 'Japanese Disney', a filmmaker as revered – and as popular – as Walt Disney or Steven Spielberg. Miyazaki, in short, is a true phenomenon in contemporary animation and in contemporary cinema, a director of animated movies that range from the lyrical, whimsical and child-like beauty of *My Neighbor Totoro* and *Ponyo On the Cliff By the Sea* to the epic sweep of *Nausicaä of the Valley of the Wind* and *Princess Mononoke*.

MEDIA, FEMINISM, CULTURAL STUDIES

The Cinema of Hayao Miyazaki
by Jeremy Mark Robinson

Spirited Away: Pocket Guide
by Jeremy Mark Robinson

Princess Mononoke: Pocket Guide
by Jeremy Mark Robinson

The Sacred Cinema of Andrei Tarkovsky
by Jeremy Mark Robinson

Liv Tyler
by Thomas A. Christie

Stepping Forward: Essays, Lectures and Interviews
by Wolfgang Iser

Wild Zones: Pornography, Art and Feminism
by Kelly Ives

The Cinema of Richard Linklater
by Thomas A. Christie

Walerian Borowczyk
by Jeremy Mark Robinson

Andrea Dworkin
by Jeremy Mark Robinson

Cixous, Irigaray, Kristeva: The Jouissance of French Feminism
by Kelly Ives

Julia Kristeva: Art, Love, Melancholy, Philosophy, Semiotics
by Kelly Ives

Luce Irigaray: Lips, Kissing, and the Politics of Sexual Difference
by Kelly Ives

Helene Cixous I Love You: The Jouissance *of Writing*
by Kelly Ives

FORTHCOMING BOOKS
Ghost In the Shell
Legend of the Overfiend
Fullmetal Alchemist
Tsui Hark
The Twilight Saga

JEREMY MARK ROBINSON

HAYAO MIYAZAKI

POCKET GUIDE

CRESCENT MOON

First published 2015.
© Jeremy Mark Robinson 2015.

Printed and bound in the U.S.A.
Set in Helvetica Neue Condensed, 9 on 11 point, and Gill Sans.
Designed by Radiance Graphics.

The right of Jeremy Mark Robinson to be identified as the author of *Hayao Miyazaki* has been asserted generally in accordance with sections 77 and 78 of the Copyright, Designs and Patents Act 1988.

All rights reserved. No part of this book may be reprinted or reproduced, stored in a retrieval system, or transmitted, in any form or by any means, electronic, mechanical, photocopying, recording or otherwise, without permission from the publisher.

British Library Cataloguing in Publication data available for this title.

ISBN-13 9781861715166 (Hbk)
ISBN-13 9781861715173 (Pbk)

Crescent Moon Publishing
P.O. Box 393, Maidstone, Kent
ME14 5XU, Great Britain
www.crmoon.com
cresmopub@yahoo.co.uk

CONTENTS

Acknowledgements *7*
Abbreviations *7*
Illustrations *9*

PART ONE: HAYAO MIYAZAKI

1 The Cinema of Hayao Miyazaki *11*
2 Hayao Miyazaki's Movies and the Japanese Animation Industry *37*
3 Aspects of Hayao Miyazaki's Cinema *55*
   Illustrations *89*

PART TWO: THE MOVIES

4 *The Castle of Cagliostro* *94*
5 *Nausicaä of the Valley of the Wind* *100*
6 *Laputa: Castle In the Sky* *122*
7 *My Neighbor Totoro* *141*
8 *Kiki's Delivery Service* *159*
   Illustrations *169*
9 *Porco Rosso* *192*
10 *Princess Mononoke* *219*
    Illustrations *258*

11 *Spirited Away* 263
12 *Howl's Moving Castle* 304
13 *Ponyo On the Cliff By the Sea* 324
14 *The Wind Rises* 348

PART THREE: ISAO TAKAHATA • STUDIO GHIBLI

15 The Cinema of Isao Takahata *369*
    Illustrations *381*
16 Studio Ghibli's Other Movies *391*

    Appendix: Quotes By Hayao Miyazaki *397*
    Resources *399*
    Availability *404*
    Filmography *405*
    Bibliography *413*

ACKNOWLEDGEMENTS

To the authors and publishers quoted.
Thanks to Peter van der Lugt at GhibliWorld.com.
Thanks to Samuel Deats.
Thanks to Emily for many conversations about Miyazaki.

PICTURE CREDITS

Illustrations are © Hayao Miyazaki. Studio Ghibli. Nibariki. Toho. Tokuma Shoten. Hakuhodo. Geneon. Buena Vista Home Entertainment Japan. Buena Vista Distribution. Walt Disney Pictures. Touchstone. Tokuma International. TMS-Kyokuichi Corporation. Toei Animation. AIP. Wild Bunch. Arista Film. ADV Films. Section 13/ Selecta Vision. Shochiku. Manga Entertainment. Eiko Kadono. New Line Cinema. Lucasfilm. 20th Century Fox. Nippon Animation. Metro-Goldwyn-Mayer. Optimum Releasing. PolyGram. Anime 18. Tokyo Movie Shinsha/ RAI. Manga Video/ Central Park Media.

ABBREVIATIONS

SP   Hayao Miyazaki, *Starting Point*

TP   Hayao Miyazaki, *Turning Point*

M   Helen McCarthy, *Hayao Miyazaki*

C   Dan Cavallaro, *The Anime Art of Hayao Miyazaki*

O   C. Odell & M. Le Blanc, *Studio Ghibli*

Cinema is optimistic because everything is always possible, nothing is ever prohibited: all you need is to be in touch with life.

Jean-Luc Godard

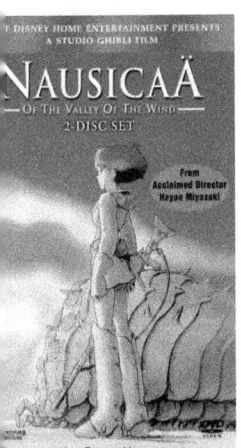

Images of Hayao Miyazaki.
(Top right by Natasha Baucas, 2009.
Second from top left, L.A. Times).
The young Miyazaki (above right).
With his mother (above).
With Toshio Suzuki (second from top).
Isao Takahata (below right). Goro Miyzaki (below left).

PART ONE: HAYAO MIYAZAKI

1

THE CINEMA OF HAYAO MIYAZAKI

> It may sound extreme, but you have to be so obsessed with the work that you think you can change the world if you make this film.
>
> Hayao Miyazaki (TP, 129)

Born on January 5, 1941 in Tokyo, Hayao Miyazaki is known as the 'Japanese Disney',[1] a filmmaker as revered – and as popular – as Walt Disney or Steven Spielberg. Miyazaki, in short, is a true phenomenon in contemporary animation and in world cinema, without equal *anywhere* in animation. Only Osamu Tezuka, the 'god of *manga*', is a comparable figure. The works of Miyazaki and Studio Ghibli[2] have dominated the box office in Japan for 25 years.[3] Miyazaki makes the guys at Disney, Pixar, Warners, Fox, DreamWorks, wherever, look like kids playing in a sand box (and they know it!). As I hope to show in this book, you will see just how remarkable Miyazaki is.

For many people, particularly in the Western world, the first Hayao Miyazaki movie they would have seen would

---

[1] But Miyazaki doesn't like being compared to Walt Disney (TP, 91).
[2] Like the Disney corporation, Ghibli scores high with audiences as a trustworthy brand: it had a trust rating of 43%, and 64.2% when Miyazaki's name was included (in a Toho survey). (J. Clements, 2006, 528).
[3] To the point where 'most other anime features are mere marketing exercises or flashes in the pan', according to J. Clements and H. McCarthy (2006, xxi).

probably be *Princess Mononoke* or *Spirited Away*.4 Those were the two films that really brought Miya-san to the attention of a big audience in the West.5 The first film I saw was *Laputa: Castle In the Sky*, with my son Jake. I think it was on the Film Four cable channel in the U.K. (in the dubbed version). Then followed *Princess Mononoke* and *Spirited Away*, and all the others.

Hayao Miyazaki may be the most talented fantasy filmmaker of his generation: not even the finest filmmakers of Hollywood could rival his films when it came to creating fantasy worlds, and fantastical characters and events.6 Let's get real here – Miyazaki is not only 'unique', 'different', a 'genius' and a 'great artist', he is a filmmaker at a whole other level from any others in the entire history of cinema.

Once you've seen a Hayao Miyazaki animated movie, you don't forget it. What I remember about *Laputa: Castle In the Sky* was a totally original vision, a unique and highly imaginative – and highly individual – blend of existing elements. Oh, we have seen all of the elements in Miyazaki's films before (and *Laputa* doesn't pretend to be anything but a classical adventure story), but not brought together in quite this way, and rarely achieved with such skill, such delicacy, such vision.

As inventive, imaginative cinema, Hayao Miyazaki's films are second to none: *Laputa: Castle In the Sky*, *Kiki's Delivery Service*, *Porco Rosso*, *Spirited Away*, *Princess Mononoke* and *Howl's Moving Castle*.

When you consider Hayao Miyazaki's output as a whole, you are awed by his imagination, which seems almost superhuman. There are perhaps only five or so all-round filmmakers in the whole history of cinema who genuinely possess the force of imagination to create entire worlds (from *scratch*, as *writers* as well as filmmakers, from *original* ideas, not

---

4 *Spirited Away* was one of Hayao Miyazaki's and Studio Ghibli's biggest hits: it was the highest grossing movie in Japanese history; it won numerous awards, including the Oscar for Best Animated Feature, and the critics adored it. Three months after its release, *Spirited Away* had sold one ticket for every six people in Japan. They also adored *Princess Mononoke* (see the reviews at the back of this book). Only a few critics came out against *Princess Mononoke*. For instance, Michael Atkinson in *Mr. Showbiz*) called it 'wacky, vividly conceived but mundanely executed cartoon fantasy'. Nobody who knew any thing about cinema or animation could possibly call *Princess Mononoke* 'mundanely executed'!
5 The Oscar and high profile of *Spirited Away* encouraged a renewed interest in *anime*: Hollywood studios bought up rights to Japanese animated product (Columbia with Katsuhiro (*Akira*) Otomo, and DreamWorks with Satoshi Kon). The works of Miyazaki (and Ghibli) are hugely important in raising awareness of *animé* outside Japan.
6 I agree with Mark Schilling who said that 'none of his contemporaries can equal the richness, depth and strangeness of his imagination' (2004).

adaptations). D.W. Griffith, yes, Orson Welles, yes, Akira Kurosawa, yes... and Miyazaki.

Hayao Miyazaki's cinema is marked by incredible fantasy worlds, which always remained grounded in recognizable realities; magical beings; action-packed adventures; the most astonishing portrayals of flight and flying machines in cinema; secret worlds and hidden dimensions; a passionate evocation of the wonders of the natural world, with a mystical reverence for elemental forces (embodied in animal spirits, or trees, or water, or clouds, or dragons); eccentric minor characters (with powerful, crazy, old women and crusty, old men a speciality); and young people (often girls) as the central characters. Miyazaki's films are very optimistic and life-affirming,[7] and celebrate the joy of being alive.

And, not least, Hayao Miyazaki's films are among the most technically breathtaking animated movies ever made. They are instantly recognizable as a Miyazaki or Studio Ghibli product – no one else makes movies like this.[8]

What Hayao Miyazaki's movies do is to bring you completely into a fantasy world that is instantly recognizable and familiar. It's as if these fantasy realms *have always existed* – very like J.R.R. Tolkien's Middle-earth or Ursula Le Guin's Earthsea (both influences on Miyazaki). The visionary and magical elements are fused with the domestic and familial and social elements, so that it seems completely ordinary and believable that, say, flying machines soar overhead which have flapping wings like an insect, or that little, white creatures pop up out of ancient trees.[9]

In Hayao Miyazaki's fantasy cinema, the immersion in the world is total, and there's nothing to lift you out of it.[10] The films of Miyazaki and his teams guide you into the filmic world with such confidence and such flair and imagination, you are happy to step inside. Partly it's because, as with the fantasy realms of Tolkien or Le Guin, Miyazaki and his teams are drawing on a long and detailed tradition of fantasy – in literature, mythology and folk tales as well as cinema. It is, in short, partly the realm of fairy tales, the classic fantasy worlds that

---

[7] Isao Takahata described Miyazaki as someone 'who never runs from or slacks off at work, who hates defeatism and who is always optimistic' (2009, 455).

[8] 'He is responsible for the entire top tier of anime's undisputed masterworks and has brought the pleasures of Japanese animation to a worldwide audience as no anime director before or since has done', noted Brian Camp in *Zettai* (21).

[9] One of the hallmarks of *manga* and Japanese entertainment was 'twisting both time and space', Miyazaki said, in order to 'create a more fantastic, magical world' (SP, 99).

[10] No winks at the camera, no sending up, no intrusive movie allusions or pop culture quotes. Let's just have the story as it is, told by a master.

seem to have always existed. It is that world of 'once upon a time', a place where people are put under spells, and magic crystals can keep castles afloat in the sky.

Hayao Miyazaki really enjoys creating imaginary worlds – that joy in creation bounces off the screen in all of his features and TV work. It's about fashioning lies and fakery so intensely it persuades the audience that it's real, that such a world might really exist.[11]

> It's an imaginary world [Miyazaki explained], but it should seem to actually exist as an alternate world, and the people who live there should appear to think and act in a realistic way. (SP, 307)

It's all lies[12] in animation (as in all cinema), Hayao Miyazaki stated in 1979, it's all a fabrication of something that the animators want the audience to believe is real:

> Even if the world depicted is a lie, the trick is to make it seem as real as possible. Stated another way, the animator must fabricate a lie that seems so real viewers will think the world depicted might possibly exist. (SP, 21)

Audiences *want* to believe, of course. They *yearn* to think that some fantasy world can really exist.[13] And they want to go there.

The animated feature films directed by Hayao Miyazaki (with the Japanese release date first) are:

> *The Castle of Cagliostro* (1979), released: December 15, 1979. U.S.A. release: Sept, 1980 and April 4, 1991.
> *Nausicaä of the Valley of the Wind* (1984), released: March 11, 1984. U.S.A. release: June, 1985.
> *Laputa: Castle In the Sky* (1986), released: August 2, 1986. U.S.A. release: July, 1987 and April 1, 1989.
> *My Neighbor Totoro* (1988), released: April 16, 1988. U.S.A. release: May 7, 1993.
> *Kiki's Delivery Service* (1989), released: July 29, 1989. U.S.A. release: May 23, 1998 (video).
> *Porco Rosso* (1992), released: July 20, 1992. U.S.A. release: October 9, 2003.
> *Princess Mononoke* (1997), released: July 12, 1997.

---

11 The world being created by the filmmakers can take on a 'greater reality than that of our own ordinary lives', Miyazaki said (TP, 226). And 'when the project is over, it seems as though that world really existed somewhere, and still exists' (ib., 323). 'I have a strong desire to be liberated from being tied down to reality' (TP, 16).

12 'Mixing fiction and nonfiction in a film to dupe the audience is the real thrill of my work' (TP, 81).

13 'I personally believe fantasy is necessary' (TP, 208).

U.S.A. release: October 7, 1999.
Spirited Away (2001), released: July 20, 2001. U.S.A. release: September 20, 2002.
Howl's Moving Castle (2004), released: November 20, 2004. U.S.A. release: June 6, 2005.
Ponyo On the Cliff By the Sea (2008), released: July 19, 2008. U.S.A. release: June 28, 2009.
The Wind Rises (2013), released July 20, 2013. U.S.A. release: February 21, 2014.

These are some of the most remarkable, inventive and entertaining movies in the history of cinema.

When it comes to the source of Hayao Miyazaki's movies, most have been original ideas, and some have been adaptions. The adaptations have included *Howl's Moving Castle*, from British author Diana Wynne-Jones, *The Borrower Arrietty*, from another Brit, Mary Norton (co-written with Keiko Niwa), *Kiki's Delivery Service*, from Eiko Kodana's book, and *The Castle of Cagliostro*, from the Monkey Punch *Lupin III* manga series.

The original scripts that Hayao Miyazaki has written (sometimes with collaborators) have included *Laputa: Castle In the Sky*, *Nausicaä of the Valley of the Wind*, *Porco Rosso*, *My Neighbor Totoro*, *Spirited Away*, *Ponyo On the Cliff By the Sea*, *The Wind Rises* and *Princess Mononoke*. That's two-thirds of Miyazaki's feature movie output: the other films have been based on books or *manga* – *Kiki's Delivery Service*, *Howl's Moving Castle*, and of course *The Castle of Cagliostro*.

To write one hit animation movie is amazing, to write *eleven* is remarkable. To write *and* direct one spectacular animated picture is very impressive, to *write and direct eleven features*, each one a hit (and some enormous hits), is unheard-of in the world of contemporary commercial animation. Toshio Suzuki reminds us that 'hit movies don't happen by accident'. Then add to that storyboarding each movie (a huge undertaking in itself). Then add to that personally overseeing drawings and cels, including drawing key animation, and you simply cannot believe one man can do it all!

And of his 11 movies as director, 5 are widely acknowledged as masterpieces – *Nausicaä*, *Totoro*, *Mononoke*, *Spirited* and *Wind*. I would add *Laputa*, *Kiki*, *Porco* and *Ponyo*. Some would add *Cagliostro*. Which only leaves *Howl*! (And *Howl* has plenty of admirers!).

There's no one in Hollywood or the West with a similar track record. (In the West, for instance, including Hollywood cinema, such as from Disney, Pixar, Warners, DreamWorks, Fox, etc, it's typical for animated movies to have whole teams of writers and story artists. Try finding a major Western animation of recent times in which *one person* created: (1) the concept, (2) the story and characters, (3) the script, (4) the storyboards – yeah, and (5) directed the sucker! Nope, *you won't find a single movie*!. So Hayao Miyazaki really is a one-of-a-kind filmmaker.[14]

Sometimes we might wish that Hayao Miyazaki had been able to produce more movies as a director, rather than the 11 between 1979 and 2011. But that's impossible in animation, and no animation director can deliver the 40, 50 or 60 feature-length movies of filmmakers like Ingmar Bergman, Jean-Luc Godard or Yasujiro Ozu (but if only he had! Imagine *fifty* Miyazaki movies!).[15]

Whatever the source (book, *manga*, etc), however, all of Hayao Miyazaki's films bear a strong imprint from the director himself. It's true that animation, like all filmmaking, is a very collaborative process,[16] and it requires a large team years of hard work to complete one of these feature animated movies.[17] But it's also true that Miyazaki is one of the very, very few film directors working in the animation industry who can truly, properly and authentically be called an *auteur*, an artist who has a major influence on his films (and whose work sustains an *auteur* analysis, who has the way of working, the skills and the talent, the themes, the motifs, the politics and the philosophy that constitute a genuine *auteur*).[18]

There are so many vital talents in making a feature-length animated film, so this is not to underplay the roles of Hayao Miyazaki's producer, Toshio Suzuki, his co-producer at

---

[14] I have been guilty in this book of comparing Hayao Miyazaki and his works too often to Western and North American cinema and TV, as if everything Japanese has to be interpreted and filtered thru Western eyes, instead of on its own terms.
[15] It's like what John Lennon said of the Beatles – we made 11 albums, how could you want more?
[16] Hayao Miyazaki recognized that directors and writers could be over-emphasized in the creation of an animated work. Animation was a team effort, and no element should be over-emphasized while others were ignored (SP, 64). And sometimes there was too much attention given to the original work.
[17] The form of Hayao Miyazaki's animation is cel animation, also known as ink and paint animation, or 2-D animation. It is a traditional form of animated film which is based on drawings and paintings. It is all done by hand, too, with each cel drawn and then painted by hand. The process moves from conceptual sketches to storyboards, to key animation and final drawings.
[18] 'If I'm going to be involved in producing a film, I want to be involved in the smallest details' (TP, 390).

Studio Ghibli,[19] Isao Takahata, or animators such as Kitaro Kousaka, Katsuya Kondô, Masashi Ando, Yoichi Kotabe,[20] Kazuo Komatsubara, Tsukasa Tannai, Akihiro Yamashita, Takeshi Inaumura and Megumi Kagawa, or art director Kazuo Oga,[21] or editor Takeshi Seyama,[22] or composer Joe Hisaishi, or colour designer Michiyo Yasuda, or sound people Toru Noguchi, Shuji Inoue, Kazuhiro Hayashi, Kazuhiro Wakabayashi, and Nobue Yoshinaga. (An important aspect of Miyazaki's career, often over-looked, is how he, Takahata and Ghibli have nurtured the talents of literally 100s of artists in the *animé* industry).

But how many true *auteurs* in feature animation of recent times are there? Not shorts, but 90+ minute features. Jan Svankmajer, certainly; Walerian Borowczyk, certainly; the Quay brothers, certainly; James Selick, perhaps. And then... who?

Of all the great names of film directors in the history of animation – Géorges Méliès, Ladislaw Starewicz, Willis O'Brien, Lotte Reiniger, George Pal, Osamu Tezuka, Tex Avery, Chuck Jones, Jiri Trnka, Paul Grimault, Ralph Bakshi, Jan Svankmajer, Michel Ocelot, and Hayao Miyazaki's friend Isao Takahata – Miyazaki's remains among the greatest. (And *very* few of the great names of animation have directed, written, drawn and storyboarded as many feature-length movies as Miyazaki. And even fewer have achieved the same critical as well as commercial success).

---

19 Studio Ghibli is an animation studio best known for the fantasy films of Hayao Miyazaki, but it also produced other pictures, as well as TV shows, TV specials and commercial work. Studio Ghibli's films, particularly those of director Hayao Miyazaki, are among the most extraordinary pictures ever made, not just in animation, and are easily the equal of the best of Disney's products, including the five films of Disney's 'golden age'.
20 Kotabe's credits include *Heidi, Little Norse Prince, Little Witch Sally, Panda! Go Panda!, Nausicaä* and other Ghibli movies.
21 Kazuo Oga has provided art direction, background art and designs on most of Ghibli's works; prior to Ghibli, Oga worked on *Wicked City, Harmageddon, Urusei Yatsura* and *Dagger of Kamui.*
22 Takeshi Seyama has more formidable credits than any other film editor in Japanese animation: as well as editing most of Miyazaki's movies, they include many masterpieces and celebrated works: Studio Ghibli movies such as *Whisper of the Heart, Tales from Earthsea, From Up On Poppy Hill, Grave of the Fireflies, My Neighbors the Yamadas, Only Yesterday, Arrietty, Pom Poko* and *Ocean Waves*, the Katsuhiro Otomo movies *Akira, Steamboy, Stink Bomb, SOS! Tokyo Metro Explorers, Magnetic Rose* and *Cannon Fodder* – plus *Votoms, Conan, Adventures of Tom Sawyer, Devilman, Dirty Pair Flash, Gintama, Himawari!, Magic User's Club, Beelzebub, Lupin III, Mahoromatic, On Your Mark, Mobile Suit SD Gundam, Paprika, Paranoia Agent, Patlabor WXIII, Serial Experiments Lain, Shamanic Princess, Sherlock Hound, Sakura Wars, Golgo 13, Rurouni Kenshin, Tegami Bachi, Space Pirate Mito, Elfen Lied, Starship Troopers, Tokyo Godfathers, Ultimate Girls, Ultra Nyan, The Whale Hunt, Wizard Barristers, You and Me, Tetsujin 28* and *Little Nemo.*

❖

The world of animation is vast, going back to Géorges Méliès, Winsor McCay and Edwin S. Porter, and taking in experimental and *avant garde* animation, the giants of Eastern Europe (Jan Svankmajer, Karel Zeman, Jiri Trnka, Walerian Borowczyk), to more recent proponents, such as the Quay Brothers, Michel Ocelot, and James Selick, or the use of animation in live-action cinema.[23]

In this study, I refer chiefly to the Western form of entertainment animation, dominated by the Walt Disney Studios, and to Japanese *animé*. Partly because there isn't space here to bring in many other forms of animation, and partly because the Western form of ink and paint animation is generally how Hayao Miyazaki's movies have been received. And also for personal reasons.

This is the third or fourth book available in English about Hayao Miyazaki: when I began writing it (about ten years ago), I thought there would be many books about Miyazaki-san and his astonishing animated works, but no. It's the same with Japanese *animé*: there is very little really good critical work available in the West.

HAYAO MIYAZAKI'S BIOGRAPHY AND CAREER

Hayao Miyazaki grew up during World War Two in Japan, and was evacuated from Tokyo in 1944; he started school in 1947 aged 6, still away from the capital (the Miyazaki family moved back to Tokyo in 1950). At Gakushuin University, Miyazaki studied political science and economics. Politics has always played a significant role in Miyazaki's career. Miyazaki was active in the union at Toei Animation, for example, becoming the Chief Secretary in 1964; at Toei he was involved in a labour dispute in 1964.

The left-leaning slant of Hayao Miyazaki's politics is evident in his cinema – in the depiction of the mining community in *Laputa: Castle In the Sky,* for instance, which drew on the mining town in South Wales that Miyazaki had visited in the 1980s (at the time when Wales and other communities in Britain were struggling to hold onto the mining industry – thanks to Margaret Thatcher and her detestable right-wing regime). Socialism, of the sort that enshrines arts and crafts

---

[23] To the point where some movies, such as the *Star Wars* prequels or *Avatar*, are virtually animated films with live-action figures added to them.

and making things by hand, can be discerned in Miyazaki's cinema in the collective of women that builds Porco Rosso's plane, or the painting and cake-making in *Kiki's Delivery Service*.

Hayao Miyazaki's involvement in left-wing politics would be unusual for someone who works in the animation industry in the West – you just don't find many film directors at the Walt Disney Studios, for instance, advertizing socialist ideology or membership of the Communist Party. No, no, no!

But Hayao Miyazaki became disillusioned with left-wing politics in the form of Marxism in the early 1980s. Miyazaki came to realize that 'Marxism was a mistake, that Marxist materialism was all wrong' (SP, 400). It was a common reaction among many intellectuals in the West, when they saw what was really going on in China with Maoism and in the Soviet Union with Communism, prior to the fall of the Berlin Wall.[24]

Hayao Miyazaki has an ambiguous attitude towards North America (but less to the West in general). It's a familiar position of many Japanese – after all, Amerika is the superpower which oversaw the dropping of two atomic bombs on Japan, to whom Japan lost the Pacific War, who occupied part of Japan, and who instigated the still controversial arms treaty. Miyazaki was furious about the Iraq War, and was unsure whether to accept the Oscar for *Spirited Away*. *Howl's Moving Castle* is partly a post-9/11 movie, and its depictions of war are Miyazaki's answer to the war-mongering of Amerika. (And *The Wind Rises* may've not won the 2013 Oscar because it depicted a designer who was among those responsible for aircraft used in Pearl Harbor).

Japanese movies are often about communities and families rather than individuals, and Hayao Miyazaki's cinema presents many ensembles and groups, with multiple charas 'who make different choices, take different paths in life, and thereby come to different ends', but are united by a common theme, as Gerald Mast and Bruce Kawin note of the typical Japanese film.

The Miyazaki family business was – no surprise here – an aviation company. Hayao Miyazaki's father, Katsuji Miyazaki (1915-93), was one of the directors of the company, which constructed parts for Japanese Zero fighter planes

---

[24] By the 1990s, Miyazaki admitted that he had 'totally forsook Marxism' (1994). Miyazaki saw his involvement with Marxism as a mistake: 'There was a time when I dabbled in the socialist movement, but I must say I was quite naive.' (2013)

during World War 2.[25]

Hayao Miyazaki married a fellow animator, Akemi Ota, in October, 1965;[26] their sons are Goro (b. 1967), who later turned to directing, and Keisuke (b. April, 1969). It was also around this time that Miyazaki met and grew friends with Isao Takahata; Ota and Takahata are perhaps the key collaborators of Miyazaki's career. Wives, husbands or lovers are often overlooked by film critics when discussing the influences on a filmmaker's life, but it's safe to assume that Akemi Ota would have had a considerable influence on Miyazaki's cinema – not least because she is an animator herself.

After he left university in 1963, Hayao Miyazaki joined the Toei Animation company,[27] where he began working in the in-between department, on TV shows such as *Wolf Boy Ken* (1963) and *Watchdog Woof-Woof* (1963). 'I'm basically three quarters an animator' (TP, 57). Miyazaki moved into key animation at Toei, contributing to the TV series *Wind Ninja Boy Fujimaru* (1964). Miyazaki also worked on *Hustle Punch* (1965), and *Rainbow Warrior Robin* (1966).

Other credits of Hayao Miyazaki's include the feature film *The Little Norse Prince* (1968), which was directed by Isao Takahata, the TV series *Little Witch Sally* (1966), *Akko-chan's Secret* (1969), the feature film *Puss In Boots* (1969), *The Impudent Frog* (1971), *Sarutobi Etchan* (1971), and the features *The Flying Ghost Ship* (1969), *Animal Treasure Island* (1971), and *Ali Baba and the 40 Thieves* (1971).

In 1971, Hayao Miyazaki and Isao Takahata left Toei to join A-Production (a.k.a. A-Pro, now Shin'ei Doga). They went on to work for Zuiyo Company (now Nippon Animation). Miyazaki's first film as director, 1979's *The Castle of Cagliostro*, was produced by Tokyo Movie Shinsha. Miyazaki also directed some of the TV episodes of the *Lupin III* series (in 1971) with his colleague Takahata. (This show ran for 23 episodes, and Miyazaki and Takahata worked on 17 episodes as directors).

In the 1970s, Hayao Miyazaki was working in television animation, the backbone of the Japanese animation industry:

---

25 Hayao Miyazaki's father worked at the Miyazaki Airplane Corporation, in Kanuma City, which was owned by his uncle, Miyazaki said, making parts for war planes (not all of the parts worked, either [SP, 208]). Certainly there's an ambiguity about Miyazaki's attitude towards what his father did for a living, in manufacturing machines that were used for war. That plays against Miyazaki's fascination for wars (C, 7).

26 He later joked that during his time at Toei Animation his wife was making more than he was (SP, 323).

27 Toei Doga was founded in 1956, as part of one of the main film studios in Japan, Toei (it changed its name to Toei Animation in 1998). Toei's productions included *Little Norse Prince*, *Ken the Wolf Boy*, *Tiger Mask*, *Little Witch Sally*, *Puss In Boots*, *Pretty Cure* and *One Piece*.

Akado Suzunosuke (1972), *Wilderness Boy Isamu* (1973), *Samurai Giants* (1973), *Alpine Girl Heidi* (1974), *A Dog of Flanders* (1975), *Three Thousand Leagues In Search of Mother* (1976), *Rascal the Raccoon* (1977), *Future Boy Conan* (1978) and *Anne of Green Gables* (1979).

For some of these *terebi* (TV) animated series, Isao Takahata was directing, with Hayao Miyazaki providing concepts, scripts, layouts and key animation:[28] *Three Thousand Leagues In Search of Mother*, *Alpine Girl Heidi* and *Anne of Green Gables*. *Three Thousand Leagues In Search of Mother* was based on Edmondo de Amici's *Cuore* (1886). *Anne of Green Gables* derived from the novels of Lucy Maude Montgomery (early 1900s). *Rascal the Raccoon* (1977) was part of Nippon Animation's *World Masterpiece Theater* TV series, and adapted from Sterling North's writings about his childhood in Wisconsin. Miyazaki worked as a key animator on it (and chiefly as a scenic designer on the other shows).

Alpine Girl Heidi was an important work for both Takahata and Miyazaki, not least because it was successful with audiences and broadcasters. The success led to a feature movie being released, culled, as so often with television *animé*, from the TV episodes re-worked into a feature-length piece. *Heidi* was based on the fiction of Johanna Spyri, and included images of life in the mountains which would influence Miyazaki's later films.

Miyazaki and Takahata collaborated on some short films about the adventures of a panda and his chums, with Takahata directing from designs and a script by Miyazaki: *Panda Go Panda* (*Panda & Child*, 1973), and *The Adventures of Panda and Friends* (1972).[29] *Panda Go Panda* has been re-issued on DVD and video.

Panda Go Panda is fun, colourful, light-hearted; the comedy is typical of Isao Takahata's work. For Hayao Miyazaki fans *Panda Go Panda* looks forward to themes, images and motifs that crop up in later outings. Such as visuals like Mimiko's hair (Dola in *Laputa: Castle In the Sky* has the same wild plaits), or Daddy Panda's wide grin and portly figure,

---

28 Both Takahata and Miyazaki have discussed the issue of whether Miyazaki might've made more movies if he hadn't met Takahata or hadn't worked for Takahata. Miyazaki thought the idea was silly, and he had been quite happy being an animator: 'I had no complaint about being an animator. If I thought about my work at such a level as expressing myself in such a form, or self-display, or showing my personality, I think I could have only done a worse job'.

29 The panda boom of the early 1970s was definitely a factor in the movie: as Hayao Miyazaki recalled, he and Takahata had submitted the proposal for *Panda Go Panda* but heard nothing back until months later, when the arrival of the pandas from China encouraged the producers to commission the film (SP, 408).

which leads on to the giant Totoro.[30]

More important for future Hayao Miyazaki movies, however, are the thematic and narrative elements in *Panda Go Panda*, such as Mimi being essentially an orphan (her grandmother leaves her for a week). It's a recurring theme in Miyazaki's cinema – that young children can survive on their own – it crops up in *Laputa: Castle In the Sky*, for instance, with both Pazu and Sheeta, or Kiki in *Kiki's Delivery Service*, and right up to *Ponyo On the Cliff By the Sea*, where two five year-old children are left on their own.[31]

In 1978 Hayao Miyazaki directed *Future Boy Conan* (a.k.a. *Conan, the Boy In the Future*) for Nippon Animation, one of his important works, and his first TV series as director (Isao Takahata and Keiji Hayakawa were co-directors, and Yasuo Otsuka was animation director). It comprised 26 episodes of 25 minutes each, with a TV movie edited from the series, entitled *Future Boy Conan: The Movie*.[32] *Future Boy Conan* was based on *The Incredible Tide* (1970) by Alexander Key. In 1999 the series was revived as *Future Boy Conan: Taiga Adventure* (directed by Keiji Hayakawa, Miyazaki's former assistant). You will recnogize many elements from *Future Boy Conan* cropping up in *Laputa* and *Nausicaä* (among others).

In 1981 Hayao Miyazaki directed the TV series *Great Detective Holmes* (a.k.a. *Sherlock Hound the Detective*), made as a co-production with R.A.I. TV in Italy.[33] It featured Sherlock Holmes-style capers in a dog world (a world populated only by dog characters). On *Great Detective Holmes* Miyazaki worked with Italian animators, including his friend Marco Pagott (he later named the character of Porco Rosso after Pagott).

Television animation continued into the 1980s and beyond for Hayao Miyazaki, although from *Nausicaä of the Valley of the Wind* onwards much of Miyazaki's work in animation was confined to his own movies: Miyazaki did key animation in *New Adventures of Gigantor* (1980), directed two episodes of *Lupin III* (1980), directed the first six episodes of

---

30 The daddy panda is a big, kind-hearted clown type: as Miyazaki put it, panda 'is a very big-hearted, easygoing character. He makes those around him happy just by being there, without doing anything in particular' (SP, 409).

31 *Panda Go Panda* was a good experience too, in terms of working on the production. And Hayao Miyazaki was delighted when he heard children singing along to the theme song when it was shown at a screening with a *Godzilla* movie. 'I was thrilled. I recall feeling very happy at the sight of those children. And I think it was because of the support of those children that I decided on the kind of work I'd do from then on' (SP, 409).

32 Released 3 months b4 *The Castle of Cagliostro*.

33 *Sherlock Hound* influenced *Steam-boy* (2004), directed by Katsuhiro Otomo; Otomo said they had looked at *Sherlock Hound* for inspiration: 'not an exact copy, but we want to recreate the same sense of Englishness' (2009, 37).

Great Detective Holmes (1981),[34] and contributed key animation to the film *Space Adventure Cobra* (1982) and the TV show *Zorro* (1982).

Hayao Miyazaki formed his own company, Nibariki[35] (Two-Horse Power) in 1984, and Studio Ghibli a little later,[36] with Isao Takahata, Toshio Suzuki and Toru Hara (former president and co-founder of Topcraft, and a producer on *Little Norse Prince*). The first Ghibli Studio was in Kichijoji in Tokyo, the second in Koganei.[37]

In 1995 Hayao Miyazaki and Ghibli made a pop music video for the band Chage and Aska. Entitled 'On Your Mark', it featured a young, female angel who's discovered by a couple of agents of the law who turn out to be her protectors. The animated promo contains numerous Miyazakian motifs, primarily flight, but also flying machines, technology, the military, etc. Miyazaki could easily have produced music videos his whole life – his kind of animation is eminently suitable for music promos, fitting in perfectly with the stream of rapid, colourful imagery on MTV and cable music channels.

MANGA.

The *manga* work of Hayao Miyazaki shouldn't be overlooked: it has provided the basis for feature films such as *Porco Rosso* and *Nausicaä of the Valley of the Wind* and has influenced movies that Miyazaki didn't direct, such as *Tales From Earthsea*. Miyazaki's most prolific years in *manga* were from the early 1980s to the mid-1990s.

Hayao Miyazaki's *manga* includes a history of food on airlines (*Dining In the Air*);[38] *Puss In Boots* (1969); *People of the Desert* (1972), a war piece; *Animal Treasure Island* (1982); *To My Sister* (1983); *The Journey of Shuna* (1983); *Daydream Data Notes* (1984-92), a World War Two story about a German tank commander; *Miscellaneous Notes: The Age of Seaplanes* (1989), which led towards *Porco Rosso*; the World War 2 story

---
[34] There was a short film released in cinemas.
[35] Nibariki was based in Suginami ward in Tokyo (from 1984), and in 1998 in Koganei City.
[36] The first Studio Ghibli film officially was *Laputa: Castle In the Sky*, but *Nausicaä of the Valley of the Wind* (1984) was really the first Studio Ghibli production (although it had been produced at Topcraft).
[37] The animation under the Topcraft ægis had been produced at Asagaya in the Suhinami ward in Tokyo (SP, 443). Topcraft was founded in 1972 by Toru Hara and others. Topcraft produced *Lupin III*, *Little Koala*, *Time Bokan* and *Mazinger Z*, and worked for the American Rankin/ Bass company, creating the animation for its TV specials, such as *The Hobbit*, *The First Easter Rabbit*, *Doctor Snuggles*, *Thundercats*, *Tom Sawyer*, *The Return of the King*, and *20,000 Leagues Under the Sea*.
[38] This was reprinted in Hayao Miyazaki's collection of essays and non-fiction, *Starting-Point*.

The Return of Hans (1994); and *Tiger In the Mire* (1998). Miyazaki and Studio Ghibli have also produced '*Art of*' books for each Ghibli movie, which are useful sources of information.

Manga weren't ideal to turn into movies for reasons such as the multiple plot-lines, Hayao Miyazaki said (SP, 62). And *pace Nausicaä of the Valley of the Wind,* Miyazaki didn't advise anyone to turn a *manga* they'd written and drawn themselves into a movie (SP, 68). Another reason was length: *Nausicaä of the Valley of the Wind* was 1,000 pages long, and *Akira* (by Katsuhiro Otomo) was 2,000 pages.

MORE ON HAYAO MIYAZAKI'S BIOGRAPHY.

What's clear is that Hayao Miyazaki certainly did his time in the trenches of the animation industry, so that by the time he came to direct his own films, he was 38, and had been working in animation for sixteen years. So he knew animation backwards. And it shows: the animation in Miyazaki's cinema is never less than inspired: Miyazaki is a filmmaker who *really* knows what he's doing. And that's important for a storyteller of his kind of pictures – because the audience needs to feel they can trust the storyteller. It's certainly one of the aspects of Miyazaki's cinema that has been vital, I think, to its success: that audiences feel they can trust Miyazaki, that he is going to deliver.

And he does. Oh, he so does.

Hayao Miyazaki is one of those highly talented people who could have had multiple careers. He could have worked lucratively for commercial aviation, for instance, or as an illustrator and animator in advertising, in print or for television. He could have been an ideas man and inventor for many industries. Interior design would have proved another lucrative avenue. And he could have directed pop promos all his life. (Too easy, tho' – not enough challenges for someone like Miyazaki!).

Hayao Miyazaki is well-known as a workaholic and perfectionist director and animator.[39] Miyazaki is very unusual in re-drawing key animation if he isn't satisfied with the quality. He personally checks[40] layouts, and produces his own

---

[39] Takahata praised Miyazaki's work ethic – a 'selfless devotion to work', which encouraged Takahata too (2009, 451). Mamoru Oshii said of Miyazaki: 'he is unbelievably energetic'.

[40] 'I am deeply involved in checking and redrawing and touching up all the work that comes from the animators,' Miyazaki said (TP, 185).

storyboards and imageboards.[41] Miyazaki is one of those film-makers who likes to be involved with every aspect of film production. This means that some of Miyazaki's actual drawings appear in his movies. 'Bear in mind that I'm a director who actually draws animation,' he said in 1993. Unlike Walt Disney, Miyazaki's own drawings appear in his films (Disney was famously a not-so-good artist, and couldn't draw Mickey Mouse, or even his famous signature).

There are costs to this perfectionism, of course, and one is the sheer amount of work that Hayao Miyazaki takes on in producing his movies. If you don't delegate tasks but prefer to do them yourself where possible, you end up slaving away all hours. And animation is a very labour-intensive kind of film-making. Thus, over the years Miyazaki has threatened to retire,[42] or to cut back on his workload.[43] But he was often enticed back into feature film production. Financially, he didn't need to: Miyazaki is a filmmaker who loves to work.

'I practically have a nervous breakdown after I complete a film, and in my experience it takes at least six months to recover' (TP, 333). To the point where Miyazaki said (in 2005) that he went onto a new project partly as a way of exorcising the hold that the old production has on him: 'unless I start working on a new one, I'll never be free from the curse of the last one. I'm serious. Unless I start working on the next film, the last one will be a drag on me for another two or three years' (ibid.).

People have witnessed Hayao Miyazaki throwing out finished artwork (during the preparation for *My Neighbor Totoro*, for example), because it wasn't good enough. Toren Smith said it was 'enough to break you heart'.[44] Another downside to the drive for perfectionism is that at times it must have been difficult for the crew working on a Hayao Miyazaki production. If Miyazaki is anything like other perfectionist filmmakers (such as Andrei Tarkovsky, Walerian Borowczyk or Stanley Kubrick), there must have been times during the production when some in the crew must have been frustrated. I would imagine that Miyazaki is the kind of filmmaker who

---

41 It's important, Hayao Miyazaki stated in 1982, 'to do our utmost to look at all the frames and give our full attention to each of them' (SP, 183).
42 Miyazaki insisted that *Mononoke* would be 'the last film that I make as an animator' (TP, 93). Miyazaki left Ghibli in 1999, but returned to make *Spirited Away* (he founded his own studio, Butaya (Pig House)). He also announced his retirement following *The Wind Rises*. 'I always make each film believing it will be my last' (TP, 189).
43 On carrying on, Miyazaki remarked, *pace Spirited Away*: 'I've got this nasty part of me that always makes me want to do a little bit more' (TP, 326).
44 T. Smith, "Interview With Masamune Shirow", *Manga Mania*, 1, 8, Feb, 1994.

demands high standards from his team, and that can be tough (particularly towards the end of production, when the work schedule goes crazy).

Making feature animated films wasn't the only aspect of Hayao Miyazaki's career, however: one was helping to run Studio Ghibli itself; another was producing his *manga* publications such as *Nausicaä of the Valley of the Wind;* working for the Ghibli Museum; and others included illustration and artwork.

Isao Takahata has portrayed his friend thus:

> Hayao Miyazaki is emotional and passionate,[45] has a friendly undulating human nature, is strongly self-assertive and tends to prompt action, has a bountiful expressiveness and curiosity, and possesses an imagination so vivid it verges on a hallucinatory vision. (2009, 459)

Hayao Miyazaki has admitted in public that he probably wasn't a very good father to his children – too absent too much of the time, for a start: 'I tried to be a good father, but in the end I wasn't a very good parent', he said in 1992 (SP, 204). His son Goro Miyazaki (b. 1967) has remarked that his father was a workaholic, that he didn't spend much time with his family, and when he was a child, Miyazaki would come home when he was asleep, and was sleeping the following morning when Goro went to school. 'I don't have much relationship with my father', Miyazaki junior admitted at the time of *Tales From Earthsea*.[46] He 'scores zero as a father, full marks as a director', Miyazaki junior added.

Very few people have criticized Hayao Miyazaki personally in public: Isao Takahata has – in his portrait of Miyazaki included in *Starting Point* ("The Fireworks of Eros"), for instance. And Miyazaki's son Goro has been very critical of Miyazaki – for example, during the making and release of *Tales From Earthsea*. These are two of the people closest to Miyazaki, of course, who will know Miyazaki very well indeed. Takahata has worked with Miyazaki since the early 1960s, and is probably quite happy to criticize Miyazaki if necessary.

However, almost everyone has good things to say about Hayao Miyazaki personally. No doubt some younger colleagues are intimidated by him – not only is Miyazaki incred-

---

[45] Isao Takahata remarked that Hayao Miyazaki is 'a truly hot-blooded fellow', who tends to overheat, and always has the air conditioning set on high in Summer (2009, 452).
[46] In C. Winstanley, 69. Miyazaki said he stayed away from the production of *Tales From Earthsea*.

ibly successful, financially and artistically, he is also clearly a very great artist, someone who knows animation inside-out.

In his wonderful portrait of his friend, "The Fireworks of Eros", Isao Takahata defined Hayao Miyazaki thus:

> Hayao Miyazaki a man who struggles. He has powerful likes and dislikes, and is extremely loving and compassionate; he weeps, is playful, loves people, expects too much of their talents, howls at his broken dreams, becomes enraged, can't bear to watch what others are doing, worries, interferes verbally and physically, becomes irritated, gives up easily, takes the hardest things upon himself, hates weak-willed and self-indulgent men and those who have no ambition, needles people but looks out for them, is often said to be a bothersomely helpful old geezer behind his back, and is generally exceedingly kind to females. (2009, 453)

Hayao Miyazaki has admitted that he can be cripplingly shy[47] – sometimes he wouldn't have the nerve to stop and look round in a town to find the right way to go, or ask for directions in a train station (SP, 382). In common with many artists and filmmakers, Miyazaki finds it difficult to watch his own movies, seeing only the mistakes and missed opportunities.[48] He is also, as Toshio Suzuki says, very shy and isn't comfortable appearing in public, so he doesn't stay for screenings and premieres. However, don't let the smiling, reserved figure you see in interviews and photos deceive you: Miyazaki is a *super-tough*, workaholic artist who makes the rest of us look like lazy, no-brain slobs.

Hayao Miyazaki is a force of nature.

And don't be fooled by the bright, summery colours in Miyazaki-sensei's movies, the simplified, 'cartoony' look of his characters, or the apparently child-oriented narratives: his themes are the grand ones of world literature: death,[49] loss, separation, corruption, ambition, family, love, childhood, creativity, and war. Thus, 2004's *Howl's Moving Castle* seems to be a children's fantasy adventure, but in fact contains images of the most horrific things humans have done to each other in their 3 million-year history: mass genocide, warfare that reduces cities to burning ash, war which corrupts and poisons the participants so much they can't even remember

---

[47] Isao Takahata has remarked that Miyazaki is 'extremely shy', adding that he is 'fundamentally childlike in his innocence, purity of spirit, selfishness, and impulsiveness' (2009, 454).

[48] Miyazaki's modesty is striking: he says he doesn't think he has the talent for making a live-action film! (TP, 91).

[49] *'I myself become terrified of death when I am in a negative state of mind. But the thought of death ceases to bother me once I become productive'* (2013).

why they went to war in the first place. So that *Howl's Moving Castle* is really in parts an *animé Saving Private Ryan* or *War and Peace* or *The Longest Day*.

Anger. Rage. Violent emotion. With his reserved, modest appearance and his colourful movies for children, we don't think of Hayao Miyazaki as a filmmaker filled with rage. But he is.[50] 'I'm a very emotional person', Miyazaki said (TP, 186), and he insists in many, many interviews that he gets *very* angry. That Miyazaki is at times angry, hot-headed, impatient and irritated is belied by his calm exterior: 'actually, I'm a person who gets angry a lot more easily than most people', he admitted (AI, 29). Anger runs deeply throughout Miya-sama's cinema, as it does in many masters of film – Orson Welles, Jean-Luc Godard, Ingmar Bergman, D.W. Griffith, Ken Russell, Pier Paolo Pasolini, Oliver Stone, etc.

INFLUENCES

Hayao Miyazaki has remarked that his influences are probably innumerable. At university, Miyazaki encountered some of the classic authors of children's fiction,[51] including Eleanor Farjeon, Phillipa Pearce, Francis Hodgson Burnett (*The Secret Garden*), and Rosemary Sutcliffe (he joined the children's literature group). Sutcliffe (1920-1992) was a British author of many historical books, including *The Mark of the Horse Lord* (1965) set in Roman Britain (highly recommended books, if you haven't read them).[52] Ryotaro Shiba, Yoshie Hotaa, and Sasuke Nakao were also influences.[53]

Treasure Island (1883) by Robert Louis Stevenson is a key literary influence on Miyazaki-san (as it has been on numerous filmmakers – the Disney Studios has made at least five versions – the 1950 movie (the definitive version), the 2002 animated remake, entitled *Treasure Planet*, and the *Pirates of the Caribbean* movies, 2003-2011).

As well as Robert Louis Stevenson, other adventure authors have provided inspiration: Jules Verne, of course (in *20,000 Leagues Under the Sea* [1869]), and Mark Twain. Also

---

[50] 'I myself haven't been able to find enlightenment, as I live steeped in impatience and irritations' (TP, 155).
[51] Miyazaki is something of an expert on children's fiction, and can discuss British authors in depth.
[52] A movie appeared in 2011, *The Eagle*, based on Sutcliffe's *The Eagle of the Ninth*.
[53] *Devil of the Desert* by Tetsuji Fukushima was another favourite *manga*.

Jonathan Swift, Maurice Leblanc, Robert Westall (*The Machine Gunners*), and Antoine de Saint-Exupéry.[54] Verne, for instance, combined an adventure story (external story) with a psychological story (internal story), as Hayao Miyazaki explained in a 1995 interview:

> Jules Verne's story of going under the sea overlaps with entering into one's own internal world. The fascination with the sea the story depicts and the idea that the sea hints at a far deeper and richer world full of secrets – this is the wonder Captain Nemo feels. At the same time, the sea shows the depth of his mind and the depth of the entire world itself. (SP, 420)

Among science fiction and fantasy authors, Hayao Miyazaki has cited Brian Aldiss (*Hothouse*), Frank Herbert (*Dune*), Isaac Asimov (*Nightfall*), J.R.R. Tolkien (*The Lord of the Rings*), Diana Wynne-Jones, and Ursula Le Guin (particularly her *Earthsea* series). He told Le Guin when he visited her in Portland, Oregon that he kept her books by his bed, and had been re-reading her works for years.

But Hayao Miyazaki has also explained that he has not been especially enamoured of outer space science fiction: he prefers to make films about nature and stay firmly on or near Earth: it's all about the Earth, about 'land, sea and sky', Miyazaki said, rather than (outer) space, which was simply darkness.[55]

Among filmmakers, Hayao Miyazaki has often cited the Russian film *The Snow Queen* (Lev Atamatov, 1957) as an important influence (which he saw when he was 23). Miyazaki wrote fondly of *The Tale of the White Serpent* (a.k.a. *Panda and the White Serpent*, Taiji Yubushita & Kazuhiko Okabe, 1958): he was 17 when it was released:

> I can still remember the pangs of emotion I felt at the sight of the incredibly beautiful, young female character, Bai-Nang, and how I went to see the film over and over as a result. It was like being in love, and Bai-Nang became a surrogate girlfriend for me at a time when I had none. (SP, 19)

Both *The Snow Queen* and *The Tale of the White Serpent* were important influences for the young Miyazaki-san. But he

---

54 Antoine de Saint-Exupéry (1900-44) was an inspiration for Hayao Miyazaki – not least because he was also an aviator. In 1998, Miyazaki was part of a television documentary which followed in the footsteps of de Saint-Exupéry to the Sahara desert. One of de Saint-Exupéry's best-known works was *The Little Prince* (filmed in 1974), and his books about flight, *Night Flight* and *Wind, Sand and Stars*.
55 Interview in *A-Club*, in M, 76.

was later critical of both movies, perhaps embarrassed by loving them so much as a kid.

Other movies that Hayao Miyazaki remembers seeing as a youth were Italian Neo-realist pictures *Bicycle Thieves* (1947) and *Shoe Shine* (1946), *Mother Joan of the Angels* (Kerzy Kawalerowica, 1961), Isao Kimura movies, *Tarzan* movies, Canadian animator Frédéric Back (*The Man Who Planted Trees, Crac!*), *Meshi* (*Repast*, Mikio Naruse, 1951), *Tasogare Sakaba* (*Twilight Saloon*, Tomu Uchida, 1955) and *Modern Times* by Charlie Chaplin. And later, the Russian animator Yuri Norstein (*Tales of Tales*, 1979), *The Shepherdess and the Chimney Sweep* (Paul Grimmault, 1953), Robert Bresson (*Journal d'un Curé de Campagne*), Andrzej Wajda (*Ashes and Diamonds*) and Yasujiro Ozu.

The early animator Winsor McCay (1869-1934), who produced *Gertie the Dinosaur* (1909/ 14) and *Little Nemo In Slumberland* (1909), was another influence on Miyazaki (the film-within-a-film in *Porco Rosso* is a *hommage* to *Gertie the Dinosaur*).

Among the animation influences on the young Hayao Miyazaki were toons such as Mickey Mouse and Betty Boop.[56] Much of the time animated films were scarce when Miyazaki went to the movies: he said maybe they would see one Disney *Donald Duck* or *Mickey Mouse* short during a Summer (SP, 123). Miyazaki has also mentioned animation coming out of Nihon Dogasha and Toei Animation, as well as the *manga* of Sanpei Shirato (SP, 194).

The influence of the art of famous Japanese artists such as Katsushika Hokusai, Kitagawa Utamaro and Hiroshige Utagawa on Hayao Miyazaki's cinema is easy to spot: their woodblock prints (*ukiyo-e*) of the 'floating world' are some of Japan's most distinctive artworks.

OSAMU TEZUKA.

A big influence on Hayao Miyazaki's early development as an artist was the comicbook artist Osamu Tezuka (1928-89), known as the *manga no kamisama* (the 'god of *manga*' – and also the 'god of *animé*'). 'I've been powerfully influenced by Tezuka', Miyazaki admitted, 'the formative experience in my life story was Osamu Tezuka-san' (TP,153), and began to draw *manga* under Tezuka's shadow (SP, 193). Miyazaki recalled that he consciously tried to move away from being

---

[56] Miyazaki has cited the Fleischers as an influence. In 1980, while discussing the Fleischers in *FILM*, he noted that the endings of the Fleischers' cartoons were poor (SP, 118).

'heavily influenced'[57] by Tezuka's comics and characters. Miyazaki has stated that: 'Tezuka's influences buried deep within me proved an extremely heavy burden'.

Osamu Tezuka is the creator/ director of *Astro Boy, Arabian Nights, Princess Knight, Triton of the Sea, Kimba the White Lion, Bix X, Black Jack, Dororo, Jungle Emperor Leo,* and *Phoenix*. While animators work under the shadow of Disney in the West, in Japan, it's Tezuka. Tezuka was very successful very quickly: by his early twenties, he was 'the biggest selling *manga* artist in Japan'. And he was immensely prolific, creating thousands of pages of *manga* (as well as developing *animé* and running production companies).

'I've been powerfully influenced by Tezuka', Hayao Miyazaki admitted, and began to draw *manga* under Tezuka's shadow (SP, 193). Miyazaki recalled that he consciously tried to move away from being 'heavily influenced' by Tezuka's comics and characters. Miyazaki has stated that 'Tezuka's influences buried deep within me proved an extremely heavy burden'.[58]

INFLUENCED BY HAYAO MIYAZAKI.

In North America, Hayao Miyazaki's films have some dedicated fans, not least animators at Pixar and Disney,[59] who have often cited Miyazaki's movies as an inspiration.[60] But that hasn't translated into big sales theatrically. For instance, when *Howl's Moving Castle* was released on 202 screens in the U.S.A. in 2005, it grossed only $4.7 million (compared to $190m in Japan). As the box office figures are so high in Japan, Studio Ghibli's and Miyazaki's films can easily sustain themselves without needing overseas sales (that is, from the time of *Princess Mononoke* onwards).[61] But it's a pity, because Miyazaki's movies would appeal to a large American audience,

---

[57] His mother told him not to copy other artists (TP, 153).
[58] And Tezuka was in turn heavily influenced by Disney: he saw *Bambi* 80 times!
[59] Films such as Disney's *Atlantis* (2001) directly took up some of Hayao Miyazaki's concepts and visuals – not least the early 20th century setting, with its world of bolts and steel and steam-powered machines. The combination in *Atlantis* of the secret world, the adventure journey to reach it, the technology employed to get there, the flying machines, the gang of characters, and the spiritual underpinnings, all of these could be found in Miyazaki's cinema. Another one was *Steam-boy* (2004), Katsuhiro Otomo's adventure tale entirely centred around steam and machinery.
[60] A recent episode of *The Simpsons* delivered a fun spoof of the cinema of Hayao Miyazaki, with send-ups of *Totoro*'s Cat-bus, the dragon from *Spirited Away*, the witches from *Kiki*, etc.
[61] Before *Mononoke*, animated movies, apart from Ghibli's, were far less prominent at the box office.

if they came to see them.[62]

The influence of Japanese animation on Western moviemaking is *enormous* – in terms of style, action, characters, settings, stories, and everything else. You can see it in the newer *Star Wars* trilogy, in *Avatar*,[63] the *Matrix* films, the *Lord of the Rings* movies, *A.I.*, the *Batman* pictures (and any superhero movies).

Admirers of Hayao Miyazaki include Barry Cook and Tony Bancroft, John Lasseter, Gary Trousdale and Kirk Wise, animator Glen Keane, director Hendel Butoy, director Kevin Altieri, and director Katsuhiro Otomo. Among critics: Andrew Osmond, Roger Ebert, Helen McCarthy, Dan Cavallaro and Jonathan Clements.

Aside from many of the key artists at Disney and Pixar, noted above, fans of Hayao Miyazaki's cinema include Tsui Hark (perhaps the greatest action filmmaker in the world), Guillemo del Toro and Akira Kurosawa: the *sensei* loved *My Neighbor Totoro* and *Kiki's Delivery Service*:

> It's *animé*, but I was so moved. I really loved Nekobus. You wouldn't come up with such an idea. I cried when I watched *Kiki's Delivery Service*.

And in Japanese animation itself, Miyazaki's influence is everywhere. You can see it in, among 1000s of other places, *Cowboy Bebop*, *Moribito*, *Ghost In the Shell*, *Fullmetal Alchemist*, *Mushishi*, *Escaflowne*, *Naruto*, *Death Note*, *Berserk*, *Macross Plus*, *Samurai Champloo*, *Final Fantasy*, *Evangelion*, and, well, everywhere.

UNMADE FILMS

A filmmaker such as Hayao Miyazaki is bursting with ideas, and over the course of his film career, like every major filmmaker, he will have produced many ideas and scripts and drawings and even filmed animation that never quite made it into a finished form or released product. There were some projects that Miyazaki began work on, but left, sometimes due to 'creative differences' between the project's producers and the director (such as *Little Nemo*). Some projects Miyazaki

---

[62] In the U.S.A., the *Pokémon* movies have generated the biggest ticket sales ($85 million gross in 1999), while Ghibli's *Spirited Away* made around $10m.
[63] Many viewers noted the influence of the floating islands in *Laputa: Castle In the Sky* on *Avatar* (2009).

wouldn't have been able to find funding for. Part of the reason for this is that Miyazaki is a perfectionist, workaholic kind of filmmaker, and he thinks *very* big! – those sorts of projects take a lot of work and a lot of time (and a lot of money) to complete.

One of the unmade projects, which Hayao Miyazaki developed with Isao Takahata, was 1971's *Pippi Longstocking*, from Astrid Lindgren's books of 1945-48 (Lindgren is one of Sweden's most well-known authors, along with August Strindberg). The company A-Pro wasn't able to be obtain the rights to Lindgren's book,[64] but Miyazaki (and Yutaka Fujioka, president of Tokyo Movie Shinsha) visited Sweden on a research trip (in August, 1971) – Miyazaki's first trip abroad.

The Swedish visit paid off later, however, as research for films such as *Laputa: Castle In the Sky* and *Kiki's Delivery Service*. And elements from *Pippi Longstocking* ended up in *Panda Go Panda* (SP, 328): this is normal for filmmakers: a project that doesn't get made isn't a complete waste of time and money and energy: many elements can be incorporated into later productions.

After visiting Sweden for the unmade *Pippi Longstocking,* Hayao Miyazaki undertook further trips to Europe, to research and photograph and sketch locations: for *Alpine Girl Heidi* Miyazaki visited Europe in Summer, 1973; Miyazaki travelled to Italy and Argentina in 1975, for *Three Thousand Leagues In Search of Mother*. Another unmade Miyazaki project was based on the American comic *Rowlf* (1971) by Richard Corben.

Miyazaki and Takahata had worked on *Little Nemo* in the mid-1980s, but had left early on. *Little Nemo* had some high profile people collaborating on it, including Jean Giraud (Moebius), illustrator Brian Froud, writers Ray Bradbury and Robert Towne and director Chris Columbus, Disney animators Frank Thomas, Ollie Johnson and Rogers Allers, with songs by the Sherman brothers (who had written *Chitty Chitty Bang Bang*). It was an American-Japanese co-production, based on Winsor McCay's comics. *Little Nemo* had a long and troubled production history, however, with collaborators coming and going.

In 2006 Hayao Miyazaki said he wanted to make a movie about Edo Castle and the 15th century period. Another

---

[64] Author Astrid Lindgren was fiercely protective of her work, and altho' there had been a TV series in 1969, and a movie of 1949, she probably didn't want to lose control of her creation.

unrealized project was about the survivors of the Great Kanto Earthquake of 1923 (the earthquake crops up in other *animé*, such as *Oshin, Doomed Megalopolis, Urotsukidoji* and *Smart-san*). In 2013's *The Wind Rises*, Miyazaki-sensei found a way to incorporate a Kanto Earthquake sequence. Prior to *Spirited Away* the project *Rin the Chimney Painter* had been developed but cancelled (Miyazaki wanted to set it at the time of the 1923 quake). A story based in the Meiji era (1868-1912), about transportation on the Shinkashigawa River, was another unmade screenplay. Another unrealized project was about a pig and a tank and love. Miyazaki also considered adapting the children's book *The Marvellous Village Veiled In Mist* by Sachiko Kashiwaba. A sequel to *Ponyo* was another possibility, as well as a sequel to *Porco Rosso*.

Turning Ghibli's films into theatrical musicals (for ex, *Totoro* or *Spirited Away*), must've been considered, as well as turning any of Hayao Miyazaki's movies into TV series, or filming them in live-action. (My top unmade Miyazaki movie is definitely an adaptation of the *Earthsea* books by Ursula Le Guin).

Hayao Miyazaki spoke in 1983 of wanting to do a version of *Beauty and the Beast* – and he would focus on the beast (as many animators would plump to do [SP, 305]). It would be a story of love cleansing someone:

> I'd like to create a film where the character is cleansed by being devoted to something, and is transformed by being cleansed, so that at the end the character becomes what we wish had been there all along. (SP, 305).

This is another way of putting the essential attribute of fairy tales: that they are not about achieving something, or becoming something more than one already was, or about the transformations that magic or wishes can bring. Instead, a fairy tale ending reveals *what the character was already like in the first place*.[65] Thus, Cinderella and Sleeping Beauty are good, kind people already, at the beginning of the fairy tales, and the ending is a *revelation* of their fundamental goodness and kindness.

Thus, it is not what a character *does* that's ultimately important, but what a character *is*.

---

[65] 'Miyazaki's gift is to convey the magic inherent in life, and nobody does it better', Helen McCarthy noted (2008, 153).

ISAO TAKAHATA

Isao Takahata (born October 29, 1935, in Ise, Japan), known to his colleagues and friends as Paku-san, is one of the most important people in Hayao Miyazaki's artistic career: they produced each other's work while the other was directing. As Miyazaki has acknowledged, they often clashed when working together, and had learnt to be very 'hands off' when they were producing the other's projects. According to the 'making of' documentary of *Only Yesterday*, while working on the movie, Miyazaki said they rarely talked – and Miyazaki was producing the film! After a screening of the finished picture, Miyazaki walked out without saying anything.

Theirs is clearly an unusual relationship, where a producer and director won't even talk to each other. How true this is, I don't know, but in the same documentary Hayao Miyazaki admitted that Isao Takahata could make him angrier than anyone else he knew. Miyazaki remarked in 1994 that he and Takahata had 'completely different' ideas about how to make movies. 'If we discuss a production, we definitely won't reach an agreement'.[66] But you also have to remember that these two directors have been working together for a long, long time, and will know each other very well. And they also produce masterpieces, no matter how different their production methods are.

Isao Takahata is the other main director at Studio Ghibli, and has directed films such as *Ponpoko, Panda! Go Panda!, 3000 Leagues In Search of Mother, My Neighbors the Yamadas, Gauche the Cellist, Only Yesterday, The Tale of Princess Kaguya* and *Grave of the Fireflies*. Also, Takahata had directing credits long before Miyazaki, helming TV shows such as *Apache Baseball Team, Heidi, 3000 Leagues In Search of Mother* and *Anne of Green Gables*. Takahata's first feature film as director was 1968's *The Little Norse Prince* (a.k.a. *Horusu: Prince of the Sun*). The financial failure of that movie led to Takahata and Miyazaki leaving Toei Animation.

Isao Takahata is a fabulously talented filmmaker,[67] especially good at comedy and broad slapstick. But his films also have an emotional depth which's really striking, and

---

[66] Hayao Miyazaki in *YOM*, June, 1994.
[67] Takahata's reputation has been somewhat over-shadowed by Miyazaki's, and Ghibli's: as H. McCarthy and J. Clements put it: 'In any other country, Takahata would be regarded as a national treasure – in an anime industry fixated on the successes of Miyazaki, the quiet achievements of this master filmmaker are often over-looked, despite a career rivalled only in length and achievement by Rintaro' (2006, 639).

some of them, such as *Only Yesterday* (*Omoide Poro Poro*, 1991), and *Grave of the Fireflies* (*Hotaru no Haka*, 1988), are deeply moving, with *Grave of the Fireflies* delivering an emotional punch that very few (animated) movies have achieved. It's on the scale of distressing emotion of *Bambi*. Indeed, *Grave of the Fireflies* is a masterpiece of cinema, the equal of *anything else* in animation – or live-action.

Acting as producer, Hayao Miyazaki produced Isao Takahata's films *Ponpoko* (*Modern-Day Raccoon War Ponpoko*, 1994), and *Only Yesterday* (1991). And also *The Cat Returns* (2002), *Kiki's Delivery Service*, *Whisper of the Heart* (1995) and *The Borrower Arrietty* (2010). He wrote (or co-wrote) some of those films, including 2010's *Arrietty* and 2011's *From Up On Poppy Hill*.[68]

TOSHIO SUZUKI.

Toshio Suzuki (born 1948, Nagoya) joined the Studio Ghibli team after meeting Hayao Miyazaki when he was managing editor of *Animage* magazine[69] (founded in 1978), which published Miyazaki's *manga* of *Nausicaä of the Valley of the Wind*. As one of the key players at Studio Ghibli,[70] Suzuki is thus one of the leading figures in the Japanese animation industry, as well as being a vital influence on Miyazaki's cinema. Isao Takahata remarked that without 'Suzuki-san, there would be no Studio Ghibli today', and that Suzuki has 'steadfastly supported Hayao Miyazaki' (2009, 460).

If you want to know what a film producer does, have a look at the 2013 documentary *Kingdom of Dreams and Madness*, which shows Toshio Suzuki tirelessly working with and encouraging numerous groups of people, promoting Ghibli's products, travelling to screenings and events, meeting the press, and talking and promoting some more. It's a sociable, hands-on job, where people skills are uppermost; Suzuki enjoys the process of filmmaking, more even than the movies themselves.

Other key collaborators on Hayao Miyazaki's movies, all of whom have made major contributions to his movies (there are many, many more) include: Masashi Andou, key animator, Hideaki Anno, key animator (and co-founder of animation studio Gainax), Mamoru Hosoda (director of two *Digimon* movies), Tomomi Mochizuki, director, Hiroyuki Morita, key

---

68 It's worth noting, however, that Miyazaki has acted as a producer only infrequently – compared to contemporaries such as Tsui Hark and Steven Spielberg, who regularly produce other filmmakers' work.
69 Suzuki worked first at Tokuma Shoten, for *Asahi Geino* magazine.
70 Suzuki was the President of Ghibli until 2008; now he focusses on production.

animator, Yoshifumi Kondo, key animator, Yasuo Otsuka, animation director, Yasuyoshi Tokuma, president of Tokuma Shoten, and Michiyo Yasuda, colour designer and head of the ink and paint dept at Ghibli.

2

HAYAO MIYAZAKI'S MOVIES AND THE JAPANESE ANIMATION INDUSTRY

Japan has the biggest animation industry in the world, and many would agree with me that it's also the finest; Hayao Miyazaki's films and those of Studio Ghibli are very much a part of it (and the most famous part). That Japan is one of the richest nations on Earth plays a role (at the height of the Bubble Economy in the 1980s, Japan had 16% of the global economic power, and 60% of real estate wealth). The famous TV shows, OAVs, specials, videos, and movies in *animé* include: *Akira, Doraemon, Digimon, Pokémon,*[71] *Dr Slump, Star Blazers, Legend of the Overfiend, Evangelion, Sailor Moon, Gundam, Speed Racer, Lupin III, Ranma 1/2, Patlabor, Macross, Dragon Ball, Urusei Yatsura, Cowboy Bebop, Mighty Atom* (*Astro Boy*) and *Ghost In the Shell*. According to Helen McCarthy, animation in Japan accounted for 6% of films released in late 1998, 25-30% of videos, and 3-6% of television shows made in Japan. This book isn't an exploration of Japanese *animé*, or the links between the films of Miyazaki and *animé*. There are excellent books on Japanese *animé* available (tho' still far too few), but I will note a few aspects which throw light on Miyazaki's cinema.

The world of Japanese animation is instantly recognizable: characters with spiky hair, red hair, purple hair, long hair, hair blowing in the breeze, giant eyes, tiny mouths, snub, pointy noses, women with pneumatic bodies, guys with buff, muscle-bound bodies, superheroes, nerds (*otaku*), grimaces showing lots of teeth, elfin ears, grizzled, old guys who smoke, child-like *shojo* figures, tall, skinny villains, people who can fly, grotesque transformations, excessive violence,[72] technofetishism, robots, *mecha*, more robots, more *mecha*, mobile

---
[71] The *Pokémon* movies have proved hugely popular in Japan, and rival Studio Ghibli's movies at the box office.
[72] Altho' Japanese popular culture is still regarded as pretty violent, Japanese society is actually more peaceful than many nations on Earth. Crime rates are low, guns are controlled, and the constitution forbids war. And in the years that *manga* sales boomed, crime rates fell (F. Schodt, 1997, 132).

power suits, giant moons, explosions, spaceships, jets, helicopters, motorbikes, guns, guns and more guns, samurai swords, lightning storms, the ocean, the colours green and silver and red, headbands, silly hats, comic sidekicks like dogs or cutie critters, Tokyo, futuristic cities, skyscrapers and mean streets (always with the skyscrapers!), neon signs, tentacles, monsters, demons, blood and guts, and last but not least: the atomic bombs dropped on Japan by the United States of America.

Hayao Miyazaki's cinema certainly has numerous links to the Japanese *animé* tradition. For instance, the *shojo* figure, the ambiguous treatment of technology, Tokyo settings, Japanese mythology, non-duality, ambiguity, unconventional narrative structures, complex characters, war (and the two World Wars), the atom bomb, and the military machine. And the motifs that crop up in thousands of *animé* products are also found in Miyazaki's films: the giant robots, flying, rapid action scenes, explosions, gadgets, steam-punk paraphernalia, young heroes, etc.

At the same time, there are many staples of Japanese *animé* that *don't* appear in Hayao Miyazaki's cinema: high school and classroom scenes, kids riding in cars or on motorcycles, teenage parties, bust-ups between kids and parents, sword fights, and sex (Miyazaki's films steer clear of pornography or even nudity, which form a staple of Japanese *animé*, earning its notoriety overseas).

THE JAPANESE *ANIMÉ* INDUSTRY

An important thing to remember about Japanese *animé* is that it is an industry that can sustain itself by producing movies and TV shows for a *domestic* audience: it doesn't need (or even usually plans for) television syndication or releases overseas (but it will always take them up if available). In other words, one of the reasons that the Japanese animation industry is the biggest in the world is because there is such a large market in Japan itself for animation. (The market is largely for home video/ DVD releases, however, and for TV of course: it's videos and DVDs that help to keep Ghibli buoyant. In theatres, Disney movies still have a huge market share in animation, with only Ghibli's pictures, and a few animated features, such as *Pokémon, Evangelion* and *Oh! My Goddess,* competing significantly).

That also means that Japanese *animé* filmmakers can make their films and TV shows for a homegrown market, and don't need to pander to an international (or a North American) audience. This certainly applies to Hayao Miyazaki's movies, which producer Toshio Suzuki has remarked on a number of occasions are very much *Japanese* movies, movies that are made primarily for the *Japanese* market. So the films can reflect and explore local or national culture, and don't need to build in elements that will appeal to a global audience (no need to shift the action of their films to, say, New York or Chicago, and turn their characters into Americans).

It's an envious position to be in for a filmmaker. European filmmakers, for instance, can similarly make films only for their own national audience, but they tend to be much smaller (or cheaper) movies. A country such as France can sustain a huge production of movies per year because it has the largest film industry in Europe (that's one of the reasons why French movies travel outside France). And it means that France can make much bigger movies (it has more government investment than many other countries).[73]

Lonely Planet's travel guide to Japan makes some useful points about contemporary Japan:

> First, Japan is an island nation. Second, until WWII, Japan was never conquered by an outside power,[74] nor was it heavily influenced by Christian missionaries. Third, until the beginning of last century, the majority of Japanese lived in close-knit rural farming communities. Fourth, most of Japan is covered in steep mountains, so the few flat areas of the country are quite crowded – people literally live on top of each other. Finally, for almost all of its history, Japan has been a strictly hierarchical place, with something approximating a caste system during the Edo period. (C. Rowthorn, 2007)

WWII and the Occupation had enormous effects on the Japanese movie industry, which still resonate today (and you can also see the effects in Studio Ghibli's output). In *A History of Narrative Film*, still the finest single book on cinema, David Cook set the scene:

---

[73] And the French love Hayao Miyazaki's movies, as they love comicbooks and fantasy art. One reason that the movies of Miyazaki and Takahata were received better and were more well-known in Europe was because Europe had imported titles such as *Heidi* and *3000 Leagues*.

[74] Miyazaki reckoned that the Japanese people have been depressed ever since the end of the feudal era, when they were forced to open up their land to foreigners (TP, 237).

> When World War II ended on August 14, 1945, much of Japan lay in ruins. The massive firebombing of its sixty cities from March through June 1945 and the dropping of atomic bombs on Hiroshima and Nagasaki had resulted in some 900,000 casualties and the nearly total paralysis of civilian life. On the morning of August 15, when Emperor Hirohito broadcast to his subjects the news that the war had ended and that Japan had lost, there was widespread disbelief. Never in their history had the Japanese people been defeated or the nation occupied, and so the circumstances of the American Occupation, 1945-52, were utterly unique. (783)

As to genres, Hayao Miyazaki's cinema has included many of the chief genres of *animé*, including action-adventure and epics (*Nausicaä of the Valley of the Wind* and *Laputa: Castle In the Sky*), war stories and fantasy (*Howl's Moving Castle*), and Japanese folklore and history (*Spirited Away* and *Princess Mononoke*). And many of Miyazaki's movies come under the umbrella of 'children's stories'. There is plenty of comedy, though no Miyazaki movie is an out-and-out comedy (that would be something to see!). Some of Miyazaki's films combine genres: *Porco Rosso*, for example, has elements of romance, comedy, war/ politics, and plenty of action-adventure.

The genres of Japanese animation include pretty much all of those in live-action, as well as some genres particular to *animé*: comedy; romance; crime; action-adventure; horror; historical drama; science fiction[75] (including *mecha*; cyberpunk; war; epics); fantasy (including comicbooks; supernatural tales; myths and legends; and superheroes); animal stories; martial arts; children's stories; epics; erotica; porn; and sports stories.[76] Gilles Poitras noted in *The Anime Companion* that *animé* has more genres than exist in Western cinema (43).

The Japanese film industry has been one of the most prolific historically, producing over 400 movies a year. The Japanese movie business has been dominated by studio conglomerates, just like the North American system, since the 1920s (the biggies are Nikkatsu, Shochiku, Toho,[77] Toei,

---
[75] More people consume science fiction in Japan than anywhere else.
[76] Although it is regarded as popular culture, Japanese *animé* draws on high culture, including woodblock prints, *ukiyo-e*, Kabuki theatre, painting, and classical music.
[77] Toho, founded in the 1930s from a number of smaller companies, is best known as the studio of *Godzilla* and *kaiju* (giant monster) movies, and Akira Kurosawa. Among Toho's output were sci-fi, *jidai-geki* and *chambara*, crime, dramas, war, youth romances and comedies. Miyazaki's later movies have been distributed by Toho (thus, Toho must've made *a lot* of money out of Miyazaki).

Shintoho and Daiei). Although the independent film sector has grown since the 1980s, the major studios continue to take up most of film production. And most Japanese film directors work for the major studios in some form or another, or for television.

Gilles Poitras explained in his excellent *Anime Companion:*

> anime is not to be confused with cartoons. Anime uses animation to tell stories and entertain, but it does so in ways that have barely been touched on in Western animation. While the U.S. continues to pump out cartoons with gag stories, musicals with cute animals, animated sitcoms, and testosterone-laced TV fare, the Japanese have been using anime to cover every literary and cinematic genre imaginable in a highly competitive market that encourages new story ideas and the creative reworking of older ideas and themes. (vii)

Japan is one of the major film markets in the world – for American movies, yes, but also for movies from everywhere. And when it comes to animation, there is a huge appetite for it in Japan. That helps to sustain an operation like Studio Ghibli, and a filmmaker like Hayao Miyazaki. Without that large, national market, and that enthusiastic response to animated movies and television, it would be more difficult for Miyazaki to make the kind of pictures he wants to make. For instance, if Miyazaki had to use foreign money, the economics would have an impact on the films: an investor from, say, Germany, might have certain requirements about the films being able to play in Europe and the U.S.A. A bank from, say, Australia, might have different provisos.

But Hayao Miyazaki's films have enjoyed a buoyant market in Japan for home-made animation: in short, the Japanese *animé* industry has enabled Miyazaki's cinema to flourish. In 2006, the bestselling *animé* titles in the U.S. of A. had 6 Studio Ghibli movies in the top 20, and 4 Miyazaki flicks in the top 11 (according to VIZ Media).

Japanese *animé* sells in the Western world via OVAs,[78] videos and DVDs, TV shows, and related *manga* comicbooks (theatrical releases are only a fraction of the market). Animated series and movies are prepared for the Western market with English language dubs (nearly always using American actors and American-style English), and also

---

[78] OVA means Original Video Animation (a.k.a. OAV = Original Animé/ Animation Video) – referring to sell-through videos, which may be linked to TV shows or movies, and, of course, *manga*.

subtitles (there is also a subculture of fans subtitling shows).

Hayao Miyazaki often discussed *manga*, and how it related to Japanese culture and entertainment. *Manga* were certainly huge in Japan, and more so than in any other country (though they are on the increase in some places). North America, Miyazaki mused, doesn't have a comicbook tradition anything like *manga* culture in Japan: in Japan, a *manga* like *Shonen Jump* might sell 6 million copies a week, enormous numbers. In a 1994 speech, Miyazaki compared that 6 million with the video sales of *Beauty and the Beast* in the U.S.A.: 20 million, for a nation with twice the population of Japan. Selling 20 million in America would be like selling 10 million in Japan, Miyazaki suggested, and *Shonen Jump* sells 6 million *manga* a week!

In Japan, the audience for *manga* is pretty much everybody: the stigma in the West attached to comics and comicbooks simply doesn't exist: everyone reads *manga*. The Japanese *manga* market is bigger than the *animé* market. *Manga* also requires far fewer personnel to create, and is cheaper to disseminate (and it's far less technically challenging).

ANIMATION IN PRODUCTION

> Those who join in the work of animation are people who dream more than others and who wish to convey those dreams to others. After a while they realize how incredibly difficult it is to entertain others.
>
> Hayao Miyazaki (SP, 25)

Hayao Miyazaki is a hands-on animation director, a workaholic who oversees every aspect of the animation process. This is unusual: many animation directors oversee projects in detail, but not to the extent of checking every piece of key animation, for instance. Miyazaki has been known to re-draw animation if he thinks it's not good enough. Miyazaki is clearly a filmmaker who can't resist getting in there and doing the work. He is a filmmaker who really likes to make films.

That's important: the *sheer joy* of making cinema really

comes across in his movies.[79] The pleasure shines through, like the elation that Hayao Miyazaki's characters experience when they fly for the first time. You really can tell when a filmmaker is having a great time making their film: you can see it in *Citizen Kane*, in *Close Encounters of the Third Kind*, in *Crouching Tiger. Hidden Dragon*, in *An American In Paris*, in *Once Upon a Time In China*. You can see the filmmakers letting their imaginations unfurl, and that helps to inspire the rest of the creative team to do better work. 'If I didn't enjoy entertaining people, I wouldn't be in this business', Miyazkai confessed (TP, 324). As his movies demonstrate, he is one of the greatest entertainers in the history of, well, everything.

Animation is a long, hard slog – *very* labour intensive, with projects like feature films typically taking three or four years to complete. It requires a particular kind of individual, then, to maintain a high level of enthusiasm and interest, to stay focussed on the project and not be distracted into doing other things (or just exhausted!). Stanley Kubrick spoke of keeping hold of his initial inspiration for making a movie all the way through the long process of development, pre-production, shooting, post-production and distribution. You have to hang on to whatever it was that really excited you about doing the project in the first place (a production that doesn't have that initial spark of excitement and fascination can all too easily lose its momentum and energy).

I haven't visited an animation studio in Tokyo, but in every 'making of' *animé* documentary, in every photo, and in every account, every animation house is a shabby building of messy desks and work stations in which animators, ink-and-paint women, in-betweeners, *mecha* designers, character designers, CG technicians and the rest of the staff, slave away at all hours. There are no plush front office buildings, as at the Disney Studios in Burbank or Pixar in Northern California. Only the new Studio Ghibli building among Tokyo animation houses has that upmarket front office feel (but on the main floors of Ghibli, it's animators and their desks and shelves crammed into small spaces again – look at the 'making of' documentary about *Spirited Away*).

It is commonplace for animators and staff to sleep under their desks in animation houses in Tokyo. Visitors from the West to companies such as Production I.G. have been

---

[79] Hayao Miyazaki had to feel excited about his work in animation: 'I never want to lose the excitement I experience when I'm working' (SP, 386). Boredom is to be avoided: 'If you watch something for three minutes, you feel like you know everything about it, even what went on backstage, and then you don't feel like watching the rest' (SP, 55).

surprised by that, and by the tiny working spaces that even high-ranking animators have: just a desk and a few shelves. Cables run over the floor, DVDs, posters, toys and photocopied timing sheets are packed in everywhere, and there's not much space btn the workers and their chairs. Staff eat their *bento* boxes at their desks (taking less than an hour for lunch). They often have multiple jobs, not just one. Look at a photo of any animation house in Tokyo, and you'll see every nook is crammed with stuff. And it's not unknown for staff to have nervous breakdowns due to the heavy workload (as with director Hideaki Anno on *The End of Evangelion*, and Tomomi Mochizuki after working on Ghibli's *Ocean Waves*).

If you dream of flying to Tokyo and working at Studio Ghibli, Sunrise or Toei or one of the other 430 *animé* houses, be prepared to work very hard, and for long hours (12-14 hours a day, plus every other Saturday), to eat your lunch at your desk (and sometimes sleep there), to enjoy few perks and benefits, to do many tasks (photocopying, say, or website design), and to make barely enough to live.

Once a production starts up, it takes on a life of its own, Hayao Miyazaki explained, and his job was to find the way that the movie wants to work, to find the direction it wants to take. As Miyazaki put it:

> The film tries to become a film. The filmmaker just becomes a slave to the film. The relationship is not one of me creating the film, but rather of the film forcing me to create it. (SP, 430)

There comes a moment during a movie's production when logic has to fly out of the window, and you have to rely on your subconscious. You have to become desperate, Hayao Miyazaki said, you have to think it's not going to work, that you can't solve the problems. At that point of desperation and hardship, the subconscious mind helps out and 'lo and behold an answer comes' (SP, 429-430).

Although you might have to draw explosions as an animator, Hayao Miyazaki said, the most important thing was to be interested in people, 'in how they live, and in how they interact with things' (SP, 125). Animators aren't just actors, Miyazaki also stated (in 1988), they have to know how to analyze, fuse and put into sequence movements 'involving gravity and momentum, elasticity, perspective, timing, and the fundamental properties of fluids' (SP, 74).

A director needs to study all sorts of things: 'Of course,

the most important thing is imagination, but you have to have a constant interest in customs, history, architecture, and all sorts of things' (TP, 132). In a 1998 directing class, Miyazaki reckoned that directors need 'a "healthy ambition", a desire to express themselves or entertain others, and make money while doing so' (TP, 129). A big ego is also a common element in directors.[80]

It's no good relying on technique, Hayao Miyazaki said, because it wouldn't help to say something if you don't really have anything to say. Rather, 'technique is something people develop in order to express something' (SP, 145). That's Jean-Luc Godard's advice to filmmakers: *have something to say*.

For Hayao Miyazaki, a shot must contain multiple meanings, and if it doesn't, it falls flat: 'unless three or four meanings are behind the decision on a certain shot, a film will not have a sense of urgency. It's amazing, but just by watching a video screen you can tell if it's an A-class or a B-class film' (TP, 131). The screen reveals all: 'you can't dodge the truth on the screen. Japanese films are boring because they are not infused with multiple meanings on the screen' (ibid.).

Hayao Miyazaki encourages his animators to look, look, look – at the real world, and at real people. Toshio Suzuki has spoken of Miyazaki's incredible facility for observation and recording the real world. To the point where a scene that Miyazaki witnessed years before might crop up in a movie.[81]

> To observe and imitate is most important. He reads books, observes, etc. He often says "Don't rush for a drawing reference book – it should be inside your head".

❖

So Hayao Miyazaki, and the key people in his creative teams – Isao Takahata, Toshio Suzuki, Yasuyoshi Tokuma, Mamoru Hosoda, Masashi Andou, Joe Hisaishi, Yasuji Mori, Yoshifumi Kondo, Michiyo Yasuda – are going to be tough, hard-working and determined individuals. Just to complete an animated feature film is achievement enough, but to make pictures that are so exquisite and visionary, is truly mind-boggling (to the point where you think, this just isn't *possible!* But Miyazaki & co. prove that it *is!*).

In 1987, Hayao Miyazaki described the typical animator

---
[80] 'One thing about film directors is that once you become one, you'll always be one' (TP, 327).
[81] Observers said the same of the artist J.M.W. Turner: he would lean out of a carriage window and sketch something very quickly. Years later, it would become a finished painting.

as young, good-natured, and poor. They made less than 100,000 Yen a month (= $1,000. There are about 100 Yen to the US dollar). They were paid ¥400 ($4) a page for theatrical movies and ¥150 ($1.50) a page for TV animation. Miyazaki reckoned there were about 2,500 animators in Japan (SP, 135). His first wage in animation was 19,000 Yen a month in 1963, Miyazaki said, when he started at Toei Animation.

In all of his lectures and writings, Hayao Miyazaki emphasized the sheer struggle of producing animation. It is an industry for workaholics,[82] to the point where Miyazaki stated: 'without workaholics, Japan's animation could never be sustained' (SP, 187). It is hard work all the way,[83] and there is no way of creating it without months of labour: 'once we start production, it's at full throttle. The schedule is always tight. I urge the staff to take no breaks, to draw, to run, while whipping myself along as well', Miyazaki remarked in 1987 (SP, 138). It means checking all of the frames and key animation, if possible (SP, 183). 'Works of art are created by those who are prepared to go to the limit,' asserted Miyazaki (1991).

And for Hayao Miyazaki, pursuing animation means pursing perfection – or something as good as one can produce. 'One has to pursue it until one is satisfied' (SP, 204). When he made *Heidi, Girl of the Alps,* Miyazaki said: 'we worked at a ferocious pace. Due to lack of sleep and fatigue, we were under such stress that we didn't even catch colds' (SP, 137). And sometimes he slept on the floor in the studio: this was more common in Japanese animation in those days than one would think: it wasn't unknown for animators to stay at work all day, and sleep there too, getting up to carry on. I would imagine that today the intensive, workaholic nature of animation is still prevalent, despite unions, labour laws and all the rest (yep, and animators still sleep under their desks).

> Animated films cannot be made as easily as live-action films [Hayao Miyazaki explained]. I can't be like John Ford, who made more than 100 films, sometimes without even participating in editing his own work. Imagine me directing at this studio for two or three hours, then moving on to another studio to direct a scene like 'there, now the pig gets on the tank,' and then moving on to draw *Nausicaä* – that's just not possible. I don't do things that way, and I don't want to. Animation just doesn't work that way by nature, and if we think it can work that way then we are finished.

---
82 For *Spirited Away*, 'the human investment was huge' (TP, 327).
83 For Hayao Miyazaki, work is all about passion and effort (SP, 385).

THE ANIMATION PROCESS.

In the Japanese animation industry, the script comes first. Storyboards and image boards are drawn when the script is completed (but sometimes before then). The storyboards are called *e-conte* (a combination of *ei*, picture, and continuity). Hayao Miyazaki likes to draw the storyboards himself (as many directors prefer to do – if they have time).

Once the film is complete in terms of storyboards, plus indications of timing (the frames),[84] dialogue and sound effects, it goes to the key animators: they put the movie together as key animation (the animation at the beginning and the end of an action). In-between work means animating the movements between the key frames which the key animators have drawn, using time sheets. This is all mostly done with drawing on paper at desks. At the same time, the drawings are cleaned up (one single outline will be chosen, for example, from a mass of pencil lines). Throughout this and all stages of animation, drawings and artwork are being tweaked and adjusted (each stage is reviewed, and directors often oversee each process – which Miyazaki does, of course).

Once the drawings have been completed, they are transferred to cels (celluloid), and inked and painted (a very time-consuming process, even with computers). Finally, they are photographed (a whole complex undertaking in itself). Photographic and special effects may be added at this stage. As expected, Hayao Miyazaki likes to check every stage in the process. (However, animation doesn't always use 24 frames per second, called 'ones' or 'singles': it often goes to 'twos' or 'doubles' (12 frames a second) or 'threes' (8 frames per second). Even Miyazaki's latest movies use those lower frame rates).

It has been a regular occurrence for Hayao Miyazaki to be storyboarding a movie while it's in production, as well as producing image-boards. That's not too much of a problem in live-action, when storyboards are often cast aside anyway when the filmmakers and actors reach the set and rehearse and work out new ways of shooting a scene. In animation, it's much more problematic, because it affects the whole process. On *Laputa: Castle In the Sky*, for example, Miyazaki recalled that he was working on the storyboards throughout production:

---

[84] In the 2013 documentary (*Kingdom*), you can see Miyazaki with a stopwatch working out the timings (closing his eyes to imagine the scene).

> My daily schedule went like this: I got up in the morning, I drew storyboards, I returned to the office. At the office, I touched-up my staff's material. At night, I went home and did some more storyboards. After that, I slept. In Japan, I'm afraid the only one who makes animation this way is me, since no one else could take it. (1987a)

Hayao Miyazaki doesn't need a script, Isao Takahata explained, and he doesn't even bother to complete the storyboards before launching into production (2009, 458). All he needs is a clear idea of his characters[85] and the imagined world he's building. As overseen by Miyazaki, Takahata said that the production 'starts to take on the elements of an endlessly improvised performance'. And he liked to work on every process in a production at the same time, instead of waiting for one part to be complete.[86] It was as if Miyazaki 'were trying to turn the creative process into an erotic adventure', Takahata said (2009, 458).

Putting a movie into words and a script at the outset is something that Hayao Miyazaki finds difficult: he doesn't want to explain it, but to go do it. Indeed, words are only the top layer of the piece: 'the part that can be explained in words and sentences is only the surface layer of what I am thinking' (TP, 143). Yes – because if a movie could all be expressed in words, there wouldn't be any need (or desire) to make it. You could just write it down. But a movie is more than a message or a series of words (ib., 144). Akira Kurosawa said the same thing to an interviewer: if he could put the 'message' into words, he'd simply hold up a placard instead of making the movie!

One of the chief reasons for Hayao Miyazaki concentrating much more on the storyboards or continuity sketches for his own movies, rather than on producing a script, or even writing out the original story, was time: *Laputa: Castle In the Sky* required 650 sketches, *Kiki's Delivery Service* 550 and *Whisper of the Heart* 450 (SP, 103). With all that work to do, there just wasn't time to write the screenplay.[87]

And Hayao Miyazaki said he couldn't work that way anyway: 'I've tried writing the story out many times before, but

---

[85] Because he works with his characters for such a long time during production, Isao Takahata remarked, Miyazaki has to identify with them emotionally (2009, 456).
[86] There is no set way of making a movie, Hayao Miyazaki asserted: it didn't have to develop from ideas to script to image boards to storyboards to animation. All of those events could be taking place at the same time, or in a different order (SP, 58).
[87] As Ingmar Bergman noted: 'I write scripts to serve as skeletons awaiting the flesh and sinew of images' (*The New York Times*, January 22, 1978).

even if I think a story works great in text, when we render it in continuity sketches it's usually unusable' (SP, 103).

Hayao Miyazaki dislikes the Western practice, developed famously at the Walt Disney Studios, of using live-action photography as a reference or a starting-point for animation. Miyazaki hates the technique. It doesn't work, Miyazaki reckoned, and pointed to the overly expressive and unnatural movements of Disney characters such as Cinderella and Snow White, who look like they're acting in a ballet. It was no good using a young, American woman as a model in pursuing realism; even more of the symbolism of the fairy tales was lost (SP, 75).

And animation and visual effects in the West is still locked into the notion of using live-action reference material: films like *Avatar* and *The Lord of the Rings* have used motion capture technology to drive the animation of their characters (and crowed about it in the publicity).

In Japan, Hayao Miyazaki preferred his animators not to become slaves to live-action photography: if they do, 'their enjoyment of their work plummets by half' (SP, 75).

MIYAZAKI'S MOVIES AND JAPAN

The films of Hayao Miyazaki and Studio Ghibli are truly a phenomenon in Japan. Every time a film by Hayao Miyazaki is released in theatres, everyone in Japan goes to see it. Or that's what it feels like: in short, every Miyazaki movie since *Porco Rosso* has been the top film that year: *Princess Mononoke*, *Spirited Away*, *The Wind Rises*, *Howl's Moving Castle,* and *Ponyo On the Cliff By the Sea*. And not just the top grossing movie, but the picture that beats all the other movies by a huge proportion. For example, in 2004, the year when big, North American movies *Harry Potter and the Prisoner of Azkaban, The Lord of the Rings: The Return of the King* and *Spider-man 2* were released in Japan (all heavyweight franchises), *Howl's Moving Castle* was the top film by a long way (in 2003, the biggest movie worldwide was *The Lord of the Rings 3,* and in 2004 it was *Harry Potter 3*).

From *Princess Mononoke* onwards, Hayao Miyazaki's movies have had very wide releases in Japan: 348 screens for *Princess Mononoke*, 336 screens for *Spirited Away,* and 450 screens for *Howl's Moving Castle* (compare that with the

3,000 or more screens in the U.S.A.). *Princess Mononoke* was the most financially successful Japanese film up to that point, in Japan itself, and including all releases, not just animation. Only *The Passion of the Christ* was more successful than *Spirited Away* as a foreign language movie worldwide (and *The Passion of the Christ* is a true oddity, being an American religious movie filmed in dead languages – Latin and Aramaic).

Once again, one should remember that it's box office *rentals* not box office *gross* that is the more accurate indicator of a film's financial returns. And figures should always be *adjusted for inflation*, otherwise they're even more inaccurate.

Hayao Miyazaki has said that he is most concerned with how his movies are received in Japan: Japan is the primary market for Miyazaki's pictures (culturally as well as financially).[88] 'I'm only worried about how my film would be viewed in Japan. Frankly, I don't worry too much about how it plays elsewhere,' Miyazaki told CNN in 1999.[89]

Hayao Miyazaki was not an English speaker,[90] and relied on other people to translate and dub his movies. His chief concern was with the Japanese audience: he hoped that the translations and dubs of his pictures would be accurate. That was the main thing – to stay true to the movie as it was intended to be seen. That most especially applied to the dictum: *no cuts*.

Hayao Miyazaki didn't want to make movies for fans who only wanted one sort of movie. It was no good for film producers to categorize fans, Miyazaki remarked in 1989, and only make films for that kind of person.

Hayao Miyazaki warned against viewers watching his movies over and over. It's not good getting obsessed with a film, Miyazaki insisted: to a friend who said his child had watched *Princess Mononoke* over 50 times, Miyazaki sent him a letter:

> saying he was making a terrible mistake. Once a year, maybe once a lifetime, is really how often you should see

---

[88] Miyazaki, like many filmmakers, takes a dim view of critics and reviews, but values audiences: 'I never read reviews. I'm not interested. But I value a lot the reactions of the spectators'. However, a filmmaker can't just do *anything* he likes. 'I think it's impossible to do everything you want', Miyazaki claimed. 'You have to make such a movie in a different place from a movie which one or two million people pay to see and get satisfied. When I watch a movie such as Tarkovsky's *Stalker*, I feel 'this SOB is doing as he pleases!' I think he is such a talented guy.'
[89] CNN, *Today*, Oct 3, 1997.
[90] According to Lonely Planet's *Japan* guidebook, few Japanese can speak English as well as most Europeans, or Hong Kong Chinese, or Singaporeans, or Indians (C. Rowthorn, 2007, 50).

any of my films.... Owning a little puppy will teach you a lot more about life than watching *Totoro* 100 times.[91]

In his writings collected in *Starting Point*, Hayao Miyazaki repeatedly complains about the current state of animation, in movies and on TV. But he doesn't have rose-tinted glasses on: animated shows weren't better in the 'old days', either: it was just that there were far fewer of them, so each one stood out more.

As well as the sorry state of current animation, Hayao Miyazaki also thinks there is *too much* animation around today, and too many channels on TV, too much of everything. So it was impossible to judge if anything was any good anymore, because viewers were inundated with it. And it also meant that animators were more overworked than ever before, having to satisfy television's insatiable demand for more material.

In 2005, there were 430 *animé* production studios in Japan,[92] and most of them were in Tokyo. (And that's one of the many reasons why so many *animé* shows are set in Tokyo, including some of Hayao Miyazaki's films). The *animé* market was worth about ¥20 billion ($200m) in 2004.

The typical 30 minute (= 22/ 23 mins with ads) *animé* TV show costs 10 million Yen. Thus, Hayao Miyazaki's movies are very high budget movies, in Japanese *animé* terms, not only compared to TV shows, but also compared with animated (and live-action) feature films: the budget of *Spirited Away* was in the region of ¥1.9-2.5 billion, or $19-25 million US dollars. So Miyazaki's pictures are some of the most expensive in Japanese animation history, and in Japanese film history.[93]

But $19m or $25m is still a lot cheaper than the North American equivalent (and $1 million for *Nausicaä of the Valley of the Wind* in 1984 is a bargain): the animated Disney and Pixar movies of recent times have included the following budgets: *Tarzan* $115m (or $142m or $150m, depending on sources); *Treasure Planet* $140m; *Ratatouille* $150m; and *Home On the Range* $110m.

---

91 Quoted in S. Fritz, 1999.
92 Animation studios themselves become the centre of attention for *animé* fans, and fans will follow particular animation houses and their work. The famous ones include Production I.G., Bandai, Studio 4°C, Gainax, Madhouse, Sunrise, Pioneer, Tezuka, Gonzo, Clamp, Toei, and of course Studio Ghibli.
93 The only reason that theatrical movies are often better than TV animation was the budget, Hayao Miyazaki asserted (SP, 55), but it didn't matter to him whether he made TV movies or theatrical movies.

These figures aren't really helpful, because movie budgets are notoriously difficult to check accurately: no one wants to admit how much money something *really* cost, or *exactly* how much they're earning (and Hollywood studios routinely exaggerate figures like budgets and grosses). But you know that if the budgets are one hundred million dollars or more, then *somebody somewhere* is making a lot of money. As William Goldman noted, there's a lot of money to be had in simply *making* a film, regardless of whether it's released or seen or not. And some people make a living out of producing movies, including existing on development deals and other deals, and many of those films aren't shot, and some that *are* filmed aren't released.

It's hard to believe that movies like *Home On the Range* or *Tarzan* from the Mouse House could have cost over $110 million or $115 million, but there are all sorts of economic factors to consider. The piece-work labour of Japanese *animé* is going to be cheaper than hiring staff on a permanent basis that occurs more in North American animation.[94] Living costs, unions and working conditions in Japan and America are further factors. The much longer production schedules of American animated movies must contribute to the higher costs too: Hayao Miyazaki and his teams delivered *Nausicaä of the Valley of the Wind* and *Laputa: Castle In the Sky* in less than a year, while Disney and Pixar movies can take 3 or more years. However, the large crews of hundreds of workers aren't hired for all of those years, but it's safe to say that the production teams in American (and Western) feature animation are larger than those in the Japanese animation industry, and that they are hired for longer periods (Disney and Pixar have much bigger front offices than Japanese studios). All of which drives costs up (at the same time, Western animation companies farm out work to outfits in countries such as Korea, Thailand and India, just as the Japanese animation industry does).

There are a number of reasons why Hayao Miyazaki can command such high budgets for his movies: one is the simple fact that, from his first film *The Castle of Cagliostro* onwards, his movies have made money. And the later ones, such as *Porco Rosso* or *Princess Mononoke*, have been hugely successful. Miyazaki has had the top grossing movie in Japan a number of times: *Porco Rosso, Ponyo, Princess Mononoke,*

---

94 Miyazaki often complained about the piecework system of producing animation in Japan, which turned out work like an assembly line, instead of the hand-crafted and personal, artistic approach that Miyazaki favoured.

Spirited Away, Howl's Moving Castle and *The Wind Rises*. That means his films can attract a lot of investment. Other reasons would include merchandizing and prestige: Miyazaki's movies are very high quality pictures, works of art in themselves, so that glory is reflected back on the investors (as in 'look at us, we put money into *Spirited Away*'). And a filmmaker who has never produced a flop is valued highly by the money-men.

❖

Like the films of Yasujiro Ozu or Kenji Mizoguchi or Akira Kurosawa, the films of Hayao Miyazaki are very *Japanese* – they are set in Japan, draw on Japanese history and culture,[95] and are about Japanese subjects (even when they're set in or about Europe,[96] and seem to portray European charas).[97] But they are also – like the movies of Ozu, Mizoguchi and Kurosawa – films which can and do travel around the world.

Most films don't. Most movies don't get released or shown outside their country of origin (sad but true – how many Egyptian, or Swedish, or Korean movies have you seen in a first-run theatre recently?). Hayao Miyazaki's movies are both very Japanese and very inter-national. Only a few filmmakers achieve that kind of flexibility.

Hayao Miyazaki is sometimes dubbed 'the Japanese Disney'; Helen McCarthy makes another suggestion, more in tune with Miyazaki's hands-on artistry: 'the Kurosawa of Japanese animation' (2002, 10). Akira Kurosawa is of course the giant of Japanese cinema: there is a marvellous series of interviews between Miyazaki and Kurosawa, which are highly recommended (published in 1993 as *What Is a Film?*).[98]

Hayao Miyazaki ranks up there with the great Japanese filmmakers, I would say. Only a few filmmakers reach those heights, but Miyazaki can rightly be placed alongside Yasujiro Ozu, Kenji Mizoguchi and Akira Kurosawa. Miyazaki does everything that a great filmmaker can do or should do – and then he does something extra, that magical or special element that raises very good art to the status of great art.

That extra or magical or mysterious or added ingredient

---

[95] Miyazaki drew on Japanese history, ancient Japanese court tales, sci-fi, fairy tales, and mythology.

[96] It was no wonder that Japanese movies were accepted in Europe, Miyazaki pointed out, when Japan's imported so much of European culture – 'literature, art, films, political philosophy, and ways of thinking' (TP, 323).

[97] Although Hayao Miyazaki's cinema employs a huge input from European culture, history and landscapes, his films are always Japanese. Even the ones set in European places, like *Porco Rosso* or *Kiki's Delivery Service*, are very, very Japanese.

[98] *My Neighbor Totoro* was one of Kurosawa's 100 favourite films; he loved the Cat-bus; Kurosawa said he wept watching *Kiki's Delivery Service;* and he also reckoned that Miyazaki's movies were more important than his own.

is a combination of (1) compassion and humanity, (2) a world vision which includes *everything*, *every* aspect of being alive, and (3) an ability to embrace and celebrate all forms of life (in Miyazaki's case, the natural world as well as the human realm).

Or, to put it another way: the films of Hayao Miyazaki are far, far above your regular, average movie. They are special, highly individual, very unusual, and deeply moving. To achieve that in any medium is *very* difficult. To do it with painted pieces of plastic seems particularly amazing. Once again, let's not forget that Miyazaki is not working alone, but has a huge team of collaborators, some young and new to the business, and some who have worked with him for decades.

CELS VERSUS COMPUTERS

The films of Hayao Miyazaki, like most of Japanese animation, are traditional cel animation, but computers and computer-generated effects and devices are employed from time to time. In *Princess Mononoke*, Studio Ghibli began to use computers, but only in small amounts. For instance, computers were applied to the time-consuming process of ink and paint for about 10,000 cels (the intention was to use the computer for around 5,000 cels, but with deadlines approaching, the production resorted to more computer work). However, there were some 140,000 cels in *Princess Mononoke*, so the computer was used to ink and paint less than 10% of the cels. *Princess Mononoke* has around 1600 shots or scenes (in Japanese animation, shots are also called cuts or scenes).

As well as computerized ink and paint, *Princess Mononoke* also employed digital technology to build 3-D models (for the Didara-botchi god, for instance), and to use particle systems to drive animation. Studio Ghibli's movies, though, never look computerized or digital, because by the far the bulk is conventional (hand-drawn) cel animation (and even when computers are used extensively in animation, drawing skills are still absolutely essential). However, cel animation in movies is as supremely *technological* and *industrial* as computers or digital technology. *Everything* in movies is *technological*, everything is fake, everything is a highly sophisticated cultural form created by humans for mass entertainment. So whether it's done with machines/tools like cameras or pencils or paintbrushes or computers isn't really the point.

It *is* important, though, I think, that Hayao Miyazaki's films don't have the plasticky look of computer-generated imagery, or the 3-D look of computer animation, or the floaty appearance of computerized additions to scenes. For instance, since the mid-1990s and the success of *Toy Story*, animated movies have shifted towards what's termed 3-D (a misleading term, as all of animation is always two dimensional, when it's projected on a screen. It's more a technical term, referring to the use of 3-D models and devices inside computer software, and the simulation of 3-D with use of 3-D goggles for viewing movies). But Miyazaki's works are refreshingly *not* like the 3-D animation that's seen in many animated movies from *Toy Story* onwards: all of Pixar's output, plus *Ice Age, Shrek, Robots, Chicken Little*, etc.[99]

It's significant, too, that Hayao Miyazaki's pictures don't employ digital additions to scenes which don't really mesh with traditional 2-D animation. For instance, Disney's *Treasure Planet, Atlantis, The Rescuers Down Under* and Warner Bros' *The Iron Man* have used computer-generated (3-D) elements placed into hand-drawn (but probably computer-inked) 2-D animation. The digital elements often look floaty and disconnected to the rest of the scenes.

Hayao Miyazaki thought it was too late for him to convert to CGI and computers; he reckoned that hand-drawn animation would never die out: there would always be someone producing it in a garage somewhere.

MIYAZAKI AND DISNEY

So many qualities of Hayao Miyazaki's cinema would endear themselves to the makers of the Walt Disney Studios' movies. For Miyazaki, *Snow White and the Seven Dwarfs* and *The Old Mill*[100] were the pinnacles of Walt Disney's achievement in animation: you can see in *Snow White,* Miyazaki said, how the animators were

---

[99] Miyazaki remarked in 2005: 'I think 2-D animation disappeared from Disney because they made so many uninteresting films. They became very conservative in the way they created them. It's too bad. I thought 2-D and 3-D could coexist happily.' However, the Mouse House brought back 2-D animation in 2007.
[100] In a lecture on animation in Osaka in 1982, Hayao Miyazaki spoke admiringly of a short cartoon he felt was the height of Walt Disney's output, a piece the studio never surpassed: *The Old Mill* (SP, 124).

clearly bursting to try out a variety of new techniques. In fact, *Snow White* demonstrates how animators can complete a work in a very healthy way, achieving a type of perfection in the process. (SP, 124)

But Hayao Miyazaki has critiqued the pandering of Disney's movies to the lowest common denominator: there must be some kind of purity of feeling in a movie, even the popular and mainstream ones. They might invite anyone in, 'but the barriers to exit must be high and purifying' (SP, 72). For Miyazaki:

> Films must also not be produced out of idle nervousness or boredom, or be used to recognize, emphasize, or amplify true vulgarity. And in that context, I must say that I hate Disney's works. The barrier to both the entry and exit of Disney films is too low and too wide. To me, they show nothing but contempt for the audience. (SP, 72)

The Walt Disney corporation itself has been involved in many of Hayao Miyazaki's films – producing the English language versions, as well as distributing them in Western territories, and on video in Japan, via its Buena Vista distribution arm (the deal was made in 1996 between Disney[101] and Tokuma, the publishing company that owned Studio Ghibli). However, the Disney corporation does not handle Ghibli's merchandizing, which would seem a perfect fit at first. Ghibli and Tokuma have held onto merchandizing rights.[102] And they haven't allowed computer games to be produced from Ghibli movies, which's very common in animation in Japan (although *Nausicaä* had two video games).

I'm sure there have been talks at Studio Ghibli about making more *Totoro* outings, including a TV series (many animation houses would've produced a TV series right away). But it's significant that when Ghibli created some animated shorts for its museum they were *Totoro* tie-ins.

Prior to the deal with Disney, Studio Ghibli had been approached by Fox and Warners (Fox had already released Ghibli movies in some territories). The chief reason that Disney was selected as an overseas distribution partner for Ghibli was that it agreed to the stipulation that nothing would be cut from Ghibli's movies. Fox and Warners hadn't agreed to

---
[101] Critics pointed out that Disney had been slow in releasing Ghibli's movies: only two (*Kiki* and *Mononoke*) in 6 years after the deal.
[102] According to Helen McCarthy, Hayao Miyazaki is not much interested in merchandizing or having his movies distributed outside of Japan. Those issues are 'completely unimportant. To him, the movies themselves, seen full-size in the cinema, are the only things that count' (M, 211).

that, according to Toshio Suzuki (the decision to withhold Ghibli's movies for ten years in the West after the disastrous treatment of *Nausicaä* has possibly harmed the reception of their movies).

JAPANESE AND ENGLISH

Another striking aspect of Hayao Miyazaki's films is the success of the English language versions. As anyone who's watched a few non-English movies will know, some dubbing can be terrible, produced with barely any care at all. The first time audiences in the West will have seen a Miyazaki movie will probably be in a dubbed version (they are favoured by TV broadcasters, for instance: if there's a choice, a broadcaster will always go with a dubbed version). The first movie by Miyazaki I saw was *Laputa: Castle In the Sky* in the Walt Disney dubbed version; my son Jake and I watched the movie and were amazed by it.

Hayao Miyazaki's films have been given the high-class treatment, with big name actors voicing the characters: Michael Keaton, Claire Danes, Jean Simmons, Christian Bale, Lauren Bacall, Jade Pinkett Smith, etc. For Disney, Miyazaki's movies are prestige projects – but they also sell well – in home entertainment formats (though not nearly as well as in Japan).

You might recognize some of the voice cast used among the secondary characters in the Walt Disney versions of Hayao Miyazaki's movies, as they appear in many animations, from Disney, Pixar and other studios: David Ogden Stiers, John Ratzenberger, Jack Angel, John Hostetter, Tress MacNeill, Sherry Lynn, Phil Hartman, Tony Jay, and Cloris Leachman.

The English language versions have altered Hayao Miyazaki's films, however, by changing some of the lines of dialogue, or adding lines (not to mention the vocal performance itself). Most Western, English-speaking audiences probably prefer the English dubbed versions (though I prefer the Japanese versions in all cases).

For instance, there are many differences between the English subtitles – which presumably translate the Japanese dialogue (though not all of it) – and the English dubbed versions. There are lines in the English subtitles which don't appear in the English dubbed version – and vice versa. Background sounds and additional lines of dialogue are also added. The Japanese filmmakers (including Hayao Miyazaki) are not present during the recordings; Miyazaki doesn't write the dub scripts (he's not an English speaker), and doesn't direct them. The dubs are produced thousands of miles from Japan (in Vancouver, Houston, L.A., wherever), months later, by teams that had nothing to do with the conception or production of the movie (so for them the dubbing is just another job).

So dubs can't count as the work of Hayao Miyazaki or the original filmmakers. This means that Studio Ghibli's films have a slightly different impact in their Japanese subtitled and English dubbed versions (regardless of where they are screened). Also, some companies have re-edited movies such as *The Castle of Cagliostro* to get rid of Japanese words and credits. Also, the English dubs use mainly American voices and American English, which inflects them with a particular cultural flavour and ideology. As these are profoundly *Japanese* movies, this can create cultural conflicts which are sometimes offensive. For me, American dubs add a layer of Americanization which's too often simply horrible. So my objections to dubbing include artistic, performance, casting and production reasons, running all the way thru language and culture to political and ideological reasons.

3
❖
ASPECTS OF HAYAO MIYAZAKI'S CINEMA

MOVIES FOR EVERYONE

A significant element in Hayao Miyazaki's cinema is that it doesn't talk down to its audience. It takes its fantastical scenarios seriously – but also allows for humour and silliness. His films are not patronizing, but also not lecturing or hectoring. Pedagogical, yes, but not over-zealous, or hitting the audience over the head with moralizing.

Hayao Miyazaki's movies, like all great fantasy movies, are not (just) for children, but for people of all ages. In fact, like fairy tales, their primary audience is not children at all, but adults. Children don't write fairy tales, don't publish books, and don't make fantasy films. Adults do. And fairy tales always were for adults, until the 19th century, when they became part of the commodification of childhood.[103]

But originally, and for always, fairy tales have been written *by adults, for adults*. Similarly with fantasy movies. That's not to say that the films of Hayao Miyazaki and his teams are not enjoyed by children, and do not contain elements that address children directly. And of course Miyazaki's films often feature children or young people as their heroes. Childhood is 'the best time of one's life' for Miyazaki [TP, 163]).

Working for children meant *beginnings*: for children, something is new for the first time: the first time you took a train journey by yourself (like Chihiro in *Spirited Away*). Hayao Miyazaki explained:

> The single difference between films for children and films for adults is that in films for children, there is always the option to start again, to create a new beginning. In films for adults, there are no ways to change things. What happened, happened.

---
[103] See any of the excellent books by Jack Zipes in the bibliography on this topic.

Hayao Miyazaki did not make movies wholly for children, but his desire to entertain children was certainly vital: 'I try to create what I wanted to see when I was a child, or what I believe my own children want to see' (SP, 50). However, he also acknowledged that producing movies for children can be even more challenging than producing movies for adults, because 'they deal with origins and fundamentals' (SP, 91).

> When I hear talk of children's futures, I just get upset, because the future of a child is to become a boring adult. Children have only the moment. In that moment, an individual child is gradually passing through the state of childhood... but there are children in existence all the time.[104]

Being a parent was certainly a spur to Hayao Miyazaki wanting to make pictures for children. Why? Because, he said in a 1995 interview, when you have a child of three, you want to show it something good. And when you see there is nothing good enough out there, you have to make a movie yourself (SP, 432).

Detractors would probably trot out the same criticisms of Hayao Miyazaki's cinema as they do of Walt Disney's films, or children's book authors: they would see only that Miyazaki's movies are very colourful and stylized and so can't be 'serious' or 'important'. They would say that Miyazaki's films are intended for children, and so can't be as serious or as valuable as films by, say, Ingmar Bergman or Wong Kar-wai. They would say that Miyazaki's pictures are 'lightweight' or light-hearted, as if the only kind of serious movies have to be heavily melancholy or dramatic or tragic (as if a comedy can't make all of the same points a serious drama can).[105] And finally they would complain that Miyazaki's pictures are fantasies, and fantasy doesn't have the cultural kudos of Shakespearean or Sophoclean tragedy.

All junk, of course.

A recurring theme in Hayao Miyazaki's writings is the ambition to make something for children that's meaningful and special, that has more value than the run-of-the-mill animation on television (SP, 187). 'I want to create works that children can enjoy, or that they can spend some quality time with', Miyazaki asserted (SP, 55).

All adults were children once, and that is partly what

---
104 Quoted in A. Osmond, 2008, 20.
105 As Mel Brooks says, he can make all of the serious points he wants to make in a comedy. You don't have to stop laughing for Brooks.

Hayao Miyazaki's movies trade on: not childishness so much as a return to a child-like view of the world[106] – which includes wonder and awe as well as fear and anxiety. In this respect, Miyazaki's cinema shares much with Disney's cinema, or many of the great filmmakers who have taken children or young people as their protagonists.

Hayao Miyazaki and his teams don't split up the audience, and they don't wink at the audience (or at the adult members of the audience). Miyazaki's movies are not self-conscious or 'postmodern' or cleverly allusive of other movies. Oh, they draw on other films often, but they don't do superficial *hommages* or spoofs of other movies. They don't deliver those in-jokes and clever satires of other films, which are so much a part of the Hollywood family movie.

Contemporary animated films are stuffed with those allusions and pop culture references: *Finding Nemo, Chicken Little, Cars, Ice Age,* and, most notoriously, the *Shrek* series.[107] But *Laputa: Castle In the Sky, Porco Rosso* and *Spirited Away* don't contain those silly references to the rolling boulder in *Raiders of the Lost Art,* or Norman Bates in *Psycho,* or the shark in *Jaws,* or numerous quotations from pop music. Hayao Miyazaki and his teams are too busy telling the story in their films to stop for jokes about *E.T.* or martial arts movies. They don't want to take you out of the story with bitter snipes at Disney or DreamWorks or Fox or Warners, or turning the film halfway through into a dumb, TV game show. They are not, in short, theme park movies, consumer movies, commodified movies, or pop culture movies.

While contemporary Hollywood cinema endlessly cannibalizes itself (remakes on top of sequels on top of remakes – when was the last time you saw a *new* American movie based on an *original idea* released in a first-run *theatre*, not on DVD or TV?), Hayao Miyazaki's cinema just gets on with making the films and telling a cracking tale. Miyazaki's pictures are boundless when it comes to ideas and inventions.

But the movies of Hayao Miyazaki and his teams are also not deadly serious – they are not po-faced and do not take

---

106 Creating *manga* for children means working at their eye-level, from their perspective, asserts Hiroshi Fujimoto (Fujiko F. Fujio), the creator of *Doraemon*: 'you have to create something you really enjoy, that they also happen to enjoy'.
107 DreamWorks' *Shrek* (2001) replayed fairy tale clichés in a knowing, ironic, postmodern and comic fashion. There were many digs at Disney films and the Disney corporation in *Shrek*. It seemed a bit odd, even obsessive, that Jeffrey Katzenberg (via DreamWorks SKG) should still be attacking Disney, his former employers. By the time *Shrek* came out, it was seven years since Katzenberg had departed the Mouse House. Some critics exalt the *Shrek* movies, but you can't even place them beside the films of Hayao Miyazaki.

themselves too seriously, like the films of Andrei Tarkovsky or Carl-Theodor Dreyer. There's just too much warmth and tenderness and *life* in a Miyazaki movie for it to be solemn for too long.

FLIGHT

Flight — the sky — transcendence. Few filmmakers have been so preoccupied with flying as Hayao Miyazaki (Steven Spielberg is definitely one). One wonders if Miyazaki would really liked to have been a pilot[108] – in World War One, and into the 1920s (just like Porco Rosso).

One of the reasons that Hayao Miyazaki is able to include so many flying sequences in his movies is surely cost: a flying scene can't be much more costly to produce than other action scenes in animation. But if you had to do those scenes in live-action, they would be much more expensive.

And it's not only flying in machines and aeroplanes in Hayao Miyazaki's cinema, although there are 100s of those – many characters fly by themselves, whether it's Totoro, Ponyo, Howl, Yubaba as a bird and Haku as a dragon in *Spirited Away*, Sheeta and Pazu (using the crystal) in *Laputa: Castle In the Sky*, or Kiki on her broomstick.

HAYAO MIYAZAKI AND FEMINISM

Not a few commentators have noted that Hayao Miyazaki is a feminist. At Studio Ghibli, Miyazaki has been concerned about the working conditions for women (the jobs in animation production have traditionally been partly arranged along gender lines: at the Disney Studios in the Classical Hollywood era, for instance, all of the key animators were male, while the inking department, which comprises dull, repetitive work, were largely female). You try naming ten major female animators. (Japan is still a rather patriarchal society: women earn 66% of what men earn (compared to 76% in the U.S.A., and 83% in Britain), and only 9% of seats in the government (in the Diet)).

Studio Ghibli has nurtured women in animation jobs:

---
[108] Miyazaki has remarked that he enjoys flying (particularly thru skies with interesting clouds), but has no ambitions to become a pilot (AI, 29).

Eiko Tanaka, for instance, now a big name in Japanese *animé*, founded Studio 4°C[109] in 1986 (she had been a producer on *Totoro* and *Kiki*); Atsuko Tanaka (a key animator at Ghibli), animated the short film *Mon-Mon the Water Spider* for the Ghibli Museum; and Makiko Futaki has been an animator on most of Ghibli's output.

Certainly a pro-women stance comes out in Hayao Miyazaki's films, in the roles that he and his writers assign to women (his mother is the source of inspiration for many aspects of his female characters, according to Dan Cavallaro [29]). Second wave feminists and third wave feminists could likely criticize the films of Miyazaki and his teams on numerous counts in their portrayal of women. But it's certainly significant that so many of Miyazaki's protagonists are female. You can search through the work of many of Miyazaki's contemporaries and struggle to find movies with a female lead. But *Nausicaä of the Valley of the Wind*, *My Neighbor Totoro*, *Kiki's Delivery Service*, *Spirited Away* and *Howl's Moving Castle* have female characters as the chief protagonist (in *Laputa: Castle In the Sky*, both Pazu and Sheeta are the heroes, in *Ponyo On the Cliff By the Sea* it's Ponyo and Sosuke, and in *Princess Mononoke* it's Ashitaka and San). And it's not only Miyazaki's films, but those of Studio Ghibli: *Whisper of the Heart*, *The Cat Returns*, *Only Yesterday*, *From Up On Poppy Hill* and *The Borrower Arrietty*, have women in the main roles, while *Grave of the Fireflies* is about a boy and a girl.

The people who put together Marco's plane in *Porco Rosso* are all women (a plane factory's traditionally a male preserve, as is the foundry where the women work in Irontown in *Princess Mononoke*), and the workers in the bathhouse in *Spirited Away* are women (there are men there too – but they are giant frogs, which's somehow apt).

It should be noted, though, that the most famous animation studio in film history, the Disney Studios, has put women at the forefront of many of their movies: *Snow White and the Seven Dwarfs*, *Cinderella*, *Alice In Wonderland*, *Sleeping Beauty*, *Lady and the Tramp* and *Mary Poppins* during Uncle Walt's lifetime, and in later movies such as *Mulan*, *The Little Mermaid*, *Beauty and the Beast*, *Pocahontas*, *The Princess and the Frog*, etc.

Having a female character in the lead role doesn't make much difference, though, if everything else in the film is patriarchal and masculinist. So the notions of feminism, and

---

109 Studio 4°C's output includes *Memories*, *Steam-boy*, *Spriggan*, *Mind Game* and *The Animatrix*.

female agency, and women's empowerment, and how women are portrayed and perceived, is problematic. It's not enough to point out that a picture has some key female characters; it's much more complicated than that.

It's important, for instance, that women are not often depicted in a very negative light in Hayao Miyazaki's cinema, as they are in so many North American movies. The images of women in Miyazaki's tend to be positive and life-affirming. Some of the women in Miyazaki's movies are very strong charas: you wouldn't mess with San in *Princess Mononoke* or Dola in *Laputa: Castle In the Sky* or Yubaba in *Spirited Away*. And the young heroines of Miyazaki's movies are also tough, practical and assertive characters: Kiki, Nausicaä, Fio, Chihiro (and sometimes they might not start out wholly confident and independent, like Chihiro, but they usually end up like that).

Why so many female characters? One reason Hayao Miyazaki offered was that when girls do something, it's kinda automatically more interesting than when boys do something:

> If a boy is walking with long strides I think nothing of it, but if a girl is walking boldly, I think she looks so full of vitality. That's because I'm a man: women might think a boy striding along looks cool. (SP, 428)

Because Hayao Miyazaki is a man: yes, it *is* that simple sometimes. Miyazaki would rather look at girls than boys, and would rather have girls as the main character than boys. Asked about his preference for female characters, Miyazaki replied that it was a complicated issue, but reduced his explanation to this: 'it's because I love women very much'.

A criticism of the depiction of female characters in Hayao Miyazaki's cinema might be that he and his writers have simply transferred male/ masculine attributes to a female character (as Hollywood movies do – consider Hollywood action movies, such as *Alien, G.I. Jane, Twilight, Lara Croft, Catwoman, Underworld, Kill Bill*, etc).

I don't think that Hayao Miyazaki's films do that, though; I don't think of Miyazaki's female characters as simply female versions of male characters. In fact, it's more that in some cases, Miyazaki's cinema doesn't make that much of gender differences. His characters don't angst about being female or male – they are too busy getting on with being themselves. There are few examples of characters voicing views such as 'girls shouldn't do that', or 'women don't do that'.

Hayao Miyazaki has commented a number of times on

wanting to provide positive role models for young, Japanese women, and *Spirited Away* was made partly to do that. It was partly a movie produced for young women, who weren't being catered for, Miyazaki thought, in movies. Certainly *shojo* characters[110] such as Nausicaä and Kiki and Fio (in *Porco Rosso*) are positive role models – they are hard-working (a vital Miyazaki characteristic), independent (also important), idealistic, optimistic, helpful, confident, warm-hearted, and (crucially) compassionate. They are characters who believe in themselves and what they are doing.

It's true they can be too idealistic (and naïve) at times, and have to adjust their hopes and dreams to fit reality; they can be irritatingly enthusiastic, and have to temper their enthusiasm; they can be headstrong, and stubborn.

But they are seldom negligent of other people's feelings; they are deferential (and remember their manners when others remind them, as Lin does to Chihiro in *Spirited Away*); they are trusting, and loyal. And, unlike too many young characters in Western animation, they are never bratty.[111] Ghibli/ Miyazaki has also avoided overly cute depictions of young women, which are everywhere in Japanese animation:[112] they do have the large eyes and tiny mouths of *animé* women, but they are not babes or dolls.[113] Large breasts are common in Japanese *animé*, but in Miyazaki's films they are reserved for older matriarchal figures, like Dola in *Laputa* or Yubaba in *Spirited Away*.

Hayao Miyazaki recognized that *shojo manga* (comicbooks depicting young women) were really psychological: the real story took place in the text and the blank spaces of the page, not in the visuals. Thus, in turning a *shojo* comicbook into an animated movie the real question was: 'how much of a person's psychological state can really be represented with visuals' (SP, 101).

Hayao Miyazaki's female characters are at their worst when they are self-absorbed, like Chihiro at the beginning of

---

110 The *shojo* character is a young girl, somewhere between a child and an adult. The *shojo* is marked by a fondness for popular culture, for cute consumer goods (*kawaii*), a wistful nostalgia, and an innocent eroticism (S. Napier, 118). Many of Hayao Miyazaki's characters are *shojo*, of course, although some critics have seen Miyazaki's young women as 'youths wearing *shojo* masks'. Cuteness is certainly a key element in Miyazaki's young female characters. It's no surprise that many of Miyazaki's *shojo* characters are linked to flight, because flying represents escape *par excellence*.
111 Hayao Miyazaki has also avoided portraying *shojo* characters as sexually objectified (called *loli*) and 'play toys for Lolita complex guys' (SP).
112 Cute characters – *kawaii* – are a staple of Japanese animation: Pikachu in *Pokémon*, for example, or young women in *manga* and *animé*.
113 A. Osmond, 1998.

Spirited Away, or Kiki when she's lost confidence in her witchy ability. When they are passive, like Clarisse in *The Castle of Cagliostro,* they conform more to stereotypes of princesses in towers who need to be rescued by dashing princes (Lupin III).

Hayao Miyazaki's women are at their best when they are brave, and kind-hearted, and compassionate, and confident in their decisions. When they trust themselves, and when they gain the trust of others. They can be just as heroic as guys, and often more heroic (Nausicaä, Kiki) – because they are the heroines, the chief characters, and no one else is going to do it if they don't. Often they have to act alone, without help or back-up, and sometimes without really knowing what they are doing.

CHARACTERS: THE LOOK

In terms of compositions and figures, the films of Hayao Miyazaki feature recurring types. The children, for instance, are wonderfully energetic, laughing characters, with large eyes[114] and enormous mouths that stretch across their whole faces when they laugh. They are squat, round body types, that bounce around a scene like basket balls.

The heroes and heroines tend to be rather intense, with the clean, pure lines of classical beauty, and the familiar features of Japanese *animé*: wide eyes (always with a couple of eye lights), tiny, button noses, small, neat mouths, and fabulous, spiky, wild hair (that usually wafts in the breeze, and not only in flying or magical scenes).[115] They are usually highly agile and dynamic, sometimes clumsy, and usually possess slender bodies like dancers.

The older men in Hayao Miyazaki's cinema run from tall, skinny, neurotic types to gruff, burly, muscular figures. Short, portly figures recur (like Marco in *Porco Rosso* or the old engineer in *Laputa: Castle In the Sky* or Jigo in *Princess Mononoke*). Some are dynamic adventurers, like Lord Yupa in *Nausicaä of the Valley of the Wind,* and some are dynamic but comic, like the Mamma Aiuto boss in *Porco Rosso*. Miyazaki loves moustaches and beards (in films such as *Nausicaä of the Valley of the Wind,* there's no mouth at all for some of the

---

[114] Why does Miya-san persist in using the big eyes of *animé*? One reason is that he finds them beautiful, and another reason is economics: to be commercial for a Japanese audience, Ghibli needs to stick to the styles of popular culture (TP, 91).
[115] When it comes to drawing women and girls, Miyazaki tends to focus on the hair above all.

male characters, just a giant, bushy shape).

Another character type that Hayao Miyazaki has made his own is the powerful, older woman, usually rather large, sometimes with a vast bosom, very big hair, and typically an enchantress. The costumes are usually skirts and dresses, with hair in traditional styles, such as buns: the crone in *Nausicaä of the Valley of the Wind,* the Witch of the Waste in *Howl's Moving Castle,* and the one that tops them all, the totally incredible, once-seen-never-forgotten Yubaba in *Spirited Away.*

Few Hayao Miyazaki heroes or heroines wear jeans and Tee shirts, crop-tops or bikinis,[116] baseball caps, tattoos or piercings. Sometimes overalls or dungarees, sometimes army uniforms, and sometimes, like Pazu in *Laputa: Castle In the Sky,* a shirt and breeches. The young women tend to wear dresses or skirts (Kiki hates her dark witch's dress).[117] The costumes are dictated very much by the periods which Miyazaki and his teams like to explore, of course: the late 19th century and early 20th century, or, occasionally, more mythical eras, as in *Nausicaä of the Valley of the Wind* or *Princess Mononoke*.

As well as using women in the lead roles, Hayao Miyazaki also likes to pair up characters, so that the hero is essentially split into two. Often, they are male and female, and are usually regarded as a couple (sometimes they actively resent being seen as a couple, like Porco with Fio in *Porco Rosso*, and sometimes they are not quite a romantic couple, like San and Ashitaka in *Princess Mononoke*). And sometimes Miyazaki likes to subvert expectations, and reverse gender roles. For instance, he makes the leader of the pirates in *Laputa: Castle In the Sky* a powerful woman, Dola. And in *Mononoke*, the tough boss of the industrial, Irontown community is not a man, but a beautiful woman, Eboshi.[118] And in *Kiki* it's the girl who rescues the boy.

CHARACTERS: TYPES.

One of the strongest elements in Hayao Miyazaki's cinema, and one of the chief reasons for its enduring

---
[116] Ariel the mermaid in Disney's 1989 flick sports one of the more preposterous costumes for a fairy tale character.
[117] There's an erotic component to this – Hayao Miyazaki has commented that he likes skirts and dresses. And like other Japanese *animé*, the skirts and dresses tend to blow in the wind all the time.
[118] A recurring motif in Miyazaki's cinema are the pairings between older women and younger women: Kushana and Nausicaä in *Nausicaä of the Valley of the Wind,* Clarisse and Fujiko in *The Castle of Cagliostro,* Dola and Sheeta in *Laputa: Castle In the Sky,* and Gina and Fio in *Porco Rosso.*

popularity, is surely Miyazaki's ability to create convincing and likeable heroes and heroines. These are young people (sometimes older people) that are resourceful, hard-working, brave, dignified, and creative, but also sometimes vulnerable, sometimes moody, sometimes doubting themselves and their abilities. They are not superheroes, however, though they do occasionally have some superhero traits – such as the ability to fly.

They are not petty, not greedy, not envious, not small-minded; they are generous, and kind, and helpful, and loyal. All of these positive qualities might make them insufferable and arrogant, but no, the characters in Hayao Miyazaki's films are very appealing. These are genuine people; sometimes they can be very serious, but they are also ready to laugh and fool around. At the level of characterization, the movies of Miyazaki are as convincing and persuasive as any of the great filmmakers – F.W. Murnau, Ingmar Bergman, D.W. Griffith, Akira Kurosawa, whoever.

Most of the characters in Hayao Miyazaki's movies are white – either Japanese or European, with one or two Americans. If they're European, they tend to be French or Italian (not so many Brits or Scandinavians, for instance). 'White' meaning 'Caucasian' – but that is a visual convention of Japanese *animé*: to Japanese audiences, they would look Japanese; to Westerners they look 'white'. And whatever they *look* like, they are all, ultimately and fundamentally, Japanese.[119]

DAILY RITUALS.

Another significant ingredient in the films of Hayao Miyazaki is their domesticity and everydayness: every single one of the interiors in these magical movies is a believable, lived-in space: there are pots of coffee or kettles and saucepans on the stove; there are onions or tomatoes on the table; there are bowls of milk on the floor for cats and vases of flowers on the table; there are clothes hanging up inside and outside; and there are pictures on the walls. These are places where real people live – the walls and floors are not spotlessly clean, the doors are scuffed at the bottom and around the handles, and the brickwork has cracks in it.

There is an emphasis on daily rituals, like eating, cleaning, cooking, and washing. And scenes of characters going to bed or getting up out of bed. The scenes may only be little slips of colour on a plastic animated cel, but you really can

---
[119] 'Japan will always remain very much the foundation of my work' (AI, 32).

believe that Kiki is lying on her back in that big, dusty room above the baker's store in *Kiki's Delivery Service.*

STYLE

In terms of style, the animated movies of Hayao Miyazaki run from conventional cinema to sudden explosions into fantastical or heightened modes of narration. Miyazaki's use of the camera is largely traditional – classical camera moves such as slow pans to reveal an environment, or slow tilts, or slow zooms, often across verticals and horizontals. Like all the best filmmakers, Miyazaki does not wave the camera around pointlessly or use self-conscious or tricky effects.[120] However, when dramatically necessary, he will employ crash zooms, or whip pans, or rapid tracking shots, or flash cuts, or extreme close-ups. In short, Miyazaki uses the camera for a dramatic reason every time. He will not cut to a God's-eye-view, for instance, when having the camera at eye-level will do just as well, or better.

One of the striking aspects of Hayao Miyazaki's cinema is how often he uses movement in space, along the right angle to the screen. Traditionally, this's trickier to achieve convincingly in animation (the flattened movement from right to left or left to right is more common. Think of the 1960s Hanna and Barbera cartoons, where characters run past recycled backgrounds).

In films such as *Princess Mononoke* or *Laputa: Castle In the Sky,* characters race towards the camera, or away from the camera, creating a dynamic sense of movement and composition. There's never a feeling that Hayao Miyazaki and his teams are limited in any way by the animation process. Characters move from and into all corners of the frame.[121] Indeed, that feeling of total freedom of movement is one of the really appealing aspects of animation.

In some pictures, such as *Spirited Away* and *Howl's Moving Castle,* there is an interior space where the production teams decide they are going to go all-out, to throw in every idea, every colour, every prop, every and any thing they can

---

[120] I'm glad that Miyazaki hasn't got into speed ramping or self-conscious editing techniques (as some fans would like to see). There's so much going on in a Miyazaki movie, you don't need that look-at-me fussiness.

[121] Characters walking towards the camera is one of the most difficult things to do in animation, Miyazaki said (SP, 320) – and Miyazaki's cinema is full of such scenes.

think of. In *Howl's Moving Castle,* this occurs in Howl's bedroom (and also the castle itself), while in *Spirited Away* it's Yubaba's rooms (and in *Arrietty,* it's the heroine's bedroom). On the visual level, the interiors are reminiscent of the highly ornate and decorative art of Symbolist painters Gustave Moreau or Odilon Redon, or the British Pre-Raphaelite artists (such as Edward Burne-Jones or John Everett Millais or James Tissot).[122]

One of the most impressive aspects of Hayao Miyazaki's cinema is invisible: the editing and pacing. Not a frame is wasted, and none of his films seem too long or slow or padded-out. One of the beauties of animation for the viewer is that because it's so expensive and so labour-intensive, animated movies are rarely too long (and animation companies haven't got time to animate anything that won't appear in the final cut). Miyazaki's pictures are as exquisitely-paced as any in the history of cinema. That is a vital element of their success. Compare, for instance, with so many Hollywood films of the same period – 1980s-2000s – and you'll find movies that drag on and on, that have every dramatic highpoint s-t-r-e-t-c-h-e-d o-u-t mercilessly l---o---n---g, each plot point will be hammered home bluntly, and the films outstay their welcome by twenty, thirty or forty minutes. (Western/ American movies can seem so *slow*! Not the *editing* – the *storytelling*. Average shot length might be shorter – there might be five shots of someone opening a door instead of one – but the storytelling is often still slow. By comparison, after 80 minutes – 40 or 50 minutes quicker than American movies – Japanese *animé* has already been there, done that – it's wolfed down all the food in the fridge and the cupboards, slashed the villains to pieces with samurai swords (amid R-rated sprays of blood), blown up the castle, transformed the crystal McGuffin into cherry blossom confetti, and soared into the heavens on angels' wings to the strains of girlie J-pop!).

Instead of including meanderings and atmospheric incidents, the best Japanese films focus on the main theme ruthlessly, as Bruce Kawin and Gerald Mast explain in *A Short History of the Movies*:

> the great Japanese films seem to rivet every incident of the plot, every character, every visual image, and every line of dialogue to the film's central thematic question or dominant mood. (1992b, 410)

---

[122] For Chris Lanier, *Spirited Away* is 'one of the most visually baroque films ever made. Its look and density are so unique', recalling ancient Buddhist frescoes or Byzantine art.

Hayao Miyazaki's movies have wonderful, enormous and spectacular endings, and that's a key reason for their success. There are quite a few major filmmakers, for instance, who had real trouble with endings (Orson Welles, Stanley Kubrick, Steven Spielberg, and Francis Coppola come to mind). But in Miyazaki's movies, the ending is fully worked out on the narrative and thematic and emotional levels: that is, Miyazaki's movies don't only deliver fantastic action and thrills and stunning set-pieces and gags and stunts, they also completely convince emotionally and thematically.

Instead of happy endings, Hayao Miyazaki said it was enough for him to have the hero deal with a single issue for the moment. It might be easier to make a movie where everyone is happy because the villain has been defeated, but Miyazaki just couldn't do that (SP).[123] 'A film should show some problem being overcome, even if it's a small one', Miyazaki remarked in 1995 (SP, 423). Just creating evil villains in order to destroy them at the end of a story to produce a catharsis makes animation 'a despicable profession' for Miyazaki (TP, 178).

> In American films, as long as it's an enemy, you can kill as many people as you want, and that's true of *Lord of the Rings* too. You can kill indiscriminately without worrying about whether they are civilians or military. As long as it can be called collateral damage. (TP, 287)

Discussing *Future Boy Conan* in 1983, Hayao Miyazaki said that he liked it when stories ended with the characters cleansed or liberated: they become, in effect, *more* child-like or innocent at the end, rather than the conventional narrative development from innocence and naïvety to maturity and knowledge. Instead of gaining something, like wisdom, or values, or morality, or a message, things drop away. So, for Miyazaki liberation is one way to go: 'I feel that viewers should feel liberated after watching cartoon films, and that the characters should also ultimately be liberated' (SP, 304).

---

[123] For Miyazaki, movies like *Pearl Harbor* and *Saving Private Ryan* were 'films like video games' (with *Ryan* as 'one of the worst films of this sort. The aerial forces do their bombing, and then it ends').

THEMES

Among the themes that Hayao Miyazaki's cinema takes in are ecology, war, politics, depression, loyalty, the loss of innocence, consumerism, and creativity (C, 1). You can add animism, good vs. evil, nature, age and youth, flight, feminism, the future, technology, and machines to that list.

Animism is the most ancient form of religion or spiritual feeling, and predates all religions. E.B. Tylor famously defined animism as 'the belief in spiritual beings'. Animism is found throughout Hayao Miyazaki's cinema, and he has referred to it in his writings. A film such as *Princess Mononoke* or *My Neighbor Totoro* is a pæan to animistic sensibilities. And animism of course is a foundation of Shintoism,[124] Japan's main religion. In Miyazaki's movies, there are offerings to spirits (*kami*),[125] sacred gates (*torii*), and Shinto shrines (*jinja*).[126]

Nature and ecology is such an all-pervasive theme in Hayao Miyazaki's cinema, and all of his films and his narratives relate to the natural world and protecting the natural world in some form or another.[127] And some movies, such as *Nausicaä of the Valley of the Wind* and *Mononoke Hime*, make ecological politics central to the narrative (*Mononoke* is the sequel to *Nausicaä* in its ecological theme). For Miyazaki, ecological issues could not be ignored from around 1960: that was the time when it was no longer possible to ignore the wider world (SP, 107).

Society isn't automatically progressive, always developing to greater and greater things. Although the utopian desire is all-powerful, and humans cannot live without it, Hayao Miyazaki reckoned there will be a time when, for example,

---

[124] As the *Lonely Planet* guide to Japan explains: 'In Shinto there is a pantheon of gods (*kami*) who are believed to dwell in the natural world. Consisting of thousands of deities, this pantheon includes both local spirits and global gods and goddesses. Shinto gods are often enshrined in religious structures known as *jinga, jingu,* or *gu* (usually translated into English as shrine')' (C. Rowthorn, 2007, 54).

[125] As well as *kami* or spirits, Hayao Miyazaki's movies – and Isao Takahata's – feature Buddhist icons, such as *jizo* statues (C. Odell, 28). In *Ponyo*, a sailor performs *kashiwade*, a prayer where the hands're clapped together twice (a Shinto custom usually performed at Buddhist shrines [G. Poitras, 1999, 63]).

[126] Although *Nausicaä of the Valley of the Wind* contains images of a messiah, there are few overt references to Christianity (*Kirisutokyo*) in Hayao Miyazaki's cinema. Miyazaki said he was shocked when he first saw the images of Christ in Western art: 'I couldn't believe what repulsive images the artists had used to represent God. I was simply aghast; there was no way I could have regarded them as beautiful' (SP, 121). Miyazaki is not the only artist of recent times to react that way. Less than one per cent of Japanese are Christian (G. Poitras, 1999, 70).

[127] Japanese want to be one with nature in old age, Hayao Miyazaki wondered, but Europeans want to confront nature and stare at it (SP, 146).

there is no electricity: there will be power lines, but no electricity (SP, 421). Miyazaki often talks about the future, how technological societies will find resources and fuel running out, with over-population a major issue.

There is no absolute good or evil in Hayao Miyazaki's cinema. This is a fundamental moral perspective. Miyazaki is critical of stories and movies which end up happily – as if everyone is now going to live happily ever after because the villain is dead. No. Miyazaki much prefers ambiguity in all of his characters – including the good guys. (Characters are often more complex in *animé* than in comparable products in the Western world. It's not unknown, as Gilles Poitras pointed out, for main characters to die, to fail, or to lose the girl/ boy [2001, 55]).

Hayao Miyazaki noted that Ursula Le Guin suggested that dark was more powerful than light in her *Earthsea* books (SP, 359), but not 'dark' in terms of 'evil'. In Japanese popular culture, heroes sometimes become villains, and vice versa.[128] The villain, however, is not the same as the enemy or the rival.

One of the reasons that the bad guys in Hayao Miyazaki's cinema are ambiguous and not wholly evil is emotional: that is, it's due to Miyazaki's tendency to empathize with his characters emotionally, so he can't see them as all bad.

> I tend to proceed on an *emotional* basis. I can't do the work unless I have an *emotional investment* in it. I tend to pour myself into the characters. And when I do so, I start to emphathize with the characters, to feel sorry for them. (SP, 299; my italics)

This *emotional basis* for Hayao Miyazaki's cinema is one of the reasons why his stories proceed at times illogically, but emotionally true.[129] His narratives do not have strictly good or evil personalities, and they often take paths which seem odd or unusual. It is an intuitive approach to storytelling which is Miyazaki's own, and one of the things that makes his cinema so extraordinary – and so different from everyone else's. 'I'm not making a film; instead, it feels like the film is making me', is one of Miyazaki's mantras (SP, 110).

Hence the villains in Hayao Miyazaki's cinema are not your usual villains:

> I'm really not good at depicting the bad guys, frankly. They always wind up to be people who are at the core

---
128 Antonia Levi, 69.
129 Plots are not always straightforward in *animé*, and often follow unexpected or unusual paths.

basically good. (SP, 303)

Only bad people, Hayao Miyazaki asserted, such as Mao Zedong, try to change history dramatically (SP, 298).

If you turn a villain into an ugly, bad guy, it's too easy to get rid of them, Miyazaki said in 1994: but if you make them more sympathetic, it becomes more complicated, a richer mix (SP, 413).

The idea of portraying good and evil in movies as simple polarities is anathema to Hayao Miyazaki:

> I know it's considered mainstream but I think it's rotten. This idea – that whenever something evil happens someone particular can be blamed and punished for it – is hopeless.[130]

Hayao Miyazaki has often said that he likes to make films he would like to see himself: 'I just want to make films I want to see' (SP, 306). Animated movies might help people feel more liberated, Miyazaki wondered, more refreshed, more relaxed: they might be able to suggest ways of liberating oneself from fears and anxieties.

Underlying the fantasy and spectacle of Hayao Miyazaki's cinema is plenty of unease and ambiguity – and sometimes Miyazaki consciously foregrounds that moral ambivalence and ideological uneasiness.[131] For instance, by making his villains not out-and-out baddies, like Eboshi, the boss of Irontown in *Princess Mononoke*, or making his heroes not wholly good guys, like Howl in *Howl's Moving Castle*.

Hayao Miyazaki's cinema is also not Gnostic or Manichæan: it does not believe that the world itself is tainted or corrupted or evil (there are more filmmakers who promulgate Gnostic philosophies than one would think, even if they are not aware of it).[132]

<u>Time</u> is a recurring concern of Hayao Miyazaki's cinema: the importance of the past, of ancestors, of earlier generat-

---

130 Hayao Miyazaki, quoted in C. Winstanley, 61.
131 'I have inherited my old man's anarchistic feelings and his lack of concern about embracing contradictions' (SP, 209).
132 But it is important to stay aware of the potentially damaging politics of fantasy. For Miyazaki, ignoring the ethnic or racial aspects of fantasy novels is dangerous. The enemies in *The Lord of the Rings* are clearly meant to be Asians and Africans, Miyazaki insisted: 'I think the people who don't understand that, who go around saying how much they like "fantasy works", are really idiots' (TP, 288).
The scene in *Raiders of the Lost Ark*, where Indy shoots the Arab with the sword, was another example of the racism of fantasy: 'it makes me incredibly ashamed to think that there are Japanese who get a thrill out of that. They're the ones being blasted in scenes like that' (TP, 288).

ions, and of the future. Read any interview by Miyazaki and he often discusses the past and the future. What the past was *really like* is a concern, and what the future is *really going to be like* is another.

The emphasis on time, on the past and the future, comes out in Hayao Miyazaki's movies in the depiction of ruins and abandoned spaces, another Miyazakian speciality, from *The Castle of Cagliostro* onwards, emphasizing a sense of history and the past. *Nausicaä of the Valley of the Wind* and *Laputa: Castle In the Sky,* for example, with their abandoned relics of earlier civilizations, offer a poignant commentary on what the past meant to the people at the time (excessive mechanization and industry), and just how much of that civilization and community has lasted.

The message is crystal clear: you might think that advanced capitalism and technological sophistication is wonderful and life-enhancing and is here to stay, but this current phase of civilization is just as transitory and ephemeral as the clouds or the wind. What is the final image of Miyazaki's final film? – a windy, cloudy, grassy plain (when humanity's gone, nature will take over).

Flight is of course a major, major theme, as outlined above.

Feminism and pro-women ethics and morality is a recurring theme, to the point where Hayao Miyazaki stands far ahead of almost every other comparable filmmaker (including in Japan). You have to look to arthouse filmmakers such as Ingmar Bergman or Pedro Almodóvar to find a (male) director so keen on placing women at the centre of their stories.

Growing up and finding one's place in the world is a theme found in pretty much every Hayao Miyazaki movie: it is given a particularly Japanese flavour, but also of course it's a universal theme (D. Cavallaro, 8). The related themes of the strong bonds of socialization and the institutionalization of the individual are set against the importance of finding one's individuality and independence. It's about being both a complex individual and being a part of a complicated society.

Social responsibility, loyalty, hard work, respect, generosity, companionship, kindness and solidarity are explored at both the individual and the social level in Hayao Miyazaki's cinema, in a manner so deep and detailed – separating Miyazaki's cinema from nearly all animation, and certainly from the Disney and American type of animation.

In short, the level of *maturity* in the outlook of Hayao Miyazaki's cinema is very rare not only in animation, but in any kind of commercial cinema. We are moving far beyond good vs. evil and good guys versus bad guys, way beyond the Western world's simplistic, moral and ethical duality which still pervades all of popular culture – *and* high culture.[133]

Youth and old age, the differences of age and of generations, is both a theme and a common motif in Hayao Miyazaki's cinema, and in Japanese animation (and not just because his movies are about children, and children and parents). Miyazaki likes to put characters of different ages together – often they are women: Chihiro and Yubaba in *Spirited Away*, for example, or Sheeta and Dola in *Laputa: Castle In the Sky,* or Kiki and Osono in *Kiki's Delivery Service*. And often communities rely on young people to do what they cannot do anymore: for instance, the Eboshi people in *Princess Mononoke* need Ashitaka to discover what is happening in the rest of the country.

Though utopian and often optimistic, Hayao Miyazaki's art is also carefully realistic and pragmatic. Not pessimistic, not defeatist, but certainly practical. His movies end with the recognition that there is plenty more work to be done. However, Miyazaki has also described himself as a pessimist, but said that he wouldn't force his own life-philosophy onto the audience of his movies, in particular children.[134]

It's important, Hayao Miyazaki said in 1979, to have characters that are fully fleshed out, who are 'life-affirming and have clear hopes and goals', and then make sure that the story 'develops as efficiently and simply as possible' (SP, 34). And Miyazaki stuck to this proviso: the *life-affirming* or positive aspects of his characters is vital, I think, to his cinema. Miyazaki doesn't want to give out 'messages', or lecture his audience (there are other places to do that than in an animated movie or TV show, he said), but he does want to send out positive, life-affirming views when it comes to his lead characters and their hopes and dreams.

Hayao Miyazaki would never, and has never, created an anti-hero as his main character, or featured characters who are nihilistic or even pessimistic. Miyazaki's characters might

---

[133] Hayao Miyazaki wondered if animators were dealing with something 'left undone in our childhood', as if they hadn't quite fully grown up, 'we must all be pursuing what we couldn't do during our childhood' (TP, 154-5). And Osamu Tezuka was acutely self-conscious, Miyazaki said, as he himself was: Tezuka was dealing with 'a gap between his inner self and the world', which Miyazaki also struggled with (ibid).

[134] At the time of *Spirited Away*, Miyazaki remarked: 'In fact, I am a pessimist. But when I'm making a film, I don't want to transfer my pessimism onto children. I keep it at bay. I don't believe that adults should impose their vision of the world on children, children are very much capable of forming their own visions. There's no need to force your own visions onto them.'

be subject to bouts of depression (like Kiki), or might be 'cursed' by the gods (like Ashitaka in *Mononoke*), or under a spell (like Sophie in *Howl* and Marco in *Rosso*), but they are not pessimists or nihilists. However, they might be anarchistic, and rebellious[135] – but usually that's part of their bid for independence and individuality, or their recognition that doing things in the accepted manner isn't going to get the best results.

A decent motive: in a 1988 lecture, Hayao Miyazaki decried the motives of characters in current animation: there are two: work and sex (SP, 84). Robots fight because they are robots, police pursue criminals because they are police, and so on. Nothing but the work ethic. Or it was sex. For Miyazaki, there had to be better motives than that.

Technology is a key theme in Hayao Miyazaki's cinema, in particular how human societies relate to technology, and how technology is being used to exploit the Earth's resources. There is also a fetishistic exaltation of technology in Miyazaki's movies,[136] which sometimes runs counter to the deeply critical treatment of technology – and the military machine.[137]

'Fan service' in Japanese animation means delivering to audiences something fetishized and glamourized: *mecha* (robots and machines),[138] for example, lovingly depicted, or something sexy – glimpses of underwear or parts of the body. Needless to say Hayao Miyazaki's movies contain 'fan service' – though almost always of the *mecha*, fetishistic kind (in the later part of the *Nausicaä manga*, however, Miyazaki does strip his heroine down to a revealing top, for no good reason).

War is one of Hayao Miyazaki's fascinations, and it crops up in many of his films, from *Nausicaä of the Valley of the Wind* to *Howl's Moving Castle*. 'I'm fascinated by wars and I read a lot about them' (SP, 399). And it fascinates his

---

[135] Miyazaki is opposed to self-righteous groups, to authorities who 'parade their righteousness': 'they restrain others through huge military power, economic power, political power or public opinion' (AI, 29).

[136] Only filmmakers such as George Lucas rivalled Hayao Miyazaki in creating myriad forms of technology. Miyazaki's films were deeply in love with machines and technology, especially vehicles such as planes.

[137] Hayao Miyazaki liked people who looked after machines, he said, who didn't trade in their cars every year for a new one. 'I prefer people who detect a kind of animistic power in the marvel of machines' (SP, 420).

[138] One could discuss at length the significance of cyborgs and robots and hybrid lifeforms in Hayao Miyazaki's cinema, in the light of the theories of Donna Haraway or Slavoj Zizek – you know the theories: the 'return of the repressed', the undead, zombies, ghosts in the machine, animated machines, dolls, puppets, computers with souls, etc etc etc… but as I've already done that elsewhere, I'll leave it up to other writers. (See, for instance, D. Haraway's "A Manifesto For Cyborgs", and *Primate Visions* (Routledge, London, 1989), and *Simians, Cyborgs, and Women* (Routledge, London, 1991).)

colleague, Isao Takahata too: Miyazaki produced the movie *Grave of the Fireflies*, which was directed by Paku-san.

'I have to admit that ever since I was a child, I, too, have been a fan of military planes, warships, and tanks. In fact, I grew up being very excited about war films and drawing military things all over the place,' Hayao Miyazaki said in 1980 in *Animation Monthly* (SP, 45). Miyazaki admitted that he spends too much time drawing tanks and military stuff in his spare time (TP, 335).

War corrupts people, it corrupts their sense of ideals and justice: *pace* the war in the Balkans of the early Nineties, Hayao Miyazaki said (in 1994): 'the thing about war is that even though people may have a sense of what is just in the beginning, once you start a war that sense of justice inevitably becomes corrupted' (SP, 399).

One thing is very striking about the cinema of Hayao Miyazaki: altho' he publicly denounces the military machine, at least half of his movies depict military forces in action and in some detail. There is a technofetishism, an adoration of *mecha* (which you find throughout *manga* and *animé*), which is at odds with the political attacks on the military-industrial complex. Yes, you could say that Miyazaki & co. evoke the military solely in order to show them in a negative light (as rampant capitalists in *Laputa*, for instance, or brutal perpetrators of pointless warfare in *Howl*), but it's also a case of artists wanting to have things both ways (as they always want to!).

MORE ASPECTS OF MIYAZAKI'S CINEMA

LOVE STORIES.

There are love stories in Hayao Miyazaki's cinema, but they tend to either be youthful and idealistic romances between teenagers, or detached, wistful relationships among older characters which are not consummated. There are many tender and affectionate scenes in Miyazaki's cinema, but only a few kisses (hugs being more common).[139] And no sex scenes. Instead, flying scenes or some other experience stands in for sexual desire, which's common in movies (dancing being the most obvious synecdoche for lovemaking in

---

[139] Although porn and *hentai* takes up a large part of Japanese animation, much of *animé* is chaste and restrained. For instance, the first onscreen kiss in Japanese cinema occurred as late as 1946 (G. Mast, 1992b).

Hollywood cinema – think of Ginger and Fred, or Leslie and Gene). As flying is so central to Miyazaki's art, it's understandable that flying scenes should stand in for sexual expression.

The typical ♥ story in Hayao Miyazaki's cinema is between two young people; they might be ten years old (as in *Spirited Away*), or thirteen (as in *Kiki's Delivery Service*), or around that age (in *Laputa: Castle In the Sky*). And when Miyazaki did portray a 'grown-up' sexual relationship – between Gina and Marco in *Porco Rosso* – it was similarly virtuous and restrained. The emotion was certainly there, but the expressions of it were demure. There's only really one scene where Gina and Porco Rosso are alone together, when Rosso visits the Hotel Adriano and eats his supper. That's a dialogue scene, without contact. Needless to say, affection would be out of place, because Gina has just heard that her (third) husband is dead (so the scene turns into a commemoration of him, as Gina and Marco drink to him).

It hardly needs to be said that the love stories in Hayao Miyazaki's movies are always heterosexual (and there are virtually no homosexual charas). And though the families he depicts might sometimes be broken, they are usually the classic configuration of mom, dad and two kids.

ACTION.

There's no doubt that a key feature of Hayao Miyazaki's cinema is fantastic action sequences. Like the filmmakers of *Akira* or *Naruto* or *Bleach* or *Fullmetal Alchemist* or the *Legend of the Overfiend* movies or *Ghost In the Shell* or other classic exponents of Japanese *animé*, Miyazaki and his teams are geniuses when it comes to staging chases, or battles between flying machines, or gun fights in enclosed spaces. It's not a question of being 'free' in animation to draw anything, or being able to do things you can't do in live-action, it's a question of imagination (and staging, and timing, and research, etc).

An action scene in a Hayao Miyazaki picture is not your usual action scene. Take the chase at the beginning of 1986's *Laputa: Castle In the Sky:* for a start, it takes place on a railroad track built from wood hundreds of feet above the ground in an incredibly deep valley surrounded by mountains. And it's a dual chase, with Muska the arch villain and his army train and soldiers on one side, and Dola the formidable pirate and her pirate gang in their car on the other. In the middle are our teenage heroes, Pazu and Sheeta, and an old-timer engineer in a slow freight train. It's a summary of every (silent) movie train chase – such as Buster Keaton or the Marx Brothers (from *The General* or *Go West*). One can imagine Walt Disney loving this chase (Disney was famously a railroad enthusiast).

After some incredible stunts, explosions, near-misses and the like, our heroes escape by falling into space (it's another literal cliffhanger moment). The question – how are they going to get out of this one? – is answered by the film's McGuffin, the magic crystal that Sheeta wears around her neck. Sheeta and Pazu float gently down an enormous mine shaft, and the picture moves into a quieter moment, setting the scene for the meeting with the wise, old man character, the old miner.

All of this is meticulously worked out, and plays like gangbusters. Although it's tempting, action set-pieces in a Miyazaki movie don't stretch belief, in the way that Hollywood movies, not only from the last 20 years or so, so often do. Simply on the level of action-adventure, the movies of Hayao Miyazaki are spectacular, and have no superiors.

COLOUR.

One of the vital collaborators in Hayao Miyazaki's cinema is undoubtedly Michiyo Yasuda (b. 1943), the colour designer. As Miyazaki's movies are among the most exquisite in the history of cinema in terms of colour, Yasuda's contribution is immense. As well as organizing the hundreds of colours used in every Miyazaki film, Yasuda and her team have also helped to create a unique look for Miyazaki's pictures. Simply, there are no other movies which look quite like these.[140] Even amongst the 1,000s of *animé* OVAs, TV shows, cartoons, pop promos, commercials and movies produced by the Japanese animation industry, the films of Hayao Miyazaki are instantly recognizable.

One of the favourite devices of Hayao Miyazaki's films is to alter between light and dark, particularly within the same scene. Miyazaki's movies love to show lamps being switched on or off, for example. Colour-wise, this means adding greys and blacks to colours, to take out the warmth and saturation.

LAYOUTS.

As to compositions and layouts, the films directed by Hayao Miyazaki are sumptuous to look at, with classical

---

[140] Colour is another significant difference between Japanese animation and Western animation, as Trish Ledoux and Doug Ranney point out: Japanese *animé* will use colour in pretty much every possible way, but Western animation tends towards flat, bright colours (1997, 3).

compositions being favoured (using the Golden Section, or the horizon along the lower third, for instance). The action generally takes place within the safe area for television and video. Sometimes, however, Miyazaki and his teams will turn in a deliberately off-kilter composition, for dramatic effect. When Nausicaä explores the underworld forest in *Nausicaä of the Valley of the Wind,* for example, she is framed very low in one shot, to emphasize the majesty of the enormous trees above her.

No expense is spared on the backgrounds and layouts of Hayao Miyazaki's movies, with a level of detail that rivals and often bests Disney's 'golden age' films. It seems that every Miyazaki movie is at the level of the finest of Disney movies from the 1937-1942 period: *Snow White and the Seven Dwarfs, Bambi* and *Pinocchio.*

For instance, the level of detail in *Spirited Away* is simply staggering. The richness of Yubaba's apartment, for example, is the densest up to that time in Hayao Miyazaki's cinema. When Chihiro runs down a corridor outside the bathroom, there are mirrors which reflect her three times (mirror shots are expensive to animate, but few filmmakers can resist mirrors – and some, such as Orson Welles and Jean Cocteau, made them central motifs in their work). *Spirited Away* is one of those pictures where you can freeze most of the frames and you have a superb image.

MOVEMENT.

The movement of the characters in Hayao Miyazaki's movies is deliberately naturalistic, and far away from the exaggerated motion of the Walt Disney canon. Miyazaki has commented that Disney's characters tend to move like ballet dancers or actors in a musical[141] – just too heightened, with lavish arm gestures, for example, and exaggerated squash-and-stretch movements.[142] Disney's characters move as if they're performing to the upper circle in a vaudeville show, while Miyazaki's characters are far, far more subtle, and naturalistic (as if they know the camera is right there, and tone down their performances).

Hayao Miyazaki's people are recognizably based on real people, even though they are stylistically drawn. In Disney's films, the figures seem to be made of dough or balloons or some squashy, bouncy material (and that's not only in the

---

141 Indeed, the filmmakers of Disney's *Beauty and the Beast* studied ballet dancers for the depiction of Belle.
142 Hayao Miyazaki also acknowledged that much of Japanese animation 'suffered from over-expressionism' (SP, 79).

'golden era' movies like *Fantasia* or *Dumbo*, but in the more recent movies like *Treasure Planet* or *Home On the Range*).[143]

Difference in scale is one of Hayao Miyazaki's recurring motifs, and it is a key element in Japanese *animé*: so in Miyazaki's cinema there are giant robots, giant babies, and giant men. The macho guys in *Laputa: Castle In the Sky,* for instance, are much larger than real people, sporting huge, barrel chests (in the fight in the street in Slug Valley, where the men pop their shirts open like Popeye or Superman). Yubaba and her son in *Spirited Away* have enormous heads, while the baby and Yubaba's bird are transformed into very small creatures.

And Hayao Miyazaki and his animators use differences in scale all the time for dramatic purposes: in some scenes, they will make their heroes appear small, to emphasize their vulnerability, say, or their fear, or their diminished dramatic influence. In particular, Miyazaki and his teams like to place something very large next to something very small: so the *ohmu* are enormous insects, and Nausicaä next to them is tiny; Tombo, hanging off the giant airship at the end of *Kiki's Delivery Service*, is a minuscule dot. In *Nausicaä of the Valley of the Wind,* Asbel flies a small fighter, but he's able to bring down most of the Tolmekian fleet.

Yes, in Hayao Miyazaki's cinema, one person *can* make a difference: his films are stories of individuals who shift the balance of power in their worlds: Nausicaä most spectacularly, perhaps, but also Sheeta and Pazu in *Laputa: Castle In the Sky,* Sophie in *Howl's Moving Castle,* Marco in *Porco Rosso*, and on a more modest scale, Kiki in *Kiki's Delivery Service.*

THE CAMERA.

Hayao Miyazaki's animation simulates live-action cinema, as if the spaces were being filmed with a real camera, as does Japanese animation (and most Western animation) in general: that is, it includes camera movements like pans and tilts (favourite Miyazakian shots), tracking shots, zooms, dynamic backgrounds, selective focus, wide angles, and so on. Western animation (including computer animation added to live-action movies) also simulates photographic elements such as lens flare.

---

[143] *Home On the Range* cost $110 million to make: what a truly dull film.

THE SETTINGS.

The settings of Hayao Miyazaki's films have included: Monte Carlo and a fictional European country (Cagliostro) in *The Castle of Cagliostro;* a fantasy land in *Nausicaä of the Valley of the Wind* (which draws on Europe and North African deserts); another fantasy realm in *Laputa: Castle In the Sky* (which also looks to Europe, with Slug Valley being inspired by South Wales, the Rhondda Valley); a fictionalized Europe is again the setting for *Howl's Moving Castle, Porco Rosso* and *Kiki's Delivery Service;* but Japan is the setting for *My Neighbor Totoro, Ponyo On the Cliff By the Sea, Spirited Away, The Wind Rises* and *Princess Mononoke*.

It's ironic, perhaps, that many of Hayao Miyazaki's movies have been set in Europe, and have dealt with European history and culture, but three of Miyazaki's biggest successes, *Spirited Away, Ponyo On the Cliff By the Sea* and *Princess Mononoke*, have been very Japanese (i.e., set in Japan, and drawing on Japanese mythology and culture). However, wherever they are set, Miyazaki's movies are very definitely *Japanese*.

They are movies made in Japan, by predominantly Japanese crews, for the Japanese film market, and financially backed by Japanese companies.[144] But the European (specifically *Western* European) *milieu* and tropes give Hayao Miyazaki's pictures a curious and fascinating cultural hybridity. And it works – Miyazaki's films never feel as if the European or Japanese elements aren't meshed at the deepest level.

And notice, too, that Hayao Miyazaki's movies are not set in North America, or about North America, or draw on North American culture, and have only used one or two North American characters. Sorry, Amerika – Miyazaki-san just isn't interested: 'I just don't seem to like American culture', Miyazaki admitted (TP, 247). 'I don't feel very beholden to America'.

SOUND.

The sound of the wind is a recurring motif in Hayao Miyazaki's cinema, as it is in the cinema of Federico Fellini and Pier Paolo Pasolini.[145] In Hayao Miyazaki's films, the sound of the wind has both a practical or 'realistic' function or meaning, but also a spiritual or magical one. It is the sound of the

---

[144] Miyazaki acknowledges that his *animé* is thoroughly Japanese, and 'much more so than I myself had originally thought' (AI, 31).
[145] The films of Fellini and Pasolini seem to use the same wind sound effect in numerous pictures – maybe there was only one wind sound effect in the library at Cinecittà.

flying scenes, of course, and it's the sound of the wind in the grass or crops, or the sound of a character's clothes in the breeze. But it is also the sound of something magical happening. As it is in traditional symbolism: the wind is the breath of the eternal, of the divine, of God... it is the Creative Word, the Word made flesh, etc. [146]

MUSIC.

The music for most of Hayao Miyazaki's films is by Joe Hisaishi (b. 1950 in Nagano Prefecture, pseudonym of Mamoru Fujisawa), and it contributes so much – especially to the emotional core of the movies: *Nausicaä of the Valley of the Wind, Kiki's Delivery Service, Laputa: Castle In the Sky, Porco Rosso* and *Spirited Away*. The collaboration of Miyazaki and Hisaishi is not to be under-estimated;[147] it may not be as well-known in film circles as the partnership of, say, Alfred Hitchcock and Bernard Herrmann, or Tim Burton and Danny Elfman, but it's certainly a vital part of the success of Miyazaki's cinema.[148] As well as Miyazaki's films, Hisaishi has also scored many other Japanese movies, including *Ario, Sonatine, The Water Traveler, Kids Return* and *Venus Wars*. In addition to film music, Hisaishi has composed electronic music, minimal music, piano music, pop music, and orchestral music, and music for the Nagano Winter Olympics.[149] Hisaishi has given concerts of Ghibli's scores, including to 14,000 at Tokyo's Budokan.

THE OCEAN AND WATER.

Pretty much every Hayao Miyazaki movie features the ocean, and sometimes it's such a prominent element: the sea in *Porco Rosso*, for instance, with its numerous islands, including Rosso's idyllic island retreat.[150] Or the coastal town in *Kiki's Delivery Service*.

And just think of the numerous towns that are set beside the sea: in *Kiki's Delivery Service*, in *Porco Rosso*, in *Howl's Moving Castle*, in *Ponyo On the Cliff By the Sea*, and in *Laputa:*

---

146 And the sound of the wind is linked to all of those manifestations of the natural world in Hayao Miyazaki's cinema – thunder, and storms, and clouds, and rivers, and oceans, and trees, and mountains.
147 It was Isao Takahata was brought Joe Hisaishi onto *Nausicaä of the Valley of the Wind* – music is one of Takahata's special skills.
148 And one should not forget that Isao Takahata has often undertaken the production of the music in Hayao Miyazaki's films, liaising with Joe Hisaishi.
149 Andrew Osmond has identified the emphasis on innocence as being particularly important to Joe Hisaishi's music, and also 'its sense of the magical, the holy' (2000).
150 And even when *Porco Rosso* moves inland, to Milan in Italy, there's a major sequence involving the chase and escape via a river.

Castle In the Sky (the military island).

And even those movies which don't contain the ocean – such as *My Neighbor Totoro* or *Princess Mononoke* – feature rivers or lakes or forests so big and juicy with life they are equivalents of the ocean. (*Mononoke Hime* has a large lake, the beautiful pool at the heart of the forest, and a river in flood).

And one of Hayao Miyazaki's specialities is the sunken land or town, which appeared in his first film, *The Castle of Cagliostro,* the Roman ruins underneath the lake. The underwater areas of the flying land of Laputa. The submerged forest in *Nausicaä of the Valley of the Wind*. The flooded railroad line in *Spirited Away*. And the deluged Japan in *Ponyo On the Cliff By the Sea*.

In short, water is everywhere in Hayao Miyazaki's cinema, for all of the obvious reasons: it adds life and beauty to scenes, it is perfect for animation in a variety of styles, it is central to human life, and it has any symbolism you want to attach to it.

And when it comes to animating water, one of the tough challenges of animation (you could portray the history of animation techniques by studying how animators depict water), Studio Ghibli is extraordinarily accomplished.

ANIMALS.

It's impossible to miss the importance of animals in Hayao Miyazaki's cinema: a staple of animation since its earliest incarnations, animals in Miyazaki's art perform a variety of functions. The cuddly, cute sidekick is a recurring animal, just as it is in the Walt Disney canon. Miyazaki is as happy to sentimentalize animals as much as Disney or Fox or Warners or any other contemporary animation studio.

Particular specialities are cats and dogs (the dog in *Howl's Moving Castle*, and the cat Jiji in *Kiki's Delivery Service,* for instance). *Sherlock Hound* was an entire TV *animé* series of anthropomorphic dogs. Miyazaki and his animators have clearly studied cats and dogs very closely.[151] Some Miyazaki and Studio Ghibli products have animals at their heart: *Ponyo On the Cliff By the Sea*, *Ponpoko* and *The Cat Returns*.

And there are also animals as nature spirits, fierce, independent, unmanageable, wild – dragons, Totoros, forest spirits, wolves. Animals as pets and friends: the red elk that Ashitaka rides in *Princess Mononoke* (which also appear in *Nausicaä of the Valley of the Wind*). Hayao Miyazaki's films

---

[151] Animation houses often have their own pets.

also invent plenty of animals – the giant bugs in *Nausicaä,* the Forest God in *Princess Mononoke*, and of course the Totoros.

FOOD.

As all great storytellers for children know, food plays a huge part in a child's life (and in many adults' lives!), and Hayao Miyazaki knows this very well. There are many scenes involving food and meals in Miyazaki's cinema:

▲ there's a humorous scene in *Ponyo On the Cliff By the Sea* where Ponyo and Sosuke eat dinner and drink honeyed tea, and the details are exquisitely realized – of children waiting patiently at a table, of being desperate to eat, of making a mess, and Ponyo's little look of disappointment when her pack of noodles comes out broken in her dish, while Sosuke's remains neatly whole.

▲ in *Laputa: Castle In the Sky*, Pazu has breakfast on the go when Sheeta wakes up, and when he returns home, disheartened, halfway through the movie, he finds Dola and her boys happily eating their way through the place. Dola's gang are over the moon when Sheeta joins them – it means good food.

▲ the breakfast scene in *Howl's Moving Castle*, in which Sophie cheers Markl up no end by providing a cooked breakfast.

▲ Kiki delivers food on her broomstick in *Kiki's Delivery Service*.

▲ in *Porco Rosso*, the pig takes a meal in Gina's hotel.

▲ in *Spirited Away*, food takes on negative connotations – the monster spirit No Face wolfs down everything, and Chihiro's parents are turned into pigs when they break a fairy tale taboo, and eat without getting permission.

HUMOUR.

It's reassuring for me that the films of Hayao Miyazaki and his teams aren't crude; they don't resort to fart jokes and toilet humour (like the farting warthog in *The Lion King* or the farting pirate in *Treasure Planet*). Nothing wrong with fart or piss or shit or whatever jokes, but they would certainly detract from the impact of Miyazaki's movies. Personally, I don't reckon that kind of childish goofing off in a fantasy movie helps any. Not that Miyazaki's films don't contain some grosser moments: *Spirited Away,* for instance, has a giant Stink God, and No Face is an imposing, black beast who vomits copiously.

EDITING

One of the reasons that the films of Hayao Miyazaki are so successful is invisible: their editing, pacing and structure. Watching a Miyazaki movie, you know you are in the hands of a master, and a master storyteller. Simply put, Miyazaki and his teams (Takeshi Seyama and Katsu Hisamura are his editors) know when to place action, when to slow a film down, when to insert backstory or motivations, and when to reveal elements of the plot (it's significant that Miyazaki has an editor credit on many of his movies).

Without this magical feeling for how time flows within a 80 or 90 minute movie, films soon become wearying and boring. A bad or disappointing movie is often one which hasn't been edited smoothly or successfully (of course, studios and producers meddle with filmmakers' work all too often).

But all of Hayao Miyazaki's pictures swim by with such grace and ease. This filmmaker does not waste a second of precious screen time. His films don't feel rushed, or disjointed, or awkward, or jagged around the edges.

The pacing of Hayao Miyazaki's movies was something that John Lasseter at Pixar found inspiring, and applied it to films such as *Toy Story* and *A Bug's Life*: 'Miyazaki-san is a master of pacing', how he lets certain scenes breathe, and doesn't rush them: 'there are certain moments in a film you cannot rush through. It's important to allow the audience to reflect on what's happening on the screen' (SP, 13).

Hayao Miyazaki derided Eisensteinian montage, where shots coalesce with other shots, combining to create a greater meaning. No, Miyazaki insisted, it's a 'totally worthless theory': rather, 'each shot should express the film in its entirety. I myself still hope to make a film like that' (TP, 131).

ILLUSTRATIONS

On the following pages: some influences on Hayao Miyazaki, and some filmmakers influenced by Miyazaki.

Some of Hayao Miyazaki's influences:
From top left:
The Snow Queen. Antoine de Saint-Exupéry. Isao Takahata.
Akira Kurosawa. Diana Wynne-Jones. Philippa Pearce.
Rosemary Sutcliffe. Moebius. Osamu Tezuka. J.R.R. Tolkien.
Ursula Le Guin. Taiji Yubushita & Kazuhiko Okabe. Lewis Carroll.
Betty Boop. Walt Disney. Frank Herbert. Chuck Jones.
Yasujiro Ozu. Robert Louis Stevenson. Jules Verne. Charlie Chaplin.

Some of the films and filmmakers influenced by Hayao Miyazaki. Clockwise from top left: Toy Story. Atlantis. Avatar. The Lord of the Rings. Batman. The Princess and the Frog. Star Wars.

Some animé products released 1980s-2000s. Only a few have a theatrical release (either in Japan or elswhere).

Some merchandize based on Studio Ghibli's films

PART TWO: THE MOVIES

4

THE CASTLE OF CAGLIOSTRO

The Castle of Cagliostro (*Lupin III: Cagliostro no Shiro = Lupin III: Cagliostro's Castle*, Toho, 1979) was Hayao Miyazaki's first animated feature film as director.[1] It was a *Lupin III* film: *Lupin III* was a big franchise based on a *manga* series by Monkey Punch (a.k.a. Kazuhiko Kato, born 1937; the first series ran from 1967 to 1972, by the T.M.S Studio, with further series from 1977-80 and 1997).[2] As well as *manga*, there were 200 TV shows, a live-action film in 1974 (a 1969 movie had been made but not released), an animated picture in 1978 (*Lupin vs. the Clone*, a.k.a. *Lupin III: The Secret of Mamo*), *The Castle of Cagliostro*, which was the follow-up to *Lupin vs. the Clone*, and more *Lupin III* films (17 features on TV and 6 movies released in cinemas)[3] after *The Castle of Cagliostro*. Plus video games, a musical, music, OVAs, TV specials, and loads of spin-off *manga* (such as Lupin in the 22nd century). And plenty of merchandizing.

So the 1979 movie helmed by Hayao Miyazaki comprised just one element in a long-running and enormous franchise that took in print, television and computer games, as well as cinema. And it began in 1967 and continued into the 2000s. Miyazaki's film was a sequel to both *Lupin vs the Clone* and

---

[1] For *The Castle of Cagliostro,* Hayao Miyazaki said he was responsible for creating the story from the basic concepts, and worked with the screenwriter to achieve the finished script. It meant changing the plot, 'unavoidable when turning the story into a film' (SP, 67).
[2] Copyright issues arose when the *Lupin* franchise was sold in the West, because French author Maurice LeBlanc had created Arsène Lupin, and Monkey Punch had used LeBlanc's character as an influence. So for video and other releases in the West, Lupin is called Rupan III or Wolf or Vidoq the Fourth. When the show was aired by Nippon TV, it was renamed *Cliffhanger*.
[3] Including: *Lupin III: Legend of the Gold of Babylon*, 1985, *Lupin III: The Fuma Conspiracy*, 1988, *Lupin III: Voyage To Danger*, 1993, *Lupin III: Pursuit of Harimao's Treasure*, 1995, *Lupin III: Dead Or Alive*, 1996, *Lupin III: Island of Assassins*, 1997, *Lupin III: Crisis In Tokyo*, 1998, and *Lupin III: Missed By a Dollar*, 2000.

the live-action film of 1974. Miyazaki had directed two episodes of *Lupin III*, numbers 145 and 155 (using the pseudonym Tsutomu Teruki), which were later released on video as *L3: Albatross: Wings of Death* and *L3: Aloha, Lupin* (a.k.a. *Farewell My Beloved Lupin*).[4] 'I often think of Lupin fondly,' Hayao Miyazaki recalled in 1980,

> for he was hungry in those days; he was a bit lecherous, fastidious, scattered, and headstrong, and he was crazy about mini-car races. (SP, 282)

The Castle of Cagliostro has many fans in Japan, where it is regarded not only as the best *Lupin III* movie, but as a classic animation in its own right.

The production schedule of *The Castle of Cagliostro* was rapid – from May to November, 1979. Hayao Miyazaki produced the storyboards – and was still drawing them when the film went into production.[5] Not the ideal state of affairs, but it would be a regular feature in Miyazaki's movies.

Cagliostro was co-written by Haruya Yamazaki, Yasuo Otsuka and Hayao Miyazaki, produced by Yutaka Fujioka and Tetsuo Katayama, production by Studio Telecom and Tokyo Movie Shinsha, with music by Yuji Ohno, animation direction and character design by Yasuo Otsuka (and Miyazaki), editing by Masatoshi Tsurubuchi, Hirokata Takahashi was DP, and art direction by Shichiro Kobayashi.

The voice cast included: Yasuo Yamada (Lupin),[6] Eiko Masuyama (Fujiko Mine), Kiboshi Kobayashi (Daisuke Jogen), Makio Inoue (Goemon), Goro Naya (Inspector Zenigata), Sumi Shimamoto (Clarisse), and Taro Ishid (Count Cagliostro).

The recurring characters in the *Lupin III* franchise included Arsène Lupin III himself, a master thief, Goeman Ishikawa XIII, a samurai warrior (in traditional dress, with a magical sword, of course),[7] Daisuke Jigen, Lupin's sidekick and marksman,[8] with an American costume, and a cigarette

---

[4] The episodes included Miyazakian motifs such as giant robots and aircraft. In episode 155, the robot that appeared later in *Laputa* has a starring role – piloted by a a young woman who resembles Nausicaä and who has, inevitably, an inventor father (who made the robot). The show includes outstanding action scenes (including a *lot* of flying) in and over downtown Tokyo.
[5] *The Castle of Cagliostro* required 43,000 drawings for a film one hour and forty minutes long (SP, 327).
[6] Yasuo Yamada played Lupin III in every movie and show until his death in 1995.
[7] Goemon refers to a legendary thief character in Japanese culture, subject of *kabuki* plays, such as *Ishikawa Goemon* of 1680 (G. Poitras, 2001, 42).
[8] Apparently inspired by James Coburn in *The Magnificent Seven*. Spike Spiegel in *Cowboy Bebop* is drawn from the same type, and is also inspired by Lupin.

glued to his mouth, Inspector Zenigata of Interpol,[9] Lupin's rival, and Fujiko Mine, a beautiful, long-haired lover[10] of Lupin's and a helper (sometimes she's on the good side or the rival side. A pity she appears so late in her super-spy mode in *The Castle of Cagliostro* – she's an appealing character, who could have contributed to more scenes. Fujiko does appear as Clarisse's governess, though).[11] All of these characters feature in *The Castle of Cagliostro* – and fans expected to see them turning up in a *Lupin III* movie (that the characters had already been established was a bonus, because scenes wouldn't be necessary to build their personalities).

Narrative elements for *The Castle of Cagliostro* were derived from both Monkey Punch's and Maurice LeBlanc's books.[12] LeBlanc had written a book called *Countess Cagliostro* (1924), which had a heroine called Clarisse who is descended from the real 18th century Count Alessandro of Cagliostro;[13] and in LeBlanc's *The Girl With Green Eyes* there is some submerged treasure.

The Castle of Cagliostro does have a Saturday morning TV serial look and feel – some of the action is in that rapidly-cut, over-the-top manner of kids' cartoons. But there are also many elements which identify it from the beginning as a Hayao Miyazaki film. One of those elements is the very elaborate Castle itself: it's another of those complex, inter-woven edifices which Miyazaki and his teams have made their speciality (like the bathhouse in *Spirited Away* or the kingdom of Laputa): enormous halls, staircases, dungeons, corridors, towers, an extending corridor, etc. There are very elaborate spaces here, a very particular sense of space, and backgrounds, and layouts.[14]

And before you reach the Castle, there is the clock tower and the ruined palace, with its abandoned gardens: this looks forward, with its wistful, melancholy and Classical atmo-

---

[9] Zenigata is a reference to the sleuth (and samurai) Heiji Zenigata, from the Edo period stories of crime writer Kodo Nomura.
[10] Fujiko knows Lupin intimately – as Helen McCarthy pointed out, she tells Clarisse where Lupin will have hidden the ring 'with all the familiarity of an old love' (M, 62).
[11] Apart from a governess, Fujiko also features as a reporter for the TV station NBK, and later in her action girl mode.
[12] Monkey Punch didn't like the 1979 *Lupin III* movie, and how it portrayed his hero as too goody-goody.
[13] Cagliostro's real name was Giuseppe Balsamo (1743-95). He was associated with alchemy and occultism (C, 39). A famous movie version of Cagliostro was the 1949 flick *Black Magic*, which starred Orson Welles.
[14] Hayao Miyazaki cited the palace in *Le Roi et L'Oiseux* (directed by Paul Grimmault) as an inspiration.

sphere, to the gardens and columns in Laputa, or the abandoned theme park in *Spirited Away*. The Greek temple, the lakes and streams, the formal design, are instantly recognizable as a Miyazakian space. It is another of the forgotten paradises that Miyazaki evokes in his films – there is one in nearly all of his movies.

And when Cagliostro is transformed by the Biblical Flood at the end of the film, it is from this area, the older, sweeter, paradisal area of Cagliostro, underneath the old clock tower, that the flood rushes (and it takes place symbolically at dawn – a literal new day).

There's a strong fairy tale component to *The Castle of Cagliostro*, too: Clarisse is very much the princess held prisoner in a tower, like Sleeping Beauty or Rapunzel. When Lupin rescues her,[15] he comments on the fairy tale-like quality of their encounter – the hero comes to rescue the princess.[16] Poor Clarisse[17] – she has come back to her home country to be married to Count Cagliostro.[18]

ACTION-ADVENTURE.

It's striking just how much of *The Castle of Cagliostro*, made in 1979, is like the action-adventure movies of today: the ironic, jokey tone, the knockabout humour, the hero and his sidekick, the romantic lover (Fujiko), who just happens to be super-girl with her gadgets and weaponry, the idealized princess to be rescued, the evil Count and his henchmen, the exotic locales, and numerous action scenes (there are several scenes where the heroes are attacked by ninja shadow warriors, one of the staples of *animé*).

The big action climax, for example, is very like the climaxes of *Pirates of the Caribbean, Indiana Jones* and *National Treasure*.[19] And there's even a sequence where a lost city is revealed – in this case, an ancient Roman city buried under water, exactly like the end of a *National Treasure* or *Indiana Jones* movie (as if embodying Lupin's dialogue about this treasure being too big for him, and it should be given to the world). And all that stuff with gadgets and cables that shoot upwards to stop the hero and his girl falling to their

---

15 But Clarisse also rescued Lupin, with her dog.
16 The circular interior looks forward to the baby's nursery in *Spirited Away*.
17 Clarisse's design is a forerunner of charas such as Nausicaä and San.
18 Clarisse was voiced by Sumi Shimamoto, who became a Miyazaki regular: she provided the voice for Nausicaä in *Nausicaä of the Valley of the Wind*, the mother in *My Neighbor Totoro*, and Toki in *Princess Mononoke*.
19 There's a big fight inside the clock tower, and outside it, a familiar setting for an action finale. The clock's cogs and mechanism, tho', has to be the largest and most complex in all cinema! (The Count comes to a satisfyingly grisly end).

death over a cliff or a tower, approaching the castle via the underground water tunnels – that's pure *Batman,* or *James Bond*, or *Star Wars*, or *Indiana Jones*. (No surprise, then, that the car chase in *The Castle of Cagliostro* is a favourite with Steven Spielberg [O, 48]).

Location-wise, *The Castle of Cagliostro* is classic Hayao Miyazaki: it's Middle Europe again – this time somewhere like Monaco, an independent kingdom on a pretty coast (the car chases along the winding coast roads are like those in thriller movies set on the French Riviera,[20] such as *James Bond* or *To Catch a Thief*.[21] In the opening scene, Lupin and Jigen have robbed a casino in Monte Carlo).

Even in his first film, Hayao Miyazaki and his team's evocation of a romanticized, heightened European region is magically achieved – these elements take *The Castle of Cagliostro* far away from run-of-the-mill, Saturday morning cartoon fare.[22]

And the back-story is a classic Hayao Miyazaki motif – how Lupin and Clarisse have met before, when Lupin tried to rob the castle and was found by a young Clarisse, ten years earlier. And the revelation of the back-story[23] occurs towards the end of the second act, again a classic place for it in both classical narrative terms, but also in Miyazaki's movies (it occurs in Miyazaki's next film, for example, *Nausicaä of the Valley of the Wind*).

There's a marvellous wedding ceremony sequence,[24] visualized with bold reds, blacks, shadows, masks, pointy hats and organ music.[25] It's depicted as an arcane ritual out of the Knights Templar or the Freemasons, the kind of decadent and obscure ritual among aristocrats and the wealthy that filmmakers such as Dario Argento, Mario Bava and Italian horror maestros like to portray. It's certainly an unusual

---

20 In one *Lupin III* episode French icon Alain Delon appears (in Paris with Fujiko, of course!).
21 *To Catch a Thief* starred Grace Kelly, whose wedding to Prince Rainer of Monaco probably influenced the church scene. As well as Cary Grant, Lupin III also draws on Batman, and of course James Bond (there's a discussion of the actors who played Bond in one episode).
22 For the landscapes Hayao Miyazaki cited the book *Italian Mountain Cities and the Tiber Estuary* as an influence on the look of *The Castle of Cagliostro* (M, 53). Helen McCarthy suggests the Japanese phrase *akogare no Paris* for the fantasy of a mysterious other-world (M, 65).
23 There are some amusing skits of Lupin as a young thief.
24 The wedding dress of Princess Sayako, daughter of the Emperor, was based on Clarisse's in *The Castle of Cagliostro*, when she married in 2005 (O, 50).
25 The music for *The Castle of Cagliostro* was composed by Yuji Ono (the main composer for *Lupin III*), and includes the TV series theme, of course, as well as jazz.

ingredient in a movie that appears to be aimed at children.[26]

The Castle of Cagliostro perhaps doesn't have the grand vision of some of Hayao Miyazaki's later movies,[27] although it does certainly feature a grandiose ending, with the revealing of the ancient Roman city in the flood. On the other hand, many of Miyazaki's movies are actually small-scale for much of the time, but when they do open out to show something larger, or fantastical and magical, they really do go to town, with some extraordinary ideas and visuals.

Although *The Castle of Cagliostro* is an action-adventure comedy and part of a commercial franchise, there are plenty of luxurious elements, which you don't find in the usual animation of this type, such as a Giovanni Bellini portrait, and sumptuous art and furniture.

---

[26] The evocations of Christianity as an exotic religion with sinister aspects is found in many *animé* and *manga*. Lupin of course impersonates the Archbishop.
[27] Hayao Miyazaki said he felt like he had thrown into *The Castle of Cagliostro* everything he done previously, going back to *Lupin* and Toei Animation, and hadn't added anything new (SP, 331). He was disillusioned after that – 1980 'was my year of being mired in gloom' (ibid.).

5
NAUSICAÄ OF THE VALLEY OF THE WIND

> Nature recovers and forgives humans, and even though "forgives" is a strange way to put it, I do think that nature creates the foundation for all life to exist so that humans (who are also animals) can go on living.
>
> Hayao Miyazaki, 1983 (SP, 290)

INTRODUCTION.
Nausicaä of the Valley of the Wind (*Kaze no Tani no Nausicaä*, 1984) is the second animated feature film by Hayao Miyazaki and his team of animation filmmakers. *Nausicaä* has been a fan favourite for years, as has the character of Nausicaä (it topped *Animage*'s movie poll for a decade,[28] and Nausicaä has always been among fans' top 20 *animé* characters).[29]

Nausicaä of the Valley of the Wind was based on Hayao Miyazaki's *manga* comic strip,[30] which was published in Tokuma Shoten's *Monthly Animage* between 1982 and 1994.[31] Only part of this lengthy, 59-chapter *manga* cycle made it into the 1984 movie (the first quarter or so).[32] As it is, the picture is packed with narrative events, maybe too many – it could easily be a long-running TV series (as many *manga* become

---
[28] Nausicaä was over-taken as the favourite female character of readers of *Animage* by Nadia in *Nadia* (also based on a Miyazaki idea).
[29] The influence of *Nausicaä* can be discerned in many, many places, such as *Green Legend Ran* (1992), *Wings of Honneamise* (1987), and *Wind of Amesia*. *Final Fantasy* (2001) is virtually a digital animation remake of *Nausicaä*. There's a spoof in *Love Hina*. The heroine of *Gunbuster* (1988) has a poster of Nausicaä on her wall (and Totoro). Totoro also regularly appears in the top ten lists of fans' favourite *animé* charas (alongside Lupin III, Heidi, Sazae-san and Doraemon).
[30] Another *manga* by Hayao Miyazaki, *Journey of Shuna* (1983), also influenced the movie.
[31] Hayao Miyazaki had been initially resistant to the idea of making an adaptation from the *manga*, but interest in a movie of the comic strip grew as it was published, and eventually Miyazaki agreed to make a one-hour movie for video.
[32] The *manga* of *Nausicaä of the Valley of the Wind* required plenty of re-shaping to make a two-hour animated movie. Characters were dropped and events were compressed or left out, for instance: when filming began, Hayao Miyazaki had written 16 chapters of his story.

in animated form).[33] *Princess Mononoke* can be regarded as a thematic sequel to *Nausicaä* (with Prince Ashitaka taking up Nausicaä's overriding objective: can't humans live in harmony with the natural world, and with each other? And *Mononoke* draws on *Totoro*, too, for many visuals).

One of the inspirations for *Nausicaä of the Valley of the Wind* was the ecological disaster of Minamata Bay in Japan, which had been polluted with mercury. The fish thrived, despite the pollution of the water. The name Nausicaä comes from Greek mythology, of course: she is 'a Phaeacian princess who appears in Homer's *Odyssey*',[34] as Hayao Miyazaki explained in 1982 (SP, 283).

Another influence, particularly on the character of Nausicaä, was the Japanese folk tale *The Princess Who Loved Insects*, produced as one of the long-running *Japanese Folk Tales* series in 1975 (Hayao Miyazaki said he read about her in *The Tales of the Past and the Present*). The princess was eccentric, individual, an aristocrat's daughter, who loved nature and didn't care about social restraints.

What's extraordinary about *Nausicaä of the Valley of the Wind*, among other aspects, is its incredibly short production schedule: it took nine months to produce[35] (and the budget, for animation, was low – about a million dollars – one of the most fruitful million dollars ever spent in animation). Needless to say, in the American animation industry, production schedules are much longer, and budgets are much higher.[36] *The Black Cauldron*, for instance, Disney's troubled 1985 production, cost $25 million (but nobody seems to have been really happy with it. For that price, you could have 25 *Nausicaäs!* That is, if you could replicate the Miyazaki and his team 25 times by magic!).

Nausicaä of the Valley of the Wind was a co-production between Tokuma and Hakuhodo (an advertising agency); it

---

33 Hayao Miyazaki had initially offered the ideas for *Nausicaä of the Valley of the Wind* in 1981 to *Animage*, which were then sent to Tokuma Shoten. The proposals were rejected (among them were the seeds for *Laputa: Castle In the Sky*), and *Animage* (and Toshio Suzuki) suggested to Miyazaki that he create a comic strip instead (H. McCarthy, 74).
34 Hayao Miyazaki said he had first read about Nausicaä in *Gods, Demigods and Demons: An Encyclopedia of Greek Mythology* by Bernard Evslin (SP, 283).
35 The film began animation on May 31, 1983, and was released on March 11, 1984. The animation used 8 frames per second, rather than 24, to cut down on the budget. Disney producer Don Hahn mentioned on the audio commentary for *Beauty and the Beast* (1991) that his movie had a very short schedule – and that was two years. *Nausicaä of the Valley of the Wind*, meanwhile, was nine months!
36 Unless you are someone like Ralph Bakshi.

was not produced at Studio Ghibli, but at Topcraft.[37] Yet although it's not the first Studio Ghibli film for Hayao Miyazaki, it is certainly the first Miyazaki/ Ghibli movie in terms of concept and collaborators: the film came from Miyazaki's own ideas and scripts, being based on his *manga* series. Although *The Castle of Cagliostro* had been Miyazaki's first picture as director, it was of course based on a popular and long-running product, the Monkey Punch *Lupin III* series.

Mitsauki Nakamura was art director on *Nausicaä of the Valley of the Wind;* Michiyo Yasuda and Fukuo Suzuki were the colour designers; Joe Hisaishi composed the music; Kazuo Komatsubara was the supervising animator; sound director was Shigeharu Shiba; sound by Kazutoshi Satou; backgrounds were by Mutsuo Koseki; the editors were Naoki Kaneko, Tomoko Kida and Shôji Sakaii; the executive producers were Yasuyoshi Tokuma, Toru Hara (of Topcraft) and Michio Kondo; and the amazing Isao Takahata was producer.[38] Many in the team became regulars on Hayao Miyazaki's movies.[39] Miyazaki said he

> felt safe with [Takahata] by my side. He is someone who understood the problem areas and everything about the project. I did cause him a lot of hardship in the problem areas! (SP, 336)

There are 56,078 cels in *Nausicaä of the Valley of the Wind*. It was seen by 916,000 cinema-goers during its 1984 release. *Nausicaä of the Valley of the Wind* was distributed in the West in 1985 with the title *Warriors of the Wind*; it played in Gotham for a week in June, 1985, and was released on New World Video in December, 1985 (and by Vestron Video in Britain in the late 1980s).[40] It had been cut down to 95 minutes from 116 mins, and the heroine was now called 'Zandra'. For years, *Warriors of the Wind* was the only version of *Nausicaä* available in the West.[41]

The later English language version by Disney (1999)

---

37 Topcraft had been founded in 1972 by Toru Hara (one of the producers of *Nausicaä*); Hara had previously worked, like Miyazaki and Takahata, at Toei Doga. Incidentally, Topcraft animated the American Rankin/ Bass TV productions of *The Hobbit*, *The Return of the King* and *The Last Unicorn* not long b4 *Nausicaä*.
38 According to Hayao Miyazaki, Isao Takahata hadn't wanted to be the producer. Miyazaki had asked him, but the director wasn't sure.
39 The animators were paid by the cel, not a salary or flat fee (because it was cheaper).
40 This was one of the first wide releases of a serious *animé* movie in the West.
41 As *The Complete Anime Guide* noted: 'surely it's one of anime's greatest ironies that one of the finest (if not *the* finest) Japanese animated films ever made is currently available in English solely thru this spindled, folded, and mutilated version.' (T. Ledoux, 1997, 169).

included voices by Alison Lohman, Patrick Stewart, Uma Thurman, Shia LaBeouf, Chris Sarandon, Mark Hamill and Edward James Olmos. (The first dubbed version was produced by New World Video and distributed by Orion). The film spawned two video games.

Critics such as Helen McCarthy have drawn attention to some of the less than wholly satisfying animation in some of Hayao Miyazaki's earlier films, such as *Nausicaä of the Valley of the Wind.* But with Miyazaki's cinema, the quality levels are so high, even where Miyazaki and his teams are not animating every square inch of the frame, they are still producing exquisite animation.

It's true that some of the scenes in Hayao Miyazaki's earlier outings are not as subtly animated as some of the later ones, but even the weakest or poorest Miyazaki movie is far superior to most other filmmakers' best efforts. *Nausicaä of the Valley of the Wind,* for instance, is already superior to the vast majority of Japanese *animé* in terms of the quality of its animation (you can check this quite simply: watch a film directed by Hayao Miyazaki and then look at any Japanese *animé* or any Saturday morning television animation of the era – or since. There's a world of difference). The difference is *storytelling*: this is where Miyazaki outstrips everybody else: he is an *absolutely fantastic* storyteller.

Nausicaä of the Valley of the Wind was treated disastrously by the distributors in the United States: New World Pictures released the film theatrically in 1985, and New World Video released *Nausicaä* on video. But New World edited the film and dubbed it in a way that appalled Hayao Miyazaki, Toshio Suzuki and Isao Takahata. The re-edit was something that the filmmakers couldn't control, and it was so bad they decided not to allow a release of one of their movies in the West for over ten years (which may've set back Miyazaki's reputation outside Japan).

Isao Takahata called the New World Pictures version of *Nausicaä of the Valley of the Wind* 'absolutely horrible!' Music and dialogue were cut or changed, Takahata recalled, which put Studio Ghibli off releasing their movies in the West. It was censorship.[42]

Moebius (Jean Giraud), the renowned French illustrator, was a fan (and friend) of Hayao Miyazaki's, and *Nausicaä of the Valley of the Wind* was his favourite Miyazaki film (as it is

---

[42] I. Takahata, in C. Littardi, "Interview: Isao Takahata", *Animeland*, 6, Paris, 1992.

for many Miyazaki fans). *Nausicaä of the Valley of the Wind* is 'a great movie, a masterpiece,' Moebius enthused. 'The work he did after continues at the same level, in the fineness, in the beauty.' [43] The influence went the other way, too (Miyazaki admired Moebius's comic strip *Arzach*). [44] In 2004, Miyazaki and Moebius took part in a joint exhibit of their work (they had met in 1987).

THE *MANGA* OF *NAUSICAÄ OF THE VALLEY OF THE WIND*.

The *manga* of *Nausicaä of the Valley of the Wind* is truly spectacular, with action and adventure on every single page. It's one of the big, prestigious fan favourites in fantasy and sci-fi *manga*, along with *Akira* and *Ghost In the Shell,* and is highly recommended if you are a fan of Miyazaki's work. (And if you haven't read any *manga* before, you can start with the best! *Nausicaä* is an ecstatically pleasurable reading experience).

The *manga* of *Nausicaä of the Valley of the Wind* was a big seller in Japan (10 million copies); [45] it appeared first in *Animage* magazine (from February, 1982 onwards); it won awards (such as the Japan Manga Artists Association); it has been translated into many languages; in the West, the Perfect Collection was a 4 volume edition published (by Viz Communications, 1995-97); a graphic novel version (7 volumes) was published in 1990-97; and a comic running to 27 issues (1988-96).

The *Nausicaä of the Valley of the Wind manga* is a large format *tankobon* (collected volumes), with the usual 6-12 panels per page in black-and-white (fortunately, in the West, Viz Media have kept the right-to-left layout of Japanese *manga*). There's also a pull-out colour map, showing Torumekia, [46] the Oceans of Salt, the Sea of Corruption, Pejitei, Tolas, Shuwa and the Valley of the Wind.

The *Nausicaä manga* is visually staggering, with densely-detailed panels in Hayao Miyazaki's distinctive, delicate drawing lines. What comes across most powerfully is the sheer genius of Miyazaki's imagination: I think an artist's imagination is their biggest asset, and Miyazaki has that times

---

[43] Interview in *Animeland*, 1, Paris, 1991.
[44] Miyazaki on Moebius: 'even today, I think he has an awesome sense of space. I directed *Nausicaä* under Moebius' influence.'
[45] Miyazaki acknowledged the encouragement of editor Hideo Ogata in creating his *Nausicaä manga*, and also in helping to persuade the backers of the movie to invest in it (TP, 317).
[46] It's Tolmekia in the movie.

a million.

Of course, as many fans as well as critics have noted, the 1984 movie streamlined much of the *Nausicaä manga*, which runs to four *tankobon*. Inevitable, of course. But much was retained for the movie. Among the elements dropped from the *Nausicaä of the Valley of the Wind manga* for the movie was plenty more telekinesis and telepathy (in the movie, it's only Nausicaä who manifests telepathic powers). The *omhus* speak in the *manga* (though only Nausicaä, principally, is able to hear/ understand them). There are further societies and relationships in the *manga*, which the film adaptation had to drop, otherwise it would be a ten-hour movie (not a problem for many fans, I'm sure – a ten-hour adaptation of *Nausicaä of the Valley of the Wind* would be just fine with me).

Whatever the source is for a movie, Hayao Miyazaki said, whether it was *manga* or a book, it would have to be taken apart entirely by the filmmakers, and then rebuilt as an organic whole (SP, 62). Besides, you can always read the *manga*.

In the *manga* of *Nausicaä of the Valley of the Wind,* Hayao Miyazaki demonstrates his total mastery of action, pace, theme and complex narrative. The *manga* has everything one could wish for in an action-adventure genre: so many cliff-hangers, face-offs, duels, sword fights, explosions, hair's-breadth escapes, flights, and chases. It is truly awesome stuff, and if you enjoy the movie, you must get hold of his *manga*.

If you want to see just how fast and loose Miyazaki plays with adapting works from other media, have a look at the *Nausicaä manga*: Miyazaki doesn't care a jot about being 'faithful' or 'respectful'; he will change whatever he needs to do, and this is his own *manga*, too.

THEMES.

Nausicaä of the Valley of the Wind is a truly enthralling entry in fantasy adventure cinema. It demonstrates the boundless imagination of Hayao Miyazaki and his team, working at their best. It's true that parts of *Nausicaä of the Valley of the Wind* haven't quite got the technical slickness and smoothness of some of Ghibli's/ Miyazaki's later animation, but the urgency of the film, the spectacle and thrills of the action scenes, the pacing, the secondary characters, and the visual invention all carry this movie along.

Nausicaä of the Valley of the Wind tackles big themes – ecological themes, of humanity existing with the Earth. It's about the way that humans tend to wreck the world, while Nausicaä represents the urge towards living in balance with one's surroundings. It was 'inspired by a kind of animism', Hayao Miyazaki remarked, a respect for all living things.[47] It is a post-apocalyptic world: in this early 1980s story, it's not nuclear weapons or a global war or a virus or an alien invasion, but the ecological imbalance instigated by humans (though there was a war which started the decline, called the Seven Days of Fire). People just can't get along with the natural world: thus there is a Sea of Decay, a poisonous blanket of ocean and desert.[48] And there are segments of jungle, which contain deadly spores. Beneath the Sea of Decay, as Nausicaä and her friends find out, is a forest of dead trees, but also clean water. The spores are a vivid and powerful manifestation of decay and evil – evil here being something that infects life and kills it, evil as life run to ruin.

The images of the community trying to save its crops by searching for the spores, which attach themselves to plants, is moving: the arrival of the crashed Tolmekian airship means possible death to the food crops of the Valley. As well as the infection of the military invasion, the Tolkmekians also bring the death of the spores. They are humans as a literal virus.

The war-mongering Tolmekians are contrasted with the gentler, rural people of the Valley of the Wind. The Tolmekians have used technology in the wrong way – building guns, airships, and, fatally, trying to revive the Giant Warriors.[49] The Tolkmekians have made the Faustian bargain with modern technology, as opposed to the in-tune-with-nature technology of the Valley of the Wind, which harnesses the wind using windmills (this is not 'steam-punk' but 'wind-punk'). The Faustian pact is also embodied by the leader of the invasion, Kushana, who is three-quarters cyborg (she first appears clad all over in heavy armour – metal armour as a cyborgian carapace hiding more cyborgization. Her arm was cut off by one of the insects, so she has a personal reason for hating them).

Existing between the Sea of Decay and the humans are the insects, a variety of bugs with the enormous *ohmu* at the

---

[47] Hayao Miyazaki, interview in *A-Club*, 19, June, 1987
[48] The notion of the Sea of Decay, as a term, came from an area of marshland in the Crimean peninsula, which has rotted away and been given the name Sea of Decay.
[49] Hayao Miyazaki said he inserted the giant robots (*kyoshinhei*) into the *manga* of *Nausicaä of the Valley of the Wind* when he was stuck with the story and didn't know where to take it (SP, 391). Giant robots are of course a staple of Japanese *manga* and *animé*. Japan still uses more robot technology than any other nation, and was also the first country to employ robotization in industry.

top of the chain. And the only person who can communicate with them and tame them is the heroine, Nausicaä.

Hayao Miyazaki didn't want the *ohmu* to have recognizable faces: he preferred them to be totally non-anthropomorphic. He didn't want the audience to know what the *ohmu* were thinking (however, in the *Nausicaä manga* they speak briefly). He was after a larger presence than humans, something totally other, something beyond humanity, something ancient, and something that could embody the spirit of the natural world. Hence he opted for a mix of anthropods and insects, rather than animals or birds or reptiles or the more usual beasts (SP, 415). He didn't want anything cuddly or anthropomorphic: bugs were chosen partly because a lot of people don't like bugs, so the *ohmu* could represent a different eco-system (SP, 416).

The one really beautiful place that's survived the ecological disaster is the Valley of the Wind, where Nausicaä lives in a community of mediæval villages. It is a sun-lit land of green fields, steep mountainsides and windmills – as if the community is harvesting the wind itself (thus the inhabitants are very sensitive to any changes in the breeze – with Nausicaä as the premier wind-poet).

The Valley of the Wind is a view of a community living in partnership with the Earth in a positive manner. It's a familiar scenario in Hayao Miyazaki's cinema – it can be found in the mining community of Slug Valley in *Laputa: Castle In the Sky*, for instance, or the fishing ports in *Kiki's Delivery Service*. (There are other lands in *Nausicaä of the Valley of the Wind*, such as Pejite and Tolmekia).

In *Nausicaä of the Valley of the Wind,* a thousand years ago, the Seven Days of Fire occurred, when the giant robots were employed as weapons: the Pacific War, the atomic bombs, and the aftermath for Japan, as well as its uneasy relationship with the U.S.A., clearly lie behind the mythology of this world. I would also suggest that *Nausicaä of the Valley of the Wind* reflects the politics of its 1980s time – the excessive militarism of the Reagan era and the Cold War, when nuclear arms were at the height of their production, and the possibility of a nuclear war was very high. No one can miss the links – not only of the giant robots and the Seven Days of Fire, but also the enormous nuclear submarine[50] the people of the Valley of the Wind take refuge in.

Once again in *Nausicaä* there's a castle, with giant three-pronged vanes. Hayao Miyazaki likes castles, if the titles and

---
[50] This has a forerunner in the abandoned ship in *Future Boy Conan*.

subjects of his films are anything to go by: castles crop up in *The Castle of Cagliostro*, *Laputa: Castle In the Sky*, *Nausicaä of the Valley of the Wind* and *Howl's Moving Castle*. And other structures are close to castles or complex, ornate and hierarchical structures – such as the bathhouse in *Spirited Away*.

In the castle the ailing King Jihil lives, Nausicaä's father, in a mediæval bed chamber, with its mythical tapestry and ceremonial suit of armour; there's also room in the castle for secret passages, and a hidden chamber in the basement, where Nausicaä is cultivating a garden of plants she's collected (the garden is another slice of paradise within the paradisal state of the Valley of the Wind. The hidden garden as paradise presents Nausicaä as Eve, the possibility of a new Eden: the end credits depict the forest transforming itself into a paradise of the future).

MUSIC AND VOICES.

Sumi Shimamoto does a brilliant job as the voice of Nausicaä (and also Clarisse in *The Castle of Cagliostro*). Hayao Miyazaki said he was 'overwhelmed' by Shimamoto's performance in the childhood dream scene: 'so vivid... so real' (SP, 336). I have to say, though, that Alison Lohman is superb, and comes out better than many as Nausicaä in the English language dub. Her voice wholly lacks the tweeness and girliness of too many voice artists who dub English *animé*. Others in the Japanese voice cast included Gorou Naya (Yupa), Yoshiko Sakakibara (Kushana), Hisako Kyoda (Obaba), Mahito Tsujimura (Jihil), Iemasa Kayumi (Kurotawa), Ichirou Nagai (Mito), Kohei Miyauchi (Goru), Mina Tominaga (Rastel) and Akiko Tsuboi (Rastel's mother). Youji Matsuda, who played Asbel; was Ashitaka in *Princess Mononoke*.

Nausicaä's soundtrack (by Joe Hisaishi), which comprises a good deal of electronica (reminiscent of Tangerine Dream and Brian Eno), is not wholly successful, and is much more satisfying when it reverts to more traditional (Westernized) orchestral sounds. Particularly effective is the sweeping cue used for Nausicaä's flying scenes. For the *ohmu*, a glissando on a sitar was used, to indicate their otherworldliness and mystery (sitar is certainly unusual in any movie soundtrack, not least an action-adventure movie). Electronic music, including drum machines, was composed for some of the action scenes. For the exploration of the Sea of Decay, Hisaishi employed electronica in slow drones, a standard approach for fantasy or science fiction, but the sounds were a departure from the usual music for 'sense of wonder' scenes.[51] (There is far less music, however, in *Nausicaä* than in comparable Western action-adventure movies).

NAUSICAÄ.

Nausicaä is another of Hayao Miyazaki's *shojo* characters, a young, idealistic, independent, energetic, brave, practical and warm-hearted woman. Nausicaä is literally as well as physically and dramatically the heart of the movie. Nausicaä is also the heart of the Valley of the Wind community – she embodies their best aspects, their conscience, their morality. She is their princess (as they often say). The *ohmu* also recognize this: Nausicaä is the only human who's able to calm them and tame them. (*Pace* the portrayal of the *ohmu* in *Nausicaä of the Valley of the Wind,* Miyazaki recalled being impressed by *Tarzan* movies he saw as a kid, when the jungle boy would holler 'AAAAAYYYYY-AAAAHHHHH' and a herd of elephants would show up (SP, 414). The idea that Tarzan had these strong animals at his beck and call was thrilling for the young Miyazaki).

Nausicaä sports a blue jacket, a short skirt, pale leggings, and wonderful, blue shin pads, which look like knee-high boots.[52] She might be about 14 or 15, maybe a little older. The filmmakers experimented with a range of costumes for Nausicaä, including Native American-style headgear with feathers, fairy tale princess dresses, and futuristic outfits, b4 deciding upon the blue dress (simple dresses crop up many times in Miyazaki's *shojo* characters – Kiki, Sheeta, Ponyo, etc).

When an interviewer remarked that the heroine's breasts were 'rather large', Hayao Miyazaki responded, well, that was so she could 'embrace all those poor old men and women in the castle when they are dying', not because of love or sex or breast-feeding (SP, 338). In the *Nausicaä manga*, however, there is an unmistakable eroticization of Nausicaä by Miyazaki (she strips down to a revealing top, and also appears nude).

Nausicaä is a wonderful pilot, too – this is a Hayao Miyazaki movie! The first time Nausicaä is seen in the 1984 film is flying her beloved glider, a small, jet-powered wing, which she rides at times like a wind-surfer or a skateboard

---

51 Electronic sounds were also used for sound fx (synthesized wind noise, for instance).
52 You see knee-pads and other leg wear in many *manga* characters. Japanese designers love to accessorize!

(and she hangs under it as well as lying on a belt).[53]

Nausicaä is a fierce fighter too: when she races to her father's rescue[54] and finds him shot[55] by Kushana's henchmen, she goes wild, and kills a bunch of them (four), before Lord Yupa intervenes,[56] to negotiate between a furious Nausicaä and the cool, cyborg villain Kushana. (Kurotawa, Kushana's second-in-command, is the recognizable military type who's really out for himself – Nausicaä smashes him against a wall). It's still unusual in this kind of movie to see the heroine murdering four men in a blind rage. On one level of plot and motive, it is vicious but understandable, as a moment of absolute fury. But it's also pretty extreme to kill not one but four people (it's rare for a Disney heroine, for instance, to act like that! Well, like never!).[57]

Nausicaä is a dreamer, too: in the jungle, early on in the movie, she lies on her back on the shell of the *ohmu*, looking up at the spores falling around her (they look like snow).[58] It's a familiar posture for a Hayao Miyazaki hero: Kiki is shown in this pose in the opening scenes of *Kiki's Delivery Service* (and within a couple of minutes of Miyazaki's first feature film, *The Castle of Cagliostro*, the hero, Lupin, is lying back on the roof of his car, and there's a shot of another classic, Miyazakian image – white clouds drifting over a sun-lit field. And Ponyo lies on the back of the jellyfish).[59]

Nausicaä is an appealing character, because she is tender-hearted and compassionate, and is incensed by the amount of killing she sees – such as when Asbel attacks the Tolmekian air fleet in his gunship. Asbel is an incredibly destructive young boy – he's furious about the death of his sister Lastelle, but he also single-handledly kills a huge number of people in those Tolmekian aircraft. As with Nausicaä's rage over her father's murder, Asbel's reaction is understandable but excessively violent. Somehow, it's more shocking that Asbel should be a boy in his teens: had it been a

---

[53] A Japanese company has had a go at building a full-size version of the glider. In the movie, they called it a *mehve*.
[54] Notice how she darts into the chamber from a hidden door – *Nausicaä* is filled with such details.
[55] We are with Nausicaä when she hears the gunshot from below.
[56] As the echoey sound of Yupa's blood drips, we move into Nausicaä's mindscreen, with Yupa in voiceover explaining why they have to wait and negotiate.
[57] The *manga* makes more of Nausicaä's remorse and inertia after the killings. But there is a scene where Nausicaä breaks down and cries with Lord Yupa – though that is over her father's death, and the invasion of her homeland.
[58] Nausicaä has a pet called Teto, like a cross between a squirrel and a fox (this may be a reference to the *otak* in Ursula Le Guiin's *Earthsea* books).
[59] Seita in *Grave of the Fireflies* also lies on his back and looks up at the sky in the most traumatic scene in Studio Ghibli's output, when he cremates his sister.

middle-aged guy, and a villain, it would have more fitted to the genre, at least in movie-movie terms.[60]

The more I see *Nausicaä of the Valley of the Wind*, the more I think the aftermath of Asbel's attack on the Tolmekian fleet is a serious psychological and moral flaw in the story: if there were say 50 people in each aircraft, then Asbel has just murdered 150 people. The flaw is that Nausicaä happily pairs up with Asbel with little more than telling him 'there has been enough killing'. Yes, we know that the princess would save Asbel from the attacking insects, because that's in her nature (and that is another spectacular aerial combat sequence, snatching the youth out of the claws of a flying bug).[61] And it's true that Asbel does look after Nausicaä when she's unconscious on landing, and also hunts for her *mehve*. But he's just killed 150 people! He's just caused three large planes to crash – the *manga* fills the sky with falling victims (some of them leap from the planes to escape the flames in the *manga* – creepy echoes of 9/11. The movie doesn't show them).

Pairing up the heroine with a suitably brave, adventurous youth is part of the action-adventure genre, of course (that Asbel is a pilot too, is typical of Hayao Miyazaki). But making Asbel a mass murderer is way too much; he's simply not worthy of Nausicaä.[62]

In the 1984 picture, Nausicaä has telepathic powers, with which she can communicate with the *ohmu*, for instance, and also know when something is about to happen way ahead of anyone else. Sometimes it's indicated by short pieces of voiceover (which Hayao Miyazaki and his teams don't use as much as one might imagine), and sometimes by depicting Nausicaä becoming aware of something offscreen before anyone else (such as when the stricken Tolmekian ship appears behind the clouds at night, and Nausicaä spots ist before the others).[63]

It's also striking just how much in the Japanese movie that Nausicaä is surrounded by men, and lives in a man's world. Apart from characters such as Kushana, who's portrayed not only as a villain but also as a partial or

---

60 Needless to say, *Nausicaä of the Valley of the Wind* has time to show the effects of Nausicaä's murderous acts, but not how Asbel feels after killing many people. That's a flaw, I think: Asbel after he's landed and come round in the underground forest needs to show some remorse.
61 But she does that also to placate the bugs so they won't attack her cohorts.
62 You could excuse this major error partly in terms of the adventure genre – by saying that the 150 people who fell to their deaths or who were burnt alive were Tolmekians, the enemies who've just invaded the Valley of the Wind.
63 The mental sensitivity is reprised in Ashitaka in *Princess Mononoke*.

artificially-enhanced human, and the grandmother Obaba, there are few women in Nausicaä's life. That she is motherless is vital (as writers know, it's much more fun in adventures to leave mom behind!), and that she loses her father in the first third of the story (however, she is helped by women – such as Lastelle's mother in the Torumekian aircraft, and there are women in her village who idolize her).

❖

When Nausicaä is first shown in both versions (print and celluloid) of the story, it is on her own, collecting plants and exploring the Sea of Decay. The scene introduces the spectacularly exotic under-realm of the Sea of Decay, the spores, and the shell of a giant insect, the *ohmu*. Nausicaä is depicted as a brave, independent, young woman, pursuing her own project of collecting plants, but also, when her reverie atop the *ohmu* is interrupted, rushing to the aid of Lord Yupa, when his gunfire disturbs an *ohmu*.[64]

These opening scenes shift from the wonder and spectacle of the Sea of Decay to an action-packed sequence where Nausicaä draws off the rampaging *ohmu* in her flying craft. They also depict how Nausicaä is able to calm the *ohmu*, and lure it away (important plot points for the climax): she is the link between the human world and these mysterious, powerful creatures (and between humans and all of nature: Nausicaä embodies Hayao Miyazaki's ecological theme – she is what people have forgotten about).

The opening sequence also introduces the desert that has enveloped much of the planet, and the unusual and ruined world of the Sea of Decay. This buried toxic world is reminiscent of the realms of H.G. Wells and Jules Verne (such as in *Journey To the Centre of the Earth* – including the 1959 20th Century Fox movie). This setting is also the classic one of modern science fiction – a waste land, a world destroyed by previous conflicts. It is the post-apocalyptic world of numerous sci-fi books, comics and films. And of course, it is also the shattered world that's so central to Japanese animation, the world of ruination following World War Two.

And the scenes also allow Hayao Miyazaki and the team to create slices of desert movie epics, such as *Lawrence of Arabia* and *The Ten Commandments*, with the scenes of the *ohmu* thundering across the sand, or Nausicaä on her glider.[65]

---

[64] The *ohmu* were animated by using pieces of card to create the impression of layers of their bodies moving.

[65] But not characters on horses (or camels) – Miyazaki consciously avoids horses, inventing creatures like the *kai* here, or using elks (in *Mononoke*), and Jihil, in the flashback, rides cattle not a horse.

So by the end of the second or third scene, *Nausicaä of the Valley of the Wind* has already established many aspects to the characters of Nausicaä and Lord Yupa, and major elements of the narrative, such as the *ohmu* insects, the high fantasy of the Sea of Decay, flight, the theme of ruin and apocalypse, and the settings.

Or put it like this: the opening scenes are masterful storytelling, backed by technically breathtaking animation. The scenes also introduce an unusual aspect of *Nausicaä of the Valley of the Wind:* the hero is a heroine – already unusual for an action-adventure – and she is not a full-grown woman (who can waste villains and have a romance with a guy), but a woman in her mid-teens. You have to think hard to find a similar sort of movie with a similar sort of heroine.[66] Yes, they do exist, but they are not common.

Hayao Miyazaki remarked that by making the hero a boy or man it becomes *Indiana Jones*, which he didn't want to do (he saved that for his '92 red pig movie). For Miyazaki, Nausicaä was not a conventional hero: she doesn't defeat a villain; rather, she is 'a protagonist who understands, or accepts. She is someone who lives in a different dimension'. And for Miyazaki it was preferable to have a woman play that role rather than a man.[67]

NAUSICAÄ AS SHAMAN AND MESSIAH.

It's striking how much is made of the people of the Valley's love for their princess, Nausicaä. The women hope their children will grow up strong like her, and throughout the movie the concern for the welfare of the princess is always uppermost in people's minds (they ask about her b4 anything else). In which case, the leap towards messiahdom is not that over-done, because the 1984 film has already prepared for it throughout the story (there's a touching moment when one of the old coots held captive by Kushana talks about his hands, ailing from infection from the spores, and how the princess had told him she liked his hands, how they were worker's hands).

But for Hayao Miyazaki, Nausicaä was something like a shaman or inspirer for her community, rather than a leader: she is something like a *miko*, 'a shaman-maiden who works at a Shinto shrine', Miyazaki explained (SP, 407). Maybe so, but Nausicaä is also an action hero in a big action-adventure

---
[66] Nausicaä was voted Number One *Animé* Character in 1991 by the readers of *Animage* magazine.
[67] Interview in *Young*, Feb 20, 1984.

picture (she can wield a sword like a demon, heft a machine gun, and fly a plane like an ace, when necessary – including steering with her foot!).

Hayao Miyazaki was not sure about the religious implications of the ending of *Nausicaä of the Valley of the Wind*. As Miyazaki recalled, 'Mitsuki Nakamura-san [art director] and I said to each other, "We've got a problem."' (SP, 333). It became Joan of Arc, a religious image, when Nausicaä came back to life. 'I wanted to get rid of the religious undertone', Miyazaki admitted, but couldn't find a way.[68] (Recall Miyazaki's dislike of Christian images – he is talking about religion in the *West* here).

Why did Nausicaä act the way she did? Hayao Miyazaki reckoned that although she did think of her community, it was really for herself that she tried to save the baby *ohmu*: 'Nausicaä felt that unless she returned the baby *ohmu* to the pack the hole in her heart would never be filled' (SP, 333).

OTHER CHARACTERS.

Lord Yupa is Nausicaä's surrogate father, partly because her own father is dying.[69] He's the familiar samurai type, a renowned warrior, noble, laconic, refined, wise and a man without a home, a wanderer. If this was live-action, he would be played by Toshiro Mifune, or perhaps Takashi Shimura from *The Seven Samurai*. (Miyazaki kills off Lord Yupa in the *manga*).

Obaba is the aged crone, a recurring character in Hayao Miyazaki's fantasy cinema: she supplies information about the history and mythology of the Valley of the Wind.[70] In touch with the ancestors and the past, she is the grandmother witch figure and advisor that is a fundamental component of fantasy and fairy tales (*Nausicaä of the Valley of the Wind* can be regarded as an ecological fairy tale).

Obaba appears at key moments to introduce the mythological themes of *Nausicaä of the Valley of the Wind,* such as when she appears in the scene in the king's chamber, and tells the story from the legend of the mysterious figure in blue walking on a gold field that will save the world. It's a piece of

---

[68] Hayao Miyazaki commented in 1994: 'when the film was finished I discovered that I was actually up to my neck in the religious zone I had always wanted to avoid; I seriously felt that I had backed myself into a corner' (SP, 393).
[69] Nausicaä has two fathers – her ailing father, King Jihil, and her surrogate father and guru, Lord Yupa. Her mother is dead (but she appears briefly in one of the flashbacks. There is more of the mother in the *manga*).
[70] Obaba also insists that the Sea of Decay must not be destroyed.

plot that will pay off big time later on.[71] Obaba also stands up to the invading army from Tolmekia, a vital moment, because she tells her people that the invaders killed their king (added to the *manga* for the movie).[72] And, unusually, Obaba (and the three children who gathered around Nausicaä when she left), are employed during the climax to comment on the action.

The bushiness of the beards and moustaches in *Nausicaä of the Valley of the Wind* is striking – these characters do have some of the bushiest and most copious facial hair of any movie (outside the giant beards of martial arts wizards or *The Lord of the Rings*). There is an economic purpose here – the beards and moustaches are so large they obscure the mouths completely, with speech being indicated by the moustaches and beards trembling slightly, avoiding the need to animate mouths to particular dialogue (saving more work).

Costume-wise, the people of the Valley of the Wind sport bulky, warm clothes, with everyone wearing a distinctive hood or a hat (there are many more unusual costumes in the *manga*). There is a permanent high wind in nearly every outdoor scene, with Lord Yupa's cloak and Nausicaä's clothes perpetually blowing around. Wind blowing hair and clothes is one of the staples of Japanese *animé*, lending life to otherwise static scenes. But in the Valley of the Wind, the flapping of clothes is exaggerated.

Hayao Miyazaki and his filmmaking teams are wonderful at creating monsters and fantastical creatures. *Nausicaä of the Valley of the Wind* abounds with them – the giant *ohmu* insects, with their multiple eyes,[73] sliding carapaces, and feelers; the numerous flying bugs, including giant dragonflies; and the two-legged, ostrich-like birds (*kai*) that Yupa uses for a steed.

WAR.

Nausicaä of the Valley of the Wind is a fantasy adventure story, yes, but it is also a war story, with a number of groups set against each other: the Valley of the Wind, Tolmekia, Pejite, and the *ohmu* (and insects). At the heart of the warring factions is Nausicaä: she is the only one who understands that the

---
[71] There are moments when Nausicaä is shown briefly in that guise. And of course she wears blue from the opening scenes onwards.
[72] An unarmed blind woman standing in front of a tank is a resonant and thoroughly modern (20th century) image.
[73] The eyes change colour, according to their mood, a familiar shorthand device to communicate *some* of the *ohmus*' feelings (but not all): red for anger, blue for calm, etc.

ohmu are protecting the forest and the Sea of Decay because the trees absorb the toxins and help to purify the water, the land and the air.[74]

The staging of the military take-over of the Valley of the Wind is particularly impressive. It is Nausicaä once again who senses the approach of the armada of airships from Tolmekia, once alerted by the guards.[75] The images of the giant grey metal hulks of the Tolmekian aircraft landing on the green fields of the Valley and smashing the buildings is a striking depiction of the destructive uses of technology. The combination of technologies, too, is convincing: 20th century aircraft and tanks are mixed with swords and spears.[76]

As in *Laputa: Castle In the Sky, Spirited Away, Princess Mononoke* and other Hayao Miyazaki films, Nausicaä is paired with a young man roughly her age: Asbel is from the neighbouring nation of Pejite (Nausicaä rescued his sister, Lastelle, from the wreckage of the crashed Tolmekian airship).[77] There's an intriguing interlude which features Nausicaä and Asbel, when they are separated from the others and crashland in the Sea of Decay, ending up falling through quicksand to the hidden world below – another slice of Jules Verne, evoking the scenes in *Journey To the Centre of the Earth* when the explorers get separated.

Socially, the Valley of the Wind is a feudal, mediæval society. But the 1984 movie happily mixes the Middle Ages with Hayao Miyazaki's beloved late 19th century/ early 20th century technology and culture, so there are knights in armour and swords, but also guns, giant robots and tanks and planes. And fantasy, too: Nausicaä's glider, the *ohmu*, the Sea of Decay, etc,

ACTION AND ADVENTURE.

Nausicaä of the Valley of the Wind has action aplenty – stupendous action, action piled on top of action – the pacing is breathtaking and very intense (Hayao Miyazaki said he delib-

---

[74] Nausicaä's experiments in her secret laboratory confirm this.

[75] The notion of the watchmen on the castle tower being able to smell something wrong in the air is inventive – it comes from the people of the Valley of the Wind being so in tune with the wind, which's central to their livelihood. They can also tell when the air is fresh and pure.

[76] No one can miss that the invaders come from the West – from, for Japan, Europe and Amerika. This is fantasy, yes, but this is very much a *Japanese* fantasy.

[77] However, Nausicaä spends just as much screen time, it seems, with Mito, one of the trusted veterans in King Jihil's company (he sports an eyepatch like a pirate). Mito's with Nausicaä during the flight over the Sea of Decay, and when Nausicaä saves the baby *ohmu*. And Mito plays a larger role in the *manga* of *Nausicaä of the Valley of the Wind* too.

erately 'kept the dramatic tension high. I had no desire to have a structure with a clear, logical development as in *Sherlock Hound* or *Cagliostro*' [SP, 337]). The air battles are staggeringly good. Miyazaki, Kazuo Komatsubara and the team can stage a duel between planes as skilfully as anybody in the history of cinema. The attack of Asbel in his gunship, coming down out of the sun, where the youngster single-handedly demolishes the Tolmekian fleet, is particularly inspired. The scene is incredible enough, but it's only one of many aerial scenes and just one of many air battles in *Nausicaä of the Valley of the Wind*. Prior to that there's the scene where Nausicaä tries to guide the Tolmekian ship down, or the scenes where she calms the *ohmu* and persuades it to return to the forest. (If you flip thru the *manga* (right to left, of course), you'll find many flying scenes – at least half the pages in the first *tankobon*).

Hayao Miyazaki and his team have clearly seen all of the great aerial combat movies, taken the finest ingredients, and the results in *Nausicaä of the Valley of the Wind* are some of the most spectacular dog fights ever put on screen.

It's striking, for instance, how Hayao Miyazaki and his animators use *clouds* as a key ingredient in an air battle.[78] Not just to make the backgrounds visually interesting, but as important parts of a battle: the planes disappear into clouds as if they're going underwater. And they rise out of clouds as if they're moving from land into the air, or from one space into another space. And when aircraft fly next to clouds, their shadows follow them as if the light is falling on solid foam. In Miyazaki's cinema, clouds aren't tinted bits of air, but have a presence (and danger) that can't be ignored (this is the era before radar and flying by wire – yet there are jet engines).

Hayao Miyazaki and his team have observed how significant clouds are for pilots, how if you can't see something like a plane right next to you, you have no idea it's there. Miyazaki's films are some of the very few pictures I've seen which accurately depict the sense of scale and depth and height in flight – think of those point-of-view shots of a character looking out of a plane window to see another aircraft far, far below, in between banks of clouds, or above them, to aircraft somewhere high above.

Clouds are deployed to extraordinary effect in the scene where a Tolmekian craft attacks then boards a plane from the

---

[78] Clouds would be one of Hayao Miyazaki's recurring motifs. He said in a 1986 interview that the really interesting effects of 'light shining between gaps in the clouds' probably only take place at 10,000 metres above the Earth. Once you get into outer space, things become much more simplified (SP, 342).

Valley of the Wind. Sequences like this are virtually impossible to achieve in live-action, using aerial photography with real aircraft. And if that isn't enough, the scene is topped by an amazing rescue by Yupa, who demonstrates his famous swordsmanship yet again, taking on the Tolmekian soldiers single-handed. The action thunders on and on – a siege, more fights, a daring escape by Nausicaä on her *mehve* into a storm, and a dog fight.[79]

The aerial scenes in *Nausicaä* are handled with such flair and attention to detail. The feelings of weight and movement are brilliantly portrayed – those large aircraft lumber through the skies, while Nausicaä's *mehve* is a graceful wing performing hurtling swoops and fly-bys. Scale, depth, speed, height, momentum and distance are expressed using every trick the animators possess.

Then there are the spectacular scenes of the enormous *ohmu* insects storming cities on fire – really apocalyptic stuff (this was a four years before *Akira* and three years before *Legend of the Overfiend*). And the epic visuals of the Pejite city ruined by attacking *ohmu* (war-torn cities are one of Hayao Miyazaki's specialities). And the final battle in *Nausicaä of the Valley of the Wind* tops everything. *Nausicaä* is the first Miyazaki film in which the apocalyptic theme of Japanese animation is staged – the reworking of the Pacific War in a fantasy context;[80] Miyazaki would return to it in pictures such as *Princess Mononoke* and *Howl's Moving Castle*.

There's a clever use of flashbacks in *Nausicaä of the Valley of the Wind*, which are a staple of Hayao Miyazaki's cinema: how the images of Nausicaä as a young girl of five or so in a field of golden wheat merges with the golden light of the tentacles of the *ohmu* in the climactic scene, in which Nausicaä is resurrected (the yellow tentacles becoming fronds of golden wheat).[81] The flashback also depicts Nausicaä caring for the *ohmu*, which foreshadows her rescue of the baby *ohmu* on the island (and her intuitive links to the natural world).

Importantly, the flashback also features the family unit, with both of Nausicaä's parents nearby: and it shows the Law

---

[79] And water – no other filmmaker has fetishized aircraft landing and taking off on water!

[80] 'In Japan we are still affected by the enormous shock of defeat in the Pacific War, which was a senseless undertaking,' Miyazaki stated in 1997 (TP, 51).

[81] For me, the only aspect that spoils the golden-hued flashbacks is the choice of using a young girl singing. The song, and the way it's sung, isn't distinctive or lyrical enough. Also, I'm not sure that the flashbacks are dramatically strong enough: there seems to be more narrative content required here, or maybe a different staging of the elements.

of the Father in action, as Jihil tells his daughter that the *ohmu* must be killed. The scene's partly intended to express how Nausicaä's sympathy for the non-human world began very early, and was strong, too: so strong that she defies the laws of her ailing father and father surrogates and goes into the toxic world alone, and also builds a laboratory in the basement of the castle to nurture her scientific findings. (Nausicaä as the idealistic scientist and explorer is a recurring type in Miyazaki-sensei's cinema, and of course in fantasy fiction and science fiction everywhere: she is Viktor Frankenstein, investigating the mysteries of nature away from prying eyes in her private laboratory).

There's no slow middle act in *Nausicaä of the Valley of the Wind*: the 1984 Japanese movie can appear as pretty much wall-to-wall action, and there is an enormous amount of action unfolding. Yet action is meaningless, and rapidly becomes just movements on a screen, a tiresome, garbled, incoherent mess of stunt following stunt, lights flashing, someone yelling – unless it is grounded with an emotion, a context, a motive, a goal, a logic, and characters. Despite the high volume of action in *Nausicaä of the Valley of the Wind,* it arises out of the themes and the characters: it grows organically from the material.

And there is so much action! No draggy second act – *Nausicaä of the Valley of the Wind* can seem like a continuous third, climactic act, from the third scene onwards. Every time you see *Nausicaä of the Valley of the Wind,* you can't believe just how much the filmmakers have crammed into the movie: the second hour is a *tour-de-force* of rising action and dramatic events, each one complicating and commenting upon the previous one. The narrative takes all sorts of unexpected turns: the princess being taken by the Torumekians along with some hostages; the ravaging of the city of Peijite by the *ohmu*; the switch when Nausicaä is captured by the Peijiteans; and so on.

The climax of *Nausicaä of the Valley of the Wind* is mind-boggling in its visuals, its parallel action, its staging and its editing. There are so many things going on at once, and so many outstanding components it's hard to pick one or two to consider: the scene where Nausicaä takes on the two soldiers carrying the baby *ohmu* as bait in the middle of an acid lake is extraordinary (the image of Nausicaä, unable to communicate with the soldiers, flying towards the gunner, standing on her flying wing with her arms outstretched, is unforgettable). Or the scene where the giant robot is revived by Kushana and launches laser fire at the herd of *ohmu* storming the lakeshore before it rots away into a bubbling, noxious mass.[82] Or the climactic pay-off of the messiah myth, when Nausicaä is healed by the *ohmu* and brought back to life, raised on masses of golden tentacles (and the flashbacks in fields of golden wheat pay off, too).

Nausicaä of the Valley of the Wind's end credits throw the narrative into the future, with scenes of the rebuilding of the Valley of the Wind and vignettes of happy, smiling people getting back to their lives. It's a format that Hayao Miyazaki would employ many times in his feature films.[83]

The end credits also return to the opening scenes: the final part of the closing credit sequence depicts Nausicaä, Asbel and Yupa visiting the Sea of Decay again (though now it looks much sparklier, more colourful, and not so spore-smothered).

ECOLOGY, THE SEA OF DECAY AND THE WALKING FOREST.

Pace Nausicaä of the Valley of the Wind, Hayao Miyazaki considered the idea of a thousand-year forest, a piece of woodland that could be left alone from any human intervention: it would begin with a carefully managed forest, and then after 50 years visitors could go there but have restrictions on what they could do: no alcohol, stores, roads or concrete (SP, 139). And whatever happened in the forest, nobody would be allowed to intervene.

The idea of a forest that moves came from *Macbeth*: Hayao Miyazaki recalled that when he heard the idea that trees could move as a child, it thrilled him: and if it's OK that trees move, then it was OK to make a movie like *Nausicaä of the Valley of the Wind* (SP, 417). Instead of defenceless plants, the trees turn the tables on humans. Nature isn't charming, Miyazaki reckoned, it could be fearsome; it doesn't need 'protecting' by humans. I agree: forests, like the rest of the natural world, have existed for a lot longer than humans. And the planet, which's been around for 4.5 billion years, doesn't need 'saving' by humans!

Nausicaä of the Valley of the Wind presents a world of interdependence, an eco-system, where one lifeform depends

---

[82] The Giant Warrior was an early animation job for director Hideaki Anno (b. 1960), co-founder of Gainax Studio and an *animé* star; Anno later directed *Evangelion, Nadia: Secret of Blue Water,* and *Gunbuster*. He was the lead voice in *The Wind Rises*.

[83] Suggesting multiple happy endings. Or, rather, the continuation of life: as Miyazaki says, *you must live*.

upon the others. Nothing can exist in isolation. Of course, the good guys are the ones who live in harmony with the natural world – the Valley of the Wind community. And the bad guys are the ones who fight the *ohmu* and the Sea of Decay – the Tolmekians and the Pejites (and they're also fighting each other. And the Pejites are not above using the *ohmu* to help destroy their enemies).

It's true that, like other movies with an ecological theme, *Nausicaä of the Valley of the Wind* can seem a little too right-on and self-righteous (and also preachy). Yes, we know that humans are slowly (or rapidly) ruining the planet. Yes we know that humans have to live in harmony with the Earth or die (the planet, tho' will simply carry on, maybe 'til the sun expires in another 5 billion years).

In 1999, Hayao Miyazaki reckoned than humanity will get worse – it will make 'more and more stupid and dangerous things', but maybe it will realize what it's done, and 'try better ways of doing things'.[84]

As to ecological messages, Hayao Miyazaki has said that he isn't interested in delivering a message in a movie. He wants the audience to enjoy themselves: 'My main aim in a movie is to make the audience come away from it happy' (M, 89). And he always succeeds.[85]

---

84 Quoted in H. McCarthy, 101.
85 But Miyazaki has also said: 'I do endeavour to make films that express my own ideas about what is important and what is wrong with the world that we currently live in' (SP, 173).

6

❖

LAPUTA: CASTLE IN THE SKY

> If I were asked to give my view, in a nutshell, of what animation is, I would say it is "whatever I want to create"... I am talking about doing something with animation that can't be done with manga magazines, children's literature, or even live-action films. I'm talking about building a truly unique imaginary world, tossing in characters I like, and then creating a complete drama using them.
>
> Hayao Miyazaki, 1979 (SP, 17)

INTRODUCTION.

Laputa: Castle In the Sky (*Tenku no Shiro Laputa,* 1986) is a perfect movie: you wouldn't want to change a single thing. Purely as an action-adventure movie, *Laputa: Castle In the Sky* is simply thunderously good – one of the greatest action-adventures ever made. It is also one of Hayao Miyazaki's marvellous films about flying: 'I personally find airplanes cool and I love flying scenes' (SP, 341). OK, the whole picture isn't about flight, but flying takes up so much of this wonderful, completely sublime adventure movie. The two heroes – Pazu and Sheeta – fall in with a bunch of pirates who live in a flying pirate ship,[86] and zoom about the sky in small flying machines (called 'flaptors' or 'ornithopters'). Elsewhere, *Laputa: Castle In the Sky* is filled with all manner of flying scenes and vehicles. Here, as in Miyazaki's other films, flight is pure release, pleasure and transcendence. It's also very dangerous (there are air battles, stricken aircraft, and many deaths in the air).

Laputa: Castle In the Sky was produced by Isao Takahata, who also produced some of Hayao Miyazaki's other movies. It was the first feature from Studio Ghibli (*Nausicaä of the Valley of the Wind* having been produced at Topcraft and Tokuma),

---

[86] The pirates' ship, called the *Tiger Moth*, was deliberately designed by Hayao Miyazaki with openings and cutaways, so it would provide more opportunities for action and drama (SP, 344).

in association with Toru Hara and Tokuma. Miyazaki wrote and directed the film; the art directors were Toshio Nazaki and Nizo Yamamoto; Yasuysoshi Tokuma was executive producer; Michiyo Yasuda was once again colour designer; Hirokata Takahashi was DP; supervising animator was Tsukasa Tannai; head key animator was Yoshinori Kanada; the editors were Yoshihiro Kasahara, Takeshi Seyama and Miyazaki; sound effects and editing by Kazutoshi Satou; visual fx by Gô Abe; and Joe Hisaishi composed the music. The production cycle was from June, 1985 to July, 1986. *Laputa: Castle In the Sky* employed 69,262 cels. It was released domestically on August 2, 1986 by Toei (shown with two episodes of *Sherlock Hound*), and received about 775,000 spectators.

The Japanese voice talent included Mayumi Tanaka (Pazu), Keiko Yokozawa (Sheeta), Nou Terada (Dola), Kotoe Hatsui (Uncle Pom), Fujio Tokita (General), Ichiro Nagai (Mentor), Hiroshi Ito (Okami), Machiko Washio (Shalulu) and Takumi Kamiyama (Lui). A version was released in 1989 by Streamline Pictures (in a limited release), and again in 2000 by Buena Vista (the Disney dubbed version). The U.S.A. Disney version included James Van Der Beek (Pazu), Anna Paquin (Sheeta), Cloris Leachman, Richard Dysart, Jim Cummings, John Hostetter and Mark Hamill as the villain Muska.[87]

The English language version of *Laputa: Castle In the Sky* is impressive (I saw it first in the dubbed version), but the Japanese version is preferable. The Japanese soundtracks capture more of the specifically *Japanese* flavour of Hayao Miyazaki's movies. Which's important, because Miyazaki has said that he is making his movies primarily for a Japanese audience, and it's far better to watch these films in the language they were made (and with the director overseeing the actors and dubbing).

Laputa: Castle In the Sky is filled with the usual Hayao Miyazaki characters: resourceful, brave, independent young heroes, gruff but kind-hearted parental figures, kooky side-kicks, robots, and formidable opponents. And the usual Miyazakian elements: eye-popping visuals, succulent colouration, moments of reflection and serenity, interludes of wonder and awe,[88] and thrilling action set-pieces.

---

87 Unfortunately, the voice actor for Pazu – James Van Der Beek – is way too old, sounding more mid-twenties than the early teenage that Pazu is meant to be. And Anna Paquin also plays Sheeta older than the Japanese version or the images from the movie. A disaster. This's when Disney's bid for well-known voice casts goes very wrong.
88 I love the vocal expression of awe of the kids in Miyazaki's movies (and other *animé*) – how they go 'whoooa!' in a soft whisper or breath.

Laputa: Castle In the Sky one of the great fantasy adventures in recent cinema – no, in *any* cinema.

And *Laputa: Castle In the Sky* is an adventure movie that doesn't wink at the audience, doesn't deliver silly spoofs of other movies, doesn't feature wisecracks and would-be witty one-liners, and doesn't have gratuitously violent scenes. *Laputa: Castle In the Sky* is very much an adventure movie in the traditional form – it's *Treasure Island* without the pop culture trimmings and the cynical targetting of the audience of many Western adventure movies. *Laputa: Castle In the Sky* demonstrates that a fantastic story told in a boldly imaginative fashion is all you need. Except that telling a story as fantastic as this in a manner as wildly imaginative as this is *incredibly difficult*.

The power of the crystal is demonstrated early on in *Laputa: Castle In the Sky*, when it saves Sheeta from death, when she falls from the aircraft. And the difference between wearing the crystal when its power is activated and when it's not working its magic is depicted in the memorable scene where Pazu catches Sheeta in his arms (poised right over a high drop into the mine workings). Here the switch to the sudden, normal weight of Sheeta is beautifully portrayed. (Even girls are heavy! The scene was used in the marketing of the film). And what a masterful way of having the two main characters meet! (That brilliantly conceived scene brings together so many elements, including the hero, the heroine, the crystal, flight, an escape and a rescue).

And it's perfectly in keeping with Pazu's character that the next day he tries out the powers of the crystal, by putting it on and leaping off the roof (crashing through it into rubble below). That tells us about Pazu's adventurous personality, how he will leap off a roof.

Pazu [97] might be a young boy (about 11 or 12), but he looks after himself well enough (partly presumably because being an orphan he's had to).[98] He is always portrayed as a practical boy: he has some coffee warming on the stove, puts Sheeta in his bed, and sleeps on the floor under his coat. Though eleven or twelve, he lives by himself in an old mining

---

[97] A forerunner of Pazu is Conan in *Future Boy Conan* (and Sheeta draws on Lana) – including the way they first meet.
[98] His father died later than his mother, who died when he was young.

house up on the hill above the cliffs and the valley.[99] He is a miner's assistant just before the mines close. He works hard, too – when the Boss asks him to do something (like fetch a wrench), Pazu does it immediately, and when the Boss leaves, turning of the lights as he goes, Pazu stays on to finish up (and that also allows Pazu to be alone to deal with the unconscious Sheeta up on the gantry).

Establishing Pazu's independence is important – it's so he can convincingly go on an adventure, because he doesn't have the ties that bind him to a family, say, or to other responsibilities (in the case of his work, looking after Sheeta takes priority over that. Besides, his surrogate mom tells him to do just that: to look after Sheeta. And he agrees, in a tiny but significant moment, to do what she says, taking Sheeta out the back way of the house).

One of the reasons that so many characters are orphans in fairy tales is that they can go on adventures easily (i.e., it's easier to write the story); it also means they are often on a father quest or mother quest or parent quest or family quest (which Sheeta and Pazu are on, in their own way, with Pazu especially passionate about his father (note how the movie emphasizes Pazu's fierce determination to follow his father many times), and they find a surrogate family in Dola's Gang).[100] Being an orphan also creates instant identification and sympathy for the hero/ine (as in *'ah, bless!, poor Cinders, poor Snow White, poor Pazu, they ain't got no mom or pa'*).

It's amusing that Pazu just happens to have aligned himself with one of the bravest and strongest families in Slug Valley (a.k.a. Slagg's Ravine): Boss (a.k.a. Chief Engineer) and his wife are both formidable figures: when Dola's boys come looking for Sheeta, Boss and his wife stand up to them:[101] Boss is a huge man, and his wife is a stout, tall, ginger-haired mother who stands at the door with a frying pan at the ready and a mean frown. She puts her children inside and guards

---

99 Hayao Miyazaki remarked that Pazu probably wouldn't have been able to live like that, in the shack by himself, but added that 'one of the essential elements of most classical children's literature is that the children in the stories actually fend for themselves' (SP, 341). And Miyazaki has stuck to this guiding principle for many of his movies.
100 That was part of Hayao Miyazaki's narrative design, he explained: to make a traditional story or children's story in which surrogate parents appear (SP, 341).
101 The fight between Pazu's Boss and Charles from Dola's Gang was inspired by the filmmakers' visit to Wales, Miyazaki recalled in 1986: 'I don't think we would have included a scene like that if we hadn't visited the area. I felt a real sense of solidarity with the mine workers!' (SP, 339) The fist fight is done in a really broad, cartoony style: Miyazaki remarked that he encouraged his head key animator (Yoshinori Kanada) 'to really go for it and not worry about the consequences' (SP, 340).

over the door. She looks like she could take on the Dola boys single-handed (in Hayao Miyazaki's world, men don't hit women – there's a chivalrous code here, which's part of the action-adventure genre, seen also in Hong Kong martial arts movies or Hollywood's action comedies. But if a guy does hit a woman, you can be sure he will be punished).[102]

Once again, it is a steam-powered, mechanical late Victorian/ early 20th century world[103] that Hayao Miyazaki, Isao Takahata, Tsukasa Tannai and the team portray in *Laputa: Castle In the Sky*.[104] A world of mines, villages, railroads, tunnels, chimneys and houses, but also the natural world in abundance: fields, trees, mountains, lakes, clouds and the ocean.[105] It's striking how much of *Laputa: Castle In the Sky* resonates with Western European culture – those rows of terraced houses in the mining town of Slug Valley could come straight out of one of D.H. Lawrence's novels set in Northern Britain, like *The Rainbow* or *Sons and Lovers* (actually, the inspiration was a mining town in Wales, in the Rhondda Valley, which Miyazaki and his team had visited).[106]

Did I mention trees? The ecological, pro-nature aspect of Hayao Miyazaki's films is very much to the fore in *Laputa: Castle In the Sky*: it is the theme of the piece. Laputa itself, for instance, is a circular flying palace dominated by an absolutely gigantic tree.[107] When the mechanical areas of the flying realm fall away in the customary climactic sequence of action movies, the roots of the tree are revealed[108] – hundreds of feet long. And when Pazu and Sheeta explore Laputa, they find

---

[102] Muska hits Sheeta, and more than once.
[103] *Laputa: Castle In the Sky* was deliberately composed as if it were science fiction written in the days of steam, Hayao Miyazaki explained: 'it's best to think of it as a work of science fiction written at the end of the 19th century' (SP, 419).
[104] The art directors Toshio Nozaki and Nizo Yamamoto have done a brilliant design job here. 'We were really lucky there, with both Nizo Yamamoto and Toshiro Nozaki in charge of the art direction', remarked Hayao Miyazaki in 1986. 'I doubt if either of them could have reached that level on their own. By having them work together we gained more than the sum of their total talents, because they inspired each other'. (SP, 345). For Helen McCarthy (in *The Anime Movie Guide*), the world that Miyazaki creates 'reaches new heights' in *Laptua*: 'every detail of Pazu's turn-of-the-century mining village (ah, but which century?), of the Government's steamtech, of the pirates' flying barge, every aspect of the minutiæ of everyday life is perfectly realised' (41).
[105] Hayao Miyazaki: 'we will fully use our imaginations and create a world that, while fictional, has a real sense of presence' (SP, 254).
[106] The art of L.S. Lowry might also be an influence (O, 64). Miyazaki also cited C.W. Nicol's writing (*The Boy Who Saw the Wind* was a 2000 *anime* made from Nicol's work).
[107] The design of Laputa itself recalls *Metropolis* and *The Tower of Babel* by Pieter Brueghel.
[108] There are two parts of Laputa itself: the lower half is technology, computers, archives, databases, and the upper half is trees, pools and gardens – growth and nature.

roots and tendrils and branches everywhere (and they use the roots to climb down to rescue the pirates, while Muska swipes at them angrily). The roots penetrating the machinery below is 'the most beautifully audacious piece of symbolism in any fantasy film', as the *SFX* special on *animé* put it. [109]

And after the destruction of the lower, technological levels of Laputa, the flying castle becomes a giant, floating tree, with a small garden around the trunk (and a few structures remain, such as walls). Trees are a recurring motif in Hayao Miyazaki's cinema, and are part of Japanese culture's positive attitude towards the natural world. When Miyazaki wants to show nature rebuilding itself, or the awesome energy and resilience of nature, or the sheer beauty of the natural world, his films often use trees. A world without trees I think would be ugly: we must have trees. In this Miyazaki has affinities with tree-lovers such as J.R.R. Tolkien, Thomas Hardy, John Cowper Powys and Ursula Le Guin.

Hayao Miyazaki's pictures often take up the notion that, left to its own devices, the world will eventually overcome everything with growths of all kinds (and the chief villain, Muska, of course really hates those roots: if you hate nature in a Miyazaki movie, that automatically marks you down as a less than human person). The robots too become overgrown (the ones that don't work anymore become absorbed into the trunk of the giant tree); the ones that survive have moss growing on them. From being laser-wielding military robots,[110] they become gardeners, the caretakers of Laputa. The robots become so kindly, they will walk up to a faraway garden to lift a glider off a bird's nest. That simple but unexpected action tells the viewer a lot about the robots without needing any dialogue. It's another example of Miyazaki and his team's economical storytelling using action and visuals.

As well as the giant tree, Laputa is a mix of classical architecture, stairways, pools, columns, gateways, arcades, gardens and lawns. It is a decaying paradise, a paradise that's gone on without anyone living there (tended only by one surviving robot. The other robots become absorbed into the tree trunk). Insects, birds, flowers, trees. In a marvellous touch, a pool beside the path that at first appears shallow is actually a very deep, clear pool, with a sunken city underneath it (a revival of the flooded Roman city in *Cagliostro*).

Once again, Hayao Miyazaki and his team have managed

---
109 C. Winstanley, 2006, 30.
110 The design of the robots draws on *Superman* by the Fleischers, and also a *Lupin III* that Miyazaki directed.

to take up instantly recognizable motifs from fairy tales and fantasy literature and imbue them with a freshness and new magic. There is always a genuine sense of *wonder* in Miyazaki's films, and somehow he and his team manage to make that sense of wonder come across convincingly (which's almost impossible to do. In fact, I'd say it's impossible, because we are so cynical, and we've seen everything – so that when it does happen, it seems miraculous). So when Sheeta and Pazu land on the grass in Laputa in their crashed kite, and see Laputa for the first time up close, it really does seem magical. This is no easy feat, and one of the most extraordinary aspects of Miyazaki's cinema is that his movies are somehow able to re-activate a sense of wonder and awe in the viewer (well, for me at least).

THE HEROES.

The heroes of *Laputa: Castle In the Sky,* Pazu and Sheeta, are both orphans, and the opening scenes, where they meet and form a bond, are very touching (being orphans helps to bring them together. They are the friends they've always wanted). Hayao Miyazaki and his team introduce elements of classic children's fiction, but somehow make them seem fresh again. And Sheeta and Pazu are an appealing pair – their scenes have a chemistry and humour and tenderness that seems natural, and isn't forced or contrived (the 1986 movie always leaves space in which Pazu and Sheeta can joke around a bit together, to take a break from the express train speed of the narrative). (The voice talent for the pair contributed so much: Mayumi Tanaka and Keiko Yukozawa). All movies are made by adults, but Sheeta and Pazu do come across like real children, without that this-is-a-child-invented-by-an-adult kind of attitude or look. And you believe that both Pazu and Sheeta are capable of the things they do in the story.

Sheeta is another of Hayao Miyazaki's familiar *shojo* figures: she is what is at stake in the film, really, what must be defended; she is the link back to Laputa, and is really a princess of the old order (with the title Lusheeta Toei Ul Laputa). But Sheeta is not wholly a damsel in distress (the *yasashii*), who has to be rescued by Pazu (though he does rescue her); she is more independent than that. In fact, this is a tough girl: in the first scene in which she features, she picks up a bottle and knocks out the chief villain Muska[111] (go

---

[111] The actual moment, however, of the bottle hitting the skull occurs off-screen: we cut back to Muska unconscious on the floor.

Sheeta!), making sure to take the crystal from him, and then climbs out of the window, thousands of feet in the air (demonstrating her immense bravery). And in her flashback, Sheeta is depicted as running a farm on her own (no mean feat), and living alone on the farm in the mountains. She's also quite capable of clearing a kitchen that looks like a bomb's gone off in it and cooking for the whole crew. There's nothing flaky about Sheeta or Pazu.

Both Sheeta and Pazu are haunted by memories of their parents: the flashbacks in *Laputa: Castle In the Sky* are particularly striking: Pazu has vivid memories of his father seeing Laputa during a storm, from his airship.[112] Sheeta meanwhile recalls how she was taken by the government men, because she had the magic crystal. Once again, as in *Nausicaä of the Valley of the Wind,* the flashbacks are portrayed with crosshatching, like storybook illustrations (recalling the opening credits). In Sheeta's flashback, she is depicted at work with the cattle on a rural farm in the snowy mountains, a familiar Miyazakian landscape, which crops up again in movies such as *Howl's Moving Castle* and *Kiki's Delivery Service.*

After a stunning chase sequence, along an elevated, wooden railroad, Sheeta and Pazu find themselves in the old mines below the village. Here they meet an aging miner (Old Pom), a prospector figure who acts as the familiar wise counsellor or wizard of folk and fairy tales. It's an affecting encounter – the kindly, old man who travels about the mines, preferring the mines to the surface, carrying his camping and cooking gear on his back. As well as exposition, Old Pom also offers a warning that the ancient power was (1) man-made (not natural), and thus (2) problematic (can be used for evil).

And, once again in a Hayao Miyazaki film, labour is a key element in the lives of the heroes: Pazu works for an engineer (Boss) at the mines, and stays on afterwards to do some extra chores. Pazu is also a dreamer and idealist in the classic manner: like Tombo in *Kiki's Delivery Service,*[113] Pazu is building an aircraft in his workshop (photos and plans of vessels line the walls).[114] So he's a practical dreamer – a dreamer who is going to follow his dream. In this case, the

---

[112] A photograph that Pazu's father took of Laputa, obscured by clouds, is on the wall in Pazu's workshop (it seems to have the date 1868 on it).
[113] Or, more seriously, Jiro Horikoshi in *The Wind Rises.*
[114] In *Animation Monthly* (in 1979), Hayao Miyazaki remarked that a character shouldn't just jump into a *mecha* (a machine) and use it to beat the bad guys, he should also he able to design the *mecha* and build it himself (SP, 20). And that's exactly what Miyazaki shows his protagonists doing: they are designing their own aircraft (in *Kiki's Delivery Service* and *Laputa: Castle In the Sky,* for instance).

quest is tied to the father: Pazu plans to fly his aircraft in search of Laputa, to follow his father. Nobody believed his pa, so part of Pazu's goal is re-instate his father's reputation.

There is something very touching about these young teenagers building aircraft – and also very grandiose, and visionary. They are literally manufacturing the means by which they can escape their lives – and grow. They are artists – crafts people and engineers (many of Hayao Miyazaki's young people are also very practical, good with tools, with cooking, and with looking after themselves). Those practical resources are important, because when they are thrust into adventures, they do not go to pieces, and break down and cry (well, they do weep sometimes – they are children, after all). But they are well-equipped, too, to deal with many of the situations they find themselves entering. For instance, when faced with a filthy kitchen, Sheeta soon rolls up her sleeves and gets to work, and Pazu's brought along food when they escape the pirates.

A Hayao Miyazaki hero is resourceful like Hansel in *Hansel and Gretel*, who leaves a trail of stones in the forest, so he and Gretel can find their way back home. A Miyazaki hero, though, would not leave behind a trail of bread crumbs for the birds to eat – they would fashion a flying vehicle from branches and giant leaves and fly away.

The pirates in *Laputa: Castle In the Sky* (they are introduced first) are a terrific bunch, led by their domineering, tough mom Dola (another of the fierce, older women that Hayao Miyazaki and his teams enjoy portraying, and brilliantly voived by Nou Terada).[115] Dola has a pair of wild plaits,[116] beady, rolling, knowing eyes, huge breasts, and a craggy, no-nonsense face. The pirates[117] are very much Dola's crew; when Pazu keeps calling her 'old woman', she retorts each time like Jack Sparrow in *Pirates of the Caribbean*,[118] 'it's Captain!'

Dola's sons are depicted as buffoons, while Uncle Pom or Pa (who might be her husband or brother),[119] hiding behind spectacles and a large moustache (another Miyazaki motif),

---

[115] It was inevitable that Dola (and her gang) would have less to do in the later parts of *Laputa: Castle In the Sky,* because the young heroes had to settle things for themselves (SP, 348). Hayao Miyazaki said he had tried to find ways in which Dola could've appeared more.
[116] Later, Sheeta has some plaits, which Muska cruelly shoots off, one by one.
[117] Each pirate is differentiated by the designers and animators.
[118] The *Pirates* movies also raided *Treasure Island*, like *Laputa*.
[119] The engineer was created by Hayao Miyazaki partly because he thought it might get a bit boring on the *Tiger Moth*. He was conceived as a kind of stepfather to Dola's boys (SP, 348), although I prefer to think of him as Dola's husband.

works as an engineer in the engine room (Pazu, handily an engineer's assistant, fits in perfectly, and the old man grudgingly accepts him. No time for introductions, they get to work straight away).

VISUAL STYLE.

Pazu sports a cap, unruly, Harry Potter hair, leather boots, dark pants (patched), a vest and a white shirt with the sleeves rolled up. Pazu is the classic young boy hero of adventure stories such as *The Adventures of Tom Sawyer* or *Treasure Island* (he might easily be Jim Hawkins). He is brave, loyal, trustworthy, energetic, thoughtful and practical (he carries a lamp for instance, which he hurries to light when he and Sheeta land in the mine, because he knows how black it will be if he doesn't light it. And he carries food, too. Sheeta remarks that his bag seems to be magic).

Sheeta wears a knee-length, blue dress (rather like Kiki's and Princess Mononoke's), with her hair in long, pig tails (tied with red ribbons and a red headband). Later, Sheeta dons some of Dola's clothes, including pink pants that balloon into the kind of pants that Aladdin or Sinbad might wear (consciously evoking the women dressed as boys or women in disguise motif in the action-adventure genre, out of *Arabian Nights*). At the beginning of the piece, Sheeta's role is very much the princess who has to be rescued, the prize that everyone's fighting for. That withdrawn, quiet and scared attitude will change as the film develops, into something more outgoing and confident. (And the plaits in the hair plus the pink pants link Sheeta with Dola).

Both Pazu and Sheeta have the open, simplified faces of Japanese *animé*, instantly recognizable as products of popular culture in East Asia.[120] And at first their qualities are somewhat functions of the plot – that is, Sheeta has to be somewhat demure and afraid and restrained at the beginning, when she's on the run from the Dola Gang and Muska and his henchmen (but she also manages to knock Muska out and climb out of the window). And Pazu has to be the brave, idealistic, enthusiastic hero-in-the-making. But as the movie progresses, their personalities are enhanced, becoming far from mere ciphers or instruments of the narrative.

That's one of Hayao Miyazaki's strengths – that he doesn't stick to one character type and leave it unchanged for

---

[120] 'Pazu and Sheeta have two of the most endearing and remarkable faces in anime history,' asserted Brian Camp in *Zettai*. 'The entire film is carried in those faces – everything that happens and everything that can happen' (71).

most of the story. He also doesn't put in unbelievable changes in personalities, and have characters do something they really wouldn't do. I don't mean plot twists, but the sudden switches in characterization which can be found in many other movies.

MUSIC.

The music for *Laputa: Castle In the Sky* (by Joe Hisaishi) comprised a variety of sounds, from soft, reflective piano music to a grand score for the main theme. A choir was employed for the climactic scenes where Laputa breaks apart. Electronic sounds, reminiscent of those in *Nausicaä of the Valley of the Wind*, accompanied some of the action scenes.[121] Hayao Miyazaki left everything concerning the music up to producer Isao Takahata to oversee, 'because he knows much more about it' (SP, 345).

The music for *Laputa: Castle In the Sky* was newly recorded and orchestrated in 1999 for the overseas release of the movie. Originally, according to Hayao Miyazaki, there was about an hour of music by Joe Hisaishi in the picture. There were sections where there was no music for 7 or 8 minutes. For foreign markets, the music was re-recorded, so that it is more conventionally spread across the whole movie.

WALES.

As someone who knows and loves Wales, I was very struck when I discovered that Hayao Miyazaki and Isao Takahata and the team had visited Cymru[122] in 1985 for research on *Laputa: Castle In the Sky:* the combination of Welsh culture and Japanese culture is an unexpected but lyrical fit:

> I was in Wales just after the miners' strike [Miyazaki recalled in 1999]. I really admired the way the miners' unions fought to the very end for their jobs and communities, and I wanted to reflect the strength of those communities in my film. I saw so many places with abandoned machinery, abandoned mines – the fabric of the industry was there, but no people. It made a strong impression on me. A whole industry with no work.

The Welsh connection is unusual and not what you expect from an animated action-adventure story made in

---

[121] However, Hayao Miyazaki asked his sound effects team to avoid the usual science fiction and robot sounds (SP, 345).
[122] It was Isao Takahata's idea to go on a research trip to Britain, partly because *Laputa: Castle In the Sky* was to be set in the era of the Industrial Revolution (SP, 339).

Japan for a Japanese audience. But when you remember that Wales is central to Celtic culture – or how Celtic culture is perceived in the modern world – it does make sense.

Needless to say, Slug Valley in *Laputa: Castle In the Sky* is a Welsh mining town Miyazaki-style: the real mining towns of South Wales can appear to some visitors as rather grim, grey places, with dark, brooding skies, grey slate roofs, endless tiny, terraced houses, narrow, claustrophobic streets, and constant rain.[123] That's one cliché of Wales and mining communities, but it's not what Hayao Miyazaki and the team put into their 1986 film: they have the rows of terraced houses and the giant machinery, but the team place the town in a deep valley with towering, vertical cliffs.[124] The green hills of Wales are there, and the Celtic look of the landscape, but the mining structures are vast, and the valley is enormous, and the palette is far lighter than the darker hues, the misty, rainy greens and greys, of the real Wales. (Miyazaki and his team haven't used the cool, soft light of Britain either).

And when it comes to the mining machinery, Hayao Miyazaki and his designers have conjured up wild exaggerations: buildings built into cliff faces hundreds of feet high, enormous pit wheels, endless pipes and a furnace, and very wide mine shafts. There's also a railroad track 100s of feet above the valley floor, which becomes the setting for the chase (it is a silent movie, Buster Keaton movie setting, but it's been Miyazakified).

The filmmakers were not only inspired by modern Welsh society, such as mining disputes in the 1980s, but also by the ancient, Celtic heritage of Wales. For Hayao Miyazaki, the Welsh people are 'at bottom Celts', a race that were 'conquered by the Roman empire as barbarians, and were continuously conquered thereafter', Miyazaki explained. Miyazaki remarked that he felt for the communities that were overwhelmed by the military might of Rome (as recounted in the *Gallic Wars* by Julius Caesar and *Spartacus* by Howard Furst). *Mark of the Horse Lord* (1965) by Rosemary Sutcliffe, set in Roman Britain, was another inspiration. That empathy with the invaded community is very much to the fore in *Nausicaä of the Valley of the Wind* too.

---

123 It was a poor town, so that the back-story about Dola's Gang only robbing the rich wouldn't have worked, Hayao Miyazaki explained; so it was dropped (SP, 340).
124 Hayao Miyazaki said he 'thought it would be fun to show a valley with lots of mine holes in it' (SP, 339). But a mining region *is* like that, with holes everywhere.

LAPUTA, A FLYING CASTLE.

The icon in *Laputa: Castle In the Sky* is the floating castle, as Hayao Miyazaki explained. It was inspired by Jonathan Swift's *Gulliver's Travels*[125] (the name *laputa* was problematic in France, South America and Spain – *la puta* means 'the whore' in Spanish; for those territories, the film was given a slightly different title for its 1999 release – often it's known as *Castle In the Sky*).

The opening credits of *Laputa: Castle In the Sky* feature a marvellous collection of Hayao Miyazaki-designed aircraft drawn and coloured in the manner of ye olde, eighteenth century European prints (i.e., simple washes of colour over black ink lines). It's yet another hymn to the early years of aviation for Miyazaki, and establishes one of the primary themes of the movie: flight.

The extravagance of some of the designs also evocatively illuminates the fantasy aspects of the world of the movie to come: some of the aircraft are impossible technically (unless you have a magic crystal or two). There are propellers everywhere, and flapping wings, and enormous props that rotate slowly underneath the flying castles. Finally, the credits depict not just one castle in the sky, but many, a whole flotilla of flying towns in a variety of designs (Italian hill towns, mediæval castles, Babylonian hanging gardens, and plenty of rice fields, etc).

Design-wise, *Laputa: Castle In the Sky* emphasizes verticals and height throughout the piece, from the incredibly high cliffs and canyons of Slug Valley, and the deep shafts of the mines, to the tall towers of Laputa, and most vividly the miles and miles of sky in which so much of the action of the movie takes place (the movie's opening shot is of a sky of big clouds). To evoke the link between the earth and the sky the movie opens with a very high fall, for Sheeta, escaping from the enemy right into the arms – literally – of her saviour, Pazu.[126]

TREES.

'Trees are so beautiful,' remarked Hayao Miyazaki (SP, 356). Trees feature prominently in Miyazaki's cinema. In discussing his love of trees, Miyazaki wondered in 1994 if it derived from the times in school when he used to look out of

---

[125] *Gulliver's Travels* is referenced in the subtitles in the Japanese print.
[126] Skies and clouds are everywhere in *Laputa: Castle In the Sky*, as in all of Hayao Miyazaki's films: 'look at those clouds!' Pazu exclaims to Sheeta early on – and the camera dutifully pans and tilts up into the sky, resting on a big, Laputa-shaped cumulus.

the classroom at a Chinese evergreen tree: 'it seemed wonderfully big and pleasant looking. I recall thinking that perhaps I could draw it sometime' (SP, 162). It wasn't a symbolic relationship with trees for Miyazaki, but something that went far back in time.[127] Miyazaki dreamt of making a movie about a single tree, showing all of the aspects of its life, but from the tree's point-of-view.

ACTION, RESCUES, DESTRUCTION.

It's striking just how much destruction there is in *Laputa: Castle In the Sky* and in Hayao Miyazaki's cinema in general. These are not *James Bond* or *Star Wars* movies, but there are many, many big explosions and scenes of buildings being destroyed. And death, too: there's a scene in *Laputa: Castle In the Sky* where the general and maybe fifty of his men are plunged to their doom by Muska (followed by the *Goliath* aircraft exploding).

In the climactic sequence, the amount of devastation on screen is enormous, as the whole, hemispherical underside of Laputa crumbles away, plus a large proportion of the classical architecture around the circumference. That's not all: inside the floating square blocks of Laputa's library are collapsing, and the airship is under attack from flying robots.

And in the scene where the reactivated robot escapes from its underground prison in the castle, the explosions and fire effects are stunning (Hayao Miyazaki is fond of depicting scenes in long, vertical shafts, which recur in *Spirited Away* and *The Castle of Cagliostro*). You can see that the visual effects and photographic effects budget is higher in *Laputa* than *Nausicaä*.

One of the stand-out pieces is a bravura *hommage* to *King Kong*, when Pazu and Dola rescue Sheeta from the giant robot when the whole military castle and everything around it is going up in flames and explosions.

The *King Kong* rescue scene in *Laputa: Castle In the Sky* is a scene that Pixar producer John Lasseter said he'd studied frame by frame: 'It's one of the greatest rescue scenes ever put on film and I love it'. So much so that Lasseter and the team considered the sequence closely when they were making *A Bug's Life*; not to copy it, but to see how it worked.[128]

The military machine in *Laputa: Castle In the Sky* has some heavyweight technology at its disposal, including an

---

[127] 'I obviously feel that a landscape with trees is preferrable to scenes without them' (SP, 163).
[128] The music cue in the rescue scene is unusual.

enormous airship or dreadnought called *Goliath*,[129] a big, armoured railroad train, and a vast castle which takes up a whole peninsula. It's all depicted in the metallic, camouflaged look of First World War and late 19th century technology (nothing much has changed there – large portions of the military around the world use the same look today). It's all about power, brute force, and the use of technology to dominate and coerce. Against all this, the world of Laputa appears paradisal – although Laputa's green, watery, Edenic exterior hides a malefic force within – a nuclear power no less, which Muska activates.

The idea, Hayao Miyazaki explained in 1986 interview, was to portray the military machine as mighty and 'large-as-life' as possible, 'because no matter what Pazu tried, there was no way he could ever have won against them', and neither could the pirate gang (SP, 346). 'I don't like the military, so I drew their nasty side' (he doesn't like nuclear power, either!).

THE FINALE.

Laputa: Castle In the Sky has as good a climactic action sequence as one could wish for: the release of vast magical forces, explosions, multiple snakepit situations for the heroes, death for the despicable villain, widespread destruction, and hair's-breadth escapes. The heroes have to be split up, so that the Laputa storyline can reach its conclusions with Muska and Sheeta; Pazu has his own journey, which's now to save Sheeta (and to free the captured pirates). There's an extended and detailed sequence where Pazu is hanging on for dear life underneath Laputa, avoiding death rays, flying robots, and snapping tree roots.[130]

Once Pazu gains entry to the underside of Laputa, he is on a quest to rescue Sheeta from the evil clutches of Muska. It's completely clichéd, but the filmmakers manage to make it play like a dream. The subsequent chases down the corridors, with Pazu blasting his way through to Sheeta in an adjoining corridor, are terrific.

Sheeta is at the mercy of Muska, meanwhile, trapped in the crystal room with a maniac intent on ruling the world.

---

[129] The flying vehicles in *Laputa: Castle In the Sky* were masterpieces of scale and weight, as John Lasseter explained: when you look at those flying ships, you know they're huge and they're very heavy: 'look at them, you can feel their weight. It's not just perspective. It's movement, it's size, it's weight. It really is amazing' (SP, 11).

[130] There are many mini-beats within this sequence, with Pazu having to use every trick he can think of. He is clambering, leaping, twisting – he never gives up. He is an unstoppable force of nature like the crystal itself.

Nuclear war rears up yet again when Muska demonstrates the power of Laputa by using the ray guns to create an atomic explosion in the ocean below. Muska is truly a nasty piece of work, but the heroes, being children, don't kill him (well, not directly): instead, they recite the secret spell that Sheeta's grandmother told her (in another flashback), which unleashes the power of the crystal (knowing that this will probably mean their own demise – but we know that a movie like this is never going to kill off its two heroes).

The staging of the very complex climactic sequence in *Laputa* is supremely confident and imaginative. The film-makers have included everything you might find in adventure movies in the final reel: stand-offs between the villain armed with a gun and the heroes; cliffhangers, with the heroes nearly falling; mayhem and explosions; gun battles; more explosions and mass destruction; leaps and dives; and miraculous escapes.

The 1986 movie doesn't quite finish off Muska properly, I don't think: he is blinded by the released light of the crystal, and staggers about the disintegrating corridors, and probably falls to his death. It would help the narrative logic of the movie to have depicted Muska's demise in a little more detail (even if it was a long shot like the one in *The Castle of Cagliostro* when Cagliostro is squashed between the giant clock hands and killed).

Because Muska is a *really* venal villain: he shows his true colours when he reaches Laputa: he kills the general and a regiment of his troops (Sheeta tries to save them), and moments later destroys the *Goliath* airship, which has hundreds of people on board. And he hits Sheeta. He is a truly scary bad guy, on a par with the meanest of Hollywood bad guys.

THE ENDING.

When Laputa transforms itself at the end of the picture, it does so according to the environmental lines that Hayao Miyazaki's characters are aiming for: it strips away everything unnecessary (such as the weapons, the over-weening, grandiose architecture, the control room, etc), and leaves the giant tree, the gardens, the robots and the magic crystal. It's nature plus a bit of magic, which's the ideal Miyazakian world. Trees, gardens, pools, a robot or two, sustained by some occult object like a crystal. It's like the ending of *Howl's Moving Castle*, when the castle casts off its land-hugging aspects, and flies in the sky.

You need a little magic to sustain such flights, but really that magic is simply the realization that life itself is *already* magical. The magic is part of the fantasy genre and format, but it isn't the whole story.

Cartoons are already preposterous, so viewers accept lies, absurd situations – it's part of the genre, the form, Hayao Miyazaki said. But even though it's all a bunch of lies and fakery in a toon, filmmakers 'still need to try hard to make their fake worlds seem as real as possible... Lies must be layered upon lies to create a thoroughly believable fake world' (SP, 307).

The endings of Hayao Miyazaki's movies recall fairy tales in which the 'happy ending' isn't *added on* by a magical transformation: the transformation reveals that the characters *have always been magical* (or beautiful, or good, or worthy, or whatever). That is, the heroic, true, pure, generous and noble characters, like Cinderella or Snow White or Hansel or Rapunzel, were always heroic and true and pure, generous and noble.

Similarly, the flying castles in Hayao Miyazaki's movies have always been magical. They don't require a *deus ex machina* element to walk in and bless everything with magic. On the personal level, the beauty and bravery in Hayao Miyazaki's characters was always there – but required the circumstances and encounters of the adventure to bring them out.

The *dénouement* scenes are rightly delightfully straightforward and traditional: our heroes re-unite happily with Dola's gang... the pirates have managed to snaffle some treasure... and the Pazu and Sheeta fly off together into the sunset...

7
MY NEIGHBOR TOTORO

My Neighbor Totoro (*Tonari no Totoro,* 1988) is a film of pure magic, film as magic, a magical film. It is a movie of endless *play*, of children playing, adults playing, and as such is close to unique in cinema. Hayao Miyazaki remarked: 'I experienced tremendous happiness as I was making this film' (SP, 377).[131] *My Neighbor Totoro* tops many people's lists of great animated movies – or any movies. It is a flawless film. A film in which you wouldn't want to change a single thing.

Hayao Miyazaki wrote and directed *My Neighbor Totoro*; it was produced by Yasuyoshi Tokuma and Toru Hara; music was by Joe Hisaishi; Kazuo Oga was art director; Takeshi Seyama was editor; Yoshiharu Sato was supervising animator; colour designer was Nobuko Mizuta; sound was by Shigeharu Shiba and Kazutoshi Satou; and the production companies were Tokuma Shoten, Nibariki and Studio Ghibli. *My Neighbor Totoro* employed 48,473 cels and was released on April 16, 1988.

The voice cast for *My Neighbor Totoro* included: Noriko Hidaka (Satsuki), Chika Sakamoto (Mei), Shigesato Itoi[132] (Mr Kusakabe), Sumi Shimamoto (Mrs Kusakabe, Shimamoto was Nausicaä and Clarisse), Yûko Maruyama (Kanta), and Hitoshi Takagi (Totoro).

Studio Ghibli produced a 13 minute short follow-up to *Totoro*, *Mei and the Kittenbus* (2002), for their Ghibli Museum in Tokyo. In 2005 the Nagoya Expo recreated the house from the movie, which you can visit. 'Totoro's Forest' is a small piece of land next to the Fuchi no Mori Forest near Tokyo which's being saved from developers by a foundation that Hayao Miyazaki helped to create in 1996.

My Neighbor Totoro became one of Studio Ghibli's biggest successes – particularly in the realm of merchandizing: cuddly Totoros and Totoro toys (including playing cards,

---
131 For Miyazaki, *Totoro* 'is where my consciousness begins. It explains how my mind works' (AI, 33).
132 Itoi is a media personality, writer and voice actor who has worked with Ghibli on the advertizing copy for their movies (including coming up with slogans).

zippo lighters, stationery, ocarinas, watches, clocks and calendars) became hugely profitable for the studio – Toshio Suzuki said that in leaner times the sales from merchandizing and toys helped to keep the company afloat.[133]

The backers of *My Neighbor Totoro* hadn't been impressed by the pitch that producer Toshio Suzuki made for the film; Tokuma Shoten didn't think the story about the big Totoro would find an audience (Hayao Miyazaki had offered the idea to Telecom in the early 1980s, but they too had declined. Think about it: how would you pitch *Totoro*?).

When Toshio Suzuki offered *Totoro* again to Tokuma Shoten, but this time to be paired with the serious animation movie *Grave of the Fireflies,* to be released as a double bill,[134] the movie was green-lit. That decision put Studio Ghibli under a lot of pressure – to deliver two productions at the same time (usually, Ghibli works on one feature only). Producing two animated features at the same time was 'almost impossible', according to Suzuki: it was 'sheer chaos'.[135] (*Grave of the Fireflies* was to be directed by Miyazaki's colleague and co-producer at Ghibli, Isao Takahata). Production began on *My Neighbor Totoro* in April, 1987.

My Neighbor Totoro was first released in the Western world by Fox Video on video and by 50th Street Films theatrically, in 1993. (The Fox version was a dub commissioned by Tokuma from Streamline Pictures and Carl Macek in 1988).

Two scenes were a problem for the North American distributors of *My Neighbor Totoro*: inevitably the bathroom scene, where Mr Kusakabe and his two daughters are all naked, taking a bath (*furo*). Western audiences, the distributors (50th Street Films/ Fox Video) argued, wouldn't understand that it was normal for Japanese families to bathe together (bathing, including publicly, is a big deal in Japan). The other was the scene where Mei and Satsuki jump on tatami mats (which are handmade and shouldn't be jumped on like that).

For Helen McCarthy and Jonathan Clements, two of the most informative commentators on Japanese *animé* in the West, *My Neighbor Totoro* is 'Hayao Miyazaki's greatest work, and hence probably the best anime ever made' (2001, 265). For McCarthy, *Totoro* was Miyazaki's masterpiece, 'and my favorite film': in *The Anime Movie Guide*, McCarthy

---

[133] *My Neighbor Totoro* has often been compared with *E.T.* And for Universal *E.T.* became a huge money-spinner in the realm of movie merchandizing.
[134] Sometimes *My Neighbor Totoro* played with *The Girl With the White Flag* (1988), about Okinawa in WW2.
[135] T. Suzuki, "*My Neighbor Totoro*", Pathea.

commented: 'I think this film is perfect. It is also my favourite movie, of any kind, in any genre, ever' (78).[136] 'It's like revisiting the happiest summer of your childhood. Oh, and it's technically as near-perfect a piece of animation as you could wish for' (28). For Miyazaki, childhood is our happiest time – and *Totoro* is his best expression of that view.

A key aspect of *My Neighbor Totoro* is that Hayao Miyazaki really enjoyed making the movie. It was a movie that didn't need tricks or gimmicks: 'it was easy to direct this work' (SP, 351).

Of *My Neighbor Totoro,* Helen McCarthy wrote:

> There are, it is true, not enough fine directors of film, but there are even fewer fine directors of animation. Anyone who can make a movie as honest, beautiful, and benign as *My Neighbor Totoro* must be cherished, because movies like this are very, very rare. In animation, though, they're even rarer. (133)

My Neighbor Totoro has most of the familiar elements of a Hayao Miyazaki film: young heroes (and women, too), magical creatures, nature mysticism, trees, rain, flying, planes, and spirituality. And, once again, although animation is a hugely collaborative process, *My Neighbor Totoro* is also absolutely a Hayao Miyazaki movie, with Miyazaki's influence all over it.

My Neighbor Totoro has no villain – it is not a story like *Laputa: Castle In the Sky* or *The Castle of Cagliostro* or *Princess Mononoke* where there are heroes and villains, and the villain is driving the plot.[137] Taking away the villain from a film like *My Neighbor Totoro* is partly why it is a different picture from action-oriented fare. It is the same with *Kiki's Delivery Service:* there are no Bad Things happening, no villains that need to be stopped and possibly punished.

PACE.

The pace of *My Neighbor Totoro* is gentle: this is a movie which unfolds gently and – for contemporary audiences perhaps – slowly. It's not the slowness of a European art

---

[136] Helen McCarthy enthused in *500 Essential Anime Movies* that 'every frame is perfectly judged' in *Totoro*, and 'in terms of story, design, animation, and music, this film achieves its aims so perfectly that it's almost absurd to give it a rating… Never sentimental, never dishonest, never preaching, and never failing to acknowledge the realities of life, he has made a film with more magic in it than any number of wizards and superpowers could create' (147).

[137] In *Princess Mononoke,* of course, the villains turn out to be ambiguous, and not wholly evil. In *Laputa: Castle In the Sky* and *The Castle of Cagliostro,* Muska and the Count are very nasty guys, and are rightly killed

movie, for instance, or the slowness of a movie that's just bad and d-r-r-r-r-a-g-s on and on. It's not the slowness of a movie that tries to milk every scene for every ounce of sentiment (as too many contemporary Hollywood movies do).[138] It's definitely not the slowness of a filmmaker trying to find their way. No, this is the slowness and gentleness of a movie that knows what to say and how to say it and is happy to take its time.

What's the rush? The rush is that in animation every frame, every second, has to count. Only a really confident filmmaker would opt to go so nonchalantly and gracefully. But *My Neighbor Totoro* is not a film of empty spaces and empty silences, like a European art movie – it's not Michelangelo Antonioni or Alain Resnais – it is a very *full* film. It's not slow because, again like some European art films, it has nothing much to say, and goes for a trendy, arty minimalism.[139]

My Neighbor Totoro is modest in scale but not necessarily in scope. Scale-wise, there are just a few characters with a modest setting and action: the family unit of a father and two young daughters, Mei and Satsuki, with the mother in hospital;[140] a neighbouring family, including Kanta and his mother; an old woman who helps out; and finally the magical creatures: Totoro, above all, plus the Cat-bus, and Totoro's two sidekicks.

Modest in scale it may be, but *My Neighbor Totoro* is also a substantial manifestation of the significance of the family, of the ties between parents and children, and between children (in this case, two sisters).[141] And as an evocation of the magic of cinema, it is colossal.

THE TWO SISTERS.

Yes, *My Neighbor Totoro* is another Hayao Miyazaki movie in which women are the primary characters: two young girls, in fact. Making them different ages is a way of allowing the filmmakers to explore different aspects of people; that is, Mei and Satsuki could have been one person (like Kiki in *Kiki's Delivery Service*, or Chihiro in *Spirited Away*), but splitting

---

[138] That's one reason why they regularly go over two hours or two hours twenty minutes, and why so many contemporary movies are actually *slower* than older movies, despite rapid editing and a larger number of shots per film.

[139] For its pacing, for its interlinking of scenes, for the flow of the narration, without doubt one of the key contributors to the success of *My Neighbor Totoro* is the editor, Takeshi Seyama.

[140] The mother is Yasuko Kusakabe.

[141] For Susan Napier, *Me Neighbor Totoro* is a classic fantasy of compensation (primarily for the children's relationship with their parents), but it's a fantasy which the girls control themselves (130).

them into two enables the filmmakers to explore aspects of being a child (Miyazaki had originally conceived there to be just one girl, a 6 year-old girl with red hair. However, Miyazaki himself has two sons).

So Mei is four, and Satsuki is around ten (Satsuki is another of Hayao Miyazaki's *shojo* figures, like Nausicaä in *Nausicaä of the Valley of the Wind* or Sheeta in *Laputa: Castle In the Sky* or Chihiro or Kiki). Having two central characters also means they can interact and exchange dialogue, which can be so much easier than having one person on their own (Kiki and Chihiro, for instance, can exist on their own, but interacting with other characters can be a quicker, shorthand way of getting into a character's state of mind – hence Kiki with her cat). 'I told the animators over and over again to watch from the window at the way children pass by', Miyazaki remarked (SP, 371).

Bravery is again an important attribute of these two children. Mei says a number of times that she isn't scared, and she proves it again and again: she stays in the attic after her sister has gone down the ladder, to investigate the dust bunnies.[142] Later, she approaches the enormous Totoro, and isn't afraid at all when he roars in her face. Instead, she laughs delightedly, and goes to sleep on his chest.

The scenes in *My Neighbor Totoro* where Mei and Satsuki yell to scare off potential ghosts or scary things are terrific: those scenes are needed, too, narratively, in order to demonstrate that Mei and Satsuki aren't timid; they are bold children. Notice how Mei, for instance, remains behind in the attic, while other four year-old children might be too scared. That prepares the audience for the first encounter between Mei and King Totoro, and shows that Mei isn't going to run away when she discovers the giant, furry creature asleep in the hollow tree.

Satsuki is a sensitive, fun, protective and brave girl, and she also has that intent and somewhat serious demeanour that Kiki and Chihiro have[143] (and male characters such as Sosuke in *Ponyo On the Cliff By the Sea* or Ashitaka in *Princess Mononoke*). The scene where a family relocates to the countryside is replayed at the beginning of *Spirited Away*, but look at the difference in Chihiro and Satsuki and Mei: to Satsuki and Mei, moving to the country is a great adventure, but Chihiro really doesn't want to move at all. She was happy

---
142 The dust bunnies are described as *susuwatari* or travelling soot by the grandmother. The dust mites from *My Neighbor Totoro* reappeared in *Spirited Away*.
143 Hayao Miyazaki thought it would be right for Satsuki to let go just once, to cry and yell (SP, 373) Her character needed that.

where she was (it's true that Chihiro is an only child, and doesn't have a vivacious sister like Mei to play with).

Indeed, the more you consider *Totoro*, the more you realize that it is the energy, the imagination and the charm of the two girls that powers it along. The movie takes its pace, its value and even its imagery from the two young girls.

In 1987 Hayao Miyazaki defined Satsuki's characterization in his notes on the movie:

> A girl bursting with vitality, seemingly growing up basking in sunshine. Limber and flexible body, stretching to its fullest. Vivacious and distinct expressions with eyes that dart about, unflinchingly looking at reality. Strong and reliable. In a family whose mother is absent, she is fulfilling the role of homemaker. Of course she is not just full of cheer. She does have some sadness inside, but for now she is full of life, her legs wanting to run, and she is eagerly impressionable. (SP, 259)

Mei has the classic Hayao Miyazaki square face,[144] and giant, auburn bunches. With her feisty, independent attitude and loud behaviour, Mei is going to grow up into Ma Dola from *Laputa* or Yubaba in *Spirited Away*.

Satsuki is given oval features, and short dark hair, like her father. With female characters, as Toshio Suzuki noted, Hayao Miyazaki concentrates on the hair, and in *My Neighbor Totoro* hair is used as a key element in the scene where Mei and Satsuki visit their mother (it's the only time in the film where they are depicted in the same room as their mom). While Mei rushes forward to embrace her mother, Satsuki hangs back; the moment when she turns and her mother brushes her hair is one of the sweetest in Miyazaki's cinema. It's very understated, but the emotion underneath is very strong (Miyazaki understands subtext as well as any filmmaker).[145]

The two heroes of *My Neighbor Totoro* – Mei and Satsuki – are a very appealing, fun couple of characters to put at the heart of a story. The whole movie is from the point-of-view of the two young girls. If he could've gone back and extended *My Neighbor Totoro* further, Hayao Miyazaki said he would've enhanced the everyday life scenes of Mei and Satsuki, rather than the Totoro scenes – so that it would even more a movie about Mei and Satsuki, not about Totoro (SP, 374).

---

144 Not the most obviously attractive design for a young girl!

145 The idea for the mother brushing Satsuki's hair came from a friend of Kiharasan's, whose mother had been ill, and she had brushed her daughter's hair (SP, 372). It fitted the scene for some affection between mother and daughter without resorting to Western-style hugs or other gestures.

The sisters' excitement as they explore their house for the first time is infectious and brilliantly done – why is it that when so many movies try to portray excited children at play they fall flat, and look contrived and forced? All adults were children once, but somehow reproducing the behaviour of children can be tricky. Not here, not in *My Neighbor Totoro*: the scenes of Satsuki and Mei rushing around the house to open windows, or find the kitchen, or creeping up to the attic, are completely wonderful (even more so when you realize that this is animation, simply drawings and coloured celluloid).

The level of *observation* here is at the highpoint of all animation: every movement, every gesture, every facial expression, is brilliantly observed. Oh yes, and *brilliantly rendered*. It is a wonder to watch the opening scenes of *My Neighbor Totoro*, to see just how graceful and detailed the animation is. Rarely has laughing, jumping, running and playing among children been so joyfully and accurately and poetically depicted. There's an elation and joy in the first twenty minutes of *My Neighbor Totoro* that is rare to find in movies, animated or live-action.

The hints at a romance between Satsuki and Kanta are beautifully portrayed – Hayao Miyazaki and his teams are absolute masters at expressing unspoken desire in a gentle manner. And what's touching about *My Neighbor Totoro* is that it's the boy who acts all shy and tongue-tied (from the moment he first sees Satsuki).[146] The traditional gender roles are reversed, as Miyazaki likes to do (Kanta says very little throughout the 1988 movie). Kanta is also depicted as another of Miyazaki's young, aerial dreamers: when he relaxes, he builds model gliders (the scene where he hides from Satsuki who calls at his house, because he's dressed in a vest and shorts, is another humorous gender reversal).

THE FATHER.

The father, Tatsuo Kusakabe, is a writer, now working on his second novel (his first book was a success). The father (who looks like Harry Potter with spectacles and wild dark hair) is an appealing character, sometimes as playful and whimsical as his children. It's a positive portrayal of a father as a protective, teaching figure,[147] who encourages his children in the belief in creatures such as Totoros or dust

---

[146] Kanta is not good at talking, Hayao Miyazaki explained, nor at fighting. But he can draw pictures. He feels tongue-tied whenever he sees Satsuki, but when he opens his mouth, something negative comes out, the opposite of what he's feeling.

[147] He works in a university in Tokyo.

bunnies.

Mr Kusakabe is a key figure in creating the warm, loving environment for the children – in this he's supported by the grandmother as someone who wants to help children. He is a fun dad, who races his children home, and plays games with them. He is a little absent-minded (Mei goes wandering off while he's at home working on his papers), but very well-meaning and affectionate.[148]

The filmmakers have rightly resisted introducing major flaws or ambiguities in the father or the grandmother or the mother or other adult figures, because this picture is about children, and childhood. They have also rightly resisted introducing major conflicts between the parents and the children. This is a happy family, even though the mother is ill in hospital. There are no flaws in the family, no hidden secrets, no chips on the shoulder, no resentments, no long-lasting tensions. The parents joke about their children, and the children joke about their parents.

Labour is again an important ingredient in *My Neighbor Totoro* – the children have their chores to do as well as Kasukabe-san. So the children are shown helping with the laundry, or cooking, or cleaning the floor, or fetching water. Kanta is depicted working in the fields, as is the grandmother. There's no griping from the children about their chores; they simply get on with it (and they make a game out of the chores too).

THE HOUSE.

The house in *My Neighbor Totoro* is another of those memorable spaces in Hayao Miyazaki's cinema, which are so clearly evoked the viewer feels like they could wander around the house for real: a living room with wooden, sliding doors (*fusama*), a small kitchen, a bathroom next door with two tubs (common in Japanese homes), the room which Mr Kusakabe turns into his office, with book shelves, and the single-room attic. The house is raised on piles, and has plenty of space in the yard around it.

Through the course of *My Neighbor Totoro*, the viewer gets to knows the house very well – but the first exploration of it is depicted entirely from the children's point-of-view: this is the house of *childhood*, the kind of house that Mei and Satsuki will remember all of their lives, the kind of house that will re-

---

[148] For the voice of Mr Kusakabe, Miyazaki didn't want the usual kind of actor: 'I heard a lot of voices of voice actors, but they are all warm, and are too much like a father who totally understands his kids… we thought that we had to cast a different kind of person.' He chose Shigesato Itoi.

appear in their dreams.[149]

Ingmar Bergman said he could recall every detail of the homes he lived in as a child, down to the paintings on the walls, the furniture, the light in Winter or Summer. When Bergman acknowledged, 'I'm deeply fixated on my childhood',[150] that was a major understatement! Bergman mined childhood in film after film.

Hayao Miyazaki does the same thing with the spaces he creates in his works, whether it's Pazu's miner's croft in *Laputa: Castle In the Sky,* or the room Kiki rents above the bakers' shop in *Kiki's Delivery Service,* or the bathhouse in *Spirited Away.* Miyazaki's spaces have the clarity and poetry of dreams, and the quality of the intense memories of childhood.[151] Miyazaki spoke of wanting to obtain vivid impressions of childhood memories, so that a scene would make what Isao Isao Takahata called 'a clear impression of what one experiences' (SP, 360).

THE SETTING.

My Neighbor Totoro was set in the regions around Tokyo, before the massive urban expansion of the 1960s. The time period, Hayao Miyazaki said, was simply a time before there was television (SP, 350). There is radio, but no TV. It was once again the era of Hayao Miyazaki's childhood, and a landscape he knew very well (Miyazaki lived in the Saitama Prefecture, in Tokorozawa City,[152] a suburb of Tokyo which had once been like the landscape of *My Neighbor Totoro*).

My Neighbor Totoro drew inspiration from a bunch of real places that Hayao Miyazaki knew, including (1) Tokorozawa, (2) the Kandagawa river, where he grew up, (3) the landscape near Sejio Sakuragaoka, and (4) Akita in the North of Japan (where the art director Kazuo Oga hailed from) (SP, 350).[153]

The shrines and temples include statues of foxes (*kitsune* are the *kami* of cereal crops in Japan, can shape-change and have supernatural powers); the camphor tree is next to a Shinto (Inari) shrine, and has rice straw and paper

---

[149] The house is really the fifth member of the Kusakabe family.
[150] I. Bergman, *Bergman on Bergman, Interviews with Ingmar Bergman*, eds. S. Björkman, *et al*, tr. P. B. Austin, Touchstone, New York, NY, 1986, 84.
[151] One reason that the two protagonists were girls was because using boys would have been too close to reality for Miyazaki.
[152] One of the early incarnations of *Totoro* was the story Miyazaki wrote in 1980 called *The Goblin of Tokorozawa*.
[153] For the location scout for *My Neighbor Totoro*, three in the production team – Hayao Miyazaki, animation director Yshiharu Sato, and art director Kazuo Oga – visited the area behind the Nippon Animation studio for a day or so (SP, 353-4).

streamers set around it.[154] The shrines and aspects of Japanese religion in the 1988 film were not intended to be taken literally or religiously, Hayao Miyazaki stated: 'this movie has nothing to do with that or any other religion', he said in 1987, in *A-Club* magazine.

TREES.

There's another enormous tree at the heart of *My Neighbor Totoro*. Yes, you're right: *no filmmaker* has put so many trees and so many magical trees into their films. Yep, not even Akira Kurosawa or Andrei Tarkovsky. In *My Neighbor Totoro*, the tree constitutes a magical realm, another of Hayao Miyazaki's mystical forests: there's a towering camphor tree at the heart of this mysterious wood, ringed by more trees.[155] The only way in – if you follow the children's route of wonder – is by crawling along a low tunnel of branches and leaves (if you go via the old religious shrine, there is more space around the tree, and if you take an adult with you, the entrance hole to Totoro's secret inner world is shut. Similarly, the adults can't see the Totoros or the Cat-bus, but both Mr Kusakabe and the nanny say they used to be able to see such things when they were children).[156]

Once again, Hayao Miyazaki and his team create a secret world inside the forest: a place of intense greens, of flowers and plants, and of butterflies. Like the heart of the forest in *Princess Mononoke*, it is blissfully quiet inside the camphor tree world. This is where Totoro lives and sleeps (he seems to spend a good deal of time sleeping – a wise creature, like a sleeping Buddha), and the place has every mark of a dream.

Discussing *My Neighbor Totoro*, Hayao Miyazaki suggested that the gods lived in such deep or dark places: they liked to be in the forests or in the mountains. Hence Totoro living inside the giant tree, or the Forest Spirit in the pool and grove in *Princess Mononoke*. Shrines, for instance, were typically situated in over-grown or dark areas: they were eerie places, where maybe a butterfly would flit by, but the silence would be deep. It wasn't darkness as something evil

---

[154] Hayao Miyazaki and his team would employ stone deities seen here in a similar fashion in *Spirited Away*, as mysterious presences, as guardians of forests and magical places.

[155] Although there maybe hadn't been a camphor tree as large as the one in the movie in his childhood, Hayao Miyazaki 'felt I had seen such a large tree' when he was young: 'we all have some tree we looked up at in awe of its size and grandeur when we were little'. So it wasn't a lie in making the tree that big, because in Miyazaki's memories 'it really was that big' (SP, 350-1).

[156] Often in stories of this kind, the adults ridicule the existence of fantasy creatures, as Brian Camp noted (226).

or sinister, however: it was an animistic religion, the sense of a presence, that something is there (SP, 359).

NATURE.

There is a truly extraordinary sense of landscape in *My Neighbor Totoro* – of trees, of skies, of clouds, of grass, of fields, of rice fields, of paths, of stones, of shrines, of a mound of trees.[157] And of light – the stormlight before rain, or the exquisite light of late afternoon. 'I am always aware of the light', Hayao Miyazaki said (SP, 376).

In the final reel of the 1988 film, when Satsuki is on a mission to rescue Mei, the filmmakers create a series of images of late afternoon and early evening light, going into sunset, which is simply breathtaking. French seventeenth century painters such as Nicolas Poussin and Claude Lorrain would love this movie – their art is full of green, tree-lined landscapes lit by afternoon suns with puffy white and gold clouds on the horizon.

The changing daylight from afternoon to sunset takes up one fourth of the running time of *My Neighbor Totoro*. As Hayao Miyazaki noted, 'it must have been difficult for Oga-san' (Kazuo Oga), the art director (SP, 376). Keeping track of the continuity in all of those shots as the light gradually changes would have been challenging.

Wind blowing across grass and trees: there is a night sequence where Satsuki slips outside the house to collect some firewood for their bath, and a breeze blows up. Only a few filmmakers can capture the feeling of mystery of the natural world, when the wind blows at night and leaves and grass rustle.[158] That breeze is also Totoro, the nature spirit, in his fiercer, nighttime form, when the wind becomes a gale that rattles the windows and scares the children (Satsuki realizes that Totoro is also the wind when she and Mei are riding along on his chest, and he flies low over the fields).[159]

For the scene of Satsuki out collecting the firewood and experiencing the gust of wind, Hayao Miyazaki said he recalled a conversation his wife had had with his son when the latter was young: 'today the beads of air bumped into us', his son had said (SP, 369). So Miyazaki put that into the scene.

---

[157] The film's first shot is a long shot of the van travelling thru rice fields under a blue sky with white clouds.

[158] Andrei Tarkovsky in *Mirror*, for instance, or Steven Spielberg in *Close Encounters of the Third Kind*.

[159] The weather sensitivity in *My Neighbor Totoro* is a part of everyday life, Hayao Miyazaki remarked, it's something that everyone feels.

It's just showing that there are sunny days and cloudy days and sudden evening downpours and nights when the wind blows [Miyazaki pointed out]. People living feeling that kind of weather and temperature on their skin. (SP, 37)

Japan, Hayao Miyazaki realized when he used to walk around the Shakujii Park after dropping his son off at nursery school, was beautiful when there was nobody about: *My Neighbor Totoro* was partly about the time when Japan wasn't so heavily populated (SP, 357).

In *My Neighbor Totoro*, humans are still living harmoniously with the forest: there is an environmental undercurrent to *My Neighbor Totoro*, but it is not the more strident ecological theme of *Princess Mononoke* or *Ponpoko*. *Ponpoko* is the political flipside of *My Neighbor Totoro*, where the raccoons make war on the humans, who are destroying their forest.

There is so much nature poetry in *My Neighbor Totoro*, it may be Hayao Miyazaki's most potent nature poetry movie, even more than *Princess Mononoke*.

The Summer is especially effectively evoked in *My Neighbor Totoro*, with, at night, mosquitoes around the lamps, a mosquito net, frogs croaking, insects buzzing, and a lazy full moon; and by day, Summer dresses, and a full-green, full-flower, full-sun treescape and landscape. Hayao Miyazaki recalled that he and his production team discussed at length how to depict the many plants in *My Neighbor Totoro*, and how to capture the feeling of Summer (including details like the direction of the sunlight during the solstice) (SP, 352).

MUSIC.

The music in *My Neighbor Totoro* is wonderful; Joe Hisaishi delivered one of the most memorable scores in the Studio Ghibli canon, with the theme song (sung by Azumi Inoue) being particularly effective, capturing the whimsy and humour of the central character, Totoro. It's introduced in its full form when Mei encounters the little Totoro in the garden near the house: as soon as that familiar melody starts up, you're already humming it.

It's simply not possible to imagine Hayao Miyazaki's movies without the music of Joe Hisaishi, because no matter how impressive the animation or story or sound effects or dialogue or characters are, the music is absolutely vital. Hisaishi told Miyazaki that the music should be light, but Miyazaki was insistent that it didn't have to be light (SP, 365).

Also, the film didn't need to have music everywhere, Miyazaki said.

THE NIGHT DANCE.

The sequence that is the signature scene in *My Neighbor Totoro*, or at least the most ecstatic sequence in the picture (and one of the stand-outs in Hayao Miyazaki's cinema), is the nighttime dance and flight. It depicts one of the most extraordinary evocations of growth and time in movies: Mei and Satsuki have been given a bag of seeds and nuts by Totoro,[160] and they plant them in the garden near their house. As Satsuki explains in her letter to her mom, Mei waters the seeds and waits for them to grow (watching them every day).

During an evening in Summer, at full moon (when their father puts up mosquito nets around their beds on the floor),[161] the children notice movement in the garden outside, through the sliding wooden doors (it's Satsuki who wakes first; the soundtrack is a delightfully playful, percussive patter).

The children rush outside when they see it's the three Totoros, engaged in a ritual dance around the vegetable patch (with King Totoro still holding the umbrella, and the two smaller Totoros holding leaves over their heads). Mei and Satsuki know instinctively what to do: they copy the stretching movements of the Totoros, and the seeds sprout by magic. First they pop up, then they grow, shooting up into the air as trees.[162]

The dance sequence is as magical as anything created by cinema's great magicians – Walt Disney, Georges Méliès, Jan Svankmajer, Orson Welles, or Akira Kurosawa. To top it all, after the trees have grown quicker than the beanstalk in the fairy tale *Jack and the Beanstalk*, so large they completely dwarf the house (with Mr Kusakabe visible at work in his room), there is a Miyazakian flight sequence. As they whirl through the sky on Totoro's chest (he stands on a whirring toy top), Satsuki calls to Mei that they are the wind – Totoro flies low over the ground, with a breeze rushing around him.[163] This

---

160 Of *My Neighbor Totoro*, Hayao Miyazaki said in 1988: 'I made it hoping that children would see it and then go out to run around the fields or pick up acorns' (SP, 35). An inspiration for *My Neighbor Totoro* may have been *The Acorns and the Wildcat* by the poet Kenji Miyazawa (who died in 1933).
161 Even that means more play – the children bounce around the nets. *My Neighbor Totoro* is a movie of endless *play*.
162 As Helen McCarthy puts it, 'Totoro has let them see the future grow and has taught them that time is only perception' (131).
163 There is a cut back to Mr Kusakabe here, working away at night at his desk, with the wind blowing in; he also hears the hooting of the ocarinas, which sounds like owls.

is pure ecstasy, filmmaking as an ecstatic, shamanic dream.

Finally, the night is topped off with a serene moment, as Mei and Satsuki join the Totoros on the tree's roof to blow the ocarinas, the soft-whoosh blowing sound is reminiscent of owls or other night noises. That moonlit-blue-night image rounds off one of the most delightful fantasy sequences in cinema. (And the pay-off is equally enchanting: when Mei and Satsuki wake the next day (late), they discover that the giant tree has vanished… But the seeds have definitely sprouted. They run outside and cavort around the vegetable patch, while their father looks on, amazed. It's as lyrical and moving an example of the power of dreaming that you'll see).

TOTORO.

The main Totoro (a.k.a. O-Totoro or King Totoro or Big Totoro), is a giant, bear-like creature, furry and blue, with a broad, white belly, long whiskers, a tail, wide-apart eyes, and an enormous mouth. There are elements of raccoons, rabbits, cats, bears and owls about Totoro. The other Totoros are called Chu-Totoro (middle-sized Totoro), a small, blue creature, that collects acorns and seeds in a little sack, and Chibi-Totoro (small Totoro). The word 'Totoro' comes from little Mei, who when she meets King Totoro thinks he looks like the troll in her storybook.

The Totoros are clearly nature spirits, guardians of the forest, with magical abilities – they can fly, raise seeds into trees in seconds, and can become invisible. They are playful and love games (like causing raindrops to fall on umbrellas with a loud roar). They play music, like to dance, and are very kind. There is no threat whatsoever when Mei enters the Totoro's secret home in the tree trunk – Totoro is Baloo the bear to Mei's Mowgli.

Totoro loves rain, and doesn't need an umbrella to protect him from it, Hayao Miyazaki explained (SP, 362). He is the lord of the forest, after all, and rain is essential for things to grow. Instead, he thought that Satsuki was giving him a musical instrument, because he enjoyed the sound of the rain on the umbrella. He was a spirit, maybe 3,000 years-old, Miyazaki mused, and maybe Kanta's grandmother met him when she was a child (SP, 368).

Hayao Miyazaki didn't want Totoro to be just another raccoon dog, another *tanuki*. He wanted to emphasize the mysterious aspects of Totoro, but not make him or it too mystical. Thus, he and Joe Hisaishi 'agonized over the music', so that it wouldn't be too spiritual or supernatural. So they chose Hisaishi's Minimalist music in the end (SP, 364).

Hayao Miyazaki was right not to show Totoro too much: he wanted to retain a sense of mystery to the character.[164] So, no dialogue for a start. He also decided that Totoro should not be shown sympathizing with Satsuki, even though she is very endearing as she searches desperately for Mei (SP, 361).

The scenes where the children encounter Totoro were meant to be ambiguous as to their reality, as to whether Satsuki or Mei really did meet Totoro, or if they had imagined it. 'Of course, I think they really happened,' Hayao Miyazaki added (SP, 364).

The Cat-bus (*nekobasu*) is one of Hayao Miyazaki's original and most memorable creations, a giant, stripey ginger cat, with eyes as headlights, and mice eyes illuminating the front and rear. As a magical transport, the Cat-bus is a perfect creation: it looks like it has always existed, like the best artworks. There must have always been a Cat-bus, surely?[165]

The Cat-bus arrives like a gust of wind, but is not the spirit of the wind, or the wind itself, Hayao Miyazaki explained, because that would make the Cat-bus not Japanese, but something European (SP, 354). Totoro climbs aboard calmly, smiling.

For John Lasseter, the busstop scene in *My Neighbor Totoro* was 'pure cinematic magic', due its pacing, the way that you 'feel the waiting and it's not tedious. It's beautiful' (SP, 12). The scene is of course among the most famous in the Miyazaki canon.

LEWIS CARROLL AND MAURICE SENDAK.

My Neighbor Totoro has the charm, whimsy and invention of the best children's literature. Comparisons with *Alice's Adventures In Wonderland* or Dr Seuss are absolutely correct, and not to lavish too much praise on the movie.

The *Alice's Adventures In Wonderland* affinities are clear: the Cat-bus has a giant grin like the Cheshire Cat (and sits in a tree like the Cheshire Cat), and can disappear like the Cat;[166] Mei chases the little Totoro like the White Rabbit; and the entrance to the magical camphor tree is along a tunnel (Mei

---

[164] It's enough to know that Totoro exists, like Laputa really exists. And 'because of his existence, Satsuki and Mei aren't isolated and helpless. I think that is sufficient' (SP, 368).

[165] The Knight-Bus in the *Harry Potter* books seems to have drawn on the Cat-bus.

[166] Japanese legends about cats were also probably an inspiration.

falls down the hole in the tree's roots[167] like Alice at the beginning of *Alice's Adventures In Wonderland*).

I also think of *Where the Wild Things Are*, Maurice Sendak's classic 1963 children's book, with Totoro resembling the Wild Things (though not as scary at first). In *Where the Wild Things Are* and other books (such as *Outside Over There*), Sendak creates encounters with mysterious creatures: one of his specialities is the magical night, especially moonlit nights, and *My Neighbor Totoro* echoes that – the ritual dance of Mei, Satsuki and the Totoro is very reminiscent of Sendak's children's books, as is the subsequent flight, and the group sitting on the top of the camphor tree and blowing ocarinas, evoking owls.

THE CHILD'S VIEW.

My Neighbor Totoro might be a 'children's film' (I don't think it is, or is usefully thought of like that), but the filmmakers cleverly weave in the adults' viewpoint numerous times, particularly that of Mr Kasukabe and the grandmother. Early on in the film, both Kasukabe-san and the grandmother explain to the children about the dust bunnies, and how you can see them when you are young. Later, Kasukabe thinks he's hearing owls hooting, but it's the Totoros and his children up on the camphor tree.

The split between the vision/ perception of children and adults is both upheld and subverted: the adults, for instance, can be as playful and as silly as the children. And maybe the adults do see what the children see: there are hints throughout the film that this is so, but the final scene clinches it in two ways: the mother thinks she sees Mei and Satsuki up in the tree, laughing, and the father finds the ear of corn that Mei has left on the window sill, inscribed with the words 'for mother'.

Those two moments bring together the two worlds, of adults and children, of age and youth, of innocence and maturity.

THE MOTHER-WORLD.

The mother is ill with tuberculosis (the novelization of *My Neighbor Totoro* makes that clear), although in the 1988 picture the disease isn't named. Hayao Miyazaki's own mother had been ill with spinal tuberculosis during his childhood.

Although absent from the family and for much of the piece, the mother is a key element in *My Neighbor Totoro* –

---

[167] Clambering over tree roots is reprised in *Mononoke*.

the family often talk about her, and sometimes it's as if she has only just stepped out of the room. The children discuss what they're going to do when mom returns from hospital.

So the Totoros are also manifestations of a maternal, protective presence, as well as being nature spirits. When Mei first meets King Totoro, she plays with him, then falls asleep on his chest, exactly like a child on its mother's lap.[168] Totoro acts as a surrogate mother at times to the two children, helping them and protecting them. But as well as Totoro and the Cat-bus, the natural world itself is a protective, nurturing mother – the night in *My Neighbor Totoro* is clearly a warm, comforting night, depicted in balmy blues and a big, white full moon (the full moon is a prime emblem of motherhood, nurturance and domesticity, as well as mystery, witchcraft, the unknown and Goddesses everywhere – Miyazaki and his team would use the full moon to stupendous effect in *Ponyo On the Cliff By the Sea*).

Instead of a succession of visits to the hospital, which would prove repetitive and perhaps tiresome, the 1988 movie limits itself to two: the first is one of Hayao Miyazaki's joyous trips by bicycle (bikes being a favourite mode of transport in Miyazaki's cinema, including the movies he scripts but doesn't direct). With Mei on the front and Satsuki sitting on the back, Mr Kasukabe rides the bike up and down hills and takes detours. The mood of the journey is sunny and optimistic.

The second visit closes the Japanese *animé*, with Mr Kasukabe answering the telegram and visiting his wife, while Mei and Satsuki have found their own way to the hospital, using the Cat-bus. The mother catching sight of them in the tree and the corn ear on the window sill brings together the two worlds: after this, with the mother getting well, the children won't need the aid of the Totoros or the Cat-bus.

Totoro's *dénouement* occurs over uplifting music, as at the end of other Hayao Miyazaki pictures, such as *Kiki's Delivery Service* and *Porco Rosso*. In it, the mother is shown returning home, and there's also a baby. So it's very much a happy ending, with the characters depicted in positive, joyous and humorous *tableaux*.

---

[168] The scene where both children fall asleep is also related to the mother: it's their way of dealing with the news that their mother was still ill and couldn't come home yet. Hayao Miyazaki wondered what children might do at such times, and thought they would probably fall asleep (SP, 375). It took Miyazaki and his team a while to find the best way of depicting the children's emotional response, but he was very happy with the result.

THE FINALE.

In the final reels of *My Neighbor Totoro*, the film becomes a quest and a chase, as Satsuki, having fallen out with her sister Mei, dashes around the countryside to rescue Mei, who has set out to see her mother in hospital (sweetly carrying an ear of corn as a gift). Satsuki's reaction to the telegram is overly dramatic – behind it lies the fear of losing their mother.

Here, Satsuki becomes the all-action hero, full of energy and determination. With the mother displaced and recuperating in hospital, Satsuki has taken on some of her mom's parental roles – she takes an umbrella to her father when it rains, she cooks for all three of them, and she looks after Mei. (The finale lasts about 15 minutes, or around half of the third act, using a three-act model).

Satsuki is entering the border zone between childhood and adulthood, and the film depicts that with the encounters with the magical elements: it is *Mei* who often sees the magical creatures first, not Satsuki, because at four years-old, Mei is completely a child, whereas Satsuki is in the process of growing up. In other words, your relationship to the magical realm indicates your child-like status (or vice versa): Mei believes instantly, and doesn't doubt her response; Satsuki is more cautious, and needs more time to be convinced. But after her initial hesitations, Satsuki is wholeheartedly a part of the magical realm, and the world of the Totoros. (Or in Miyazakian terms, you might say: do you want to be a magical child or a boring adult?).

Totoro's quest and chase brings together a number of themes, including the primary ones of the sisters' relationship, and their relationship with their parents, this time with their mother. It is at this point that Satsuki rushes to the camphor tree, to beg Totoro for help (she has already tried every road and possibility, and the locals are dragging a lake, fearing that Mei has drowned, after what seemed to be one of her shoes was found – an ominous image in a children's film).

But it isn't the story which one takes away from *My Neighbor Totoro,* it's the sweet characters, and the poetic evocation of a magical Summer and childhood, and the feeling of a radiant, shining, playful movie.

8
▼
KIKI'S DELIVERY SERVICE

1989's *Kiki's Delivery Service* (*Majo no Takkyubin*)[169] is a masterpiece about a young person growing up and learning about the world.[170] It centres on a 13 year-old witch[171] who leaves her family in the country to start a year of working in a new town, Koriko.[172] 'I thought it would be nice for a change to work on a small-scale film about regular life', Hayao Miyazaki said of *Kiki's Delivery Service* (SP, 383). But what Miyazaki calls 'small-scale' turns out to be very big indeed!

Yasuyoshi Tokuma, Mikihiko Ysuzuki, Morihisa Takagi, Toru Hara and Hayao Miyazaki were producers; Joe Hisaishi provided the music; Shinji Otsuka, Katsuya Kondou and Yoshifumi Kondo were animation directors; Michiyo Yasuda and Yuriko Katayama were colour designers; Hinoshi Ono was production designer; Eiko Tanaka was production manager; Shigeo Sugimura was DP; Takeshi Seyama was editor; and sound was by Naoko Asari, Kazutoshi Satou and Shuji Inoue. Nippon TV/ Ghibli/ Yamato Transport/ Tokuma Shoten produced. The initial budget was 800,000,000 Yen (= $800,000 – i.e., *very* low!).

---

[169] This translated as: *Witch's Special Express Delivery*.
[170] *Kiki's Delivery Service* was fundamentally about a girl who comes to a big city, has to find a room and settle in. Kiki might be a witch, but really the movie was about 'ordinary girls who come to Tokyo from the countryside', Miyazaki said (SP, 378). Similarly, someone coming to Studio Ghibli for the first time might find it labyrinthine, Miyazaki commented, this time referring to the bathhouse in *Spirited Away*.
[171] Kiki is designed along the Western conception of a witch, with a magic flying broom, black cat as a witch's familiar, black dress, etc. But there are no negative connotations attached to this representation of witchcraft. *Kiki's Delivery Service* was attacked for promoting 'divination' and undermining family values by a right-wing group in the U.S.A., the Concerned Women For America, which also criticized the Walt Disney Company for earlier movies such as *Peter Pan* and *Fantasia* (M, 143). And it was also the target of another right-wing group, this time in Japan, which attacked *Kiki's Delivery Service* for undermining family values.
[172] In this fantasy world, witches leave home at 13 and have to work for a year in a town they find themselves, which doesn't have a witch in it. They have to use their magic to help out the inhabitants.

Voice talent included Minami Takayama[173] (Kiki – *and* Ursula), Rei Sakuma (Jiji), Mieko Nobuzawa, Keiko Toda (Mrs Osono), Kappei Yamaguchi (Tombo), Jaruko Kato (Madame) and Hiroko Seki (Bertha).[174] The Yamato Transport Company was a sponsor of *Kiki's Delivery Service* – the movie used the company's name and referred to its black cat logo (M, 143).

Kiki's Delivery Service was written, directed and produced by Hayao Miyazaki[175] from a 1985 novel by Eiko Kadono.[176] (Kadono disliked[177] many of the changes that Miyazaki and his team made to her book).[178]

Kiki's Delivery Service had some 2,640,000 spectators during its theatrical release in 1989, which put it at the top of Japanese movies that year. *Kiki's Delivery Service* has sold very well on video (M, 143), including in the U.S.A., where it's shifted more than 1 million copies, beating *Akira*.

Carl Macek produced the first English language version of *Kiki's Delivery Service*, and Jack Fletcher oversaw the Disney dub (co-written with John Semper).[179] A live-action version of *Kiki's Delivery Service* was being prepared by the Walt Disney company in the mid-2000s, at the time when the books by Eiko Kadano were being translated into English.

Kiki is part of the 'magical girl' genre, which includes shows that Hayao Miyazaki worked on – *Little Witch Sally* (1966) and *Akko-chan's Secret* (1969) – as well as *Gigi, Creamy Mami, Comet-san, Marvelous Melmo, Cutey Honey* and *Little Witch Chappy.* (The influence of *Bewitched* and *I Dream of Jeannie* on the Japanese 'magical girl' genre is substantial).

On a technical level, *Kiki's Delivery Service* is absolutely

---

173 Minami Takayama (b. 1964) has also appeared in *Escaflowne* and *Detective Conan*, and was part of the pop act Two-Mix. Takayama was way too old (at 25) to play 13 year-old Kiki, yet Japanese voice actors seem to be able to get away with that more than their American/ English counterparts.
174 *Kiki's Delivery Service* employed 67,337 cels.
175 Hayao Miyazaki stepped in to direct the project, having planned at first to produce it. But Studio Ghibli couldn't find a suitable director (Miyazaki also wasn't satisfied with the script that had been written by a younger member of the Studio Ghibli team (M, 140). According to Helen McCarthy, the director chosen to helm *Kiki's Delivery Service* had been intimidated by the thought of working from a Miyazaki script.) This wasn't the first or last time that someone has been awed by working with Miyazaki.
176 Kadono also wrote *Cobby the Cute Little Cat* (1998), a TV animé. There have been four more books about Kiki published since the first one.
177 If that was me, I'd be ecstatic beyond belief to have Miyazaki making a movie of my book! He could change everything if he liked, the title, *anything*!
178 There is no depression in the book, for example, which is much lighter than the movie (M, 142).
179 The American version included Kirsten Dunst, Janeane Garofalo, Debbie Reynolds, Matthew Lawrence, and two of *The Simpsons'* stalwarts: Phil Hartman and Tress McNeille.

breathtaking. This is filmmaking at its very height – the staging, the compositions, the density of detail, the lighting, the colours, the movement, the architecture and props... *Kiki's Delivery Service* is mind-bogglingly inventive. There is so much crammed into every frame, *Kiki's Delivery Service* is a film that demands to be seen again and again. 'The detail is presented with a light hand, but its accumulation and precision lend the massive weight of reality to every frame,' wrote Helen McCarthy (M, 155).

The recreation of a European *milieu* is spellbinding. It is Hayao Miyazaki's customary Middle Europe – a mix of France, Italy, Germany, the Czech Republic, Spain, etc (the inspirations included Lisbon, Naples, Stockholm, Paris, and San Francisco, with Stockholm being a key influence – the filmmakers visited it, and took a large number of photos for reference). It was a Mediterranean coastal town on one side, and a Scandinavian city on the other. A totally convincing world, with once again an emphasis on technology (cars, planes, airships, bikes, telephones, gadgets). It's set somewhere in the 1950s or 1960s, but it is at once timeless and time-specific.[180]

The flying sequences, as in the rest of Hayao Miyazaki's work, are incredible in *Kiki's Delivery Service*. This is *the* film for witches flying on broomsticks (yes, even more than *The Wizard of Oz* or *Harry Potter,* which offer strong competition). And Miyazaki and his team add all sorts of quirks to the flying scenes – such as having Kiki not being the best flier in the world – the way she kicks off buildings or bounces on roofs is marvellous.

So with a film like *Kiki's Delivery Service,* Hayao Miyazaki and his team of filmmakers have produced a movie that is fabulously entertaining on the level of story, character, action and drama, plus it has mesmerizing visuals and *mise-en-scène*, it has compelling themes, and it works on multiple levels. *Kiki's Delivery Service,* as Helen McCarthy remarked, is 'a warm, gentle and very beautiful film, and should be in every family's collection, as well as that of every animation buff' (M, 157).

Kiki is a fabulously appealing individual, another of the *shojo* characters that Hayao Miyazaki and his teams are so brilliant at depicting. She is resourceful, independent, hard-

---

[180] Miyazaki said it was in a make-believe 1950s in which the Second World War never happened (in K. Eisner). Consciously and indulgently retro, the town has old-fashioned villas which have bread ovens, as well as apartment blocks. The airships come from the 1930s, the cars from the 1940s, and some of the machines from the 1950s. Studio Ghibli revisited this era again in *From Up On Poppy Hill*.

working, enthusiastic, and highly individual. She is also a capable, young girl who rises to challenges. But she is troubled too, and doubts herself, and has periods of detachment from her surroundings; that also makes her appealing. She sports a black dress (which she doesn't like, tho' it's rendered as purple), and a giant, bright red bow which she wears in her hair.[181]

When is the first time we see Kiki? She is lying on her back in a field in the hills near her home, looking up at the white clouds, listening to the weather forecast. That's significant: she's not surrounded by her family (her mother, father and grandmother are introduced in the following scenes), or by friends of her own age (they come a few scenes later, when Kiki leaves).[182]

So from the first Kiki is identified as someone separate, someone who spends time on her own, and time in the countryside.[183] She is linked to the natural world, and in particular to the sky: the scene emphasizes both the wind blowing through the grass (a superb effect), and the clouds and the sky (very low angles are employed, looking past Kiki's head up at the sky).[184] At this point, we don't know that Kiki is a witch who can fly, but when that's revealed, the opening scene makes even more sense.

It's important, too, that Kiki makes the decision to leave her home on her own, and doesn't discuss it with anybody (apart from Jiji, her cat). And when she tells her parents, though they make some gentle comments (her mom thought she was going to wait another month, and her dad has brought the camping gear for the weekend), they accept her decision (indeed, they are soon preparing for Kiki's departure – her dad phones up neighbours and relatives).

Hayao Miyazaki defined Kiki's characterization in his 1988 notes on the movie:

> Kiki, the thirteen year-old protagonist of this story, is a witch with only one particular strength: her ability to fly through the air. In her world, witches are not unusual at all. The real challenge Kiki faces is that, as part of her training, she must live for a year in an unfamiliar town and get its inhabitants to recognise her as a fully-fledged

---

[181] Kiki was partly based on Toshio Suzuki's 13 year-old daughter.
[182] That Kiki's ma and pa let Kiki go freely, without any big sentimental scenes, is important: these are parents who understand what Kiki is and what she has to do. There is some anxiety, of course – her mother gives her her old broom, for example.
[183] Kiki's mom is a witch, but her father is a regular father.
[184] Yes, once again, it's that favourite Miyazakian setting of lush meadows beneath blue skies.

witch. (SP, 262)

'Kiki's magic,' Hayao Miyazaki said, 'is something that all real girls possess – limited abilities that hint at some sort of talent' (SP, 263). It was not much more 'than that possessed by any real-life girl', Miyazaki added (1989).

Hayao Miyazaki enhanced the search for independence beyond the original story, partly to make the movie connect more deeply with the contemporary world of Japan. That also means that the film would exaggerate the loneliness and frustration that Kiki experiences (SP, 263).

Like the fairy tales of Charles Perrault, the Brothers Grimm and Hans Christian Andersen, *Kiki's Delivery Service* emphasizes the importance of hard work. Kiki is a worker – she earns her keep at the bakers' premises (the Osonos' place), she cleans her room, cooks for herself, and forms her own business. She stays with the bakers, who are usually shown at work. Kiki says she thought at first that Tombo was a layabout (and one of Tombo's friends remarks that Kiki working for herself is enterprising). In *Kiki's Delivery Service*, though, the emphasis on working isn't presented in the sometimes crude, somewhat self-righteous fashion of some of the fairy tales of the Grimms, Andersen or Perrault (it isn't backed up by Protestant references to God, for instance). However, *Kiki's Delivery Service* undoubtedly has a pedagogical goal, but its lessons are delivered in a wholly convincing, wholly unpatronizing manner (partly because Kiki is always at the centre of the narrative, and partly because the authority figures that Kiki encounters do not labour moral lessons, and partly because Kiki is such an independent character: she is not someone who can be told what to do – although, when she's asked to do something, like clean the painter's room in exchange for Ursula mending the toy cat, she does).

For Hayao Miyazaki, *Kiki's Delivery Service* was about young girls in Japanese society making their way in the world, growing up, trying to achieve independence. The point was there was a cost – including to the notion of flight. That Kiki can fly is amazing, on one level, but on another, it's not much different from having any other talent, Miyazaki thought. 'It is usually felt that the power of flight would liberate one from the earth, but freedom is accompanied by anxiety and loneliness,' Miyazaki explained. That is, even being magical has its problems, can isolate the heroine from other people, up there in the sky, and life itself always has a cost.

Kiki's Delivery Service is really a movie about depression, about losing one's powers – whether they be creative and artistic, or the power of health, to be alive in the first place.[185] This is the central dilemma or obstacle that Kiki has to face in *Kiki's Delivery Service*: in the final reels, she finds her magic waning to near-nothing (but not to completely nothing). As Hayao Miyazaki said, 'Kiki's heart wavers between isolation and longing for human company'. The *external* story is about Kiki rescuing Tombo from the drifting airship – that is the action climax (and terrifically done it is too – Miyazaki and his teams are masters of action, staging, suspense, timing and sheer drama). But the *internal* struggle for Kiki is whether she can regain her magic. It's true that one of the motives for the renewal of her powers is to rescue her friend in peril, Tombo (Kiki never loses her willingness to help others throughout the film). But the real goal or function of the action climax is to demonstrate that Kiki has found her magic again.

The finale with the dirigible is not tacked on to *Kiki's Delivery Service*, but is part of the fabric of the narrative. And not just because there was an earlier scene involving the airship,[186] when Kiki and Tombo go to see it (and a later one, when the airship flies over the town and Tombo is waving from the cabin), but because the airship is all to do with the theme of flight (again, this applies not only to Kiki but also to Tombo).[187] The finale reverses genders – now it's the princess who saves the prince.

Rather than a happy ending which depicts Kiki overcoming all obstacles, Hayao Miyazaki said he wanted to suggest that Kiki would become depressed again in the future, but she would bounce back each time (SP, 379). Depression isn't something that can be solved by defeating the villain (if only!): and in the Miyazakiverse, no big obstacles can be dissolved by killing the bad guy.

The coda included a number of things that Hayao Miyazaki wanted to show, such as the Osonos' baby, Tombo, and Kiki making friends with girls her own age (SP, 379).

That *Kiki's Delivery Service* is about depression and hiding away from life and how that's not really a good way to live is demonstrated vividly: for instance, when Kiki and

---

185 *Kiki's Delivery Service* was also meant to show 'the weakness of [Kiki's] determination and shallowness of her understanding', Miyazaki explained in *The Art of Kiki's Delivery Service*.
186 This is a world in which the Hindenberg disaster never happened.
187 The climactic rescue includes numerous Miyazakian touches, including a giant clock and clock tower (from *The Castle of Cagliostro*); and the clock tower doesn't just appear to function as an extra element in the spectacular rescue scene – it was introduced earlier, when a workman in the clock tower told Kiki when she arrived in Koriko that there wasn't a witch in the town.

Tombo go to visit the airship, Tombo's gang of friends turn up in their car. Kiki remains on the beach, and Tombo calls out to her to join them. Kiki wavers, but opts to walk home alone. No need for narration or dialogue here: the filmmakers portray Kiki walking home, slipping by the bakers (kind of her adopted parents) and falling onto her bed. Her room is quiet and dull and boring – the contrast with the laughter and conversation of Tombo and his friends is striking. (And there are scenes where Kiki hangs around in the shop, bored and listless: work is sometimes like that).

At this point, *Kiki's Delivery Service* demonstrates that one's choices do affect one's life: Kiki could have joined Tombo's crew, and probably had a much better time. But she *chose* to go home on her own, and stay in. To emphasize the depression, and the loss of Kiki's magic, her cat, Jiji, hops in through the window and meeows to Kiki, but she has lost the ability to understand her cat.[188]

At this moment in the story, some of Kiki's problems are self-imposed; that's partly what makes *Kiki's Delivery Service* so interesting: that is, it's not a movie about someone who finds themselves up against difficult obstacles like monsters or aliens, or in tough circumstances. There is, for example, no villain in *Kiki's Delivery Service*, no one that the heroine is battling against. No wars, invasions, huge social injustices, etc. There are potential obstacles – like the policeman who is going to fine Kiki for her dangerous flying (but Tombo saves her from him), or the birds that get in Kiki's way when she's on her first delivery flight. But the true obstacles are inside Kiki herself. It's a psychological movie.

To make sure the audience really does get the point of the story, *Kiki's Delivery Service* adds a parallel character to Kiki: the young, female painter Ursula who works in the woods outside the town:[189] the artist visits Kiki, and helps her out of her depression by taking her into the countryside for a break. And, importantly, Ursula tells Kiki that sometimes artists can lose their inspiration (and she offers Kiki some advice about that). Kiki's shocked reaction – that artists can have blocks too – is very touching.

Ursula is important in the picture, and in Hayao Miya-

---

[188] There's a great touch when Jiji approaches Kiki in bed when Kiki's ill, and the girl simply points silently to the food. A minor sub-plot has Jiji making friends with another cat, Lily, and becoming a father, with kittens (Miyazaki's movies like to put families and offspring into the closing credits).

[189] The name Ursula might be a nod to Ursula Le Guin, the celebrated author of the awesome *Earthsea* books, and acknowledged by Hayao Miyazaki as a literary influence.

zaki's cinema, obviously, because she is the most prominent artist in his *œuvre*. She is shown sketching some birds and using Kiki as a model for a big canvas she's painting of a girl on a flying horse at night (the painting was called *The Ship Flying Over the Rainbow*; it was created by pupils at a special school; Miyazaki added the face of Kiki). Having Kiki as a witch who flies about on a broom delivering things is much more exciting, perhaps, from a visual and action point-of-view, than a painter working at an easel or sketchpad, but they are exactly the same thing. *Kiki's Delivery Service* could be about a painter trying to paint. But a witch who can fly makes for a more impressive and thrilling animated movie.

Discovering Ursula was vital in Kiki's psychological development, Hayao Miyazaki said: Ursula was someone who understood her, and what she was going through. She was also a friend who visited her in her rooms. Meeting Ursula was probably more significant than whether her business would succeed (SP, 381).

There are other parallel characters: Tombo,[190] for instance, is a boy of Kiki's age who's mad about flight: he's building a pedal-powered aircraft with his friends. Tombo is part of an aviation club, with his chums. And he's right in the middle of the people trying to stop the airship flying off by hanging onto the last rope. One of the stand-out sequences in *Kiki's Delivery Service* is an equivalent for a love scene between Kiki and Tombo (the romance between Kiki and Tombo is sweetly done). Instead of having them dancing, one of the classic (Hollywood) tropes for an erotic scene, they are, of course, *flying*. What is more erotic in Hayao Miyazaki's cinema than two people flying together? It begins with a bicycle ride (next to the sea, to see the airship). The bike journey itself, with Kiki riding along behind Tombo, would be obvious enough as an image of joyful and tender togetherness (the way they lean together around the corners, for instance, the speed, the legs pumping, the panting, the exhilaration, are further stand-ins for love-making), but this is a Miyazaki movie, so they have to fly. Tombo pedals like mad, the propeller spins wildly, and the bike takes off.

To depict that the youngsters aren't quite mature lovers yet, the bike crashes, of course (a classic way of suggesting that theirs is not yet an accomplished kind of loving). And in a kind of post-coital scene, as Kiki and Tombo talk together after

---

[190] It's easy to see in Tombo a version of the young Miyazaki – Tombo even has the thick-rimmed square spectacles that Miyazaki sometimes wears. And he's goofy, he likes girls, he's clumsy, he's persistent, he's a dreamer, etc.

the crash, there is an element of sexual jealousy – when Tombo's crew turns up, part of the reason that Kiki decides not to join them might be because there are a couple of girls in the gang. Yet none of this is overtly stated, and the movie works on many levels simultaneously.[191]

Yet another level to *Kiki's Delivery Service* is food and cooking. It's one of Hayao Miyazaki's recurring motifs; food is a key to fairy tales, too. It can represent affluence or success, or plenitude, or just good, pleasurable things (and food of course has its erotic components – the pleasure of eating being one of the tropes for sex in fairy tales). Kiki ends up at a bakers' business; she visits a grandmother (Madame) and helps her bake a special cake for her granddaughter's birthday party;[192] she delivers a toy cat to a house where the family have a meal; she has food from home that she doesn't feel like eating; she is shown cooking and eating; the baker Osono makes her some porridge when she's ill; Tombo buys a cake; Kiki delivers a cake to him, etc.

It's really startling just how extraordinary *Kiki's Delivery Service* is, if you think about it: not only does it have a young female main character (already unusual), it concentrates on her pretty much exclusively. The entire story is depicted from Kiki's point-of-view. It's amazing, too, that Kiki *isn't* shown as a young child who yearns for her parents, Kokiri and Okino, back home. The Disney Studios would probably not resist, for instance, putting in a scene where Kiki breaks down and cries and longs for her mom and dad. The Disney Studios would not allow a thirteen year-old girl to be on her own in a town without some home sickness. But no, *Kiki's Delivery Service* is far less sentimental (though just as emotional). Kiki doesn't even get in touch with her parents for a long time in the 1989 film – only towards the ends does the movie switch locations from Kiki and Koriko to her parents back home, who have received a letter from her. (However, *Kiki's Delivery Service* does have Kiki finding shelter with a loving couple who act as her adoptive parents – the bakers, Osono and her husband. Yet while Osono-san is motherly (and expecting a child herself), she also leaves Kiki to her own devices – Kiki looks after herself, cleaning and cooking for herself and her cat. Kiki does bring connections to her parents with her – her broom from her mom, the radio from her dad, while the cat is an aspect of

---

[191] It doesn't descend to the level of crudity of many a movie.
[192] The scene where the birthday girl rejects the delivery of the cake from her grandmother was something that happened in real life, and Kiki had to deal with it, Hayao Miyazaki commented (SP, 380). It might have really upset her, but it was something she would encounter in her delivery service.

herself).

Further, *Kiki's Delivery Service* depicts a young woman struggling with herself – struggling to find a place for herself in the world, which's the external problem (but one that Kiki solves rapidly, when she decides that her witch's skill is flying, and sets up her delivery service). But also struggling internally.

And the way that *Kiki's Delivery Service* depicts the inner toiling is brilliant: as well as the scenes of depression, described above, the movie also has an enchanting and moving sequence where Kiki tries to regain her magic: she takes up her broom in her room and forces it to fly.[193] Her powers aren't completely gone, but they are weak (she hovers for a little, then crashes to the floor). In the next scene, Kiki is running down a hill, like a child with an umbrella or a kite, trying to fly. This is classic Hayao Miyazaki, and he captures with such grace, such humour, and such *insight* how young people (or anyone) try to attain transcendence. And the subtle elements are beautifully realized – how Kiki flies her a short distance then lands again. How she climbs back up the hill to try again. And how she winds up crashing, and breaking her broomstick.

Here Hayao Miyazaki and his team portray with hypnotic lyricism the reach and fall of artistic endeavour, of magic, of life itself. Without her magic, Kiki realizes, she is not really alive, she is not a complete person, and she can't do what she was meant to do, what she wants to do. An artist paints and makes art, a witch flies and uses magic, a baker bakes bread and cakes, a boy who wants to be an aviator builds planes – but without that, they are not whole people.

---

[193] It didn't matter what the reason was for Kiki losing her ability to fly: the fact that she couldn't fly anymore was what counted in the movie, Hayao Miyazaki insisted (SP, 380).

ILLUSTRATIONS

Illustrations on the following pages are from the movies directed by Hayao Miyazaki (two pages for each movie).

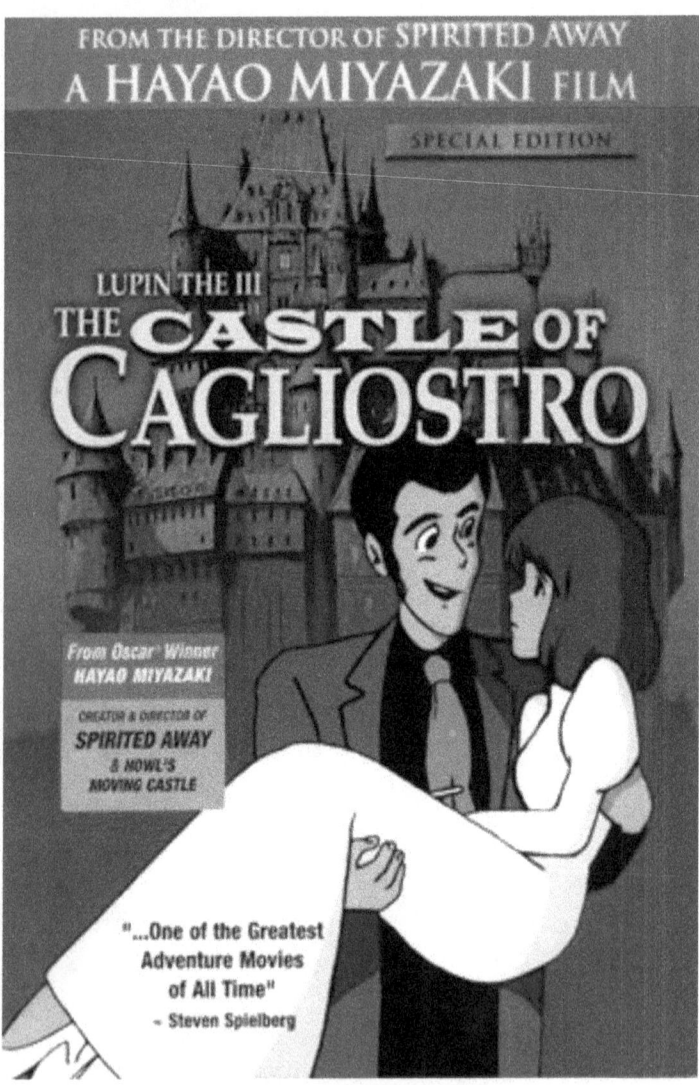

(© TMS-Kyokuichi Corporation/ Monkey Punch/ Manga Entertainment 1979)

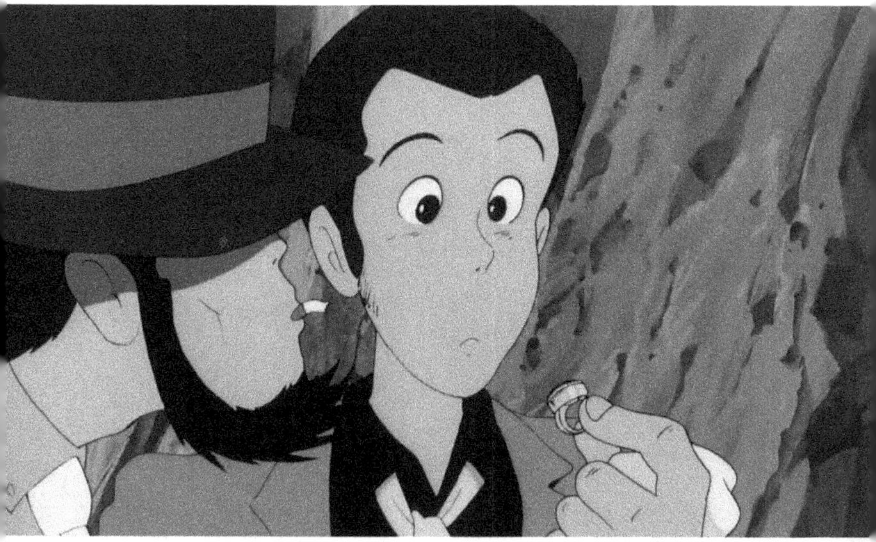

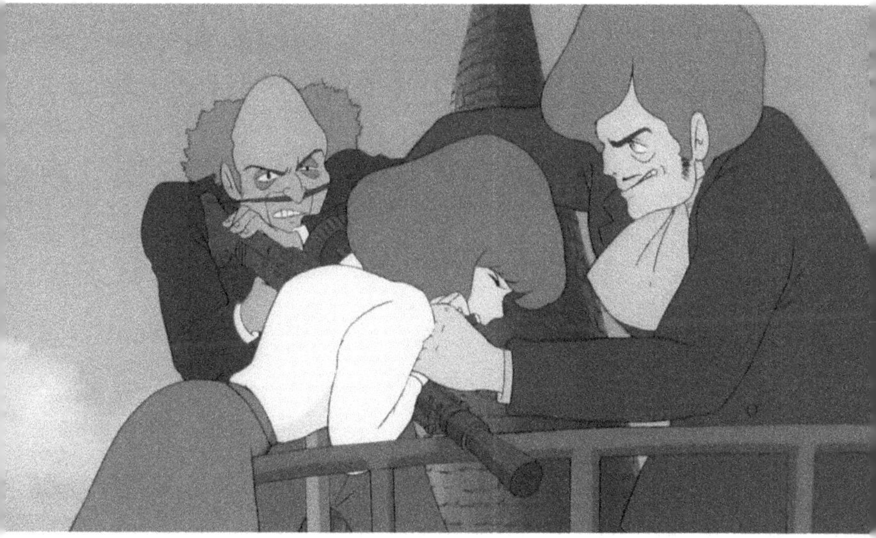

(© Nibarki/ Tokuma Shoten/ Hakuhodo, 1984)

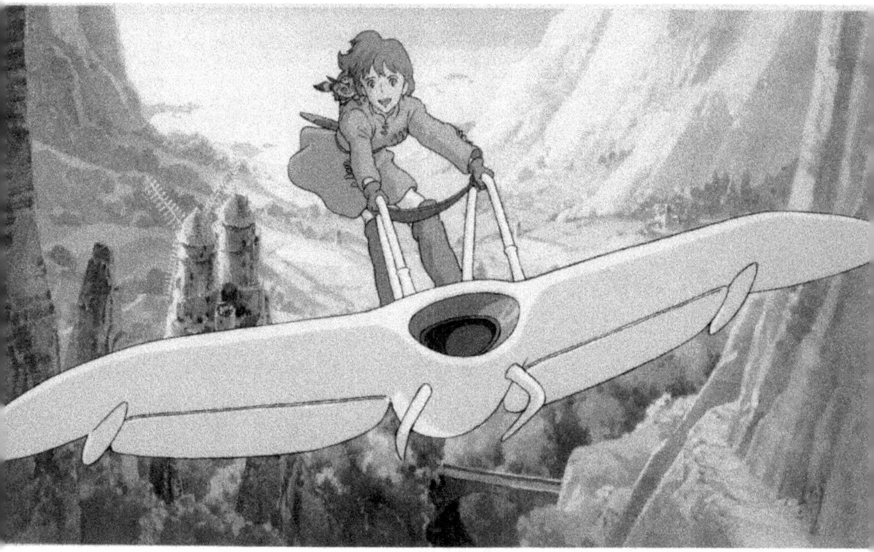

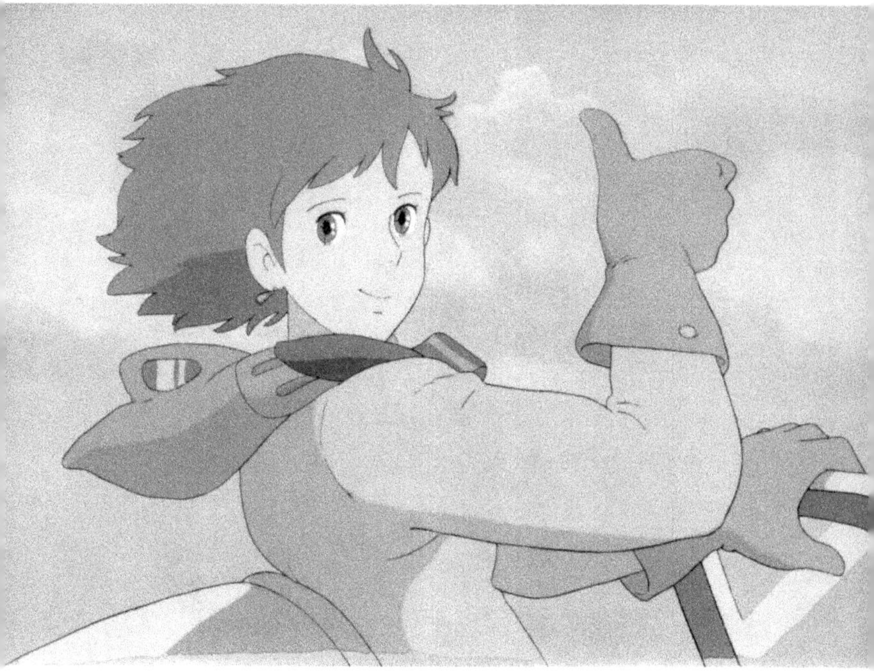

(© Nibariki/ Tokuma Shoten, 1986)

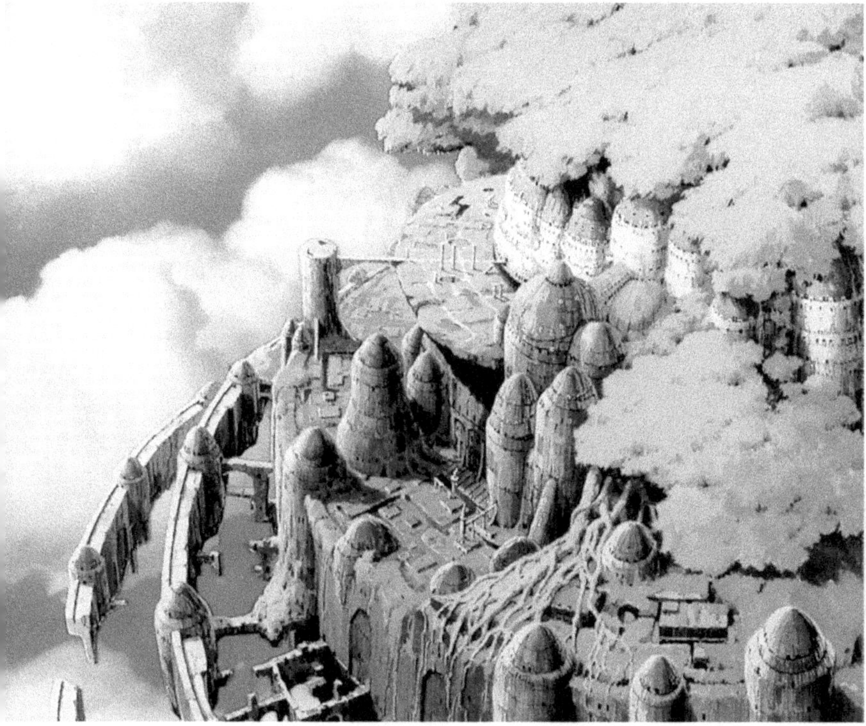

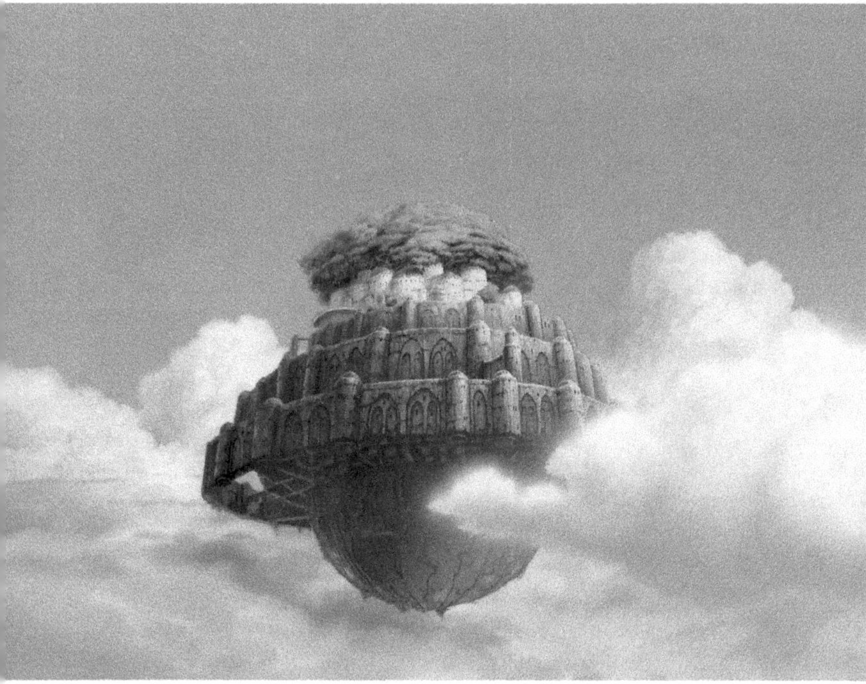

(© Eiko Kandono/ Nibariki/ Tokuma Shoten, 1989)

(© Nibariki/ Tokuma Shoten, 1988)

(© Nibariki/ TNNG, 1992)

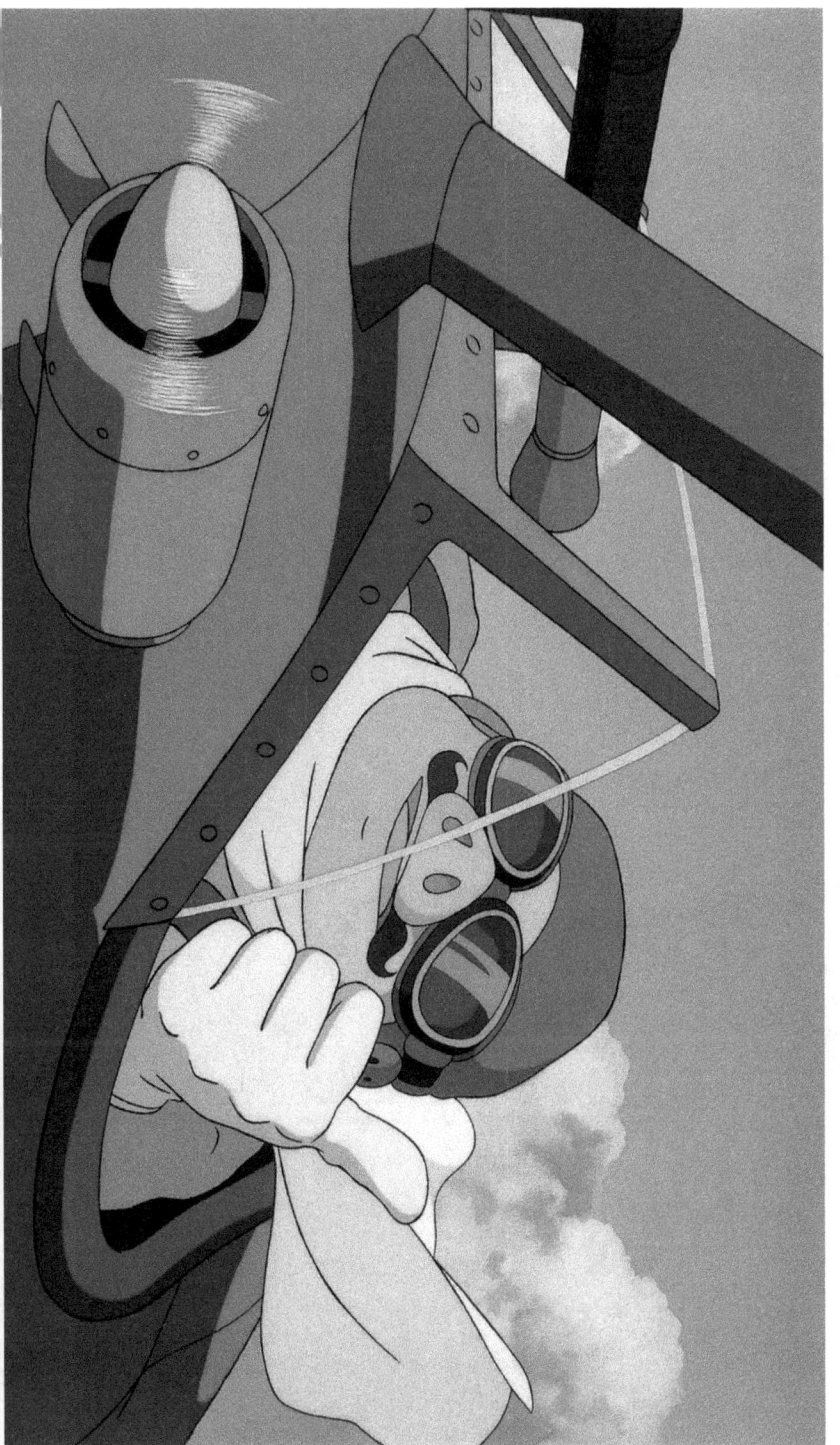

(© Nibariki/ TNDG. 1997)

(© Nibariki/ TNDGDDTM, 2001)

(© Toho/ Walt Disney Pictures/ Wild Bunch, 2004)

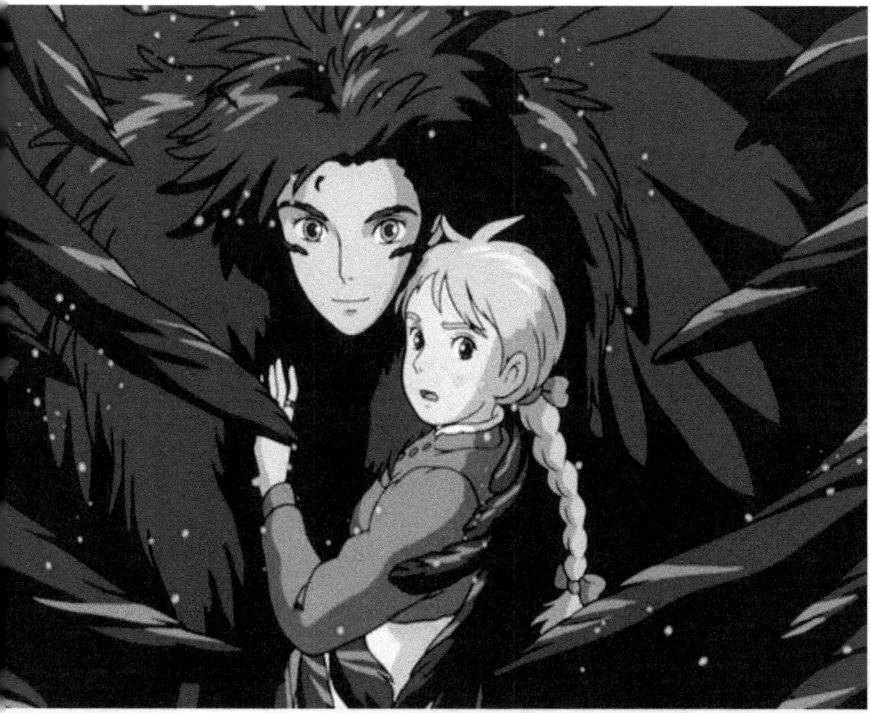

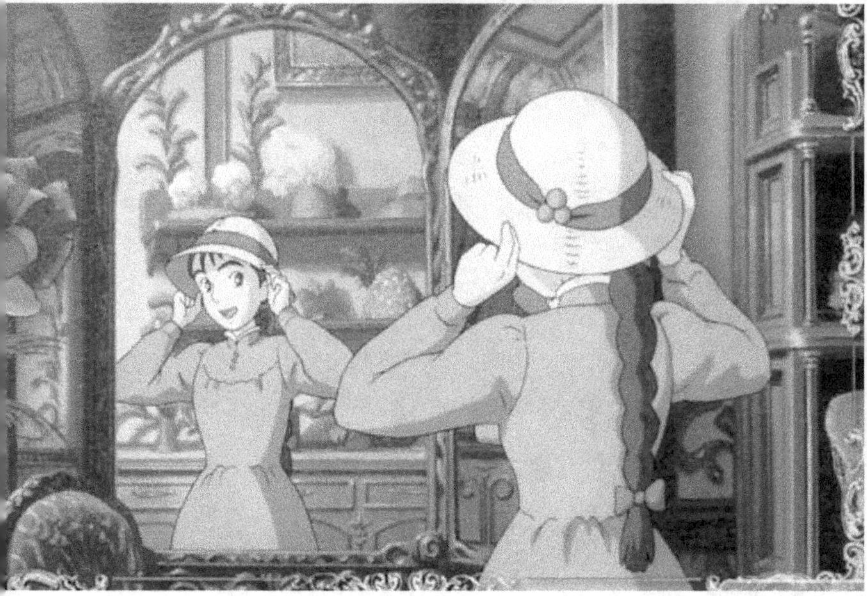

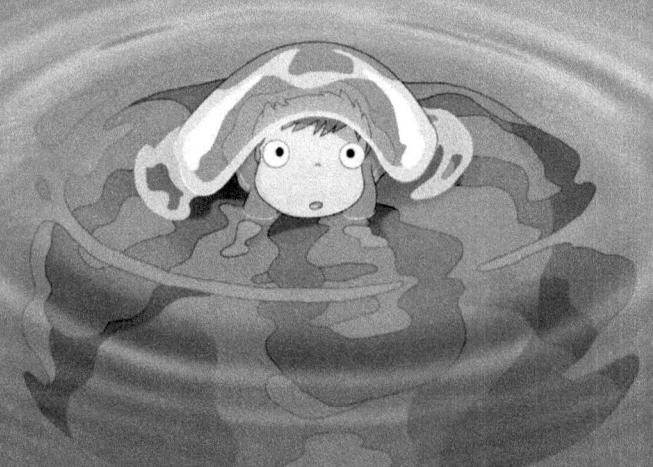

(© Toho/ Studio Ghibli, 2013)

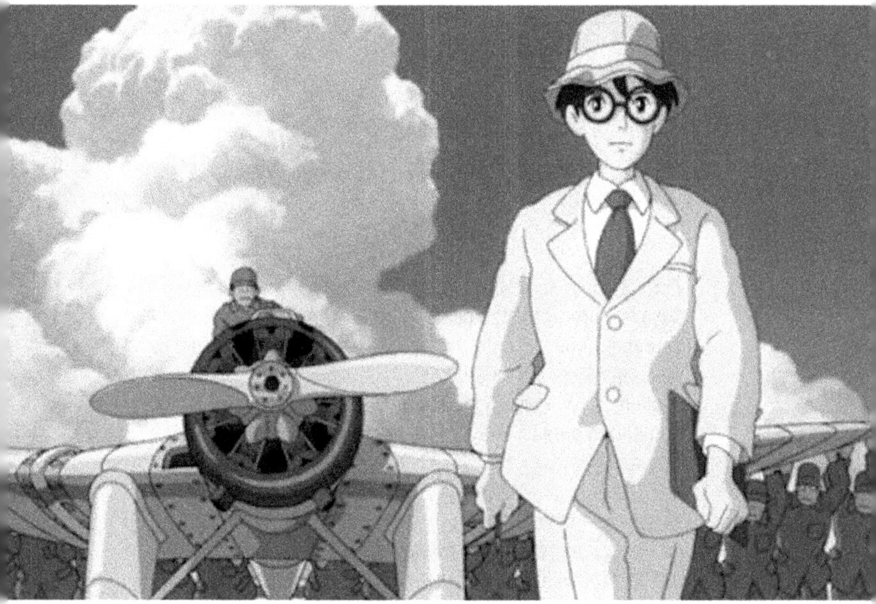

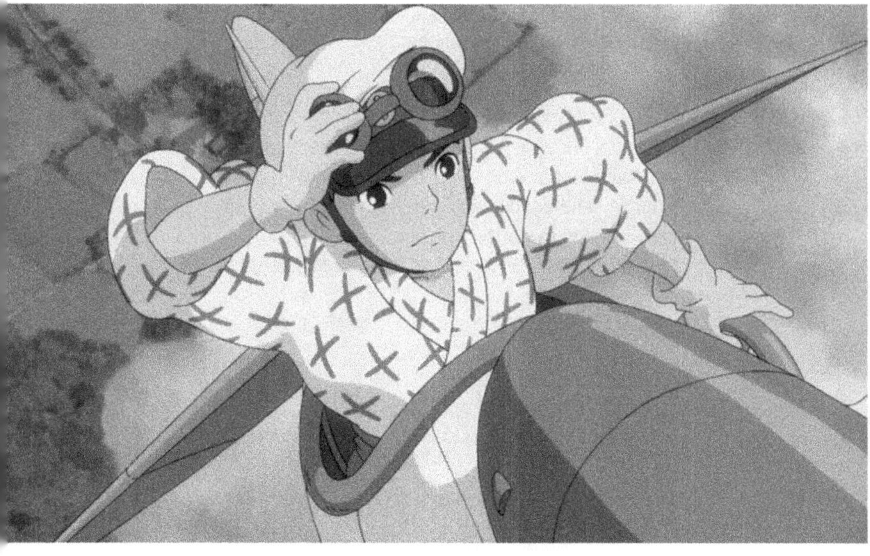

9

PORCO ROSSO

Porco Rosso (*Kurenai no Buta,* 1992) has a classic Hayao Miyazaki protagonist: a pilot. No ordinary pilot, though: the title character (Marco Pagott)[1] is a pig. Or rather, a man with a pig's head and face, a man under a curse (which's never really explained). (Not wholly a pig's head – it's very much a humanized version of a pig, rather like the frog men in *Spirited Away*).

Once again, it's one of Hayao Miyazaki's *intuitive* decisions, which makes sense when you see it in the movie (Marco's the first character introduced in the picture). If you had to *explain* it, though – say to a film producer or financier – it might sound dumb.[2]

> Filmmaker: Our main character is a pig.
> Studio mogul: Eh? I thought it was an action movie about pilots? (I'm spending 2 mil tops!).
> Filmmaker: Well, a pig-man, actually... Half a pig... No, a man with a pig's head.
> Studio mogul: Are you nuts?
> Filmmaker: Trust me!

But it works. Partly because, although many characters draw attention to it (including Pagott himself), it's woven in to the reality of the world of the movie (there isn't a scene, for example, where a character meeting Marco for the first time dissolves into hysterical laughter).

Porco Rosso began life as a 30-45 minute movie for

---

[1] The main character has a number of names: he's Marco Pagott, a.k.a. Marco Porcellini, a.k.a. Porco Rosso (the 'Crimson Pig', on account of his red seaplane, and his appearance). The Mamma Aiuto gang call him the Pig, while Gina refers to him as Marco. He was born in 1893, and flew a plane first at 17 (as he explains to Fio). He fought in the First World War for the Italian Air Force (becoming Captain), where he lost many of his friends.
[2] And a Western animated movie would certainly prefer to explain it.

Japanese Airlines,[3] which was expanded to a feature film (it was commissioned by an airline company, then, and was intended to be in-flight entertainment).[4] Hayao Miyazaki had produced a *manga* (comic) titled *Hikoutei Jidai* (*The Age of the Flying Boat*, 1989),[5] published in *Model Graphix*, a magazine of model-building, which was the basis for the film, although it's a lighter piece[6] (he also drew a history of airline food, *Dining In the Air*).[7] Because Isao Takahata was making *Only Yesterday*, much of the responsibility for producing *Porco Rosso* was down to Hayao Miyazaki.

When it was going to be a lighter sort of movie, with another director making it, it would have involved the hero as a tank commander, who kidnaps a woman and falls in love with her. It would have been called *Pig's Tank* (a.k.a. *Anchor*), 'a silly movie which will show my embarrassing side', Hayao Miyazaki admitted.

The upbeat, life-affirming nature of *Porco Rosso* was fundamental to the project:

> In the film we will make, the male characters are always upbeat and lively, the women are always charming, and everyone enjoys life; the world they inhabit is always cheery and beautiful. (SP, 267)

The idea was to produce a movie of a beautiful world, a once upon a time world, which would contain places that people would like to visit, a sky through which people would like to fly, and 'a secret hideaway we ourselves would want' (SP, 268). The movie would emphasize movement, the joy of being in motion, Hayao Miyazaki said.

Porco Rosso was produced by Tokuma Shoten, Japan Airlines, Nippon Television Network and Studio Ghibli. The supervising animators were Megumi Kagawa and Toshio Kawgauchi. Yoshitsu Hisamura was art director, Katsu Hisamura was production designer, with colour design by

---

[3] When it was a 45 minute film for Japan Airlines, Hayao Miyazaki said in his production memo that: 'we must never forget that first of all it is a cartoon movie for tired, middle-aged men whose brain cells have turned to tofu' (SP, 267). The journey towards production wasn't easy – the project grew, a lot more money was spent, and there was trouble with the animation (AI, 28).

[4] There are references to a TV series that Hayao Miyazaki worked on, *Three Thousand Miles In Search of Mother*, which featured characters called Marco and Fiolina.

[5] It was later published in an English translation in *Magazine* and *Animerica*.

[6] The initial concept of *Porco Rosso* as something in a more light-hearted and knockabout vein was dropped as Miyazaki developed the project.

[7] Hollywood movies about flying linked to *Porco Rosso* would include *Wings* (1927), Howard Hughes' epic, and *Only Angels Have Wings* (1939).

Michiyo Yasuda. Atsushi Okui was DP. Sound was by Naoko Asari and Makoto Sumiya. Music was by Joe Hisaishi.[8] Toshio Suzuki was producer, and executive producers were Yasuyoshi Tokuma, Sokai Tokuma, Matsuo Toshimitsu and Yoshio Sasaki.[9] As well as writing and directing, Miyazaki is also credited with editing, along with Takeshi Seyama and Katsu Hisamura. In short, it was the regular Miyazaki team.

Porco Rosso's Japanese voice cast included Shuichiro Moriyama (Porco), Akemi Okamura (Fio), Tokiko Kato (Gina), Tsunehiko Kamijô (Aiuto Gang Boss), Akio Otsuka[10] (Curtis), and Sanshi Katsura (Piccolo). The English voices in *Porco Rosso* include Michael Keaton, Carey Elwes, Susan Egan and Brad Garrett (one of the better American English dubs).

Porco Rosso was described in a documentary on Studio Ghibli as Hayao Miyazaki's idea of what it was to be really cool: Porco Rosso certainly embodies that. There are definitely aspects of autobiography in the character of Porco Rosso, which's an idealized version of aspects of Miyazaki himself[11] (while the aircraft builder, Mr Piccolo, has affinities with Miyazaki's producer, Toshio Suzuki.[12] Maybe there's also some biographical purpose behind Rosso being a pig-man, and Piccolo being a mole-man).[13]

Hayao Miyazaki acknowledged that he was being self-indulgent when he made *Porco Rosso*. It was a personal film for him, and he worried if audiences would take to it. They did.

Porco Rosso was a big hit for Studio Ghibli and Hayao Miyazaki – it was the top grossing film in Japan in 1992.[14] It was released theatrically in Japan on July 20, 1992. 93 minutes. At the box office, *Porco Rosso* trumped *Hook* and *Beauty and the Beast*. (In many other territories, the top film of 1992 was, unusually, an animated movie: Disney's *Aladdin*,

---

8 By 1992, Joe Hisaishi was really getting into his stride in composing scores for Studio Ghibli movies. The music is marvellous in *Porco Rosso* – there's a plaintive, Italianate, folky piece of solo guitar; a humourous brass band cue for the Mamma Aiuto gang scenes; lush strings for the peaceful flying scenes; and Joe Hisaishi's customary soft piano (for the romantic scenes).
9 *Porco Rosso* used 58,555 cels.
10 Akio Otsuka is one of the great voice artists in Japan – he is the amazing Batou in the *Ghost In the Shell* series, for instance (and the King in *Howl's Moving Castle*).
11 Hayao Miyazaki sometimes caricatures himself as a pig, and also has the nickname of 'pig' (*Buta-Ya*).
12 Look at the scene where Marco and Piccolo sit in Piccolo's office and discuss budgets and bills and money – that's a recurring scenario for film directors and producers the world over. And it's typical of the producer-director relationship that Piccolo says that Marco is short, money-wise, but will have time to pay it back.
13 Piccolo is also a wholly Japanese characterization, in an Italian setting.
14 The fans of *Animage* magazine put *Sailor Moon* at the top of their readers' poll, the first time that a Hayao Miyazaki film hadn't been at the top.

which topped *The Bodyguard, Basic Instinct, Lethal Weapon 3* and *Batman Returns* at the global box office).

Once again, there are differences between the English language dubbed version (produced by the Walt Disney corporation) and the subtitled Japanese version. Ferralin mentions that the Italian authorities have been throwing accusations at Porco Rosso, including pornography. Well, you can bet that the Walt Disney corporation didn't mention porn in its English dub of *Porco Rosso*.

On a milder level, there are numerous differences, in which the culturally specific Japanese elements of the dialogue are Americanized in the English language version. Piccolo tells Rosso that you can teach him anything about aeronautical engineering, because it would be like teaching Buddhism to Buddha. Those sort of remarks (which aren't particularly esoteric) are dropped from the Disney dub of *Porco Rosso*.

Porco Rosso is another favourite Hayao Miyazaki movie for me – well, *all* of Miyazaki's films are favourites. This is a filmmaker (leading a team of filmmakers) who has not produced a single dud picture: every one of Miyazaki's films is a gem.

Somehow, Hayao Miyazaki has distilled every adventure comic, every war comicbook, and every action hero that kids grew up with in the past 100 years and put them into one character and one movie.[15] George Lucas, Paramount and 20th Century Fox did the same with the *Indiana Jones* and *Star Wars* films.[16]

The narrative and thematic levels in *Porco Rosso* include:

1. Porco Rosso's job, and the rivalry between Porco Rosso and the Mamma Aiuto gang.
2. The rivalry with Donald Curtis, in the skies and as a pilot, but also for Gina's love.
3. The on-off romance with Gina.

---

[15] As Helen McCarthy remarked: 'Every frame is well crafted, with some of the most marvelous aerial sequences ever animated and skies so exquisite the background painters should be designing for God. Hisaishi's score is perfectly matched to the flow of every scene' (2008, 152). In *The Anime Movie Guide*, McCarthy further enthused: 'The backgrounds are fabulous, the animation first class – look particularly at the way water is handled, since it has rarely, if ever, been done better […] The action sequences include aerial battles that have never been bettered in live-action film, and the comedy is superbly placed' (28, 167).
[16] However, Porco Rosso is a superior creation to Indiana Jones in some respects. The relentless violence of the *Indiana Jones* films does wear you down. And the *Raiders of the Lost Ark* movies, fabulous as they are, have all sorts of dubious ideological and political elements to them.

4. The buddy/ father-daughter relationship with Fio.
5. Flight.
6. The First World War.
7. The military, and build-up of fascism.
8. The past, haunted by past deeds.

Central to *Porco Rosso* is the experience of flight. As one of the Studio Ghibli staff commented, Hayao Miyazaki is mad about airplanes.[17] I think we gathered that from his movies! It's not just planes in *Porco Rosso*, it's *seaplanes*. That brings together two of Miyazaki's favourite things: aeroplanes and the ocean (the sky and the sea... the air and the water).[18] And seaplanes means there are sequences of aircraft landing and taking off from the sea, as well as being parked on it. There's something romantic about just that, let alone the planes themselves and the pilots. (Of the numerous scenes of take-offs and landings, the loveliest is where Porco lands his sea-plane at the Hotel Adriano at sunset. This is pure, olde worlde glamour).

Porco Rosso (voiced by Shuichiro Moriyama (b. 1934), and by Michael Keaton in the English version) is a brilliant pilot who used to work for the Italian Air Force. He is a classic maverick figure – a loner, an outsider, a rebel, but also with a warm and friendly side which comes out when he lowers his defences. He is a classic gruff, heroic character, who often grunts rather than talks, and he smokes continuously (another link to Miyazaki-san himself).

In opting out of everyday society – the island retreat couldn't be more clear (a man on an island) – Marco Pagott may also be withdrawn in other ways. He's not a depressive personality, but his situation can appear like the withdrawals of depression. Don't let the sunny *mise-en-scène* of *Porco Rosso* mask the downbeat elements. Marco isn't only the 'reluctant hero' of conventional narratives, he doesn't want to be a part of the ordinary world at all. Yet he also knows that he can't get by without it – and he needs the real world out there to make a living.

Note how, though he lives on an island in the Adriatic, he also has two vital communication links to the outside world: a telephone and a radio. Both devices have a key function in the film, narratively, delivering exposition and also calls for help. But they also link Marco to the outside world to the point where he can't ignore it.

---

[17] The name Ghibli is linked to a plane and the Italian Air Force, and it also means the 'hot wind' that blows across the Sahara.
[18] Seaplanes crop up again in *The Wind Rises*.

But Marco Pagott has turned into a bounty hunter – he won't shift his butt unless the price is right. His initial response to the phone call, as he suns himself in his deckchair at the beginning of the film, is to negotiate a price. Only when the caller mentions that children have been taken hostage does Rosso decide to act (yeah, and his price goes up).

Because, on the face of it, Rosso's life seems idyllic: he's first seen lying back in a deckchair on a beach under a hot sun. That is a fantasy for many people: it's a vacation dream (and surely a dream for the filmmaker, Hayao Miyazaki – some wine, some cigarettes, music on the radio, warm sun, an island hideaway and a plane nearby). He seems to have few worries (but that is also part of his dilemma: he may have nothing to worry about, but he also has *no one* to worry about. His solitude cannot last, because he can't be a complete human being if he remains alone. That's partly what Fio and Gina do – they remind Marco that to be fully human, one must be with people, one cannot hide away).

Porco Rosso contains one of the coolest hideaways in cinema – Marco holes up on a small, uninhabited island in the Adriatic. That's cool enough on its own, but Hayao Miyazaki and the designers Yoshitsu Hisamura and Katsu Hisamura have fashioned an idyllic, hidden cove, open to the sun, but enclosed by cliffs. There's a sandy beach, a tent, an umbrella, a chair, a table, a radio, some wine and some cigarettes (a small building nearby suggests the site has been occupied some years ago, maybe by pirates). And Porco Rosso has his famous, red seaplane moored right next to the beach. It's perfect. It's where every kid would love to hide away if they were an ace pilot in the 1920s.

And of course the first time that Porco Rosso is introduced, it is relaxing in the sun in his island hide-out, with his feet up, a magazine over his face, with the radio playing music.[19] This serene vacation scene cannot continue, of course: pretty soon, Rosso receives a telephone call about some damsels in distress which he has to go rescue (in this case, five year-old girls). That scene depicts Rosso as a heroic pilot – he's not only a gruff, cynical bounty hunter who only works when the price is right. He goes to save a bunch of children.

The second totally fabulous setting in *Porco Rosso* is Hotel Adriano, Gina's hotel and restaurant: a beauty shot depicts the small, rocky island after sunset, with Porco

---

[19] Porco Rosso sports a baggy flying suit for much of the film, complete with cap and goggles.

Rosso's plane landing and riding up to it. It has high, stone walls, a 19th century exterior and some jetties for boats and seaplanes. It was probably built as a private getaway for some millionaire. The Hotel Adriano is the ultimate in exotic eateries – it has the same narrative function as the diner, bar or hamburger joint in American movies (as a watering-hole scene), but it's way classier.[20]

The setting of *Porco Rosso* is once again the alternative universe of Hayao Miyazaki's other works, but very close to the real Europe of the 1920s-1930s (the date 1929 can be seen on the magazine, *Cinema*, that Pagott has over his face in his introduction scene. The *manga Hikoutei Jidai* had been set in Summer, 1929). That puts *Porco Rosso* into a precise, historical context, quite different from any of Miyazaki's other movies (O, 93) – up to *The Wind Rises*. This time it's not 'somewhere in Europe', but the Adriatic and not too far from Italy. It has been identified as maybe near Rijeka in Croatia, Dovrok City, and the Croatian islands. (Miyazaki shifted the location from the former Yugoslavia when war broke out there during production).

Hayao Miyazaki teams Porco Rosso up with a young woman, Fio (who just happens to be an engineer, otherwise the pig wouldn't take her along – most of Miyazaki's heroes are very practical). Fio acts not only as Pagott's buddy, but as his conscience, his heart – Fio represents his spirit, what he's fighting for (a key line of dialogue is Marco's remark that Fio reminds him that she is an aspect of humanity is worth fighting for).

Fio is portrayed as a 17 year-old woman, idealistic, energetic, hard-working. She has bushy, ginger hair, tied back in a single bunch (a recurring motif in Hayao Miyazaki's cinema). She wears a check shirt, pants pulled below the knee, red stripey socks, and an apron. Yet again it's the attractive tomboy in *animé*, a girl who's great with machines.

Fio is also a helluva worker: when Porco Rosso arrives with his plane, she is quick to back in the truck, and happily gets the plane off the truck on her own. When the deal is made between Pagott and Piccolo, aided by Fio's enthusiastic contributions, Fio stays up all night to design Pagott's new plane at the drawing board (it's an idealized image of the dead keen film animator, who will work through the night to get a scene finished before the director comes in the next morning).

---

[20] In the real world, it would be 100s of bucks a night and booked up years in advance.

Fio is not Porco Rosso's lover, however[21] – that is Gina, who runs a hotel and restaurant on an island in the Adriatic. The love relationship of Pagott and Gina is a wistful, nostalgic one, a love affair of separation, love from afar: Marco seldom lands and meets Gina; he is the drifter, someone always on the move, the man who won't be tied down. But of course he carries a candle for her, and she for him.

The love relationship of Rosso and Gina is depicted in flashback, with Gina as a young girl. The concept of the spell is introduced in the intimate scene where Rosso is eating alone upstairs in the restaurant and Gina joins him. Here we find out that Gina has lost another husband to combat (she has a thing for pilots, and has lost three, no less).

In the dinner scene, Gina refers to a photograph, with the young Gina surrounded by four pilots standing in front of a plane, of course – three are now dead. It's also the only photograph of Marco (taken in 1912) as a human (his face has been scribbled over, presumably by Marco; Gina tells him to leave the photo alone, as it's the only one she has left of him).

Gina is a terrific character – clearly modelled on Hollywood stars of the 1930s and 1940s – such as Lauren Bacall, Rita Hayworth and Mary Astor (Hayao Miyazaki was a fan of Bacall – who isn't? She's divine!). Rita Hayworth singing "Put the Blame On Mame" in *Gilda* (1946), one of the hottest moment in all cinema, is another affinity. Gina is very slim, sexy, and classy; she wears a dark purple evening dress (the same colour as Kiki's witch's dress), lipstick and eye shadow.

Gina runs the Hotel Adriano and the restaurant alone; and she's a chanteuse, too, singing in a setting redolent of countless movies of the 1930s and 1940s,[22] where, as Woody Allen said in *Radio Days*, everyone seemed to live in penthouses and hang out in classy nightclubs and restaurants. Older women are a recurring ingredient in Hayao Miyazaki's cinema, as are mothers (to a lesser extent), but not single, mature and ostentatiously sexual women.

(The relationship between Porco and Gina recalls that of Bogart and Bacall in *To Have and Have Not* – Gina is an independent woman who can fend for herself, like Bacall's Slim, and Rosso is very much the gruff, tough, laconic hero in the

---

[21] Earlier concepts of *Porco Rosso* had Marco lusting after Fio.
[22] The song, 'Le Temps de Cerises' (*The Time of Cherries*, lyrics: J.B. Clement, music: A. Renard), is the Communards' anthem, about the Paris Commune (C, 99). As well as Lauren Bacall and Rita Hayworth, the song in *Porco Rosso* also evokes Marilyn Monroe in *The River of No Return* (Otto Preminger, 1954), when she sings 'I'm Going To File My Claim'. The voice of Gina was Tokiko Kato, a famous Japanese singer (and environmental activist), she also sang the song.

Humphrey Bogart mode. Like Slim, Gina is surrounded by guys who admire her, and look at her longingly. And Gina can effortlessly tame them, even though they are hardened gangsters and pirates: when she approaches them in her bar, they crumple into little boys).

As Gina sings[23] there's a beautiful montage of images of Porco Rosso flying his red seaplane to Hotel Adriano: a perfect, golden sunset, and an exquisite long shot of the hotel on its island in a deep blue sky (facing away from the sun), with the plane approaching from behind the camera, leaving a wake of white foam. And when the Red Pig moors his plane at a jetty (tipping the guy at the quay, a nice detail), he notices Curtis's blue sea-plane, the *Rattlesnake*.

Donald Curtis is Porco Rosso's rival – a classic flyboy Yank character (who's also a rival for Gina's affection, although Gina's pretty clear that Curtis hasn't got a chance. As she tells him, when he approaches her in the Hotel Adriano's garden, love is more complicated in Europe than it is in the U.S.A. Gina swiftly and easily laughs away Curtis's claim over her).

Piccolo is a short guy wearing a cap and spectacles: for no explained reason, he is characterized as a mole, with a wide mouth and whiskers. He is portrayed as a wily engineer and businessman – and he's quite happy to have his granddaughter Fio design Rosso's new plane, and to have it built by an all-female crew.

It's significant, perhaps, that neither Gina nor Porco Rosso have children. That is a movie convention, of course, where many filmmakers prefer to have their heroes and heroines able to dive into all sorts of situations, without bringing along their kids. If you're flying planes in dogfights or escaping from the Italian militia, it's simply better not to have kids tagging along. (And Gina, though married three times, doesn't have children.)

The 1992 film, though, does give Marco Pagott children: Fio is a surrogate daughter, and she regards Porco Rosso as something of a surrogate father. (Where are Fio's parents? Piccolo says that the men have left the country to look for work, which accounts for Fio's pa, or maybe he also died in the First World War, but Fio's mother isn't shown either). The potential sexual issues that might arise between Marco and Fio are undercut immediately when Fio is introduced by Piccolo warning Rosso to keep his distance from Fio. There is a hint, though, that Fio idolizes Marco a little, and is maybe

---

23 Tokiko Kato, the voice of Gina, sang the song.

partly in love with him (an element of the romantic attraction of being a pilot which's part of the aerial combat genre).

Meanwhile, Porco Rosso is a reluctant surrogate father to Fio: certainly he grows to feel very protective of her. And the 1992 movie also gives Rosso another set of children – the group of kids that Rosso rescues from the pirates. (Note, for instance, how it seems to be the fact that the Mamma Aiuto gang have kidnapped some young children that galvanizes Rosso into action when he receives the telephone call at the beginning of the picture).

There's an an engaging playfulness about the Fio-Rosso relationship, which kicks in after Rosso has accepted that Fio will design his new plane. The antagonism is never serious (until Fio decides that she will be coming along with Pagott), and there are some amusing details depicting Fio getting the better of the world-weary, seen-it-all-before seaplane pilot (like when she winks at him at the table during Mr Piccolo's prayer). Porco has a particular view of Fio – somewhat old-fashioned, and sexist, too – that she's (1) a young kid, and (2) a woman. The script plays around with the age and gender elements many times.

Porco Rosso is full of memorable images and sequences (like all of Hayao Miyazaki's pictures). The very moving scene of the air force pilots flying up to heaven was inspired by Roald Dahl, one of the great 20th century authors for children (and also a pilot himself). It comes from *They Shall Not Grow Old*, from *Over To You: Ten Stories of Flyers and Flying* (1946).[24]

In that scene, lines of aircraft climb gently up to the heavens, while Porco Rosso struggles with the controls, half-way between life and death. He's been in the worst dog-fight of his life, during a reconnaissance mission in World War One. At the end of the dogfight, with three German planes on his tail, he falls unconscious – but his plane flies itself. The aircraft enters a cloud, and rises through a white mist (and, once again, the cloud is portrayed like water, as if the plane is rising from the ocean). It is a white prairie, extending to the horizon. Far above, there is a long, long line of aircraft, flying up to (or maybe in) heaven. A closer view shows the aircraft to include British, French, Italian and German planes. And there are thousands of them.

The music is one of the indicators of how this sequence

---

24 However, Miyazaki is not so fond of Dahl's stories for children, which remain very popular.

should be interpreted: during the dogfight, which might be a spectacular action scene, a melancholy and soft piano and strings cue is employed (and the camera stays back for part of the scene, showing a very long shot of the planes weaving in and out of each other). But when Rosso flies upwards into the white cloud, the music shifts to electronic washes of sound, including synthesized choral effects, which emphasize the unreality of the scene: it is not meant to be realistic at all: it is a scene about death, about dying in combat.

The scene also depicts Porco Rosso as a true hero – he knows that Berlini has just married Gina (two days earlier, and Rosso was best man), and he wants Berlini to be saved, for Gina, and death to take him instead. (Sacrifice is one of the hallmarks of heroes). Needless to say, the scene depicts Marco Pagott in his human guise.

It is another example of the genius of Hayao Miyazaki and his team in taking on a serious subject – death in war – and rendering it in animation. Miyazaki's movies are a constant and vivid reminder that animation can tackle the most serious issues of the day. This sombre tone reflected what was happening at the time in the former Yugoslavia (in the early 1990s); the film had been conceived as lighter in tone, but the war in Eastern Europe persuaded Miyazaki and his team to go for a more serious mood.[25] And later, the Iraq War would influence *Howl's Moving Castle*.

Critics (such as Helen McCarthy) have suggested that there isn't a villain in *Porco Rosso*. That's true – well, not the conventional movie villain who goes around killing people and blowing things up. The Mamma Aiuto gang aren't true movie villains – they are rivals for Rosso's business, but they are more like buffoons than mobsters (that's portrayed in the first scenes, which show the gang's seaplane being overrun by five year-old girls).

No, the villains of the piece are really the Italian Air Force and the Italian government: they are the ones who are hunting for Rosso when he enters Italy to fix his seaplane, they are the ones who are spying on him, and try to shoot his plane down as he escapes from Milan. And it's clear that Rosso regards the Italian government as moving too far towards fascism ('better a pig than a fascist,' he tells his friend Ferralin). There are anti-fascist and pro-republican images and references in *Porco Rosso*.

---

[25] Other filmmakers responded to the crisis in the Balkans, including, memorably, Jean-Luc Godard in his film *Notre Musique* (2001).

And the event that haunts all of *Porco Rosso* is the First World War: war is really the main problem, because *Porco Rosso* is set in 1929, when the full-blown rise of fascism in Europe was only a few years away. Rosso recognizes this, and chooses to opt out of the whole political mess. It is the epoch itself that is difficult or even evil, with Europe sliding towards another great war, after barely recovering from the last one. So Rosso simply doesn't want to be a part of that world, even though he finds himself being drawn into it.

Some of the memorable sections of *Porco Rosso* are where Marco Pagott is travelling around the Adriatic and Italy. The sequence, for instance, where he travels to Italy with his smashed-up aircraft: there are scenes of Rosso on a cargo ship, sitting next to his plane under its tarpaulin, and smoking. Or on a train, with the plane tied down to a flatbed truck.

And when the plane is repaired and on its way, there's a scene where Rosso and Fio refuel the plane on a quiet, hot, sunny coast (with a youth[26] who rows out to the plane carrying fuel in barrels).

I've always really liked these interludes or linking sequences that Hayao Miyazaki and his teams put into their movies. They are gentler, not action-filled, but add some evocative atmospheres and textures to the film. And *Porco Rosso* is a wonderful movie for moods and textures.

And it's cool the way Porco Rosso knows everybody by name, as if he's Humphrey Bogart[27] or James Cagney, and has been around that area for years. Critic Mark Schilling remarked that *Porco Rosso* is 'mock-Hemingway pretentious, with Porco as a mucho macho Papa figure' (1992). Oh no, it isn't like that. (Though the macho Hemingwayesque, Bogartian elements are definitely in there, consciously so.)

Porco Rosso takes his plane to Milan to be repaired (by an all-female engineering crew), at the Piccolo S.p.A. aircraft company. The workers all turn out to be relatives of Piccolo's large extended family (a joke on the big families of Mediterranean countries). Fio is his seventeen year-old granddaughter.

Porco Rosso is doubtful at first, he doesn't think the local women will be able to build his plane: Mr Piccolo reassuring Pagott that the women are good workers is a classic example

---

[26] The boy exclaims, when he sees Fio – wow, a girl riding a war plane! (It's a Miyazakian dream come true!).
[27] In the scene where Marco goes to a secret rendezvous with his friend Ferralin in the theatre, the pig wears a hat and trenchcoat exactly like Humphrey Bogart. He might have stepped out of *The Big Sleep*.

of Hayao Miyazaki's feminism (which was reflected in his views on the women who work on his films). (Notice too how some of the women are consciously drawn to look like Gina, to remind Pagott of her).

It's touching (and right) that when the women arrive to sign on to build Porco Rosso's plane, the first thing they do is to get the pots and pans out and cook a big meal (of spaghetti, of course), rather than going straight into starting work on the plane. It's one of those things that groups of artists sometimes do before embarking on an enterprise like putting on a theatre show (or making a movie). And it's quite right that Rosso should tuck in immediately, until he looks round to see the women waiting while Mr Piccolo offers a short prayer (and the prayer itself has a political slant to it, when Mr Piccolo mentions that Rosso's commission has saved the company from bankruptcy – *Porco Rosso* was made in the early 1990s, a time of global recession).

Workshops of one sort or another are a recurring motif in Hayao Miyazaki's cinema – clearly evoking the animation studio (and Studio Ghibli) itself, but also the co-operative spirit. In *Spirited Away* the workers band together to help the River God, for instance, and in *Porco Rosso* the workers build a plane, just like the animation team puts together a film. And Marco, walking around and smoking and watching the women at work, recalls the film director (and perhaps Miyazaki himself) over-seeing his/ her film crew working.[28] (In those scenes, Rosso is not the driving force: he has commissioned the project, but he is not wholly in control of it. He has to stand back and watch other people do the work.)

In response to criticism about the treatment of women in *Porco Rosso* and the implied anti-feminism, Hayao Miyazaki replied that Gina is an appealing character because

> she is trying to be herself; even in a man-dominated society, she tries to express her own feelings and wishes. Even under difficult circumstances, a woman can express herself if she's strong, and I think Gina is like that.[29]

Some of the key personnel on *Porco Rosso* were women,

---

[28] Some of the women on the Studio Ghibli production team thought that the representation of women in *Porco Rosso* could also hint at the exploitation of women, rather than pro-feminism, because it was still Piccolo who was in charge. The boss was male, the client was male, and the product – a plane – was distinctly masculine. However, the project is overseen by a woman, Fio, and she later on becomes the president of Piccolo S.p.A.
[29] Quoted in H. McCarthy, 1999.

including the colour designer, supervising animator and art director.

One of the great set-pieces in *Porco Rosso* is the breakneck, hair's-breadth escape from Milan (right out of *Lupin III*): the Italian government spies are lurking outside, and start firing as soon as the women shove open the aircraft hangar doors and the plane emerges (as dawn breaks). Once the rebuilt seaplane is on the water, there's a fantastic chase along the canals of Milan, with the heavies shooting at the plane, the aircraft making a turn to miss a barge, lifting off the water to avoid another barge, and eventually pulling up, just missing one of the bigger bridges. It is a textbook chase and action sequence, just about impossible to do in live-action (and difficult to achieve with models too – it's got high speed and water, tricky elements to make convincing. And CGI? Well, that's animation too, but with a photorealist finish).

It's a scene which animation can achieve with eye-popping results: narratively, it's simply an extension of the truck chase a few minutes earlier, when Rosso and Fio were followed by the government spies in a car, and Rosso forced them to crash.[30] But although the Milan escape scene doesn't add much to the 1992 movie in terms of plot or story, it does deliver a breathtaking slice of action. (And there is some plot information, if you want it: to avoid the first slow-moving canal barge, Rosso struggles with the controls, until Fio tells him to use the new devices, the tabs, which she's installed. That piece of information – and the device itself – saves them from crashing).

The Milan in *Porco Rosso* is not the tourist Milan of the Cathedral, the piazzas, Leonardo da Vinci's *The Last Supper*, etc. It is a heavily industrial area, with canals, barges, bridges, factories, warehouses, and plenty of chimneys. Only later, during the spectacular escape, is the rest of Milan glimpsed (but not the Duomo). And this is an idealized Milan, quite a bit more spectacular than the real Milan – at least along the river, which features a series of fabulous bridges.

Hayao Miyazaki described *Porco Rosso* as a movie made for adults, while his other films have been aimed at children. I'd say rather than all of Miyazaki's films, or certainly his feature animated films, can play to multiple audiences. They

---

[30] That chase is pure spy adventure stuff, with the black car tailing the truck until Rosso tries to out-manœuvre the goons with some wild cornering and a rapid U-turn (he drives a truck like he flies his plane). Notice how Rosso has Fio scoot over, so that he can be driving the truck when the chase begins.

can dazzle viewers of any age. But *Porco Rosso* does appear more 'grown-up' in some respects – the age of the hero, for instance: the Crimson Pig is definitely not one of Miyazaki's young, idealistic hero/ines. He's no ten or twelve year-old. He is very distinctly a world-weary guy, someone who's been around, someone who lives by a code of bounty hunting and cynicism, though his noble side does come out too. (And his romantic side – as Helen McCarthy explained, he 'has a deeply romantic nature and old-fashioned, chivalrous view of women – which Fio and Gina both find infuriating' [2002, 168]).

That's partly why this middle-aged, seen-it-all-before guy is paired with Fio, an impossibly charming, enthusiastic – and very talented – engineer. Part of her function is to remind this old cynic about having ideals and hopes. Fio is unfailingly optimistic, and unflaggingly energetic, while Porco says just looking at her tires him out (when Mr Piccolo warns Porco not to touch her – several times).

The love relationship in *Porco Rosso* is not the idealistic romance of youth, too: both Gina and Pagott have been with other people (well, you can presume Porco has. But, on his island, he has retreated from love too). The only time they are really together, on their own, is at Hotel Adriano, when Gina joins Pagott as he's eating. Pagott doesn't keep to Gina's promise of joining her in the garden at Hotel Adriano – he stays away.

However, he does fly over her garden, his way of saying hello. That is the film's true love scene, and it's typical that the love scene in a Hayao Miyazaki movie is once again a flying scene! You don't need to know anything about Sigmund Freud to understand what's going on here – how Porco Rosso shows off his big, red plane, doing loop-the-loops, and circling Hotel Adriano in one of Miyazaki's most spectacular flying sequences. Who needs a sex scene when you've got animation this good?[31]

And notice the timing of the flying/ love scene: it comes just as Donald Curtis has sneaked into Gina's garden, to propose marriage to Gina. It's quite correct, dramatically, that Gina should rebuff Curtis *before* Porco Rosso's makes his appearance, and it's entirely apt that Rosso should trump his rival for Gina's affection. It's right too that Curtis should witness Gina's warm feelings for Rosso, which adds to his motives for competing with Rosso in the skies.

---

[31] Once again, Joe Hisaishi and the orchestra provide the vital ingredient to the scene – a lovely, romantic melody the starts on flute then is backed by strings.

Porco Rosso is glimpsed as his true self, as Marco Pagott, in a couple of scenes: in the very moving nighttime sequence, where Rosso tells Fio his story of the dogfight and nearly dying, and Fio sees him for a moment as a middle-aged guy with a moustache, checking the bullets by lamplight, when he lets down his guard[32] (and in the flashback itself).[33] In the second scene, at the end of the movie, Curtis sees Porco in his human guise.

And both those scenes are related to the fairy tale kiss: after Fio's kissed him, he's seen as his former self (at the end), and just before she kisses him on the island. It seems that Rosso can change back into appearing as a regular human – maybe only at night (he only visits Gina and the Hotel Adriano at night).

But it's a great touch that the spell on Porco isn't really explained[34] – what did he do to become a pig (or what was done to him)? Was it because he should have died in the First World War, and not his friend, Berlini? If so, who put the spell on him? Or was it self-imposed? That makes more sense: Marco does seems to be someone who is a little disgusted with himself. He has moved away from being human partly because he has lost faith in himself, perhaps, and in humanity. It was World War One, presumably, which finally shattered Marco's ideals and hopes and dreams (the war does seem to be the time in which Marco became a pig-man. The 1914-18 War could be interpreted as proof that humans are utterly stupid. And a second world war was only 20 years away).[35]

It is suggested in *The Art of Porco Rosso* book that it was Marco Pagott who made himself into a pig-man, as a kind of penance. The event is told in a flashback on the island, when Fio begs for a story. But instead of explaining what happened

---

32 Fio is lying on the beach in her sleeping bag, and Marco is sitting at his little table, checking the bullets he's bought. Like a child who can't sleep, Fio asks Marco to tell her a story. When he's seen as a human, Marco is not the portly size he is as a pig-man.
33 Fio says her father was in the same squadron as Marco Pagott.
34 Miyazaki remarked: 'when a man becomes middle-aged, he becomes a pig'.
35 For Miyazaki, war corrupts the souls and hearts of people, no matter what ideals they start out with.

with the curse or spell, the film leaves it ambiguous.[36] Fio is convinced that Rosso is a good man, though, and she leaps up from her sleeping bag to throw her arms around him and kiss him. That is the close of the scene: Rosso is startled by Fio's reaction, but her idealism and optimism and faith are beginning to work on him. (He tells her she helps to restore his faith in humanity).

Pigs of course have all sorts of negative connotations, some political and ideological – satirical cartoons of the Nazis, or Josef Stalin and KGB officers, for instance, sometimes portray them as pigs. The greedy capitalist in America and Europe is routinely caricatured as a pig (usually in top hat and tails, smoking a cigar). In the negative view, pigs snuffle around at ground level, live in their own waste, etc.[37]

In traditional symbolism, the pig or swine connotes gluttony, greed, anger, lust and dirt, as well as fertility and prosperity. The Goddess of ancient times was linked to the sow, with lunar and sky symbolism. In Buddhism, the pig represents ignorance and greed. In Celtic mythology, the pig is one of the symbols of the Celtic Goddess Cerridwen. In Christianity, pigs are associated with gluttony and sensuality, and Satan. In Greek mythology, pigs were sacrificed to Ceres and Demeter as fertility goddesses. The sow was sacred to Zeus, who was suckled by a sow. And so on.

So making the hero a pig-man is quite different from, say, making him a wolf-man, or a bug-man, or a bird-man. For Hayao Miyazaki, the pig isn't wholly negative. Miyazaki said he had wanted to have a film with a pig in the lead role for many years (there are pig motifs at his studio).

The pig caricature fits in with the notion of the main character as a middle-aged man who has become disillusioned with life, who has let go of his dreams and ideals, who is no longer the dashing hero of youth. As Hayao Miyazaki explained:

---

[36] Miyazaki said once that Marco became a pig when he couldn't resolve the conflicts between personal and social duties and desires: he intended to marry Gina, but she was living on an island, part of an enemy country during the First World War (Austria), so he declined. 'As a military officer, he could not bring himself to marry an enemy national. Torn between his loyalty to his home country and his love for Gina, he chose his country.' After witnessing the deaths of his companions in the war, 'including that of his best friend (Gina's husband), he started wondering about the meaning of his actions, and the meaning of flying and dying for his country. Unable to resolve the conflicts in his mind, he became a pig.'

[37] The pig-man was intended to embody some of Miyazaki's ideas about humanity – about humans being foolish, not divine.

I'm disgusted by the notion that man is the ultimate being, chosen by God. But I believe that there are things in this world that are beautiful, that are important, that are worth striving for. I made the hero a pig because that was what best suited these feelings of mine. (1993)

That is one of the primary roles for Fio and Gina in the film: to re-humanize Porco Rosso, to remind him that he was once Marco Pagott, and is not a bad man.

And it's terrific too that the filmmakers keep Porco Rosso's fate ambiguous to the end: although Donald Curtis sees Rosso as a human, there is no scene of the curse being lifted. (Or maybe there *is* a hint at the spell being broken, because Rosso has now 'done the right thing' – sent Fio off with Gina, and planning to draw off the Italian Air Force).

The 1992 film's romantic story also ends on a wistful and ambiguous note: Gina has been waiting for Porco Rosso to land and visit her in the garden. That's the time when they would marry. But instead of returning with her and Fio to Hotel Adriano, Rosso retains his independence, and puts Fio on the plane with Gina.

The ending of *Porco Rosso* is narrated in voiceover by Fio: as well as describing her own fate (now she is president of the Piccolo aircraft company, overseeing a prototype jet plane),[38] she relates that it's a secret whether Gina and Porco Rosso finally got together. That's left up to the audience – but the final shot in the film is the garden at Hotel Adriano, a paradisal image, and the site of the courtship, if it occurs (perhaps Rosso's red seaplane can be glimpsed at the other end of the garden in the fly-over shot).

The climax of the 1992 Japanese movie is a duel in the air and the water between Porco Rosso and Donald Curtis. It's a giant, spectacular scene, a festival on an island organized by the Mamma Aiuto gang (and fellow outlaws) in the Adriatic. It has the festive air of a championship race or a wrestling match. A big bag of money (to cover Porco Rosso's debts) on the one side, and Fio on the other (the two bets are placed on chairs on the platform). But the fight is also about Gina, of course, with Curtis irritated that he's been rejected in favour of Rosso. And pride, too – the pride of being the best pilot in the Adriatic Sea.

---

[38] Fio is seen flying the white jet (so she's become a pilot herself, perhaps with some training or hints from Marco) over Hotel Adriano. The jet was modelled on a real Italian aircraft, the Caproni C-22J, designed by Carlo Ferranin.

The sequence is milked by the filmmakers for every ounce of build-up and suspense and action – and comedy. There are numerous comic gags here, such as the gangsters firing guns into the restless audience to quieten them down (and chucking in a bomb).[39]

As well as the climactic battle itself, the filmmakers also add further suspense elements – such as the imminent arrival of the Italian Air Force, with Gina rushing to the island to tell everybody. That is a classic scriptwriting device of linking the duel to larger (political) issues.

In its set-up and the action and the pay-off, it is a traditional (and Hollywoodesque) sequence, but the spin on it is totally Miyazaki's own, the filmmaking team's own, Studio Ghibli's own. You've seen fights before, you've seen aerial battles before, you've seen crowds of extras gathered at some festival scene, but not quite like this.

The dogfight itself is about as splendid as Hayao Miyazaki and his teams have ever got in terms of aerial action scenes.[40] It is a loving and detailed recreation not of movies, but of real planes making complex manœuvres in the sky.[41] As well as choosing some awe-inspiring camera angles and movements, the filmmakers have also used the sea, with large, blue waves sweeping below the planes, as a significant ingredient (these are both seaplanes, after all).

In some of the dogfight scenes, the filmmakers allow the planes to drop down out of the frame, without moving the camera, and wait for them to fly back into the frame. Many another filmmaker wouldn't allow an empty shot, and would probably cut to another angle (especially in an action scene).

Of course, being the hero, Porco Rosso can't behave in the expected manner in a big, climactic fight: instead, he tries to encourage Donald Curtis to use up all of his ammo, by flying close to the waves, where he's more difficult to hit. And Pagott is the nobler fighter of the two, as well: when he has Curtis in his sights, when he's on his tail, he opts not to shoot, because he might kill Curtis (he wants to wait until he can hit the engine, not the pilot). Curtis, meanwhile, is the all-out

---

39 A call-back to the Dola gang in *Laputa*.
40 There are two dogfights between Donald Curtis and Porco Rosso: in the first, Curtis bests Rosso, and shoots his engine and plane up, forcing Rosso to ditch his plane (but he has time, flying out of Curtis's sight below a cloud, to pull it up a beach and hide it under a tree, on a small island). In the second dogfight, at the climax, Rosso gets the better of Curtis, by hanging onto his tail (in classic dogfight style), but withholding his gunfire, because he doesn't want to hurt Curtis.
41 'It is difficult beyond imagination to aim at a target that is moving in three-dimensional space in an irregular manner from a moving aircraft and shoot to destroy it. It is impossible without having an immense talent for it' (TP, 177).

villain, who's trying to shoot down the Crimson Pig any which way.

In any decent Errol Flynn-style fight, or a martial arts duel, there has to be a few moments when the opponents yell insults at each other. This is comically depicted in *Porco Rosso* when the pig and the Yank shout at one other as they fly together, then hurl spanners.[42]

Eventually, the duellers (and the audience below) are exhausted, and the seaplanes land. Then follows a good, old fist fight, in the traditional, Hollywood manner – it might be Clark Gable or John Wayne here. Except the staging of it occurs in the water, another touch that takes the scene into a slightly different area.

As the men slog away at each other, falling into the ocean, they become pulpier and bloodier, losing teeth and gaining bruises. It's caricature, but it fits – you can go this over-the-top towards the end of a movie (if the audience are going to carp about 'realism' now, they've completely missed the point).

They hurl insults at each other still, but now they're much slower and close to collapsing from exhaustion. It's sweet the way that Fio encourages Porco Rosso in his corner in this *Raging Bull* fight.[43] There's not the slightest twinge of girlie reluctance about the violence of the fight – Fio urges Rosso to beat the hell out of Curtis (and, after all, if Rosso loses, Fio'll be married to Curtis).

The sucker punch comes not from Donald Curtis's fist, though, but his generous (though grudgingly given) statement that Gina really wants – and loves – Porco Rosso, not him. Of course Rosso doesn't believe him (they're in the midst of a vicious fight), but some sort of realization does get through eventually.

HOLLYWOOD CINEMA.

There's a scene in a theatre in Milan, where Porco Rosso arranges to meet his buddy from the Italian Air Force. And what do Hayao Miyazaki and his team chose to have playing on the screen? An animated film, of course – it's clearly meant to be a nod to *Gertie the Dinosaur* (Windsor McCay, 1914) (though it's the animators' version of it), and to the Fleischer Studio (in particular, the character of Betty Boop). And to early Disney shorts. And Rosso and Ferralin comment that the movie stinks, but then they get to like it (well, Ferralin does).

---

42 And anything else they can grab (after both their guns jam).
43 There's even a chair placed in the ocean.

Significantly, the film-within-a-film ends with a kiss between the heroes (the Betty Boop character and the pilot character): the film is a commentary on *Porco Rosso*, and Marco, of course, and in particular on Pagott's role as heroic pilot, and the romantic plot[44] (and it reminds us that *Porco Rosso* is very much a movie-movie, a movie about other movies).

Another cinema reference occurs in the character of Donald Curtis. Of anyone in *Porco Rosso*, Curtis is perhaps the most clichéd: he is the stereotypical American, a cowboy of the skies: loud, brash, bold, patronizing, naïve, dim and somewhat obnoxious. He's John Wayne or Clark Cable to Porco Rosso's Humphrey Bogart (and it's clear which one the film favours). Curtis thinks he's cool, but he isn't: Porco Rosso is. Curtis tries too hard, does too much. Whereas Rosso is an image of effortless cool, the kind of cool that some people have without trying.

So, after he's been spurned by Gina in the garden, and he and Porco Rosso have had their big fight, Donald Curtis goes back to the United States of America to become what he told Gina he would be: a big movie star (in the garden, he tells Gina that he has already written a film script, and has a film studio interested). He even brags he might be President! An actor as U.S. President! This particular storyline pays off in the final scenes, when a poster for Curtis's first movie (entitled *Triple Love*) is shown: of course he's playing a rugged hero, with his gal by his side (and in the background, improbably, is a dinosaur, a reference perhaps to *King Kong*, and, more correctly, the kind of movies Hollywood was making in the 1950s, not the 1930s).

Although it's not immediately obvious, if you only watch the English language version of *Porco Rosso*, but the film is primarily about Italians: Fio, Piccolo, Gina, the gangs and Porco Rosso himself are all Italian (Rosso was born in Genoa).[45] Donald Curtis is very American. Like other English language versions of Hayao Miyazaki's prepared by the Disney Studios in California, mainly American voice talents were used. But this is a European movie – a Japanese interpretation of a European story. The setting is Italy and Croatia and the Adriatic Sea, and the great event that haunts the picture is the First World War. (Ultimately, of course, it's a profoundly *Japanese* movie).

---

44 There are some really fun images of the children in the audience reacting to the picture, ranging from delight to fear and hiding their eyes.
45 The film opens with a teleprinter in different languages (Japanese, Chinese, English, Italian, Arabic, Russian, etc) offering some exposition.

THE MAMMA AIUTO GANG.

The Mamma Aiuto gang are some of the rivals for Porco Rosso and his work. As *Porco Rosso* explains, the Adriatic Sea has succumbed to the tyranny of pirates, who regularly raid ships. This's depicted in the opening sequence, with the Mamma Aiuto gang raiding a ship, including taking a bunch of young children as hostages.

The Mamma Aiuto crew, though, are not serious rivals for Porco Rosso, nor are they to be taken wholly seriously. For a start, they are depicted in the broad, comic manner of Hayao Miyazaki's other films: a bunch of guys who are actually more like buffoons, only barely kept in check by the gang boss. And when the children are taken on board, they cause havoc – a delightful scene, which contains many humourous gags.

When the Mamma Aiuto gang's seaplane is airborne, there is another dogfight, which mirrors the one at the end of the film: Porco Rosso triumphs in both, of course. The scene demonstrates that Rosso is a feared and brilliant pilot, that everyone knows him, and that he's the hero who saves a group of children.

The sequence also emphasizes that *Porco Rosso* is going to be a picture largely about men, what men do, men getting into fights, men and their machines, and brotherhoods of men (the gangs, but also the Italian Air Force, a gang on a governmental, military scale). Indeed, there are only two significant women in *Porco Rosso*, Fio and Gina – though there are secondary characters, such as the three crones at Piccolo's factory, and the large group of women who re-build Porco Rosso's seaplane. (But the inclusion of the young children in the opening scenes indicate that although men and machines and guns and macho competitions are central to the movie, it is also for children, and children are also part of this world).

FLYING

The films of Hayao Miyazaki are rivalled only by the *Star Wars* movies for the sheer number – and variety – of flying craft. Aeroplanes are a favourite, as they are in the films of Steven Spielberg, particularly older planes, bi-planes, and seaplanes. Propeller-powered planes of all kinds. But there are also gliders (such as the one Nausicaä has), and kites (such as the one that Pazu and Sheeta ride in *Laputa: Castle In the Sky*). There are flaptors or ornithopters (in *Howl's Moving Castle* and *Laputa: Castle In the Sky*). And autogyros (in *The Castle of Cagliostro)*. There are flying castles. There are broomsticks, too, in *Kiki's Delivery Service*. Paper planes in *The Wind Rises*. Airships are another favourite craft.

And many characters fly on their own, without vehicles of any kind: the flying dragons and Yubaba in *Spirited Away*, Howl in *Howl's Moving Castle,* the Cat-bus and Totoro in *My Neighbor Totoro*, and the mermaid in *Ponyo On the Cliff By the Sea*.

Clearly flying and aircraft have a special fascination for Hayao Miyazaki, that goes very deep. Most of his major characters fly at some point or other in his movies. Sometimes they are flying to travel to other places, sometimes to escape from villains, but sometimes just for the pleasure of it. That is emphasized by the cinematic apparatus employed in some of the flying scenes: the big swells of music, the framing and compositions, the sense of movement within the frame, and the rushing wind sound effects.

In a 1979 article in *Animation Monthly*, Hayao Miyazaki spoke about Igor Sikorsky, one of the heroes of aviation: when an engine failed on a flight over Russia, Sigorsky was clambering about the four engine biplane, checking his engines. That's the way people should really fly, Miyazaki said, because they simply yearn to fly (SP, 24).

In traditional symbolism, flight connotes transcendence, escape, the movement into a higher plane of existence, a release from the Earth, from matter, and superhumanity. In Hayao Miyazaki's cinema, flight is not wholly positive; escape is not always the answer. But it is a deep impulse in Miyazaki's characters.

Flying also has its erotic component – the sheer freedom and release. (Sigmund Freud noted that dreams of flying were erotic dreams – but *all* dreams and dreaming for Freud had an erotic element).

Flying is of course one of the hallmarks of archaic shamanism (and shamanism is the origin of all religion). The spiritual flight of the shaman is the central act of shamanism. The shaman travels to other worlds by drumming or dancing her/ himself up into a magical, ecstatic state, and by climbing up the 'World Tree', which is the *axis mundi*. The Cosmic Tree or Column or mountain is the connection between the three realms of Heaven, Earth and Hell.

Flying scenes in Hayao Miyazaki's movies definitely have these shamanic connotations of transcendence, the yearning for a 'magical flight' to other worlds, other states, other modes of being. They are scenes of ecstasy, formed from the ecstasy of the shaman who rises up, spiritually, into the sky.

Archaic shamans dress in feathers, like birds, to emulate and take on the magic of birds, while souls are everywhere in religion associated with birds, and the soul was thought of as covered in feathers. Howl and Yubaba turn into bird-like creatures in Miyazaki's films. As the Romanian historian of religions, Mircea Eliade, explained (in *Shamanism*):

> Birds are psychopomps. Becoming a bird oneself or being accompanied by a bird indicates the capacity, while still alive, to undertake the ecstatic journey to the sky and the beyond. (1972, 98)

As well as flight, the sky is another hugely significant element in Hayao Miyazaki's movies. Every one of Miyazaki's works contains marvellous imagery of skies – his are not films confined to interiors, like some of the films of Yasujiro Ozu or Carl-Theodor Dreyer, for instance. Miyazaki's films are Fresh Air films, they are Big Sky films.[46] If Miyazaki had produced his stories in live-action, you can bet that they would include months of location shooting, in all weathers, like the movies of Akira Kurosawa or Werner Herzog. In live-action, Miyazaki would simply have to get out of the studio.

Ironically, as Hayao Miyazaki has commented, his pictures are actually manufactured by people sitting at desks and easels, indoors. There are location visits, sometimes, for research before starting a film (if the budget allowed for it – usually it doesn't), but the movies are the products of people working indoors for months on end. Maybe *that's why* there are so many open spaces and big skies in Miyazaki's pictures – it's the filmmakers yearning to get outside.

In Hayao Miyazaki's cinema there are not only skies a-plenty, but images of clouds, too, with big, fluffy, white cumulus clouds being a favourite. And the wind, too – from soft breezes that play around the legs to hurricanes. And not forgetting thunder and storms and lightning.

EARLY FLIGHT AND DESIGN.

The flying scenes have 'a beauty beyond mere realism. This is how flying ought to look and feel,' remarked Mark Schilling (1992). One of the aspects of aviation that Hayao Miyazaki's films are so adept at capturing is the early days of powered flight: not the jet age, but the propeller age, the

---

[46] *Porco Rosso* is a unique film in cinema history because it contains probably more images of skies than any other film.

diesel engine age, and the glider age. *Porco Rosso* is partly a hymn to the early aircraft and pilots of aviation's history. The pilots are daredevils and rough and tumble guys. They are heroes to some of the younger generation (the cynicism following two world wars hasn't yet set in).

And *Porco Rosso* is also keen to show the *genius* of design: not for nothing is the movie set partly in Italy, and celebrates Italian design. The Piccolo company is intended to represent not only real companies (such as Piaggio and Caproni),[47] but also the spirit of Italian (and European) industrial design in that period. The age of the aeroplane in *Porco Rosso* is a time when one person could influence aircraft design, when 'a person's intuition, sense, experience, or even passion could have an overall effect on a plane's performance', Miyazaki-san commented (SP, 384). Miyazaki revisited all of this in 2013's *The Wind Rises*.

Having the designer of Porco Rosso's new plane a seventeen year-old woman is a classic Miyazakian touch. And having the plane built entirely by women is another Miyazakian flourish.

That section of the 1992 movie is all about building an aircraft – not just the plane itself, but the *building of it*. Another filmmaker might've cut this section of the movie down considerably (a short, musical montage, say), and zipped straight to the dramatic escape along the canal. But this is a Hayao Miyazaki movie, so there are scenes at the drawing board, discussions of the new design elements that Fio is introducing, remarks about details such as the angle of the wing, conversations about the cost of the whole operation with the boss, Piccolo, and many montage sequences showing the women constructing the aircraft.

There's also a fun sequence where Mr Piccolo reveals the new Folgore engine he's acquired (don't ask how), which's part of the technofetishism in *Porco Rosso*: and how it's going to cream Donald Curtis's plane (it just happens to be the engine that lost to Curtis in the Schneider Cup, but, as Piccolo explains to Rosso, that was because it wasn't mounted right, and wasn't tuned up right. Needless to say, Piccolo prides himself on being the engineer to really refine the engine for maximum performance. You can't teach Buddha Buddhism, he says).

In the following scene, Piccolo demonstrates to Pagott just how good the new engine is going to be: he mounts it on a stand with a prop attached and winds it up; part of the shed's

---

47 Caproni appears as a character in *The Wind Rises*.

tin roof rattles and flies away. The engine (which has the name 'GHIBLI' on it) is crucial: it's one of the chief reasons why Rosso goes to Milan.

FLYING MACHINES.

Hayao Miyazaki is clearly deeply in love with the aircraft in *Porco Rosso*.

> I like that style of aircraft. Although I make films for children, that particular film is really because I wanted to express my love for all those ships. Until finishing *Mononoke Hime*, I felt a little – not really guilty, but that I'd indulged myself in *Porco Rosso*.[48]

Hayao Miyazaki admitted to *Comix Box* magazine that he could quite happily write about aeroplanes for eons. 'The truth is that I am happiest when I am writing about stupid airplanes and tanks in magazines like *Model Graphix*'. But animation required money and resources: it wasn't something that Miyazaki could produce on his own. He did ponder in 1989 making his tank pig story as an OAV, with his own money.

The aircraft in *Porco Rosso* are based on real planes, but Hayao Miyazaki created his own versions of them. Donald Curtis flies a real plane, based on the Curtiss R3C-2. (You can see a very similar aircraft in London's Science Museum). The Curtiss R3C-2 was a racing plane, and won the Schneider Cup in 1925 (beating an Italian plane, the Macchi M33).[49] The Schneider Cup is referenced in the dialogue when Rosso encounters Curtis at the Hotel Adriano. The Italian Air Force planes are based on real aircraft. Ferralin flies an MC-72, which drew on the Macchi M-39 and M-52. There are also a host of First World War One aircraft, used in the dogfight flashback sequence (Porco flies a Macchi M5).

The chief plane in *Porco Rosso* – and the main gadget or McGuffin or cool device – is of course Porco Rosso's bright red seaplane, the Savoia S-21.[50] It is a long, elegant boat, with a single, large wing mounted above the cockpit (Fio admires its graceful lines when she sees it for the first time). The single engine is fixed above and just in front of the pilot (the engine, plus the wing, makes for tricky visibility). There are struts at the end of the wing, for landing on the water. Two

---
48 Quoted in H. McCarthy, 1999.
49 The Schneider Cup, inaugurated by Jacques Schneider in 1913, was a seaplane race, and ran until 1931 (apart from during WW1).
50 Miyazaki had found a good diagram of the Italian seaplane, and preferred to imagine the interior for himself, instead of visiting a museum in Italy and seeing it for real (1993).

guns are mounted inside the fuselage at the front.

Pagott's seaplane has much attention lavished on it by the filmmakers (Hayao Miyazaki could easily have a second career working for an an illustrator or designer for commercial airlines). It is shown off to its best in many sequences in the piece. The choice of red of course fits in with the title, *Porco Rosso*, 'the Crimson Pig' (a stupid colour for a plane, Donald Curtis moans, and he's right, but it also means that the red hue pops out of the blue and grey sky backgrounds). And the unusual design means that the seaplane has a distinctive silhouette.[51]

However, there are many other planes in *Porco Rosso* with similar designs of the engine mounted above the wing, with the fuselage suspended below. But Pagott's plane has other features which distinguishes it from every other plane in the film (and any other plane in Hayao Miyazaki's output).[52]

Technology is better when it's well designed, for Hayao Miyazaki, and with planes that fly under 190 miles an hour, there is a possibility for individual designs (above 190 m.p.h. and factors such as engineering and materials take over).

Self-indulgent? Is *Porco Rosso* self-indulgent? For me, as a fan, Hayao Miyazaki can indulge himself any time he likes. The movie works. It entertains. It thrills. It amuses. It moves. *Porco Rosso* does everything a movie should do, everything a movie *can* do.

---

[51] Animators often talk about creating characters with instantly recognizable silhouettes.

[52] The Mamma Aiuto gang have multi-coloured seaplanes – aircraft that they've customized themselves with patterned paint jobs in orange, purple, green (there's even a plane in blue with white polka dots). Few gangsters in history would suffer such colourful getaway cars or planes! But the gangsters are even embarrassed that the Aiuto gang haven't painted their re-built plane yet!

10
❖
PRINCESS MONONOKE

> I will depict hatred, but only to show that there is something more valuable.
> I will depict a curse to show the joy of liberation from it.
> I will depict the boy's understanding of the girl and the process by which the girl opens her heart to the boy.
>
> Hayao Miyazaki, 1995 (SP, 274)

A WORK OF GENIUS.
Princess Mononoke is a work of genius. It is a masterpiece. It is one of the most staggeringly incredible films you will ever see. By *any* standards you want to apply, the levels of imagination and artistry and detail and insight and energy in this movie are simply astounding.

As well as being a visionary piece, with the highest quality animation achievable, with fascinating characters, stupendous action, brilliant set-pieces, and with some deeply poetic episodes, *Princess Mononoke* is also a thematically, politically and philosophically rich movie. There are many levels to this wonderful picture.

Princess Mononoke (*Mononoke Hime,* 1997, Tokuma Shoten/ Nippon Television Network/ Dentsu/ Studio Ghibli) was written and directed by Hayao Miyazaki, produced by Toshio Susuki, Seichiro Ujiie, Yutaka Narita and Yasuyoshi Tokuma, with music by Joe Hisaishi, cinematography by Atsushi Okui, sound by Kazuhiro Wakabayashi and Muchihiro Ito, computer graphics by Yoshinori Sugano, Yashiyuki Momose, Mitsunori Katama and Masafumi Inoue, the animation directors were Masashi Ando, Yoshifumi Kondo, Katsuya Kondo and Kitaro Kosaka,[53] the art directors were Nizo Yamamoto, Naoya Tanaka, Yoji Takeshige, Satoshi Kuroda and Kazuo Oga, editing was by Miyazaki and Takeshi Seyama, the ADs were Koji Aritomi, Masakatsu Ishizone and Hiroyuki Ito,

---
[53] Kitaro Kosaka has credits on *Angel's Egg, Akira, Metropolis, Grave of the Fireflies, Nasu, Pon Poko,* and Miyazaki's movies.

and colour design was by Michiyo Yasuda. Most of the principals in the crew had worked with Miyazaki and Suzuki before. Pre-production for *Princess Mononoke* began in August, 1994.[54]

Toshio Suzuki recalled that the financial backers of *Princess Mononoke* were against making the movie because: (1) the budget was too big, (2) there was a similar Hollywood movie coming out the same year (*Jurassic Park 2*), and (3) it was a historical drama (thought to perform poorly at the box office).

The budget for *Princess Mononoke* was $19.4 million,[55] and the box office rental was $92.7 million (the gross was $154 million), with approximately 13.53 million admissions in Japan (between July and November, around 12 million people had seen the film in theatres – about 10% of the population).[56] The film was released on July 12, 1997. *Princess Mononoke* was also the first Hayao Miyazaki movie to be released in a wider release in theatres in the U.S.A. (on October 7, 1999), as part of the 1996 agreement between Tokuma and the Walt Disney Company.[57]

The filming schedule at Studio Ghibli for *Mononoke Hime* ran from August, 1994 to June, 1997. Hayao Miyazaki began writing *Princess Mononoke* in August, 1994, completing the first treatment in April, 1995. Production kicked in with the creation of the storyboards from May, 1995 onwards. In July, 1995 the animation schedule began, and was finished in June, 1997.

Princess Mononoke became the biggest grossing movie in Japan (unadjusted for inflation), the previous movie being *E.T. The Extraterrestrial*.[58] *Titanic*[59] knocked off *Princess Mononoke* from the top spot,[60] but *Spirited Away* trounced

---

[54] The origins of *Princess Mononoke* went back to at least 1980, when Hayao Miyazaki began drawing image boards for elements that would be used in the movie.
[55] The biggest undertaking by Studio Ghibli up until then. Miyazaki noted that the team at Ghibli was ready for this movie: they were at their peak, and if they didn't make it now, they wouldn't make it at all (TP, 44).
[56] And Japan at the time had 1/10th of the cinema screens of the U.S.A.
[57] Although *Princess Mononoke* is regarded as a Studio Ghibli production, other companies were involved, including: sub-contractor Production I.G., Telecom Animation Film, Studio Killy, Trace Studio M, IM Studio, Toei Animation, and Takahashi Production/ T2 Studio.
[58] *Princess Mononoke* broke *E.T.*'s record in a quarter of the time that *E.T.* had taken to make its record.
[59] Sometimes I like to believe that *Titanic* never existed – a movie that audiences went nuts over and had so much about it *not* to like.
[60] As well as *Titanic*, the big American movies of 1997 were *Jurassic Park 2* (*The Lost World*), *Men In Black*, *Tomorrow Never Dies*, *Air Force One* and *As Good As It Gets*.

Titanic in Japan (quite right, too!).

On video, *Princess Mononoke* fared amazingly well, selling two million cassettes in 3 weeks, and four million by the end of 1998.[61] In January, 1999, *Princess Mononoke* premiered on television in Japan and gained a 35.1% share of the audience (which is a very large audience).

144,043 cels were produced (using 550 colours). Hayao Miyazaki personally checked around 80,000 of those cels, including re-drawing or adjusting many of them (that is an astounding amount of work).[62]

Personally checking over half of the cels took its toll on Miyazaki: he explained, after the film was released, that it was an exhausting process:

> A pictorial animator has to make pictures move. Even if I have others do it, I end up having to fix a majority of it anyway. This is the most exhausting aspect of my day-to-day work. Physically, I just can't go on. I suffer from everything from poor eyesight to shoulder tension and hip and thigh pain.[63]

Voice-wise, Yoji Matsuda (b. October 19, 1967)[64] played Prince Ashitaka, Yuriko Ishida[65] (b. October 3, 1969) was Princess Mononoke, Yuko Tanaka was Eboshi-gozen, Kaoru Kobayashi was Jokio-bo, Tsunehiko Kamijô was Gonza, Sumi Shimamoto[66] was Toki, Tetsu Watanabe was Yamainu, Mitsuru Satô was Tatari-gama, Hisaya Morishige was Okkoto, Akira Nagoya was Usi-kai, Akihiro Miwa was Moro, Mitsuko Mori was Hiisama, and Nishimura Masahiko was Kouroku. (Both Matsuda and Ishida have done very little *animé*. For two such crucial roles, in a very important production, many producers would select veteran voice actors. But Miyazaki often casts voices that aren't heard everywhere in *animé*).

Recording the voice actors on the same stage as the technical staff proved difficult (introduced for the first time on this show), but the direct interaction between the filmmakers and the performers was immediate and useful.

English voices were provided by Gillian Anderson, Billy Crudup, Claire Danes, Keith David, John DeMita and John Di-

---

[61] According to *Screen Digest* (Nov, 1998), only children's animated films usually sell above 200,000 copies.
[62] About 80,000 of the cels were key animation.
[63] Hayao Miyazaki in *Asia Pulse*, May, 1997.
[64] Yoji Matsuda was Asbel in *Nausicaä*.
[65] Yuriko Ishida also appeared in *Pon Poko* and *From Up On Poppy Hill*.
[66] Sumi Shimamoto was a Miyazaki regular, appearing as Clarisse in *The Castle of Cagliostro*, the mother in *Totoro*, and the lead in *Nausicaä of the Valley of the Wind*.

Maggio (Jack Fletcher oversaw the English dub, and Neil Gaiman[67] wrote the English language script).[68] The American version was released by Disney in 1999.

Joe Hisaishi provided music before animation was completed for *Princess Mononoke*, so the production team had music they could draw inspiration from. Usually, Hisaishi would create the music after the film was finished (as with most Western movies). The collaboration between Hisaishi and Miyazaki and his team was much closer on *Princess Mononoke*.

There are percussive cues using drums for the Kuro-sawan battle scenes in the last third of *Princess Mononoke* • a haunting, soft piano cue for the rebirth of the landscape in the final moments (one of Hisaishi's beloved musical modes, which he employs a good deal) • mysterious, bubbling wood-wind sounds for the appearance of the *kodama* • and a beaut-iful, melancholy cue using sustained strings in the scenes involving the Forest Spirit in its stag form.

Princess Mononoke was the first Hayao Miyazaki production to employ computers and CGI on a big scale. They were used on *Princess Mononoke* to colour the cels – about 10,000 out of 144,000 cels. Around 10 minutes of *Princess Mononoke* used digital ink and paint work, and 15 minutes overall employed CGI (C, 127). Computer composition to combine elements of animation was deployed, as well as particle animation, morphing, 3-D rendering, and texture mapping.

The computer dept at Studio Ghibli for this show in-cluded computer graphics director Yoshinori Sugano, animators Yashiyuki Momose, Mitsunori Katama and Masa-fumi Inoue, and digital paint artist Horoaki Ishii, among others. The computer work was done in-house at Studio Ghibli, using 21 computers, two servers, and systems such as Silicon Graphics and Avid.

THE CURSE.

Hayao Miyazaki had apparently had the idea for *Princess Mononoke* a long time – back in the Seventies he had wanted to do a movie about a princess who lives in a forest with a beast. The *mononoke*[69] was an animal spirit that the young

---

[67] Actually, it was translated by Steve Alpert or Ian McWilliam, according to Jonathan Clements, with Gaiman acting in an editorial role; Gaiman got the job because he was recommended by Quentin Tarantino (2009, 239).
[68] *Princess Mononoke* was marketed as a prestige project, and using name actors was a key element in selling Japanese *animé* to a U.S. audience.
[69] 'Mononoke' can be translated as a spirit, as animism.

woman was forced to marry. The echoes of *Beauty and the Beast* were obvious (the fairy tale, most famously in the version by Charles Perrault, is the basis for many stories, and 100s of movies).

To the initial *Beauty and the Beast*-type narrative Hayao Miyazaki added many layers, such as the political struggle for power in mediæval Japan, the industry/ human versus nature/ environment conflict, and a love story. (The most difficult part of *Mononoke* was the story, Miyazaki confessed [TP, 80]).

Hayao Miyazaki also wanted to have a character with a curse: 'for the longest time I wanted to make her the heroine of a movie,' Miyazaki recalled.[70] The princess would have had a birthmark; over time, the curse shifted to a young prince (Ashitaka's curse, the *tatari,* has the look of a birthmark, of course; also, for a moment, both San and Ashitaka have the cursemark on them, when they hold up the Forest God's head during the finale).

As well as having a symbolic or philosophical aspect, the curse or mark Ashitaka bears is also a real wound that hurts, particularly at crisis moments, like the village massacre, or the first sight of the Forest Spirit. For Hayao Miyazaki, Ashitaka's curse could be linked to contemporary diseases such as AIDS.[71]

> Ashitaka was cursed for a very absurd reason [Miyazaki explained in 1997]. Sure, Ashitaka did something he should not have done – killing Tatari Gami. But there was enough reason to do so from the humans' viewpoint. Nevertheless, he received a deadly curse. I think that is similar to the lives of people today. I think this is a very absurd thing that is part of life itself.

Hayao Miyazaki described Ashitaka as someone who has no home anymore, has no place to live, is not particularly welcome anywhere, cannot go back to his village, who fights alone and usually without thanks, who has to live with a curse and with conflicts. It is no easy path, and there are no easy answers.

> Ashitaka is the kind of person who is willing to live with the thorn. So, I think that Ashitaka is a person of the 21st century, who decided to live with the thorn, San. He does not say 'well, I can't do anything about it'.

---

70 In H. McCarthy, 2002, 183.
71 Hayao Miyazaki in H. McCarthy, 2002, 192.

Ashitaka is part-god himself. Or at least, some of the crazed god's powers have infected Ashitaka. Unfortunately, they are the kind of powers that anyone could do without, unless they happened to be a warrior intent on slaughtering people. The powers give Ashitaka added strength during combat, enabling him to decapitate soldiers with one arrow from afar. Ashitaka, though, is much more of a peacemaker than a war-monger, and he has to keep those powers firmly in check.

Notice too that the Forest Spirit does not cure Ashitaka of his god-curse: when the Forest God heals Ashitaka of the gunshot wound, which kills a normal person, it does not also heal the curse of the boar god on Ashitaka's arm. Ashitaka checks both wounds when he wakes by the lake in the forest glen. There's no doubt that the Forest Spirit could heal Ashitaka's wound if it wanted to – it is the master of life and death, as San explains. It's left the curse in place maybe because it's something that Ashitaka has to deal with and heal himself.[72]

THE WOLF PRINCESS.

Princess Mononoke evokes all sorts of mythological and legendary narratives. One of the strongest is the wolf girl, the feral child, the human who grows up amongst wild animals in a forest or jungle. It's *The Jungle Book* or *Tarzan*. In the 1997 film, San was left behind by her parents as a child, and is brought up by Moro[73] and her children, the wolves. She is also part of the prehistoric era, a human who might be found 10,000 years ago in Japan. (That *Princess Mononoke* was either about San or Ashitaka was reflected in Miyazaki's two titles for the movie in his 1995 memo for the project: *Princess Mononoke* and *Ashitaka Sekki* (*Ashitaka Story*) (SP, 272).)[74]

Wolves are powerful symbols, which cinema has regularly employed. *Princess Mononoke* is one of those less frequent outings which evokes the maternal, nurturing side of wolves, as well as the more usual predatory, aggressive, hunting aspects. And the elements of wildness, of otherness,

---

[72] The slogan for *Princess Mononoke* was simply 'Live'. It is a phrase or concept that is dear to Miyazaki: repeatedly he insists that humans must live, they must walk on. It was the message of the final scene in his last film, *The Wind Rises*: 'you must live'.

[73] Moro is 'the wolf goddess is a survivor from the old world' (TP, 22).

[74] Her name is San, which also means three (she can be regarded as the 3rd child of the wolf-god Moro [P. Drazen, 2003]). The name 'mononoke', which means 'evil spirits', is given to her by the people of Irontown. As a princess, San is in the fairy tale mold: a princess without a king or queen as parents, a princess in spirit and attitude, a princess without the usual kind of realm to rule over – she has the ancient forest.

of mystery. These are no ordinary wolves, though, and their mighty forms place them very much in the realm of spirits or gods.[75] They are the wolves of fairy tales and fantasy fiction.

Together with the wolf girl, Mononoke, the wolves constitute a family or community of their own, obeying their own laws, and roaming where they will. Moro is an enormous wolf, all white, while the brothers are smaller and blue-white. The image of San riding Moro or one of the brother wolves, with her hair streaming back, wearing her mask and white fur cloak and clutching a spear, is unforgettable, one of the icons of Hayao Miyazaki's cinema.

The first proper view of Princess Mononoke, when she turns to the camera (which takes Ashitaka's point-of-view, across the river), is extraordinary. She stands proud and glares at Ashitaka, with blood smearing her mouth. This's no ordinary heroine: that defiant look, her unusual costume, the blood around her mouth, and the giant form of the white wolf behind her, all spell otherness and wildness. And San remains true to that first image: she stays with her wolf family after the events in the narrative, including her encounter with her equal, Prince Ashitaka.

Princess Mononoke is one of the toughest of all Hayao Miyazaki's female characters – certainly the toughest of his younger, female characters. She is a rough and tumble woman, tomboyish, untameable, fierce in combat, incredibly brave and boundlessly energetic and athletic.

The Princess is a very appealing character: she has little or no fear: she hurtles down on the caravan of cattle led by Eboshi and her men, with only a dagger for a weapon (but it does help that she rides a mighty wolf). Later, she makes an assault on Irontown completely alone, taking on soldiers on the battlements and roofs, fighting with Gonza, and finally duelling with Ashitaka and then Eboshi herself (before Ashitaka steps in). San's hatred of humans never lets up, and she is eager to kill Eboshi right up to the end.

For Hayao Miyazaki, part of San's journey was to show 'the kind of development that makes them a good person in their heart', to grow as a character to the point where she can feel affection for one human, if not the rest of humanity (this

---

[75] In *Mononoke*, and in *Spirited Away*, Miyazaki and co. attempted to portray something abstract and unknowable – gods. Miyazaki said he wasn't quite sure how to depict the gods and the spirits.
The gods in the forest exist apart from humans, with no relation to humans: they are not petty gods who guide souls to heaven after death: the forest 'is the central core, the navel, of the world, and we want to return in time to that pure place' (TP, 36).

journey was reflected somewhat in Chihiro in Miyazaki's next film, *Spirited Away,* where the ten year-old girl moves from selfishness to compassion for Haku, another prince).

The appearance of Mononoke Hime is expressive of an earlier historic period: she has short, roughly-cut hair, a necklace of white teeth (probably wolf teeth), white, shell earrings (which tinkle), and a white tunic over a knee-length, dark blue dress (roughly made, it looks as if San's created her own clothes). Most impressive is her warrior costume:[76] a spirit mask that evokes a wolf, a white fur cloak (presumably wolf fur), with a white fur headdress at the top (and wolf ears). Plus a very sharp dagger, and a spear.

Where does Princess Mononoke live? In a spectacular, granite boulder wolf lair, high up in the hills, overlooking a narrow, river valley below. This is where San takes Ashitaka to recuperate. Some of the tenderest scenes in *Princess Mononoke* occur here, when Ashitaka wakes and watches San sleeping next to him, covered in a wolf fur. It's apt that Ashitaka wakes at night, into the quiet world of the forest, where Moro the wolf-god stands guard in the moonlight. The conversation between Moro and Ashitaka is unusual but important (and lengthy, too). It develops the themes of the film, and also offers some back-story into San's past (Moro says she was abandoned by her parents when they fled, so was brought up as a wolf. It would be interesting to see flashbacks of San' childhood). Ashitaka states simply his guiding moral: can't humans and animals get along? Moro is doubtful: humans have one advantage: technology.

I have a lot of sympathy with Princess Mononoke's point-of-view: for her, humanity is cruel and stupid and is destroying her home, the forest, and trying to eliminate the gods, her friends. Though human, San has good reason for despising humanity.

San is right: humans are without doubt the most violent, the most idiotic, the most aggressive, and the most dangerous species on the planet (they are also the most neurotic, the most damaged, and the most messed up).

And there are far too many of them, and they are consuming everything in the world.

That's part of the ecological message in Hayao Miya-

---

[76] One of the enjoyable aspects of *Mononoke* was the design of the clothing: Miyazaki drew on reference, of course, but also made up many of the costumes.

zaki's cinema,[77] but the scientific facts bear it out.[78] The true size of the human population, if it were in correct proportion to other mammals and natural resources, should be about the size of a London suburb. 50,000, or 100,000 or maybe 300, 000. But not 10 million in one city, and not 6,000,000,000 spread across the planet.

This is the world we live in, Hayao Miyazaki wanted to say in *Princess Mononoke,* and that 'we share this despair', whether we are adults or children.

> It's not like we can coexist with nature as long as we live humbly, and we destroy it because we become greedy [Miyazaki explained]. When we recognize that even living humbly destroys nature, we don't know what to do. And I think that unless we put ourselves in the place where we don't know what to do and start from there, we cannot think about environmental issues or issues concerning nature.

The problem of ecology and the environment is a complex one, Hayao Miyazaki wanted to stress in *Princess Mononoke*: he talked about the historical aspects of Japan's forests, how in the Edo period forests were planted, but not for beauty or ecology, but to finance feudal domains (called *Hans*).[79] That is, it wasn't as simple as saying that bad people have ruined the planet: hard-working people have been doing it too.

LOVE.

For Helen McCarthy, *Princess Mononoke* is also about love and loss:

> Miyazaki is making a film about love, the extent to which love involves loss of many kinds, and how that loss can be borne. San and Ashitaka, the human embodiments of love and loss, come to an agreement that is ideal for neither but respects both. (2002, 200)

Princess Mononoke once again depicts a love relationship in which the lovers remain apart, as in *Porco Rosso*. Once

---

[77] 'I've come to the point where I just can't make a movie without addressing the problem of humanity as part of an eco-system,' Hayao Miyazaki said in 1997 (*Asia Pulse*, May, 1997).

[78] Miyazaki admitted that as the *Princess Mononoke* project developed, he found humans less and less appealing: 'I wanted to punish human beings. Part of me is disgusted with hordes of people' (TP, 58).

[79] Miyazaki noted in 1997 that 'for the power balance between humans and animals, that was decidedly changed when humans started using gun powder. Really, though, the biggest reason why mountain animals decreased so much is agriculture'.

again, it is self-imposed. Because *Princess Mononoke* is a love story: in amongst all the action, the giant gods, the warring factions, there are two people who grow to love each other. But this is a more 'grown-up' version of the idealized love relationships depicted in *Laputa: Castle In the Sky* or *Spirited Away* or *Kiki's Delivery Service*. For a start, San and Ashitaka are a little older – maybe 16 or 17 or more. While Chihiro in *Spirited Away* is meant to be 10 years-old, and Haku a little older, and Kiki is thirteen, and Tombo about the same age, and the heroes of *Laputa: Castle In the Sky* might be twelve or so, both San and Ashitaka are at an age when they could get together and make love, get married, have children, etc. But no, there isn't even a kiss.

Yet this love story is convincing and tender – and especially moving from Mononoke's point-of-view, how she eventually realizes how much Ashitaka means to her, and how he accepts her as she is, and isn't trying to change her into something she isn't. It's true that the love story is subordinated to the action-adventure plot – *Princess Mononoke* is definitely not first and foremost a love story (however, it is highly romantic: the romanticization glows out of every frame). But the romance is an important element in the piece, because it is part of San's re-humanization, if you like, part of her journey of coming back to humanity.

And only someone noble and heroic and kind-hearted and brave is going to be her equal, and Ashitaka is certainly that. Ashitaka is a more suitable mate for San than Asbel is for Nausicaä in *Nausicaä*. And that San and Ashitaka decide to stay apart for the time being is a more satisfying resolution of the narrative than the Hollywood happy ending of togetherness, partly because it is true to their characters, and partly because it doesn't rule out them being together in the future (Ashitaka says he will come to the forest to visit San, for instance).

There's an intimate moment in the 1997 film between San and Ashitaka – some of my favourite scenes in this movie are those between San and Ashitaka when they are alone together. He lies on his back on the grass in the sacred glen, with Yakul nearby, and San has brought him some healing plants to eat (a subtle touch has San appearing with the light foot of a forest spirit – she steps swiftly on a little clump of grass – *manga* and *animé* often include images of feet).

We sense that the princess of the spirits is intrigued by this human that was shot by his own people e (as she puts it – though we know that the people of Irontown aren't Ashitaka's people), and who carried her away from Tatarba (San lumps all humans together). She sends her wolf brothers away and decides to deal with him herself. The Forest God has brought Ashitaka back to life, but he is still very weak. And he can't chew his food, so San chews it for him. Here is the kiss – well, it's a good reason for what is really a kiss (if you want a love scene between San and Ashitaka, this is it, right here – but it's typical of Hayao Miyazaki that it ain't a conventional love scene! – although it is intimate. It's also classic Miyazaki that it's the *woman* who initiates the intimacy, not the man).

Instead of chewing the leaves and placing them in Ashitaka's mouth, which would probably do the job just as well, San leans down and passes the chewed leaf into his mouth (like an animal mother might do with its offspring). Notice how the camera stays back to keep them in a two shot, from behind (so there's an ambiguity about whether Ashitaka is conscious when San is pressing the food into his mouth.) The subtle touch of having Ashitaka starting to weep and, significantly, San's bewildered reaction, says more about her increasing interest in this brave youth (a warrior who weeps... San is also startled because she is a girl who has never shed tears. She is too busy surviving to bother with tears).

ASHITAKA.

Although the movie's title is *Mononoke Hime,* the chief protagonist is really Prince Ashitaka: the 1997 film begins and ends with him, the narrative spends more time with Ashitaka than anyone else, and much of the plot is seen from his perspective (the titles suggested for the film were *The Legend of Ashitaka* and *Princess Mononoke*). But this is a movie with so many memorable characters competing for attention – not least the Forest Spirit (Shishigami), or Toki, or Lady Eboshi, or Jigo, or Moro.

Princess Mononoke the wolf princess is the other main character, although she appears after Ashitaka has been well-established (some twenty minutes into the first act). Mononoke is one of Hayao Miyazaki's young women, tough, independent, fearless, energetic, athletic, practical and skilled.

Ashitaka is another Miyazakian type: a young hero – brave but thoughtful, energetic and athletic but also tender and compassionate. Miyazaki and his team of animators give the hero a number of unusual attributes to differentiate him from other movie heroes. He rides a red elk (from the *Nausicaä manga*) which sports two enormous horns, for instance, rather than the regular horse. He has an unusual, red hood and mask,[80] and a *mino*, a rainwear cloak made from woven, dried straw.

Note how Ashitaka appears to be an orphan – he has a sister, Kaya, who idolizes him, and who says goodbye to him as he leaves, giving him her precious dagger (however, Hayao Miyazaki remarked that Kaya calls Ashitaka brother meaning someone older in her clan).[81] Apart from that, Ashitaka has few or no relatives, and his allegiance is to the village; when the village elders reluctantly tell him he must leave, he follows their request. But there is no mom or dad in Ashitaka's life. Hiisama is clearly a surrogate mother, or at least a mother or grandmother figure, and the man who's keeping look-out in the wooden tower at the edge of the forest is a kind of father figure (note how Ashitaka protects him when they fall from the look-out tower).

Narratively, the quests in *Princess Mononoke* pile up for the hero: he begins the film as the young prince of the community, but is soon marked and cursed by the boar god Nago (the Tatari-gami or cursed god),[82] and has to leave the village. At that point, his narrative goal is to make good his curse: if this were a simple fairy tale, that would be one of the primary goals. But as Ashitaka travels to the West, the goals and quests alter: he becomes involved in an attack on a community, encounters the wolf princess San, meets Eboshi and the denizens of yet another community, Tatarba, and so on.

It's the classic storytelling device of opening out the world of the hero as he undergoes a journey.[83] Along the way the goals (and motives) develop, so that by the end of the movie Ashitaka (and Princess Mononoke) are both changed. (Thus, from a storytelling perspective, Ashitaka being an outcast from his village serves to push the hero on his way, in the usual first act manner: yes, it is a curse that must be healed, but it is a way for the filmmakers of getting the hero in

---

80 A little like Lord Yupa in *Nausicaä of the Valley of the Wind*.
81 Kaya is also a brave girl: when the rampaging boar-god Nago is hurtling towards the village, she draws her sword and turns to face it.
82 The boar-god can be regarded as a 'death god' (*shinigami*), who also crop up in *animé* such as *Naruto, Legend of the Overfiend, Yu Yu Hakusho, Descendants of Darkness, Death Note* and *Bleach*.
83 In the next village, there's a market scene, where Ashitaka meets Jigo; these sorts of films always have a bustling market scene; they're typically an opportunity for the hero to meet new characters, some who might help her/ him, as well as to obtain information. They also allow the filmmakers to show off some of the movie's production values. They're called 'watering hole' scenes in screenwriting manuals (famous examples would include the cantina scene in *Star Wars*, and any saloon scene in a Western).

motion).

And the ending too of *Princess Mononoke* isn't the classic, Hollywood ending: there isn't a kiss and a hug and a wedding for Ashitaka and Mononoke: instead, the wolf girl, who can't forgive what humans have done to the forest, returns to her homeland, and Ashitaka says he will go to Tatarba to help them rebuild it. (However, these two heroes are shown in a scene on their own, and they do promise to see each other again).[84]

Similarly, the two people who are daubed villains and by rights should perish, if this were a regular (Westernized) movie, Eboshi and Jigo, don't die. *Princess Mononoke* is not as clear-cut as that, and won't follow the conventions of action-adventure movies. It's true that Eboshi is maimed (the wolf Moro bites off her arm), but neither Mononoke and Moro don't get to kill her, as they are desperate to do, and Jigo survives intact (even though in some respects he's been the worst villain in the piece, using Eboshi to kill the Shishigami, and playing off the warring factions of the people of Tatarba, Lord Asano and the Emperor's forces against each other. Jigo is the familiar adventurer-mercenary and treasure-hunter: he's in it just for the reward. His goals are the lowest and basest – pure capitalism).

Ashitaka is a peacemaker, an intermediary between warring communities; he tries a peaceful solution *first*, before reacting with aggression. His is the familiar liberal message of 'can't we all just get along?' Why can't the animals and gods of the forest and humans get on with each other? It's a familiar question, and the answer is simple: they can't. Or they won't. Anyway, they don't.

It's important that, although Ashitaka is an outstanding warrior, he isn't depicted attacking too often – he defends, or he reacts, or he helps, but he doesn't attack. Early on, he kills some of the samurai (who are scorned as thugs by other characters), but only after warning them off, and only reluctantly (and feels remorse afterwards). It's also the curse which's enhancing his actions – maybe he was only trying to wound or scare the samurai, or to defend the villagers.[85] (And Hayao Miyazaki did not want Ashitaka to be a samurai: 'I wanted to have a boy, not a samurai boy, in the movie'. Hence

---
84 'I expect San will repeatedly break Ashitaka's heart after this' (TP, 83).
85 The writhing, glowing movement of the curse around Ashitaka's arm when it's activated in moments of crisis, such as the scene where Ashitaka rescues San in Irontown, recalls the way that *ki* or life energy is portrayed in *animé* and *manga*. *Ki* appears as flames, as Gilles Poitras noted, 'a larger-than-life image of a person's "battle aura," or as someone sensing a person's "battle spirit"' (1999, 67).

he rides Yakul, not a horse, and doesn't wear a samurai costume).

It's often Ashitaka who's standing physically in between the characters, trying to get them to negotiate or at least talk. San does the same – between Lord Okkoto and Moro, for instance, towards the end of the film. And when San is white with anger at the apocalyptic climax, and wants to kill Eboshi, just after Ashitaka's saved her and carried her through the lake, Ashitaka again steps between them.

There's less humour among the main characters in *Princess Mononoke* than in other Hayao Miyazaki movies. Ashitaka and San (and Eboshi) smile or joke or laugh far, far less than, say, Tombo in *Kiki's Delivery Service* or Pazu in *Laputa: Castle In the Sky* (they don't laugh once in *Mononoke*, and smile rarely). Instead, the humour is diverted to the secondary characters, such as the husband-and-wife bickering of Toki and Kohroku, or the wry quips of Jigo.

I guess for some viewers Ashitaka is a little solemn and serious. I don't think so; but he does take his quest of reaching the far West seriously. Hayao Miyazaki commented that Ashitaka

> is not a cheerful, carefree boy. He is a melancholy guy who has a destiny. I feel that I am that way myself, but until now, I haven't made a film about this kind of character.

The *sadness* of Ashitaka is so central to his character. It is a fundamental melancholy in his personality, not in his circumstances (or as a result of his curse). The introspection is one aspect that differentiates Ashitaka from heroes in Western, Hollywood movies.

One of the clues to Ashitaka's character occurs in the opening sequence: not just the battle with the crazed god Nago, which reveals Ashitaka in his heroic, action mode: we see he is a fearsome warrior (although he does try to negotiate with Nago first). But just as significant is the aftermath: the scene in the hut with the wise woman and the village elders is the key scene: here the witch woman gives Ashitaka his task (to discover the solution to his curse in the West), the familiar exposition of a million movies (and to learn to see unclouded by hate,[86] an important moral precept).

But notice Ashitaka's reaction; he sits quietly and listens. He does not argue with the wise woman, nor with the elders.

---

[86] Ashitaka repeats this to Eboshi; she laughs, then she decides to show him other sides to Irontown.

He accepts what she says. And when he is given his task, he cuts off his topknot,[87] places it on the altar, rises, bows and walks out. He is calm and polite: this prince is definitely not a spoilt brat, and not a selfish guy either: he is going to do what's best for the community.

The way that Ashitaka acts in that whole scene says a huge amount about his character. (This is great storytelling).[88]

Towards the end of the 1997 movie, Ashitaka has become more like one of the gods – or at least, the god-curse has now infected more of his body (one of the reasons that Ashitaka takes off his jacket, to keep San warm, is to reveal that the skin-stain has spread to his chest. And he's also one of those male heroes who strips down like in North American action flicks). And the design of the Forest Spirit in his decapitated state also evokes Ashitaka's skin curse: the swirling colours of purple and black link with those on Ashitaka's arm. Certainly, the movie is clear that both Ashitaka and San are not your average sort of person, and are closer to divinity in some respects than humans.

Another intriguing aspect of Ashitaka's characterization is his ability to sense what's happening to San at key moments. Yes, it is a dramatic device, developed sometimes to get information across, or to leap over gaps in the narrative. But it never seems contrived here (the scene where Ashitaka senses that one of the wolves is buried under a pile of dead boars, for instance, some way off, would be just silly in some other movies).

It also pays off to introduce the audience to the flashbacks to scenes which Ashitaka did not witness. And it pays off at the end, when the wolf mother Moro asks if Ashitaka wants to save the girl he loves.

OTHER CHARACTERS.

Jigo is an ambiguous character: a monk in red and white garb, squat, rotund, gnarled, with a large wart on his face, he is also one of the Emperor's men. He has a bunch of motives: one is to gain the head of the Forest God, because the Emperor thinks it will grant immortality. So he has the greedy instincts of the treasure hunter, a familiar character in the adventure genre. But he's also playing the different commun-

---

87 Cutting off the topknot in this village means that Ashitaka is a non-person, Miyazaki explained, and he is forced out by his community.
88 The filmmaking might be something out of the classic Japanese movies of Yasujiro Ozu or Kenji Mizoguchi: the camera is stationary, at waist height, in medium shots – the way that actors have been filmed millions of times in Japanese movies (often sitting on cushions on the floor around a low table).

ities against each other, pitting Lord Asano and his soldiers against Eboshi and her people. Their internecine war helps to weaken their communities, which's what the Emperor wants.

And it's Jigo who craftily tells Ashitaka just enough, to entice the youth to search for the land of the Forest Spirit. Jigo's a canny judge of people's characters, and – importantly – their values, and what they want. But he's wrong, at the end: the bigger picture is that somehow humans and nature have to get along. You can't win against fools, is how he puts it, but his cynicism and materialism is out-done here by higher values.[89]

For Hayao Miyazaki, Eboshi[90] was a tough woman who had had a hard life,[91] and that helps to make her uncompromising in her efforts to build a better life for her people. The problem is, she is one of those people who will stoop to means beyond the law, and beyond what reasonable people would do. It's not a problem for Eboshi that she is going to try to kill a god (the Forest Spirit), or the animals that get in her way (the boars), or the soldiers of Lord Asano, or the wolf girl, San.

Eboshi and Irontown embody the contradictions at the heart of the themes in *Princess Mononoke*: Eboshi offers shelter to prostitutes and lepers, but she is also actively developing weapons and heavy industry (such as ironworks). In a conventional (Westernized) movie, she'd be a villain with a cigar and a nasty attitude.

One of the curious omissions from the 1997 film is the non-appearance of Lord Asano. We see his samurai and his soldiers, and his emissaries, but there isn't a scene with Asano himself. Maybe there was and it was cut b4 animation. But it is curious that Asano's army plays an important role in the piece, during the siege of Tatarba, but the leader isn't really portrayed. (Asano wants some of the iron that Eboshi is mining).

The *kodama*, the tree spirits, are a Miyazakian spin on traditional sprites or woodland fairies. They are small, doll-

---

[89] Miyazaki explained: 'I made the character of Jiko Bou without knowing what kind of role he would play. He could be a spy of the Muromachi government (the Samurai regime which was ruling Japan at that time), a henchman of some religious group, or a Ninja, or he could actually be a very good guy. In the end, he became a character who has all of those elements.'

[90] The name Eboshi comes from where Miyazaki has his mountain cabin. There was also a Tate Eboshi in legend.

[91] They made Eboshi a woman also because the staff said they preferred to draw a beautiful woman to a man (TP, 61). The costume (suggesting she was a courtesan) was part of the move towards beauty. Eboshi was a modern person – and to people of old, 20th century people might seem like the devil, Miyazaki thought (TP, 57).

like, white, with black spots for eyes and a mouth. They spin their heads and rattle like toys. The stand-out scene with the *kodama* is when they lead Ashitaka and the two wounded soldiers into the forest: Ashitaka is trying to reach Tatarba on the other side of the mountains, but the *kodama* guide him to the heart of the forest.

Hayao Miyazaki's movies are wonderful with sidekicks and odd minor characters that pop up and disappear again, and the *kodama* are no exception. And the filmmakers give them all sorts of unusual attributes, such as fading from view, or mimicking humans (as when the *kodama* copy, like children, Ashitaka carrying the soldier on his back). Another magical scene with the *kodama* occurs at the appearance of the Nightwalker, when thousands of them materialize on the tops of the trees, and start to rattle and spin when the Nightwalker arrives.[92]

One of the most unusual elements of *Princess Mononoke* is the ape tribe, a gorilla-like version of the legendary beast of China, the *Shoujou*. The portrayal of the apes is deliberately odd, with deep, slowed-down voices, and a stylized, silhouetted approach to the animation. The apes are depicted as proto-humans: they want to absorb the power of humanity by eating them. These beliefs are actually historical aspects of real incarnations of humans in prehistory. The idea that eating the bodies and particularly the brains of your enemies will give you their power was a belief that lasted for many thousands of years (and into the modern period, with the religious rituals of the Aztecs). So *Princess Mononoke* is excavating ancient prehistory with headhunting cults in the characters of the apes. (San protests, telling the apes that those beliefs are false, that the apes would become something less than human).

The boars represent another level of animal life, and have their own morals, ethics and gods (Nago and Okkoto). Significantly, both the giant boar-gods, Nago and Okkoto, go mad, when they are shot with iron bullets by the troops of Asano and Eboshi. Moro the wolf-god is also shot, but notice how she doesn't go mad, but bears her fatal injury with dignity (she saves up her strength to bite off the head of Eboshi, but in the end decides that San needs her help more, so she launches herself at Okkoto, to save San).

The boars are the only characters in *Princess Mononoke* that don't appeal to me so much, but that's no fault of Hayao

---

92 Miyazaki described the Forest Spirit as 'nature's night': 'the creature is gathering and giving out lives during the night'.

Miyazaki and his filmmaking team: it's what the boars represent. Each of the animal groups depict some aspect of humanity: the wolves are fiercely independent and fine warriors, but also have a nurturing, wise aspect, the *kodama* are the spirits of the trees, or humans who are in tune with the natural world, like the Spirit God himself, and the boars represent the foot soldiers of humanity, the workers or proletariat, perhaps, whose negative traits are aggression, stubbornness, ignorance and a mob mentality. All of the animal groups are proud – it's debatable whether the wolves are prouder than the boars – and that pride and unwillingness to compromise leads to problems.

So it's not because the boars are badly visualized or dramatized in *Princess Mononoke* that I find them less than appealing, it's because of the aspects of humanity that they embody. However, the boars are certainly brave – when they go to war, they *really* go to war, launching themselves in their hundreds against the human forces. But in *Princess Mononoke* the boars, although they have their reasons, are also misguided. Miyazaki's point is that when a war starts, noble motives are debased.

One of the curious scenes is where San goes to help Lord Okkoto, the leader of the boars. Like Ashitaka, San acts here as an intermediary and a helper. San might not agree with their tactics and ethics but she wants to help the boars, and avert a catastrophe.

THE COMMUNITIES IN *PRINCESS MONONOKE*.

Hayao Miyazaki's world has been described as a fantastical, vaguely European space, with Western-looking characters and architecture. *Totoro, Ponyo, The Wind Rises* and *Princess Mononoke*, though, were set in Japan (but a Japan of the past – *circa* the 1950s in *Totoro*, mediæval feudal Japan in *Princess Mononoke*). Miyazaki chose the 14th century for *Princess Mononoke* because, he explained, it was a time when 'people changed their value system from gods to money'. It was an era of transition, when

> life and death were sharply delineated. People lived, loved, hated, worked and died. Life was not ambiguous. Even in the midst of hatred and slaughter there were still things that made life worth living. Marvellous encounters and beautiful things could still exist.[93]

---
93 Hayao Miyazaki, quoted in S. Napier, 181.

The Emishi,[94] being the oldest community in terms of history in *Princess Mononoke*[95] (aside from San, Moro and the wolf family), are not a matriarchy, but women hold a much higher place than the more conventional views of prehistory as patriarchal. The Emishi are linked in the 1990s film and by the filmmakers to an older group of people who lived in Japan, who were possibly the ancestors of the Japanese people. In the scene in the hut with the elders, it's mentioned (by one of the eldest of the village elders), that the Emishi were wiped out 500 years ago (by the Emperor), and are the last survivors of an ancient people.

That women held key positions in the social hierarchy of the Emishi is part of a movement in some archæological circles towards pro-women social structures. You can find it in the work of anthropologist Chris Knight, British poets such as Robert Graves and Peter Redgrove, with their evocation of the 'White Goddess' and the 'Black Goddess', and feminist writers and artists such as Catherine Elwes, Monica Sjöo, Elinor Gadon, Geoffrey Ashe[96] and Barbara Walker, who believed that women were often leaders, and that some ancient societies were matriarchies. There isn't space here to go into the vast area of Goddess studies, but I have noted some useful starting points below.[97]

The world of *Princess Mononoke* is both prehistoric and mediæval, both mythological and historical. It is a world of self-enclosed communities – Ashitaka travels from his homeland in the East of Nippon through a number of tribes, including the town under attack from the samurai warriors, to Irontown, and the forest itself. The filmmakers combine a variety of periods, from prehistory to the Renaissance.

THE FOREST.

The forest. What a forest! The research trips that Hayao Miyazaki and his team made to Yakushima in Japan for

---

[94] In making Ashitaka the hero, Yoshihiko Amino noted that Miyazaki 'decentered the Japanese state', because the Emishi were a small tribe in the North, while the bulk of the Japanese people were the Yamato (TP, 61).
[95] The other races are the Jomon and the Yamato.
[96] We publish a book by Geoffrey Ashe about his American course on the female deities of old, *Discovering the Goddess* (Crescent Moon, 2007).
[97] G. Ashe: *The Virgin: Mary's Cult and the Re-emergence of the Goddess*, Arkana, London, 1987; E. Gadon: *The Once and Future Goddess*, Aquarian Press 1990; M. Gimbutas: *The Language of the Goddess*, Thames & Hudson, London, 1989; S. Nicholson, ed. *The Goddess Re-awakening: The Goddess Principle Today,* Theosophical Publishing House, New York, NY, 1989; E. C. Whitmont: *Return of the Goddess*, Routledge, London, 1987; M. Sjöo & B. Mor: *The Great Cosmic Mother*, Harper & Row, San Francisco 1987; E. Neumann: *The Great Mother*, Princeton University Press, NJ, 1972.

Princess Mononoke certainly paid off:[98] this is one of the great forests in cinema (Yakushima has rainforests which includes cedars 1000s of years old; 75% of the island is forested mountains. It's off the coast of Kyushu, in South-eastern Japan, and is regarded as a mystical island).[99]

Ancestors of *Princess Mononoke*'s forest are obviously the submerged forest in *Nausicaä of the Valley of the Wind* and the giant tree in *Laputa: Castle In the Sky,* and the neighbourhood woods in *My Neighbor Totoro* (is there a Miyazaki movie which doesn't include trees and woodland? No). And in 2010's *Arrietty*, Ghibli returned to the dense vegetation and green world of *Mononoke*.

In *Mononoke Hime* the forest is a vast, lush, green world, extending for many miles in the valleys below the mountains. It is a place of renewal, purity, growth, and a deep spirituality.[100] In short, life. It is both a fairy tale woodland and a real place, drawing on botanical studies. Dragonflies fly by and butterflies flutter by in this peaceful, dreamy place. Shafts of light beam down, there are toadstools and giant, moss-covered trees.

From a design point-of-view, the forest in *Princess Mononoke* is exquisite: large, glacial boulders, enormous trees, tree roots, and thousands of tiny plants and flowers. The level of detail in the forest is beyond obsessive. As the characters walk or clamber through the forest (the forest floor is always uneven, until the central glade is reached), the viewer's eye wanders over one of the most densely detailed woodlands in movies.

And it's not just the small flowers and plants, which might have come from an Early Netherlandish painting of the Madonna sitting with the baby Jesus in the *hortus conclusus* (enclosed garden), it's also *the light*. This is one element that is tougher to capture on celluloid: the soft light that filters through canopies of leaves. This is a misty, golden light, not the harder light of Hollywood action movies set in forests, which typically fill the area in front of the camera with smoke machines, and shoot into the sun.[101]

---

[98] The background artists 'worked frantically' on the forest, Miyazaki said (TP, 45). Japan has about 70% of forests (compared to 12% in Britain).
[99] Kazuo Oga, the art director of *Princess Mononoke*, and therefore one of the stars of the movie, visited the Shirakami mountains, in Northern Honshu, Japan. One of the background designers was from Akita, and another from Kyushu.
[100] If you go beyond worldly desires, Miyazaki suggested in 1994, and want to go somewhere pure, you might end up with something as simple as a stone or drops of water. There's a wealth of Asian philosophy and mysticism behind such a view.
[101] Since the 1970s, forests in Robin Hood or King Arthur or mediæval flicks always have tons of smoke and backlight. Are woods really that misty and smoky? Occasionally. Most of the time, no.

Sometimes the forest in *Princess Mononoke* is lit by Godrays, and sometimes the light is softer and mistier. The signature colour of *Princess Mononoke* is green (complimented by blue; for the human world, it's red, inevitably). Colour designer Michiyo Yasuda and her team saved the brightest, richest greens for the sacred glen, which complements the golden light. But there are so many varieties of green throughout the movie (550 colours were used in *Princess Mononoke*, and 549 of them were green). This really is 'the green and the gold' that British poet Robert Graves spoke of that poets use to evoke their childhoods.

And you know that the completely clear water in the forest glade is pure and healing, and uncontaminated by humans. (And it proves so for Ashitaka and the soldiers). This is a place where you can find rest and nourishment and healing.

As well as woods and mountains, *Princess Mononoke* is also a movie of rivers: these are the cold, rushing streams of rural Japan, filled with enormous, granite glacial boulders, rounded and smooth, and often covered with moss. Some of the best scenes from the point-of-view of atmosphere and design are those set beside the river, where Ashitaka encounters San for the first time, and where Ashitaka rescues the soldiers from the water. It's also striking how the filmmakers include rivers in spate after rain, capturing the brown, muddy water churned up into waves.

Design-wise, at times *Princess Mononoke* looks like a Zen Buddhist garden, with its rocks and trees, and its atmosphere of spiritual serenity. The famous Zen gardens at Kyoto might be reference points.

And when the spiritual centre of the forest is reached, the art directors (Nizo Yamamoto, Naoya Tanaka, Yoji Takeshige, Satoshi Kuroda and Kazuo Oga) have created a magical space that is at once instantly familiar and unworldly: there is juicy, green grass bordering a pool filled with perfectly clear water. Small clumps of grass form islands (presumably growing atop small rocks). It is a familiar sort of pool that one might find on a granite tableland (but the rocks and water are definitely not red with iron ore – there's no iron here in this part of the forest – the iron is left to Irontown).[102]

The forest is typically the place in fairy and folk tales where characters enter in order to encounter obstacles and mystery. The forest is the site of initiation and trial. It lies on

---

[102] The sacred place of the movie was also meant to be a historically real place, a holy spot which some historians believe existed.

the edge of the familiar, everyday world of the fairy tale. It is where the protagonist gets lost, meets strange creatures, undergoes transformations and spells. It is, typically, one of the first places the protagonist enters on the journey outwards from the home, in *Snow White, Little Red Riding Hood* or *Hansel and Gretel*, for example.

In *The Brothers Grimm*, Jack Zipes writes of the forest in fairy tales:

> Inevitably, they find their way into the forest. It is there that they lose and find themselves. It is there that they gain a sense of what is to be done. The forest is always large, immense, great, and mysterious. No one ever gains power of the forest, but the trees possess the power to change lives and alter destinies. (43)

The forest is a zone of otherness, strangeness, enchantment and the unknown. In (Jungian) psychological terms, it is the unconscious, or confusion, a realm of instability, a *regressus ad uterum*, a place of re-creation and re-birth, where the ego/ soul/ hero/ine is tested and initiated. The enchanted or dark forest is a place of wild things, such as dragons in caves, or witches in their gloomy houses; it is also a land of death (and dragons, witches, caves and darkness are linked with death or the 'dark side' of life).

The forest also has a feminine/ uterine/ womb association, for it is the place of rebirth. The places in fairy tales linked with the dark forest (caves, marshes, deserts, wells, seas, underworlds), are also feminine and birth spaces. Entering the dark forest is essentially the 'descent and return' process of mythology (Orpheus, Jesus, Theseus, Persephone, Isis and others descended into the Underworld or Hell and returned changed and/ or reborn). The descent is towards the foundation of life, to the secret heart of nature. The initiate (whether Orpheus, Hansel, Little Red Riding Hood or Persephone) has to overcome fear and doubt, and learn courage and resourcefulness. Often a monster has to be encountered and sometimes slain (Theseus and the Minotaur, Perseus and St George against the dragon, Marduk and the monster Tiamat, Zeus and the Titans, Jack and the giant). In *Princess Mononoke*, Ashitaka undertakes this journey, with all its mythological associations.

The Grimm Brothers, in their *Children's and Household Tales*, expressed some of the Germanic love of forests, which is fuelled by awe and mysticism. There are clichés that abound about the Germanic, Bavarian mystification of groves as places of ritual and magic, sites of notions of community, race and origins. However, these clichés about the dark forest do form much of the background of fairy tales, in Jacob and Wilhelm Grimm's books especially.

But what's striking about *Princess Mononoke* is that the story doesn't develop *beyond* the forest – to a mountain top, for instance, or some castle or temple where a magic jewel or Grail is kept. Rather, the forest (and the spiritual heart of it, the glade), is the final destination of the story (although the action climax does move out onto the hills – partly for dramatic and staging reasons).

In folk and fairy tales it is often the other way around: the forest will be encountered early on, but the narrative will move on to courts or castles or an ogre's cave or a witch's house. But the most magical place in *Princess Mononoke* is a glade and a pool in the forest.

NATURE VERSUS INDUSTRY.

For Hayao Miyazaki, *Princess Mononoke* was intended to be a movie of pre-industrial Japan. A country which had not yet been industrially exploited, a Japan

> when it had thick forests, few people, and a purity of nature, with distant mountains and deep valleys, abundant and clear flowing streams, narrow dirt paths unpaved with gravel, and a multitude of birds, beasts, and insects. (SP, 273)

Tatarba[103] ('Irontown' in the English language dub) is another of Hayao Miyazaki's workshops or factories or institutions, recalling the Piccolo aviation company in *Porco Rosso* or the bathhouse in *Spirited Away*. Like the bathhouse, Tatarba is presided over by an older woman. Eboshi[104] is an ambiguous character: on the one hand, she provides food and work and accommodation for (female) prostitutes, and also a group of lepers. The community at Tatarba seems to be thriving. On the other hand, Eboshi is developing weapons in order to kill the Forest God, and is happy to cut down the trees to support her iron works. (The ambiguity is heightened by making Eboshi a beautiful, well-mannered woman – she is not your average movie villain).

Tatarba is in direct opposition to the forest: it is an iron works, felling trees to feed its furnace (and Tatarba is built

---
[103] The iron foundry was way too big, Miyazaki admitted: he had been inspired by a photo he saw as a youth of a foundry built in China's Great Leap Forward (TP, 97).
[104] Forerunners of Eboshi include Kushana in *Nausicaä of the Valley of the Wind*.

from wood, too, to add to the injustice). And it's iron that drives the gods mad when the bullets pierce them.

Tatarba is an emblem and manifestation of humanity and what humans do: it is not an agricultural community, where people live off the land and cultivate crops. It is not a place where people live more harmoniously with the earth. It is, in short, industry: Tatarba embodies Industry, and Progress, and Capitalism.

Put it another way: Tatarba (and Eboshi and her people) embody exploitation: that is their *raison d'être*: they exploit the resources of the world. If that means clearing the forests of trees, so be it. If that means killing the Forest Spirit, so be it.

So with the community of Tatarba, Hayao Miyazaki and his team of filmmakers are exploring cultural and social oppositions such as nature vs. industry, trees/ wood vs. iron/ machines, and, ultimately, nature vs. humanity. The film's eco-friendly subtext is clear: animals live harmoniously with the world, and do not seek to exploit it. But humans can't help exploiting the Earth. Humans, in short, don't know how *to live*.

Instead, humans have to impose themselves and their will upon the Earth. The contrast is between the serenity and cycles of growth and decay in the forest and the industrialization of the humans. And it's the human creation of iron in bullets that drives the gods crazy. Eboshi maybe has respect for the gods, but she has no problem with killing them if needs be. Yet, also, humans are simply living, so it's not a direct opposition, it's more ambiguous.

Princess Mononoke shows that many of the groups are resisting change, and want things to stay the same. The humans in Irontown want to be able to exploit the natural resources of the area, for instance. Part of the thematic project of *Princess Mononoke* is to demonstrate that change is inescapable – and usually beneficial, too (the Forest Spirit embodies change – it is continually changing from a Day Spirit to a Night Spirit).

With Tatarba's ironworks, *Princess Mononoke* explores two historical periods: the first is the mediæval period, when the film is set (the Muromachi period, 1392-1573 [SP, 272]), with the emergent industry of working metal and the creation of modern weapons such as guns (called 'flint-fire-arrows' in the movie, because the word for 'gun' wasn't known in the Muromachi era, guns were imported by the Portuguese later, in 1543).[105] The Muromachi era was the time of the first developments of industrialization on a big scale.

The second historical period is the early origins of Japan itself, a prehistoric time, roughly 10,000 B.C. to 300 B.C., known as the Neolithic Jomon period (this is also the time of early Shintoism, and Shinto's nature mysticism lies behind much of *Princess Mononoke*). The Emishi, where Ashitaka comes from, have affinities with both the mediæval and prehistoric periods, while Princess Mononoke herself is consciously depicted as a girl who 'resembled a Jomon pottery figure', as Hayao Miyazaki put it (SP, 273).[106] She is portrayed as someone from a very ancient time (her headdress, for instance, and her wolf family, underline that connection with the deep past).

In contemporary Japan, the Ainu (24,000 of them), now living mainly in Hokkaido in North Japan (they used to live in Northern Honshu), are the last links to the ancient Jomon societies; they are sometimes called Caucasian, and are related to the peoples of Siberia.

So as well as a clash between nature and industry, *Mononoke Hime* also explores conflicts between different historical periods, between the mediæval era and prehistory, and between the early modern period and the mediæval period. (And working with metal of course goes back thousands of years: there is a 'Bronze Age', an 'Iron Age', a 'Stone Age').

THE FOREST SPIRIT.

During the daytime, the Spirit God (Shishigami) is a stag with enormous antlers and a mask-like, quasi-human face.[107] At night, it becomes the Nightwalker, Didarabotchi, a giant in blue-white-violet, comprised of glittering points of light inside a translucent body, trailing tendrils of energy.

The design of the Forest Spirit consciously evokes the stag, an animal with a host of symbolisms attached to it, like the snake or the lion. In traditional symbolism, the stag's associated with the dawn, renewal, fire, creation, and the sun.

---

[105] Miyazaki described the gun thus: 'It's called a 'Kasou' or 'Fire Spear'. In reality, it had a longer rod, and it often exploded and injured the shooter. It was often made from copper, and was used in the Ming dynasty in the 15th century. It had been brought to Japan before matchlock guns were.'

[106] Hayao Miyazaki and his team used the research of archæologists such as Eiichi Fujimori. 'Jomon' means 'cord pattern', the patterns that are found on prehistoric pottery (SP, 148).

[107] 'With its double countenance, human eyes in an animal muzzle, and the ineffable and mysterious smile of Greek *kuroi*, the Forest God appears to represent the supreme balance of Yin and Yang, death and rebirth, disrupted by men's blindness', as critic Alessandro Bencivenni put it (2003).

(In Japan, the dragon is the 'celestial stag'). And the stag's linked with the cycle of the seasons, because it sheds its antlers each year. The stag form is also very ancient, and distinctly shamanic (shamen wear antlers, for instance).

There's a very famous prehistoric painting, dating to the upper palæolithic era, in a cave in France. It depicts a dancing shaman or sorcerer, a figure with a man's legs, a lion's body, and a stag's antlers. The Forest Spirit in *Princess Mononoke* evokes this image both in its day and night guises – the film is a beautiful expression of prehistoric shamanism, mana and animism (animism is the foundation of all religions, including Japanese Shintoism – as E.B. Tylor defined it, animism is 'the belief in spiritual beings').

One of the unforgettable images in the 1997 Japanese *animé* – in a movie crammed with them – is Shishigami's feet walking towards the camera and sprouting flowers, grass and plants. It was one of those images that no other film has ever done.[108] And it occurs twice (once underwater, and in the black space of Ashitaka's dream). This is a god that walks on water.

It was a key decision to keep the Forest Spirit mute – it might have been tempting to have the Shishigami speak, in the usual low, echoey voice of cinematic deities. But the silent looks that the Forest Spirit gives – towards the camera, into the eyes of the audience as well as into the characters' eyes – become all the more powerful. It's the same tactic that was employed in Biblical movies of the 1950s and 1960s, which portrayed Christ as a silent figure, relying on the reactions of other characters to enhance the sense of the sacred.

The head of the Forest Spirit is the film's McGuffin – this is what Eboshi and Jigo (and the Emperor) are after. This tells you what kind of movie this is: it is no ordinary flick in which the McGuffin is a suitcase full of money, or a treasure map, or the secret plans for nuclear missile sites, or the blueprint of a time travelling machine, as in your average contemporary action-adventure movie. No, it's the head of a god that can grant immortality (however, there have been movie villains of course (it's always the villains) who've wanted to obtain the secrets of immortality – it's Lord Voldemort's ultimate aim in the *Harry Potter* series, for example, or Walter Donovan's goal in the third *Indiana Jones* flick).

---

[108] The computer animators of Treebeard the ent paid *hommage* to this scene in *The Lord of the Rings: The Two Towers* (2002). There's also a slight pause in the medium shot of the grass, before the god's feet enter the upper part of the frame, to give the moment even more power.

THE NIGHTWALKER.

The most miraculous sequence in *Princess Mononoke* is perhaps the Nightwalker scene, where the Forest God first appears as the Didarabotchi. It's just before dawn, and the Nightwalker is returning to the sacred centre of the forest (there is a full moon right behind it). The god is imagined as a giant creature of light. Moving very slowly and very gracefully, wading through the trees as if through a pool of green.[109] It's an image of a nature god, the embodiment of the forest and the night.

The arrival of the Nightwalker is signalled by the appearance of the *kodama* in their thousands – the little, white figures pop up in the trees. No one else witnesses this scene: it is a secret contract between the filmmakers and the viewers, with the human and beast characters absent (Jigo and his cronies are somewhere in the distance, and spot the Nightwalker. There's a marvellous touch of strong gusts of wind blowing down from the circular gap in the trees, until it creates ripples in the pool). Only Ashitaka is there, but he is maybe fatally wounded or dead, lying half in the water (that's another stroke of genius in this magical movie – that San should ensure that the wounded boy is lying half in the lake. She also cuts a plant and posts it above his head, perhaps to act as a guide for the Forest God. But when the Forest God appears in his deer form, Ashitaka has now sunk below the water).

The Nightwalker sequence continues with the transformation of the giant god into the deer with the human face (which occurs at sunrise), which materializes on the island in the centre of the pool. The filmmakers have created an authentic sense of wonder and spirituality here, which's almost impossible to do (and with painted plastic!). The number of *genuinely* religious or spiritual films is very, very small. You need a filmmaking team working at their very best with superlative material to be able to evoke this kind of heartfelt mysticism.

Hayao Miyazaki and his team pull it off by using every cinematic trick at their disposal – and one of the chief of these is the *absence* of sounds and only the softest of music cues. The Nightwalker sequence unfolds in near-silence: there are electronic choral effects, and very quiet sounds (such as water and wind).[110] The episode is lit with a golden, pink light

---

[109] This is an image which recalls the appearance of the god Pan in *The Wind In the Willows* by Kenneth Grahame.

[110] Silence is recurring aspect of Japanese animation – moments when nothing is being said, and there is no music or sound effects.

(the light of dawn), which helps too, as does the slow, graceful movement of the Forest Spirit.

In *Princess Mononoke*, the bringing back to life of a character has an authentic emotion to it, which's usually lacking in similar scenes in movies (it's quite a common scene, and not only in fantasy cinema). The filmmakers are somehow able to re-invest a resurrection scene with the spiritual feeling it deserves.

THE NARRATIVE SWITCH.

Halfway through *Princess Mononoke* there is a complete switch in the narrative, but it's so deftly done you might not notice it first-time round (I didn't the first time I saw the movie). It occurs when Ashitaka has rescued San from the clutches of Eboshi and her chums in Irontown. This is one of the big set-pieces in *Princess Mononoke*, of course, involving numerous action beats, extras, and stupendous fights. With San now unconscious (Ashitaka stuns both Eboshi and San to end their ferocious duel), the prince carries her out of the village, to the amazement of the onlookers (a brilliantly staged scene, worthy of Akira Kurosawa, and rightly extended beyond the requirements of the narrative). But not before one of the irate women has fired at Ashitaka and shot him in the chest (her husband was killed in the wolf attacks – the women in *Mononoke Hime* are certainly gutsy).[111] But the wound doesn't kill Ashitaka, however, and he is able to force open the enormous, wooden gate, and leave the village on the backs on the wolves.

Then comes the switch: San wakes, and Ashitaka falls off the galloping elk (Ashitaka takes a fall on his back onto boulders that would be very difficult to achieve in live-action – it would kill a stunt guy doing it for real).[112] On the ground, face-down, Ashitaka is now near-death, there's blood down his back and over Yakul – but San is now back on fighting form, and taking charge (including preventing her wolves from chewing Ashitaka's face off).

The dramatic switch is complete, and it's *San* who's leading the action, making the decisions, and pushing the narrative forward. And I, for one, find San a very intriguing character, and an appealing one too: right from her first appearance, she is one of Hayao Miyazaki's great heroes: independent, strong, resourceful, brave, fierce. But also

---

[111] It's also unusual for a minor character to get to shoot the hero. And because it's a minor chara, the hero can't be vanquished (apart from all the other reasons).
[112] Although Akira Kurosawa's *Ran* features some incredible horse falls.

tender – and the compassion comes out in the following scenes, where San takes Ashitaka into the heart of the woods, where the Forest Spirit can heal him. Whenever San is in the foreground of *Princess Mononoke*, the film is even more engrossing – the prince is a fascinating hero, too, but doesn't have the same appeal as San. Partly because you don't know what the feral San is going to do.

Some of the most striking scenes in *Princess Mononoke* occur next, exquisitely staged: the way that San leads Yakul into the clear water of the forest glade, and pulls the unconscious Ashitaka off the animal, floating him to the island at the centre. And the way that she doesn't drag Ashitaka out of the water, onto the bank, as one might expect, but leaves him partially in the water. It's details such as this that help to make Hayao Miyazaki's films far beyond your average action-adventure (down to the detail of the forest spirits appearing around the plant that San cuts, as if puzzled by what she's done – cutting a plant to heal a human).

WOMEN AND SEX.

There is more cleavage[113] in *Princess Mononoke* than in any other Hayao Miyazaki movie: the women who work in the forge in Tatarba are former prostitutes that Eboshi has rescued from brothels.[114] The kimonos they wear are left open at the neck, emphasizing their breasts (they also go about in bare feet, and headscarves).

The eroticization of the women who work in Tatarba is part of the proto-feminism of the world of *Princess Mononoke*: the women in Tatarba are more assertive and confident than the men; the ruler of Tatarba is a woman; Toki at Irontown stands up to Gonza and the other men; a woman fires a rifle at a man with intent to kill him (shooting him in the back); the witch doctor of the Emishi is an old woman (called Hiisama), and the elders of the Emishi defer to her; and the wolf family is ruled by women – San and Moro. In 1997, Hayao Miyazaki explained some of his thinking:

> It's not that I wanted to make it modern. It's just that depicting Tatara Ba under the rule of men would be boring. And if I made the boss of Tatara Ba a man, he would be a manager, not a revolutionary. If it's a woman, she becomes a revolutionary, even if she is doing the same thing. So I didn't make them women who have to be

[113] And more nudity – even Ashitaka goes nearly naked at one point (when crossing a river).
[114] The talk of brothels and prostitution puts *Princess Mononoke* in a very different place from a typical children's animated movie.

protected by men, or women in their families. I intentionally cut them off (from such things).

The feminism and pro-women angle of the film is depicted strongly in the first scene at Tatarba, when Ashitaka arrives in a boat with the two soldiers he's saved. While Kohroku tells everyone that Ashitaka has saved them, and should be thanked, Gonza (captain of the guard), soon arrives to take charge. The distrust of outsiders and the way the scene is staged is thus far expected in the adventure genre. But it's rapidly subverted when the wonderful character Toki appears. She's a young, formidable presence in a red kimono, who first lays into her hapless husband Kohroku for getting wounded so he won't be any use at work. And when Gonza tries to rein Toki in, she rounds on him too (and all this is in front of everybody).

Toki standing up to Gonza and dressing him down with some choice remarks is a humourous but also important subversion of the genre. Tatarba, it seems, isn't much of a patriarchal system: at the end of the scene Toki talks with Eboshi, who watches from up the slope. Ashitaka is an observer in all this, but the introduction of Eboshi here makes it clear who is in charge (only now is Eboshi revealed as the leader of her people, although she was introduced earlier, in the caravan attack scene, and was in charge of that party).

The subversion of the action-adventure genre, the switching of gender roles, and the reversal of expectations continues throughout the 1997 movie: it's Toki and her women friends who do much of the important work at the ironworks in Tatarba; it's Toki and the women who lead the defence of Tatarba; it's Toki and the women who repel the emissaries of Lord Asano.[115]

And right away there's an erotic flirtation between Ashitaka and the womenfolk of Tatarba. As soon as Toki meets him by the lake, she wonders if he's handsome, and of course she thinks he's gorgeous. The flirtation is light-hearted, but Ashitaka stands out amongst the other men as a distinctly attractive prospect. They have him in their sights: he is young, brave, handsome, a warrior, apparently unattached, and someone new. And the women waste no time in making Ashitaka know that (there's more erotic banter in *Princess Mononoke* than in any other Miyazaki movie).

Hayao Miyazaki's films don't show sex, but there is a

---

[115] Though the men resent the gender reversal, and grumble that Eboshi has spoilt the women.

clear stand-in for a sex scene that's very obvious and bawdy. On his way back from Eboshi demonstrating the lepers who are manufacturing rifles for her, Ashitaka passes the forge, where the women are singing as they operate the bellows for the furnace by pressing down in rows of four on an enormous, wooden contraption.

So when Ashitaka shows up and decides to try his hand (or rather his legs) at the women's work, the women gather round to watch. It's a sex scene in all but name – the heat, the rhythmic movement, the squeak of the wood, the firelight, the nighttime setting, the bare feet and partially naked breasts, the giggling and laughing of the women (even down to the way that Ashitaka is a little too eager at first, and the women talk about him keeping up that rapid pace).

Yet despite all of the feminism on display in *Princess Mononoke*, and the powerful character of San, it is also very much a boy's movie, with warriors, sword fights, battles, and tons of action.

AKIRA KUROSAWA AND HAYAO MIYAZAKI.

Mononoke Hime is Hayao Miyazaki's Akira Kurosawa movie: in it Miyazaki and and the finest team of animators in the world consciously rework and pay *hommage* to some classic scenes from Kurosawa's cinema: sword fights, arrows fired from galloping horses, samurai attacking peasants, sieges of castles, and pitched battles, involving explosions, sword fights, fire, smoke, and fluttering flags and standards. Or simply riders galloping in misty mountains. Soldiers carrying banners (a Kurosawa favourite). Rain. Forests. Wooden forts.[116] And yet more mist (the amount of smoke and mist and atmospheric effects provided by the special effects department in *Princess Mononoke* is marked, and a striking development from Miyazaki's previous movies, which had already employed clouds like no other filmmaker. Nearly every long shot in *Princess Mononoke* has cloud, mist, fog or smoke effects added to it. And from *Princess Mononoke* onwards, Miyazaki would utilize rain and wind just as much as Kurosawa, who is famous for it).

It's easy to discern in *Princess Mononoke* elements from Akira Kurosawa's cinema such as *The Seven Samurai, Throne of Blood, Yojimbo* and *The Hidden Fortress.* Like Kurosawa's

---

[116] In this mediæval world, the communities are fortified – the Emishi village has look-out towers and walls, and Irontown resembles a military fort more than a factory for extracting iron ore. It has a heavy gate that takes ten men to open, and the surrounding area has been fitted with pointed wooden stakes to repel invaders.

cinema, *Princess Mononoke* is storytelling on a big canvas, with the filmmakers creating scenes with a boldness and energy that are difficult to sustain (no wonder Hayao Miyazaki said he was exhausted after making *Princess Mononoke*. Ironically, *Princess Mononoke* may have been easier to shoot in live-action, though that would have been very tough too).

If you like *Princess Mononoke*, I'd recommend any of Akira Kurosawa's samurai and historical movies, such as *The Seven Samurai, Sanjuro, Yojimbo, The Hidden Fortress, Throne of Blood,* and the later, colossal epics: *Kagemusha* and *Ran*. Kurosawa's 1985 adaption of *King Lear, Ran,* contains two battles which rank among the greatest ever filmed, conflicts so extraordinary and so desperately tragic you can't believe they were produced.

For Hayao Miyazaki, you only need to see a few shots from a really good movie to know it's really good: from just a few shots you can discern

> the creator's philosophy, talents, resolve and character. In other words, no matter where you cut the film, you know right away whether you have hit the jackpot or not. (SP, 158)

When Hayao Miyazaki reviewed *Ikiru*, one of Akira Kurosawa's masterpieces, he talked about just one single shot in a scene which impressed him, that when he saw the scene (involving the protagonist stamping a mountain of documents), he knew that *Ikiru* 'was a film that had to be viewed with utmost respect', a movie that a filmmaker makes rarely in their career (SP, 159). The sadness of the man going through the routine of his daily work, the repetitiveness and dullness of it, was captured by Kurosawa:

> the man's dutiful, sad performance of his work is the sadness that we have in our own lives. Our lives do not take on meaning because of something we have accomplished. (SP, 160)

In taking on Akira Kurosawa in *Princess Mononoke*, Hayao Miyazaki and his team were tackling the greatest Japanese filmmaker, and you can only do that if you're feeling mighty confident. You wouldn't expect a filmmaker to mount a full-blooded, Kurosawa-style epic as their first movie, for instance (no one ever has). However, by the time of his second film (*Nausicaä of the Valley of the Wind*), Miyazaki was already staging action and narrative on an enormous canvas.

But *Princess Mononoke* does full justice to Akira Kurosawa's cinema, and the 1997 movie also understands the poetry of Kurosawa's films, the nature mysticism, the psychological and emotional drama, and the very important moral and ethical elements. Although Kurosawa's associated with *chambara*, sword-play, mediæval and 16th century historical epics, Toshio Mifune, and all the rest, those other elements are actually more significant in many respects – the nature mysticism and adventure and companionship in the astonishing *Dersu Uzala*, for example, or the themes of morality and psychology in *Ikiru* or *The Seven Samurai*.

The amount of blood and bloodshed in *Princess Mononoke* is striking: Hayao Miyazaki's movies have never shied away from portraying violence, and they are often more violent than viewers expect, not least because they are animation, which's often thought to be family-oriented, toned-down fare (the Walt Disney Studios, for instance, is very reluctant to show blood, and presents death on screen very carefully.)

But in *Princess Mononoke* the body count and on-screen violence is severer than usual in a Hayao Miyazaki movie (or it's more in close-up now): there are quite a few decapitations, arms being chopped off, people being stabbed and battered, samurai being blown to bits by gunfire, and grave pits with lines of corpses (not only dead humans, but slain boars too).[117]

There's a lot of blood being sloshed around in *Princess Mononoke* too: Moro the wolf, Okkoto the boar, Ashitaka, San, and many other main characters have blood on them (and some, such as the wolf and the boar, have multiple. bleeding wounds, the blood gushing everywhere). And San is so memorably introduced with blood on her face – a highly unusual character introduction.

The violence in *Princess Mononoke* is introduced early on – when Ashitaka comes across a village under attack from Lord Asano's samurai, he rips off a guy's arms and pins them to a tree with an arrow, and decapitates another samurai on horseback.[118] From then on, the audience is going to realize they are not watching your usual action-adventure animated movie (the mad boar Nago in the opening scene has already suggested that too).

The violence I would align with the cinema of Akira Kurosawa again – Kurosawa, aside from being a genius at portraying violence and conflict, was right to portray it because his

---
117 The gravepits are disturbing images, with many modern affinities such as world wars.
118 Notice that it's the samurai who are often the targets of Ashitaka's vehemence; they are not the heroic warriors of lore, but hired guards.

movies were evoking violent historical times. In those days, a samurai fight could be a bloody affair (although Kurosawa was happy to use violence excessively when employed in a symbolic fashion, too – *viz.*, Washizu's death by a thousand arrows in *Throne of Blood*, a much-copied screen demise).

In a 1985 article, Hayao Miyazaki was critical of Akira Kurosawa's stylizations of battles: in *Kagemusha*, Miyazaki pointed out that the troops were set out in groups, and they charged like unified cavalry. In reality, Miyazaki reckoned that the soldiers would've all charged together (SP, 133). Also, most battles tended to be depicted in big, wide-open spaces, not in rice fields, along footpaths, or in the undergrowth: 'won't someone make period films that more carefully depict scenes with these kinds of details?' Miyazaki asked (ibid.). And he proceeded to do just that, twelve years later, in *Mononoke Hime*.

The battles in *Princess Mononoke* run from the epic vista to the swift, fierce hand-to-hand fight (both reveal the influence of Akira Kurosawa). The rapidity of the sword fights and sword-and-dagger duels is lightning-swift (the filmmakers seems to have been studying Hong Kong martial arts movies for some of the moves). All in all, the staging of the action in *Princess Mononoke* is a big step-up from the knockabout humour of *Porco Rosso* or the sometimes vaguer conflicts of *Laputa: Castle In the Sky*.

And the action in *Princess Mononoke* is as accomplished as the best martial arts movies – the duel between Ashitaka and the four samurai pursing him from Irontown, for instance, is a stunning example of using space and distance and speed and camera angles and point-of-view shots. If only all action movies were this good.

Princess Mononoke is Hayao Miyazaki's Akira Kurosawa epic, yes, but it's also his *Tarzan* and *Jungle Book* movie, an action-adventure picture with the kind of characters and action that you can find in the fiction of Edgar Rice Burroughs, Jules Verne, H.G. Wells, Mark Twain and Rudyard Kipling (and thousands of comicbooks going back to the early days of magazine publishing for young people in the first part of the 20th century).

Although *Princess Mononoke* might be the only Hayao Miyazaki movie *not* featuring flying sequences (or flying vehicles), there is plenty of action up in the air, with characters leaping about – and of course much of the climactic sequence takes place in the sky, as the Nightwalker searches for its head.

THE FINALE.

The climax of *Princess Mononoke* is unbelievably spectacular. You know it's going to be, when the rest of the movie is so good: you know the filmmakers are going to top everything that's already appeared. And they do. The filmmakers are throwing everything they can think of into the mix: there are incredible scenes of mass battles, some intricately intercut as flashbacks with the scenes set in the present (when Ashitaka asks the haunted soldier crouched by the graves what happened, for instance). Scenes of the boars charging, with San on a wolf riding between them. Explosions and fire and smoke from mines and grenades. And deeply moving scenes after the battle, as Ashitaka explores the carnage. *Princess Mononoke* is a movie that depicts the consequences of war and the costs of violence, as in the rest of Miyazaki's cinema.

It's intriguing that the filmmakers leave Ashitaka out of the big battle towards the end of the second act of the movie: Ashitaka is riding through wind and rain as the storm breaks and the battle commences (he's heading for Irontown). But only after he's reached Irontown over the river (at some peril, avoiding soldiers, samurai and arrows – no A to B trip is easy in an action-adventure movie), and spoken to the women on the battlements, does he find out what's happening.

At this point, the 1997 movie takes all sorts of interesting twists and turns – Hayao Miyazaki-sama and his team do everything you'd expect in an action-adventure picture – such as plenty of action, for a start, but also plenty of obstacles for the heroes, plenty of snakepit situations, plenty of cliffhangers, and quieter interludes (though, thankfully, not the wisecracks and one-liners and silly bits of humour of too many Hollywood flicks).

Hayao Miyazaki and his animation house do all of that, and *then some*. But they also *do more*: they keep the action pinned to the major themes of the movie, which's vital; it's not simply action for the sake of it, action emptied of purpose or value or consequence. They fill the screen with amazing spectacles. And finally they add quirky, unusual turns to the narrative.

One of the most interesting scenes in the *tour-de-force* finale of *Princess Mononoke*, for example, takes place when all of the major characters arrive at the forest glade (and what a collection of characters they are – three gods, no less, plus a cursed hero, a wolf princess, wolves, cynical treasure hunters, soldiers, and a woman who's intent on killing a god).

Dramatically, this sequence of scenes needs to do many

things, including:

(1) to bring the action to a satisfying climax,

(2) to play out many of the characters' goals,

(3) to resolve many conflicts between the groups of characters,

(4) to explore the themes of the film, and

(5) to deliver entertaining cinema.

And it does all of that, but it does it all in Hayao Miyazaki's highly individual way. How many filmmakers, for example, would choose to play out some of the action *inside* the body of a god? But Miyazaki and his team do just that when they have San being absorbed into Okkoto's body (now he's nearly all demon), and being smothered by those wriggling, red, squishy, worm-like thingies.

Ashitaka acts of course like the prince or hero of fairy tales, and dives into the writhing mass of scarlet tendrils, to save his wolf princess. The imagery alone is just astounding, but the dramatic moves that *Princess Mononoke* takes continually surprise the audience. Ashitaka, for instance, is unsuccessful, and is ejected far out of the mouth of the beast, to fall into the lake, sinking to the bottom, unconscious.

In the midst of all this thrilling drama, the filmmakers are also orchestrating other elements, such as the reappearance of the Forest Spirit, and Eboshi and Jigo waiting for their chance to kill it. There's so much going on, but the climax of *Princess Mononoke* never feels rushed or contrived or cheated or silly. It has a dramatic and visual logic, features truly astonishing imagery and details, and possesses a momentum that works like gangbusters (the editing, for instance, is exquisitely pin-sharp).[119]

How delightful, for instance, is the way that San is finally rescued – by Moro speaking to Ashitaka in his mind, as he floats underwater unconscious. That works because the movie has already shown how Ashitaka is telepathically linked to San and the wolves (but it's still a struggle for him to extricate San from the crazed Okkoto).

But no, it's not over yet (though the preceding act would be enough for many a movie): the biggest, wildest scenes in *Princess Mononoke* are still to come: out burst the special effects, costing hundreds of thousands of Yen per minute, as the Forest Spirit mutates into a purple, blue and black giant searching for its head with enormous, gloopy blobs spreading

---

[119] It's worth recalling that Miyazaki has the editor credit on *Princess Mononoke*, along with the incredible Takeshi Seyama.

over the mountains, into the lake, thru the trees. Blobs, tendrils of energy, colours, decaying trees and grass, characters fleeing in every direction – the imagery floods the screen.

You'd think that the dark goo issuing from the headless Forest Spirit would be a positive life-force – but it makes thematic sense as well as dramatic sense that the energies inside the Shishigami should be so powerful that it's death for a human who touches them. Because we are dealing with massive elemental powers here – the power of nature itself.

This section of *Princess Mononoke* is completely crazy, with the action now frantic and broad (though the human-scale dramas are still being played out fiercely back down on the ground – for instance, the scene on the island (enveloped on all sides by walls of bubbly god-stuff), where San is determined to finish off Eboshi, and Ashitaka does all he can to dissuade her. We are in a mythic zone now: when San stabs Ashitaka in the chest (with Kaya's gift knife, note), it has no effect (because the cursemark has spread further). They embrace).

The climax of *Princess Mononoke* is absolutely apocalyptic – it has everything except distant atomic explosions over Tokyo like so many Japanese *animé* (actually, there are scenes of debris and hurricane winds reminiscent of nuclear bombs, when the Forest Spirit topples into the lake). Giant hands flying over trees, a mass of immense hands on elastic arms diving into the trees from far above, a flood of dark purple liquid like lava smothering the mountains and flowing everywhere, characters dodging out-lying tendrils speeding towards them, San and Ashitaka hurtling around on wolfback, Jigo, Gonza & co. hurrying off with the Forest Spirit's head in a metal box, the frantic exodus from Irontown, the village being demolished – the action is breakneck.

It's quite right that the Forest Spirit appears to die *after* it's recovered its head. Many storytellers and filmmakers might move from that point to the happy ending, with the land reborn. No. It makes sense that after the god has found its head, it should topple into the lake. That adds a suitably jumbo-sized piece of action to close this so-spectacular part of *Princess Mononoke*, but the dramatic function is clear: the Forest Spirit's collapse seems to destroy plenty of the landscape around it, but most of the destruction is directed at Irontown (witness the shot of the remains of Irontown (and some of the banners of Lord Asano) flying off into the mountains – as if it's the timber returning to its origins, in the trees).

Only *after* Irontown has been (partially) demolished does

the rejuvenation of the earth begin. The *ecological* theme (or message) of *Princess Mononoke* seems clear at this point: humans can begin again, they can have a second chance, but they'd better build something *in tune* with nature, rather than set against it. As Ashitaka states, the Forest Spirit isn't dead, it isn't all over, as San worries, because the Forest Spirit is all around, is life itself. (That piece of dialogue is what I would call 'on the nail', very blunt; but it's only stated once; in a Hollywood flick, it would be rammed home with a sledgehammer).

And when the rebirth occurs, rightly held for some moments in the extreme long shot of the mountains and the lake, and Joe Hisaishi's piano music plays (Hisaishi is credited as pianist), it is a deeply moving ending. It is the right ending, and it is a happy ending, and it comes out of everything that has gone on before. It has the satisfying logic of a fairy tale, as well as the beauty and poetry of a mediæval romance.

THE ENDING.

The ending of *Princess Mononoke* is not about resolving every element in the movie and rounding it all off with a happy ending, as Hayao Miyazaki insisted in his 1995 memo:

> *Princess Mononoke* does not purport to solve the problems of the entire world. The battle between rampaging forest gods and humanity cannot end well; there can be no happy ending. Yet, even amid the hatred and slaughter, there are things worthy of life. It is possible for wonderful encounters to occur and for beautiful things to exist. (SP, 274)

The *dénouement* of *Princess Mononoke* quite rightly doesn't go on and on as it so often does in American or European movies of this kind: rather, the 1997 film makes all of the pertinent points with a series of brief visits to each of the major characters: the most important scene is the two-hander between Ashitaka[120] and Mononoke, where he says he will help build a new Tatarba, and San tells him she will return to the forest because she can't forgive humans for what they've done.[121] But Ashitaka promises to visit San in the forest, and she smiles. A kiss isn't necessary here, after all they've been

---

[120] We can see that the cursemark is diminished, and presumably halted.
[121] 'The problem presented to me was whether San's hatred of humanity could be softened by Ashitaka's love' (TP, 83).

through.[122]

The imagery of shoots, plants and flowers growing rapidly is spiritual – authentically, properly spiritual. It really is one of the most impressive and convincing scenes of rebirth in cinema. The waves of green, and deeper greens, and then deeper greens still, are highly poetic. And when the film cuts to San and Ashitaka hugging each other on the ground in the long grass, it is the greenest, juiciest grass in movies.[123]

Princess Mononoke then cuts to the other main players: (1) Eboshi, sitting in the ruins of Tatarba, surrounded by her people, vowing to build a new and better town, and wanting to thank Ashitaka; (2) Jigo and an aide on the rock, with Jigo providing a little comic relief after all the climactic scenes, and finally (3) to the sacred centre of the film, the pool and glade.

The way Eboshi is sitting in a quiet, tired manner, and her attitude, suggests that she is humbled by what's happened. She realizes that San and the wolves helped to save them. It's not certain here if Eboshi is going to change her ways (she's still going to build a new town, which will presumably have to have some kind of industrial labour at the heart of it), but maybe she's realized that San and her wolf gods and the other animal gods had some good reasons for doing what they did.

There isn't a happy ending for the conflict between humanity and the gods, Hayao Miyazaki wrote in his proposal for the film: it is always an uneasy, ambiguous relationship: gods will never do exactly what humans want them to, and vice versa.

But the final image of *Princess Mononoke* is quite rightly the spiritual core of the piece, the lake and glade: it's still devastated but on the way to being renewed: there are new shoots growing out of the soil, and the fallen trees are sprouting new branches. But the clincher, of course, is the reappearance of the little *kodama* – a single one, seen in long shot near the clear water, which materializes and rattles its head.[124]

And that, folks, is the last image of one of the most truly, mind-bogglingly beautiful movies ever made.

---

[122] 'I have no way of replying to children who… ask why Ashitaka can control his hatred when they are unable to control theirs. That is the very reason I wanted to make this film' (TP, 84). 'The main reason I made this film is because I felt children in Japan harbor doubts as to why they need to live' (TP, 79).
[123] And if there's one thing that Studio Ghibli can do, it is beautiful trees, flowers, plants, fields and grass.
[124] The renewal of a land has been done in movies before, but rarely as convincing on a dramatic as well as a thematic level as in *Princess Mononoke*.

Miyazaki drawing the Nausicaä manga (above).
The Nausicaä storyboards (below).

Miyazaki working on the storyboards for The Wind Rises

Miyazaki working out timings for animation using a stopwatch.
This is how large parts of Ghibli's movies are made:
sitting at a desk with a pencil and a piece of paper.

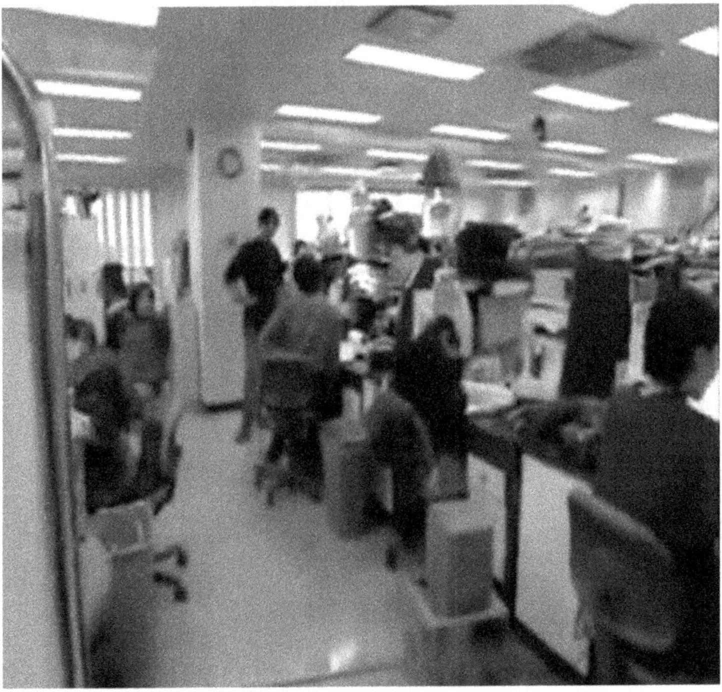

Studio Ghibli during the production of Princess Mononoke.

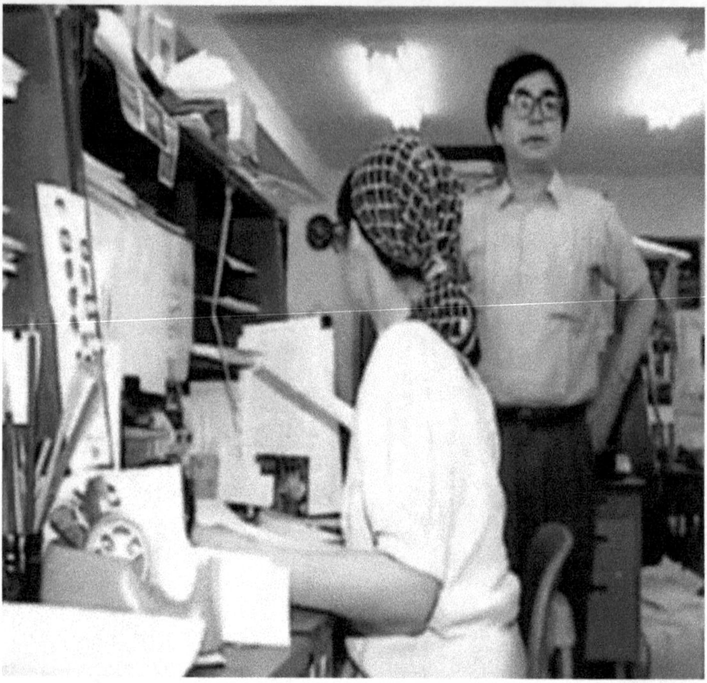

Miyazaki working the animation staff at Studio Ghibli.
At the time of Kiki in 1989 (above), and during
The Wind Rises in 2013 (below).

11
*
SPIRITED AWAY

INTRODUCTION.
Spirited Away (*Sen to Chihiro no Kamikakushi* = *The Spiriting Away of Sen and Chihiro*, 2001) is without a doubt a masterpiece of cinema, and one of Hayao Miyazaki's great works. It is one of the most spectacular films of *colour* you will ever see. And of storytelling, of imagination, of characterization. It's the movie that brought Miyazaki to a global audience, even more perhaps than *Princess Mononoke*.

Art direction in *Spirited Away* was by Norubu Yoshida and Youji Takeshige. Motohiro Hatanaka was casting director. The animation directors were Kitaro Kousaka, Masashi Ando and Megumi Kagawa.[1] Music was by Joe Hisaishi (the music was produced by Kazumi Inaki and Tamaki Kojo).[2] Colour design was by Michiyo Yasuda (assisted by Kazuko Yamada). Takeshi Seyama edited the movie. Atsushi Okui was DP. Masayuki Miyagi and Atsushi Takahashi were ADs. Digital animation was by Mitsunori Katama. Sound was by Kazuhiro Hayashi and Toshiaki Abe. Takeshi Imaizumi, Tetsuya Satake and Tsukuru Takagi were sound mixers and recordists. Michihiro Ito produced the sound fx. Toru Noguchi recorded the characters' sounds. Shuji Inoue's team recorded ambient sounds for *Spirited Away,* including a real bathhouse.

The voice talent for *Spirited Away* included Rumi Hiragi, 14 years-old (born August 1, 1987, as Chihiro), Miyu Irono (Haku),[3] Mari Natsuki (Yubaba and Zeniba), Bunta Sugawara (Kamaji),[4] Yumi Tamai (Lin), Tatsuya Gashûin (Aogaeru), Takashi Naitô (Chihiro's father), Yasuko Sawaguchi (Chihiro's mom), Ryûnosuke Kamiki (Baby Boh),[5] Yumi Tamai (Rin), Yô

---
[1] There were some 40 animators working on *Spirited Away.*
[2] Others in the music team included Takashi Nagai, Masayoshi Okawa, Masaki Sakjme, Shinichi Tanaka, and Futoshi Ueda.
[3] Irono, an *animé* actor, was 13 at the time. The English dub wrongly used an older actor.
[4] Toshio Suzuki reckoned that it had to be Bunta Sugawara for Kamaji, because he was the only actor who could say the line, 'it's love. Love' (TP, 209). Sagawara was also Ged in *Tales From Earthsea.*
[5] Kamiki was a celebrity at 7 years-old.

Ôizumi (Bandaigaeru), Koba Hayashi (the River God), Tsunehiko Kamijô (Chichiyaku), and Takehiko Ono (Aniyaku). The English dub,[6] produced by Kirk Wise, John Lasseter and Donald W. Ernst at Disney in 2002.[7]

The production companies, apart from Studio Ghibli, were Nippon Television, Dentsu, Buena Vista, Tohokushinsha Film, Mitsubishi Corporation and Tokuma Shoten. Toshio Suzuki, Yasuyoshi Tokuma, Takeyoshi Matsushita, Seiichiro Ujiie, Yuraka Narita, Koji Hoshin, Banjiro Uemara and Hironori Aihara produced *Spirited Away*; and Hayao Miyazaki wrote and directed the film.[8]

It's worth emphasizing that last credit: the movie was *not* an adaptation of a book,[9] a play, a *manga,* a radio series, a comicbook, a biography, a board game, a musical, a ballet, an opera, a theme park ride, a TV show, a computer game, a remake of an earlier film, or a sequel: it was an original script by Miyazaki.[10] And, no, it wasn't written by a committee, or ten 'story editors', or went thru in development hell and many producers and writing teams before reaching the screen. That in itself is pretty astounding for a movie this pricey.[11]

> There are 1415 different shots in *Spirited Away*. When starting the project [Miyazaki explained], I had envisioned about 1200, but the film told me no, it had to be more than 1200. It's not me who makes the film. The film makes itself and I have no choice but to follow.

Spirited Away was a good experience for Hayao Miyazaki: that's important, especially for movies which mean a lot to the filmmakers.

---

[6] Subtitles were by husband and wife team Cindy and David Hewitt.
[7] It included actors Daveigh Chase, Suzanne Pleshette, Jason Marsden, Susan Egan, David Ogden Stiers, Lauren Holly, Michael Chiklis, John Ratzenberger, and Jack Angel.
[8] Part of the in-between segments of *Spirited Away* were farmed out to an animation company in South Korea, D.R. Digital, because the production schedule of *Spirited Away* proved to be too much for Studio Ghibli. Other companies involved in *Spirited Away* included Anime Torotoro, Oh Production, Studio Cockpit, Studio Takuranke, Group Donguri, Nakamura Production, Gainax, Studio Kuma, Production I-G, Studio Musashi, Studio Hibari, Kiryu, Mugenkan, AIC, Liberty Ship and Madhouse. Some of those are celebrated *animé* houses in their own right.
[9] However, one of the starting-points for *Spirited Away* was *The Mysterious Town Behind the Fog* by Sachiko Kashiwaba (1995), which depicts a girl in a strange world filled with eccentric characters.
[10] *Spirited Away* was conceived much longer, running to three hours. Miyazaki cut the movie down, simplifying it and eliminating the 'eye candy'.
[11] Moebius remarked: 'when I saw *Princess Mononoke*, and even more *Spirited Away*, I was struck by the fact that I couldn't imagine a producer, any producer in the world, accepting the script.'

Creation is always a series of regrets, but *Spirited Away* was an exception. I felt really good when I was creating it. I'd always wanted to visualize a train running on the surface of the sea, and I think we came up with the scene that perfectly matches that image.

Spirited Away is a movie of many outstanding sequences, but also many modest and intimate moments.[12] There isn't an ounce of fat or waste, and nothing is too long in its 124 minute run (it's one of Hayao Miyazaki's longest films). And you can see why this production cost JPY 2.5 billion – the money is up there on the screen, in every exquisite, hand-crafted frame.

Spirited Away was enormously successful – like *Princess Mononoke*, it fared incredibly well at the box office in Japan. In fact, it was the biggest box office success in Japan's history, making around $250-300 million or ¥30 billion (unadjusted for inflation – only figures adjusted for inflation really make sense).[13] Its audience was in the region of 23 million, about one-sixth of people in Japan (bearing in mind that there are 127 million people living in Japan).[14] Released on July 20, 2001 in Japan, *Spirited Away* went on to win the Best Animated Film Oscar, and numerous other awards, such as the Golden Bear in Berlin, best film at the Japanese Academy Awards, and top awards from the New York Film Critics, Los Angeles Film Critics, Annie Awards, Critics' Choice Awards, National Board of Review, Golden Satellite, Saturn, Hong Kong Film, International Children's Film, etc (of course, it shoulda won the Best Film Oscar – which went to *A Beautiful Mind* that year. *Spirited Away* beat *Ice Age* (Blue Sky/ Fox) and *Lilo and Stitch* (Disney) for the Animation Oscar).[15]

In 2001, the big movies globally were *Harry Potter 1*, *The Lord of the Rings 1*, *Pearl Harbor*, *The Mummy 2* and *Jurassic Park 3* (the usual – YAWN – sequels and franchise movies).

---

12 Andrew Osmond speaks of its 'vibrant imagination, its immersive world, inimitable idiosyncrasies and eloquent fables' (2008, 106).
13 The box office for *Spirited Away* was equivalent to a picture making $1 billion in the U.S.A.
14 *Spirited Away* also became the first movie to reach $200m b4 opening in the U.S.A. When it was released in America in 2002 it grossed about $10m.
15 But the awarding of Oscars is a very odd business – for instance, *Howl* was nominated in 2005, but *Wallace and Gromit* won. Well, Aardman's stopmotions are fun and easy to like (and Miyazaki enjoys them), but they are certainly not finer than *Howl*! Same again in 2013: *The Wind Rises* was nominated, but *Frozen* won! (The Oscars favour North American movies, with Pixar and DreamWorks product dominating).

And two other huge animated movies,[16] both digital: Disney's *Monsters, Inc* and DreamWorks' *Shrek*. *Monsters, Inc* and *Shrek* battled it out for the first animated movie Oscar (*Shrek* won), but had they gone up against *Spirited Away*, the competition would've stood no chance (*Spirited Away* is at a whole other level from anything in Western animation). As it was, *Spirited Away* won the Oscar the following year.

It's all the more remarkable when you consider who the hero of *Spirited Away* is: a ten year-old girl. If you asked some film studio executives or marketing experts about producing the Ultimate Money-spinning Movie, they would probably advise you to have a teenage boy (white, American) for your hero or identification figure, who teams up with preferrably some older, male figure who can kick ass action-wise, plus some delicious eye candy in the form of a sexy, young starlet. *Spirited Away* has none of that. It has action in abundance, and magic, and the hint of a romance, but it breaks the rules in many other respects.

Joe Hisaishi (and his team of music editors, music supervisors, music scorers, orchestraters, recording engineers and music mixers)[17] provides a marvellous score for *Spirited Away*, one of his best, by turns haunting, sweeping, plangent, creepy, percussive and heartfelt. The music rightly provides both the emotional state of mind of the heroine, Chihiro, but also the third person views of the fantasy world of *Spirited Away*. The theme song, 'Always With Me', was by Yumi Kimura and Wakako Kaku, who had sent in the song to Studio Ghibli on spec.[18]

Spirited Away is a masterpiece of what is sometimes called 'traditional' or 'classic' cel animation. That is, drawings and ink and paint (although computers had been employed, for instance, in earlier Studio Ghibli movies, such as in *Mononoke Hime*). *Spirited Away* would be – or should be – in many critics' top ten animated films. It can happily stand beside the finest of Western animation, such as the films of Walt Disney's 'golden age', and more recent movies, such as *Beauty and the Beast* or *The Lion King* (and for some will be held in higher regard. Certainly thematically and psychologically, it is way beyond Disney or Pixar). Artistically, *Spirited Away* is pretty much superior to every ink and paint

---

16 The other big, Western animated movies of 2001 were *Atlantis, Jimmy Neutron* and *Final Fantasy*, although parts of *Evolution, Planet of the Apes, Artificial Intelligence, Dr Doolittle 2*, and *Spy Kids* were animation, like so many high budget movies.
17 The music was recorded by the New Japan Philharmonic Orchestra.
18 This would've been included in the cancelled *Rin the Chimney Painter* project.

animation you can think of – and you have to search hard to find films that can match it.

Anyone can spot the increase in the *subtlety* of emotion in Hayao Miyazaki's later movies – in particular, the preponderance of conflicting feelings in the hero/ines, and the shading in those emotions. The later pieces are more emotionally complex, and contain far more conflicting motives and goals for the hero/ines than the earlier films. Which makes them satisfying in different ways. Not more 'realistic' or 'true to life', necessarily, but certainly enough to complicate the narratives even further.

And the subtlety of emotional responses also bears directly on the plots of the later Hayao Miyazaki movies, so that the hero/ ines have more to consider at each move: their goals are not now simply to 'save the princess' or 'find mom' (notice also how, in the later movies, Miyazaki's hero/ines gather a bunch of characters around them as they progress; so that it's not just about themselves).

Spirited Away operates on so many levels. Dan Cavallaro points out some of them: 'a coming-of-age quest, a reflection on alter egos, an adult fable' and adventurous experiments in animation and technology (C, 146). There are many other layers to *Spirited Away*. For fairy tale expert Jack Zipes, *Spirited Away* depicts 'a bizarre counter-world', in which the normal world is turned upside-down.[19]

Hayao Miyazaki insisted that although *Spirited Away* was wild fantasy, it was 'true', it was not a lie: 'I'm dealing with real issues'.[20] Audiences respond to that: the issues are real and true, they are easy to relate to: if you want to stay in Yuya (the bathhouse), you have to work. If you want to save your parents, you'll have to stay and work it out, and it won't happen instantly. There are no easy solutions.

CHIHIRO.

One of the inspirations for *Spirited Away* was the ten year-old daughter of a friend of Hayao Miyazaki's (and her father was an inspiration for the father in the film. One of the sources for the mom character was a Ghibli employee). Producer Toshio Suzuki was partly responsible for persuading

---

[19] 'Everyone wants to take part in the cleansing. Nobody is purely clean. The world is chock-full of ambiguity. Deep down all the creatures want love and friendship. Humans, a spidery grandpa, ghosts, giant chicks, frogs, mice, and other creatures are drawn as unconventional characters that follow rituals without anything codified. The detailed depiction of the interior and exterior buildings is exquisite, and the images metamorphose before our eyes.' (2011, 108)
[20] Quoted in S. Adilman, 2002.

Miyazaki to make a movie for children, rather than the film he was planning for young people.

> What made me decide to make this film [Miyazaki remarked] was the realisation that there are no films made for that age group of ten-year old girls. It was through observing the daughter of a friend that I realised there were no films out there for her, no films that directly spoke to her. Certainly, girls like her see films that contain characters their age, but they can't identify with them, because they are imaginary characters that don't resemble them at all.

The heroine is another of Hayao Miyazaki's very appealing characters.[21] Chihiro is very much a reluctant hero, an introverted, nervy, passive,[22] somewhat selfish, scared and spoilt child of about 10.[23] She doesn't want her life shaken up, doesn't want to move house, and misses her friends (who have given her a bunch of pink flowers and a farewell card – which handily reminds her of her name later on).

At the beginning of the film, Chihiro might grow up to be Woody Allen or James Stewart in one of their neurotic roles (Stewart in *Vertigo* – Allen in any of his movies). Chihiro is definitely not like the practical, brave, independent young women in *Kiki's Delivery Service* or *Nausicaä of the Valley of the Wind*, or the vivacious and energetic girls like Ponyo or Satsuki in *My Neighbor Totoro*. But by the end of the piece, she is.

That was the intention: Chihiro wasn't meant to have some magical power, like flying, or something she was really good at. Hayao Miyazaki and his team were keen to keep Chihiro realistic, in terms of what a young girl of ten or so would really be capable of doing (they asked themselves questions, such as, would a ten year-old girl be capable of doing this?).

Hayao Miyazaki wasn't convinced that Chihiro was appealing enough, or cute enough, although he avoids overly *kawaii* characterizations (true, Chihiro's visual characterization is not instantly appealing). By the end of production, he recognized that Chihiro wasn't dull and was charming.

Andrew Osmond (2008) draws attention to the scared, passive Chihiro of the earlier scenes (a characterization which

---

[21] Miyazaki has said he tends to think about the characters and their situations for a long time b4 beginning to sketch them.
[22] Her passivity or inaction is important: she is not one of Miyazaki's all-action heroes. Severl times in the first act, Chihiro is hunkered down, unable to act.
[23] Miyazaki said in his statement for *Spirited Away* that it was 'for the people who used to be 10 years-old, and the people who are going to be 10 years-old'.

was developed with animator Masashi Ando's input), and which was supplanted by the more familiar Miyazakian heroine: heroic, brave, energetic. In Osmond's reading, the more heroic Chihiro won out, as the movie was altered during production (2008, 21). Osmond even suggested that some viewers (probably adults) may have been alienated by this alteration in Chihiro's character (89). No, I don't think so at all.

Chihiro wears a white Tee shirt with a green stripe, red shorts, and sneakers. She has her bushy hair in a single bunch.[24] She is a very skinny kid, with long, spindly legs (a Hayao Miyazaki favourite form – also employed in Nausicaä and Satsuki). Chihiro has a round moon-face, with eyes set wide apart, a tiny nose (a mere filip in profile), and large cheeks (the middle section of her face is expanded, to allow for more expressions – at times there's three inches between her mouth and her nose). In the second part of the film, Chihiro sports the uniform of the bathhouse workers: a red jacket and pants, tied with a belt (and usually in bare feet – in this picture, characters are traditionally Japanese, taking their shoes and socks off indoors).

Hayao Miyazaki spoke about two of the key scenes in the 2001 film being the first one, where Chihiro is depicted in the car, afraid of the world outside, and the final scene, where she has faced the world, and is much stronger:

> But there are two scenes in *Spirited Away* that could be considered symbolic for the film. One is the first scene in the back of the car, where she is really a vulnerable little girl, and the other is the final scene, where she's full of life and has faced the whole world. Those are two portraits of Chihiro which show the development of her character.

It's important for Hayao Miyazaki that Chihiro is portrayed as spoilt as well as afraid: she is a person who doesn't appreciate all of the things her parents are doing for her. Chihiro is not someone, one imagines, who has to do household chores, which she has to do in the bathhouse (and at first she's useless). She really doesn't have much of an idea about how the world works – or rather, everything has been done *for* her, so she hasn't had to deal with the world much.

One of the views embodied in *Spirited Away* is that you already possess everything you need to do whatever it is you

---

[24] At the end of the movie, Zeniba gives Chihiro a hairband, which she's made. Miyazaki animated the moment when Chihiro puts it on (Aki Kagawa, one of the animation supervisors, recalled that some in the team thought the shot was suggestive).

need to do, or to *be* whatever you want to *be*. You don't need anything *more*. Thus, Chihiro met Haku once, but has forgotten about it: but the memory is still there, inside her (Haku says somehow he knew her name, but she doesn't know his). The sister witch Zeniba tells Chihiro: you'll have to help your parents and Haku on your own. Use what you remember about them.

THE JOURNEY TO THE BATHHOUSE.

One of the delights of Hayao Miyazaki's movies are the elaborate opening credit sequences (such as in *Laputa: Castle In the Sky* or *Ponyo*). But there are no opening credits in *Spirited Away* like that: instead, after the Studio Ghibli credits and the production company credits (white lettering over pale blue, as usual), the movie goes straight into Chihiro in the car. The main title comes up over a shot of the car driving up a side road on a hill (no hints, then, of what's to come!).

Once again, Hayao Miyazaki and his team introduce the fantastical world of the film (the bathhouse) gradually: the movie opens with a car journey, set in the contemporary world (in Japan),[25] and shifts in stages to a more fantastical realm – first when the tarmac road becomes a rough track, and the city is left behind for the forest; then through the tunnel into the green fields (cue the classic Miyazakian image of clouds drifting over green hills – an image Miyazaki has made wholly his own – it's the final image of his final film); across a riverbed; into the abandoned theme park; and finally to the moment when Chihiro steps onto the bridge that leads to the bathhouse.

The elegant transitions (each one a threshold) lead the heroine and the audience from the 'real world' into the secondary/ fantasy world of the bathhouse one step at a time. The movie could easily have jumped from the tunnel, for instance, to the bridge across the canyon to the bathhouse. Instead, the filmmakers take the audience by the hand, just as Chihiro hangs on to her mother too tightly in the tunnel, and leads them step by step into the magical world. It is a gentler journey than suddenly thrusting the audience (and the heroine) into the magic realm.

And the *length* of the journey also serves to highlight Chihiro's emotional journey: she really is resistant to the whole idea of even entering the tunnel (she runs back towards

---

[25] There are no big shots of Tokyo, however, which many another filmmaker would've unable to resist: instead, the car's depicted driving along modest suburban roads, turning off to go up a hill.

the car, but gets scared, looks at the weird statue next to her, and joins her parents),[26] let alone crossing that eerily empty (though sunlit) entrance hall, or walking over the grass and the rocky stream (notice how Chihiro clambers gingerly over the rocks; notice too that her dad and mom only smell the enticing food when they have crossed the water – another example of the many fairy tale[27] motifs in *Spirited Away* – that the river (later a lake) is the border zone of the magical world). Gusts of wind (a Miyazakian favourite motif) are deployed twice, which scare Chihiro even further.

And Chihiro's reluctance and suspicion and fears continue up to the moment her parents turn into pigs and on and on, into the second act of the film (for a long, long time, Chihiro is having A Really Bad Day). All of that narrative work makes Chihiro's transformation into someone brave and kind-hearted and compassionate possess all the more impact (however, unlike some Miyazaki characters, Chihiro stays in the same form throughout the movie – she doesn't transform, but everyone around her does).

This *really is* a film about the journey of an individual from being selfish and self-absorbed to someone heroic and compassionate (unlike some other movies which advertize that spiritual journey, but don't deliver it). In *Spirited Away*, Chihiro is not only going to save her parents Akio and Yûko Ogino, she's also going to help Haku, *and* No Face, *and* the River God, *and* Zeniba, *and* baby Boh. *And* she even manages to teach Yubaba a lesson that bullying people isn't so good.[28] *And* she has to re-discover her name to leave the spirit world and return to her world. *Spirited Away* pulls off this remarkable narrative feat (remarkable because it's actually difficult to do convincingly), with such grace, such elegance, such skill, you can't believe it.

And look at the *mise-en-scène* of the opening half of the first act of *Spirited Away*: it's all positive, uplifting, sunny: the sky is blue, it's a warm, Summer's day, there's a sunlit forest. The feelings of starting a new life in a new home (and even the adventure of leaving the tarmac road and hurtling along a forest track) ought to be fun for Chihiro. And once the family're outside the entrance foyer, the theme park is a sunlit realm of green fields and white clouds. But Chihiro resists

---

[26] And how the movie exaggerates the confident walking styles of Chihiro's mom and dad enhances Chihiro's insecurities.
[27] 'Like all the best fairy tales, the film is innocent, child-friendly, and psychologically disturbing all at once', for J. Clements and H. McCarthy (2006, 606).
[28] In an early conception, Chihiro would've fought with Yubaba and defeated her, and then gone up against an even more powerful adversary, Zeniba.

everything. She is resisting *life itself*.

In scriptwriting terms, the first act of *Spirited Away* climaxes with Chihiro's meeting with Yubaba: when the agreement is made that Chihiro will have to work at the bathhouse to save her parents, the narrative set-up is complete. (Halfway through the first act, as usual in movie scripts, there's a turning-point: it's when Chihiro encounters her parents turned into pigs).

OTHER CHARACTERS.

Spirited Away is convincing on every level – dramatically and narratively, as well as visually or technically. All of the characters, for instance, have totally convincing personalities, from the main characters, such as Chihiro, Yubaba and Haku, to the secondary characters, such as Lin, Kamaji and the foreman. They are not types, not stereotypes, nor mere ciphers, as secondary characters (and main characters) are in too many movies. *Spirited Away* depicts a fantasy world, of course, but it's a realm where you really can believe that characters such as Yubaba the formidable, out-size witch or Kamaji the gruff, six-armed engineer exist. It's not only that if they don't exist, then they *should* exist: it's also that, within the world of this movie, they really *do* exist.

In other words, Yubaba and Kamaji and Haku and the gods are not simply fantastical creations (though they are products of an almost superhuman imagination working at its height), they are also grounded in modes of convincing behaviour, and motives, and character traits. Hayao Miyazaki and his team don't just invent amazing-looking creatures, they clothe them, give them movements, gestures and behaviour, all tailored individually. Or to re-state the obvious: *Spirited Away* is filmmaking of the highest, highest order.

As with Sophie in *Howl's Moving Castle,* Chihiro collects friends as she goes along: there is a very odd group of creatures around her which are drawn to her: there's Master Haku, the confident, prince-like boy who's also a flying dragon and ultimately revealed as nothing less than a river god. He has the blowing hair, the sleek features, and the intense stare of conventional Japanese animation. There's Lin, an older sister figure and helper for Chihiro, who, though she resents having Chihiro thrust upon her by the foreman, soon gets to like her. There's No Face (*Kaonashi*),[29] an ambiguous deity that Chihiro inadvertently allows into the bathhouse (when it's raining

---

[29] Art director Yoji Takeshige was partly responsible for suggesting that No Face should form a large part of the 2nd half of *Spirited Away*.

outside, and she leaves the door open), who creates pandemonium, but it turns out that only Chihiro can really tame him – or at least, get rid of him.[30]

Two unlikely characters that become part of Chihiro's menagerie of odd companions are the baby Boh and Yubaba's bird – but they are transformed by Zeniba into a pudgy mouse and a fly, respectively.[31] Like Sophie in *Howl's Moving Castle,* Chihiro accepts these new companions, and takes them with her, carrying them on her shoulder. That acceptance is very important.

Once again, there are surrogate parental figures: with Chihiro's parents, the Oginos, out of the way (and turned into pigs,[32] along with many other humans – straight out of Homer's *Odyssey*),[33] stand-ins present themselves: Kamaji is another of the father figures in Hayao Miyazaki's cinema: he is gruff, practical, a worker, but also kindly once you get past the crusty exterior. Design-wise, Kamaji has the requisite Miyazaki moustache and spectacles. Oh, and he happens to have six arms, which he walks on (yet his body is human), and uses to operate the boiler for the bathhouse (he turns a wheel, and mixes the water flavours from three glass jars below).[34] The arms can also extend a long way. (The more fatherly aspects of Kamaji come out, for instance, in the scene where he wakes to find Chihiro asleep on the floor of the boiler room, and picks up a mat to cover her and keep her warm. Kamaji also lies for Chihiro – he tells Lin that she's his granddaughter. Although he doesn't have any work for her, he encourages her to try Yubaba, and asks Lin to take her to see the boss. Later, Kamaji gives Chihiro the train ticket he's been saving).

The black spiders that carry the coal to the boiler, one by one, are a marvellous comic invention (cousins of the dust bunnies in *My Neighbor Totoro*), and they also play a part in the plot: when one spider is squashed by the piece of coal it's carrying, Chihiro helps it. There's an aspect of labour disputes

---
30 Some critics have suggested that the relationship that No Face has with Chihiro is ambiguous to the point of having a sexual component (C, 139).
31 The mouse and the fly are pure Miyazaki, and Miyazaki liked to animate the comedy between them himself.
32 Miyazaki on pigs: 'I think they fit very well with what I wanted to say. The behaviour of pigs is very similar to human behaviour. I really like pigs at heart, for their strengths as well as their weaknesses. We look like pigs, with our round bellies. They're close to us.'
33 The theme park also has hints of *Pinocchio*, in which boys are turned into asses.
34 And Kamaji's introduced using the German Expressionist technique of the 1920s which filmmakers have exploited for decades: out-size shadows on the wall.

and unions here, which Hayao Miyazaki alluded to in films such as *Laputa: Castle In the Sky* – because the other spiders see Chihiro throwing the coal in the furnace, and they all want to be helped.

The lesson here, which Kamaji teaches Chihiro, is that you can't interfere with people's work unless you know what you're doing, and can handle the consequences. (And it's sweet how the spiders become Chihiro's friends too – looking after her shoes, which they hide in their cubby holes, and surrounding her as she sleeps). They also play a part in a later scene, when the little, black bug inside Haku looks for somewhere to hide, and the spiders gather in their cubby holes and hiss and block its path.

Lin is something of a mother figure for Chihiro, but is also like an older sister, showing Chihiro the ropes (finding her clothes, showing her where to sleep and work). It's important that when Lin first encounters Chihiro in the boiler room, she doesn't freak out like many of her cohorts do at the sight (or smell) or a human; instead, she accepts her (though grudgingly at first). Hayao Miyazaki knows that it's not only *characters* that're vital in storytelling, it's also their *relationships* to each other.

The main surrogate maternal presence in *Spirited Away* is Yubaba – and the device of Yubaba having a twin sister (Zeniba) is another example of splitting one character into two opposing personalities.[35] Yubaba and Zeniba clearly (and vividly) embody the good mother and the bad mother. Both witches, Yubaba and Zeniba are two halves of one person. Yet Yubaba is not an evil witch: her softer side is revealed in the interview scene, when Chihiro asks for a job, and it's disclosed that Yubaba is also a mother (with a very large baby that she dotes on).[36] As the story unfolds, it's revealed that when it comes to her baby, Yubaba is as gooey and indulgent as any mother.[37] Chihiro cleverly manipulates Yubaba's soft spot for her baby (as Haku does too). Her baby is the only person who can really get the better of Yubaba; at the end of the piece, Boh reminds Yubaba that if she isn't nice to Chihiro, he will cry (and Yubaba only grants Chihiro permission to work in the bathhouse during a tricky time when she's trying to calm her big baby Boh down: one of the tests that Chihiro overcomes and wins at this moment is to keep persisting in

---

[35] There was an economic reason for this, too: it was simply cheaper to have the sisters look the same.
[36] The Duchess in *Alice* has a large baby – which becomes a pig.
[37] But who is the father of Boh? The film doesn't depict anyone who has a relationship with Yubaba – man, she's gotta be difficult to live with!

demanding a job from Yubaba. If Chihiro had bottled that difficult moment, it might all be over).[38]

As in *Howl's Moving Castle*, *Kiki's Delivery Service* and *Nausicaä of the Valley of the Wind* and other Hayao Miyazaki films, in *Spirited Away* compassion is a key theme: indeed, this is one of the elements that makes Hayao Miyazaki such a great director. It is a rare component among filmmakers, but it's one of the elements that distinguishes their work from run-of-the-mill directors.

Hayao Miyazaki does not lecture his audience, but he is keen to demonstrate that compassion for others is one of the most vital of all emotions. Characters such as Nausicaä and Kiki and Sosuke and Pazu have it immediately – they don't have to learn it, like Chihiro. But when it kicks in with Chihiro, her empathy with others and eagerness to help make her a noble and worthy individual.

Like Hayao Miyazaki's animations from *Nausicaä of the Valley of the Wind* and *Laputa: Castle In the Sky* onwards, *Spirited Away* teams Chihiro up with a boy of about her own age (making Haku slightly older is part of the dramatic function he has, which is to introduce Chihiro to the magical world of the bathhouse. One of Haku's functions, for instance, is simple but essential: exposition, as with Lin, to explain the world that Chihiro is entering). The scene in the elevator, when Haku and Chihiro are alone together, and Haku reminds her not to babble and distances himself from her, reminds Chihiro that Haku has problems of his own, that he is a separate person, and that she hasn't known him that long, and can't help her with everything (*Spirited Away* contains quite a few elevator scenes – the most amusing being when Chihiro is squashed against the wall by the enormous Raddish God. And even the Raddish God helps Chihiro in a way: he goes to the top floor with her, and she remembers to bow to him, after he's bowed to her. The bathhouse is a community when the niceties of ritual, gesture and deference are upheld, and oil social interactions. Notice how Lin has to remind Chihiro to say 'thank you' to Kamaji).

YUBABA.

Spirited Away is a *tour-de-force* of animation, and for me it's the equal of any of the greatest animated films – whether that's Walt Disney's *Pinocchio* or *Bambi* or Jan Svankmajer's *Alice*. *Spirited Away* is a picture crammed with outstanding

---

[38] 'When Chihiro says out loud, "I'll work here", her words are so powerful that even a witch like Yubaba can't ignore them', noted Miyazaki (TP, 198).

set-pieces. But not all of them are the big visual effects and action sequences. There is plenty of small-scale, intimate animation here which is equally staggering.

Yubaba[39] is a super-abundance of design, concept, animation[40] and execution.[41] She is the equal of any of the great animated characters in the history of cinema (tho' she'd insist on being Number One!). Yubaba is a sorceress who's larger-than-life in every respect, an out-size diva of a witch with her giant, grey hair in a bun, her enormous, deeply-lined face and bloodshot eyes, her wrinkled fingers encrusted with colourful, jewelled rings, her long, red finger nails, her loud, raucous laugh, her piercing stare, her long, hooked nose, and her genius with magic (which includes hurtling through the air, zipping up Chihiro's mouth, making objects dart about, controlling three bouncing heads, and flying as a bird – rather like Howl in *Howl's Moving Castle,* though it's not explained where Yubaba goes on her night flights). Even without her magic, Yubaba is a formidable presence, who rules over the bathhouse with a rod of iron, strikes fear into everyone around her, has a fierce temper, yet has the softest of soft spots for her over-size baby.

Yubaba is the grandmother from hell, the really fearsome teacher you were always scared of, the great aunt from far away who comes to stay and makes your life a waking nightmare. And she knows how bad she is – and like a true diva, she loves it!

The interview scene in *Spirited Away* is one of the greatest in Hayao Miyazaki's cinema – and therefore one of the finest in all animated cinema. The inventiveness, the timing and pacing, the drama, the characterization, the interaction, the movement, the shapes and outlines, the backgrounds and layouts, the fusion of dialogue and motion, the props and colours, all are at the highest level of filmmaking.

You know it's going to be something special when the production design racks up to a dense level of decoration and colour – lavish and ornate European 18th century to early 20th century furnishings, with colours saturated. Shiny, brass fittings; spacious, painted cases; imposing, wooden doors; intricately-patterned carpets and rugs.

---

39 The Japanese word 'yu' means 'hot water', and 'baba' means 'old woman'.
40 Animator Atsuko Tanaka was a principal contributor to Yubaba's animation.
41 Supervising animator Masashi Ando said that the Queen in *Alice's Adventures In Wonderland* definitely influenced Yubaba (via John Tenniel's famous illustrations). Miyazaki acknowledged an indirect influence from Lewis Carroll. *Rin the Chimney Painter* was a production cancelled before *Spirited Away* which featured a character similar to Yubaba.

The scene begins with Chihiro outside Yubaba's rooms, and being dragged along by magic (as if she's got a cable attached to her navel),[42] through a series of luxurious rooms and corridors (the doors flying open by magic, with each room being lit up in sequence). This was one of the scenes that was employed in the marketing of the film. It truly is a multi-million dollar scene.

The 2001 movie shows that Chihiro has already come quite a long way in the scene in Yubaba's rooms: Chihiro is terrified of Yubaba but is determined to get a job at the bathhouse (Chihiro's stubbornness, which we saw in the scenes with her parents, when she does *not* want to enter the tunnel, emerges here, but in a different manner – now she's going to defiantly demand a job. And it's bravery, a key component of all Miyazakian heroes).

So even when Yubaba has told her *no*, Chihiro keeps asking. Even when Yubaba is trying to calm down her baby next door, and is getting angrier, Chihiro still insists. Even when faced with a truly formidable opponent, a shape-shifting sorceress, Chihiro still has the guts to demand a job! (What keeps Chihiro so insistent? Presumably the motive of rescuing her parents – because Haku has told her it is the only way of saving them). The scene is also the Faustian bargain, the deal made with a witch of fairy tales, and the movie's set-up: everything needed to make the story work's included in the scene. [43]

During that incredible scene, Yubaba tells Chihiro that she hadn't expected the girl to get that far; and later, Lin tells Chihiro that she got further than she expected (Lin admits that she thought that Chihiro was pretty dumb). Yubaba enjoys putting Chihiro down in the interview scene, which marks her down as a particularly spiteful character. Not truly vicious – Yubaba doesn't kill anyone in the narrative, for example – but you wouldn't want to get on the wrong side of the sorceress.

When Chihiro first encounters Yubaba, the witch is doing some administrative work – signing papers and putting money in a purse in a box (the witch as film producer and financier). One of her first acts is to zip up Chihiro's mouth so the girl can't interrupt her: Yubaba is a prima donna who likes to hold forth, with nobody else having their say. Notice that it's Yubaba's curiosity about who helped Chihiro to get so far in the bathhouse that makes her unzip Chihiro's mouth; yet now

---
42 Chihiro forgets to knock first – she just tries the door – fatal in approaching a witch's dwelling.

43 For instance, Yubaba confirms that Chihiro's folks have been turned into pigs, that they took her guests' food without permission.

Chihiro is free to ask for a job again.

One of Yubaba's finest moments of rage is in the scene in her office, when Haku turns up (now without Yubaba's controlling spell inside him), and tells Yubaba that she doesn't seem to be missing what she really values. Notice how Yubaba's attention turns *first* to the gold and *then* to her baby. But when she realizes that her child is gone her fury is magnificent to behold, with the steam and fire literally billowing from her nostrils.

The team of animators and crew use the Miyazakian hair to maximum effect at this point, with Yubaba's locks engulfing Haku in a torrent of writhing tendrils.[44] But the prince stands his ground. And the movie tops itself again, with Yubaba's diva-like deflation at the mention of her dreaded sister, Zeniba, and she crumples from witch-in-a-frenzy to an old, exhausted woman.

THE GODS.

Once again in Hayao Miyazaki's cinema, there are monsters aplenty in *Spirited Away*.[45] Here, the monsters are gods or spirits, nearly all of which are *not* traditional Japanese deities, but were invented by Miyazaki:[46] they include the enormous Raddish God (*daikon*),[47] a cross between a grey elephant and a sumo wrestler (another Totoro-type), a bunch of giant, yellow Bird or Chicken Gods (*Ootori-sama*), a portly figure enclosed entirely in a large, yellow cape and a little, red hat, and his/ her smaller companion, *ushioni* in traditional costumes and antlers,[48] and a bunch of wild critters recalling Maurice Sendak's Wild Things. The *Kappa* are trickster water gods. Yubaba has three green, bouncing heads as kind of pets, Kashira, in her office (for no explained reason). The male workers are giant frogs[49] – well, not completely frogs (though there is a small, green frog), but men with frog-like heads. Once again, these characters are instantly recognizable as Japanese men, like other creatures in Miyazaki's cinema. The women workers are equally stylized but recognizably human (they have elongated faces, for instance, and have bright

---

[44] And earlier, her hair's stuck with pieces of the green door that her baby Boh demolishes.
[45] In the Gifu and Shizuoka area a festival called *Shimotsuki* occurs where spirits from all over Japan are invited to bathe (TP, 218).
[46] The only ones that drew on Japanese traditions were the masked phantoms, the masks being at the Kasuga Taisha Shrine in Nara, of dancers.
[47] The Raddish God is *Oshira-Sama*.
[48] These are Cow Goblins or Spirits with Antlers, *Ushioni*.
[49] Maybe another *Alice* reference.

clothing and resemble slugs).50

There are so many secondary characters, and in scenes that're so crowded, you have to watch *Spirited Away* a few times to see them all. And the sequences which introduce the gods – arriving on the steam boat, and walking across the bridge – are so packed with animation it's impossible to take it all in. (And because even in these scenes the viewpoint is wholly with Chihiro.)

THE SETTING.

The presence of the natural world suffuses *Spirited Away* – the first image of the 2001 film is a big close-up of a bunch of pink flowers, which Chihiro holds in the back of the car. Fairly soon, the movie has the family entering the classic forest of fairy tales – it's announced by a tilt down shot of a giant tree, where the road becomes a stony lane. After the journey through the sunlit woods (with its statuary and little houses), *Spirited Away* makes the natural world a vital force in this story, much of which takes places indoors, in a bathhouse.51 (The bathhouse, Yuya, is a place where eight million gods visit.)52 Hayao Miyazaki had been thinking about a movie set in a bathhouse since he was a child. Miyazaki submitted two proposals based on a bathhouse, b4 the third one was accepted and developed into *Spirited Away*.

But the bathhouse has trees around it, is set upon a rocky outcrop, is filled with water flowing into baths and pipes, and in the second half of the narrative is surrounded by the ocean after heavy rains. None of the reverse angles of the bathhouse depict the distant suburbs of 'real life', for instance, where Chihiro is going to live, and where her school is. Once the bathhouse is reached, the 'real' Japan falls away.53

The abandoned theme park is a marvellous touch – it's as if we're exploring Hayao Miyazaki's fantasy films themselves, with the statues covered in moss and the partially decayed environment representing the rich history of Miya-

---

50 Some of the women are inspired by the Heian period (794-1192) – the dots above the eyes, for instance, echo the painted eyebrows of the period. There are also prostitutes in *Spirited Away* – that was unintentional, Miyazaki explained. But there is a scene where one of the bathhouse workers is leading a male figure.
51 Bathing in public is an ancient and still familiar practice in Japan (you see it everywhere in *manga* and *animé*). In Tokyo in the 1960s there were 2,700 *sento* (public baths), and 18,000 or so in Japan (A. Osmond, 2008, 70).
52 Some Japanese viewers found the bathhouse more Chinese than Japanese. It also contained Western influences (also drawing on the period when Japan was Westernized). But they recognized that it was a fantastical place, like no bathhouse that has ever existed.
53 As she walks to see her parents, Chihiro catches a glimpse of what seem to real houses, on a distant bluff.

zaki's pictures (the squat, mossy statues emerge from the ground like fish – and sometimes they *are* fish).54

Yubaba's apartment is the most luxurious space in Hayao Miyazaki's cinema: it includes giant, painted vases, carved balconies, chandeliers, a spotless, marble bathroom, a white, marble fire-place, bookcases, sideboards, lamps, a screen, paintings, and a desk which includes a telephone made out of a human skull (a wonderful Gothic touch).

There's also one of the richest rugs in movies (an intricately woven red carpet, where much of the action in the apartment takes place). So much time and attention has been lavished on Yubaba's apartment because of Yubaba's significance in the story. It functions as the villain's lair, and embodies Yubaba's power and prestige. As she tells Chihiro, her bathhouse is a classy operation.

It's one of the most opulent spaces in recent cinema (even the ceiling is carved in wood). It's as if the producers and director have told their crew: go nuts, do anything you like. But it all works, it all fits together and – like all of the spaces in Hayao Miyazaki's cinema – it convinces as a place where people could really live. It's an extravagant (and feminine) setting, of course, but it's not like many expensive sets in live-action movies, which are so obviously sets, where no one would want to live or could live. Miyazaki's cinema, for all its heightened fantasy, is always grounded in a liveable reality. Yubaba, for instance, isn't only a powerful witch and ambiguous villain, she's also a mom who goes around her apartment clearing up (you don't see Darth Vader or a *James Bond* villain picking up the cushions off the floor in a *Star Wars* or *James Bond* flick! Maybe they should – someone's got to do it!).

Spirited Away is one of those films where you can freeze most of the frames and you have a superb image (not true of even many classic movies). Or rather, *Spirited Away* is one of those movies where you *want* to freeze a frame, because by the time of *Spirited Away,* the production team led by Hayao Miyazaki is layering their output with so many levels of detail, so many parts of the composition to look at, you really do need to pause the flow to admire it all, or watch the movie again.

---

54 The Edo-Tokyo Architectural Park in Koganei, a favourite place for Hayao Miyazaki to visit, offered inspirations for the theme park. The film also drew on the Taiwanese hill-towns of Jiufen and Jinguashi.

THE NURSERY.

One of the more remarkable spaces in *Spirited Away*, in a film jammed with fascinating places, is baby Boh's nursery at the top of the bathhouse. Its ancestor is the circular room at the top of the isolated tower in *The Castle of Cagliostro*, where Clarisse was held prisoner. In *Spirited Away*, the circular room also has celestial objects (clouds, a sun) painted on the ceiling, a rural storybook diorama around the walls, and is littered with giant cushions (all individually and colourfully patterned). There's also green padding around the walls, and on the floor, a colonnade, unopened presents, a red toy car, a flying pterodactyl, soft toys, candy in boxes on a green table, a bookcase, a giant rag doll, a large bed with a mediæval canopy, etc. It's another piece of quaint Victoriana that features so often in Hayao Miyazaki's work, but here kitted out with rich patterns and hues. It's the Ultimate Victorian Nursery. (The number of toys, including the unopened gifts, are further expressions of the attention that Yubaba lavishes on her beloved baby. So much mother-love; her employees don't get it, so it all goes to baby Boh. Boh is spoilt to bits by his mom, who goes OTT with her affection).

A wonderful moment has Chihiro diving into the mound of cushions, to escape from Yubaba, a classic image of childlike behaviour. Meanwhile, the reveal of the giant baby Boh[55] who's inside the cushion mountain is beautifully timed.[56]

WORK.

Work is another theme in *Spirited Away* – people have to be given work to do at the bathhouse, otherwise they can't stay there.[57] So one of Chihiro's primary tasks, in the first act of *Spirited Away,* is to somehow get work. She tries first with Kamaji the engineer, but he won't give her a job to do. Eventually, she has to go to the top, to beg for a job from the boss, the witch Yubaba. And in *Spirited Away* Chihiro is depicted at work in many scenes. (In this respect, it is a kind of follow-up to *Kiki's Delivery Service*: and like that 1989 movie, the viewpoint also stays mainly with the young girl character. And it's

---
[55] Boh may be a spoof of Kintaro, a Japanese hero who wore a *harakake* (a red apron) with his name on it.

[56] That Boh wants to stay indoors and not go outside, because of germs, might reflect Japanese youth, Andrew Osmond suggested, who prefer to stay in and indulge in the virtual reality of television, computer games and the internet (2008, 13).

[57] That labour can encourage a sense of responsibility and integrity and purpose might be lecturing and 'dreary moralism', as Andrew Osmond (2003) put it, but *Spirited Away* rises above that with its 'witty riffs on the theme'. But it's also a sly comment on advanced capitalism: that you have to work, otherwise you can't live. That is, you have to *do* something, and be seen doing something, all the time.

about a young woman finding her place in a strange, new environment).

Hayao Miyazaki's pictures do not stint on emphasizing the work ethic – labour is always a significant and not-to-be-ignored ingredient of the path of the hero/ine. In no way are Miyazaki's hero/ines lazy aristocrats, who loll about on couches and hammocks in the hazy, afternoon sunshine, ordering servants to bring just one more cocktail. They always have to put in the basic work hours, whether that means cooking and cleaning, or walking and running and flying for miles, or digging and planting and harvesting.

To illustrate just how completely essential hard work is to the Hayao Miyazakian hero/ine, compare his movies with any similar action-adventure flicks, particularly those in the Western tradition. Few heroes in *Indiana Jones, Star Wars, Harry Potter, Lord of the Rings, The Mummy* and other movie franchises are depicted hard at work: they will feature one token scene of work (if at all), then move on to the story, to the action and adventure and explosions and chases and all the rest. [58]

Talking about hard work – Kamaji is such a devoted worker, he doesn't even have a bedroom – he simply sleeps where he works (like an animator!),[59] in front of the boiler, where he prepares the herbal leaves for the bath water. (The unions would have something to say about that – but I guess the bathhouse, as run by dominatrix Yubaba, isn't unionized. Any workers threatening to go on strike would be vaporized). [60]

The economic downturn in Japan (and around the world), when the Bubble Economy burst in the late 1980s, is clearly one of the elements behind the work theme, as it was with *Howl's Moving Castle*. The references to the abandoned theme park, for instance, are vivid manifestations of a boom-and-bust economy: Chihiro's father mentions that the theme parks were built in the early 1990s – not that long ago from 2001, when *Spirited Away* was released. Daddy Ogino also tells Chihiro not to worry because he has money and credit cards (living on credit being another manifestation of a shaky economy).

Although the bathhouse is a community of workers (and

---

[58] Jean-Luc Godard pointed out that people are seldom depicted at work in movies. And so he proceeded to show them working in films such as *Slow Motion* (1979).
[59] 'I feel like I've made a movie about the inner workings of Studio Ghibli itself', Miyazaki remarked)TP, 241).
[60] Yet there a potential union dispute when Chihiro helps out the coal spiders and is dressed down by Kamaji for interferring.

hard workers too), the greedy aspects of capitalism soon erupt when the possibility of gaining some gold occurs (then the devotion to the ideals of community and society break down, and it's every frog for himself).

LOSING THE PARENTS.

It's significant that the first magical person that Chihiro meets is Haku, on the bridge (that is, someone that Chihiro comes to trust, and seems to be on her side, though he remains ambiguous). And as soon as Chihiro meets Haku, the magic begins: in short, night comes. A magical night. The music rolls in with an impressive cue; the shadows lengthen behind Haku in a time-lapse effect; he turns and blows something like white petals in the direction of the bathhouse (only later are these petals linked with Haku's dragon form); Haku tells Chihiro to run.

It's one of Hayao Miyazaki's most impressive sequences, combining a visionary imagination with emotionally convincing reactions (Chihiro in fear), and incredible action. Once again, it is the blob-men, a Miyazakian staple – but they are just one element in this very complex sequence, which includes the black spirits floating around the amusement park (partially invisible), the lights coming on (strings of deep red lamps), night falling, Chihiro running away, and so many other stunning images: the illuminated steam boat,[61] for instance, sailing out of the night (the stream has become an ocean, and Chihiro runs right into it – she is literally out of her depth), with the gods on board, who materialize from floating masks as they walk onto the land, or the images of the stalls and restaurants lit up for the night (in this theme park, everything happens at night).

When Chihiro encounters her parents, now giant pigs still stuffing themselves at the food counter, it is a truly horrific image – particularly when her father slowly turns and falls to the ground. The addition of a shadowy figure behind the counter wielding a utensil like a whip adds even more horror to this already horrific scene. It's not as shocking as Chihiro seeing her parents die before her eyes, unable to help, but it is pretty distressing. Chihiro refuses to accept that these giant pigs are her parents, and hurries away to find them.

When Akio and Yûko Ogino smell the magical scent of cooking, in classic cartoon style, it gets them into trouble:

---

[61] It's wonderful that the gods arrive in a steam boat of all things. And the gold and scarlet lighting is deliberately exaggerated.

Spirited Away employs the fairy tale trope of the heroes breaking a taboo or prohibition. In this case, it is to eat food uninvited (as Yubaba explains to Chihiro later. In fairy tales, you don't take stuff from magical beings without invitations!). Chihiro doesn't want them to do it, and hangs around outside the restaurant. She won't even take the few steps under the awning (her instincts prove right here – and most of the way through the movie: she doesn't take the food, doesn't step onto the bridge, and doesn't enter the bathhouse, until guided by Haku). Her father says, don't worry, he's got money and a credit card (in a capitalist society, money is deemed to solve all problems. Her father is all instinct, like an animal, following his nose).[62]

The loss of the parents is a classic fairy tale device,[63] as well as a classic motif of films and novels. It renders the hero/ine suddenly alone, without protection, without a safety net, without help, without advice, without warmth and comfort. Now Chihiro has no mom's arm to cling onto. Many fairy tales of course begin with the parents gone by the start of the tale – as in *Cinderella* or *Snow White*, and as in Hayao Miyazaki's films, such as *Laputa: Castle In the Sky*. But to show the parents being dispatched on screen, in the fore-ground of the story, is a traumatic event, about as severe a trauma as you can have a child character under-go.

In *Spirited Away*, though, the parents have become pigs, and one of Chihiro's chief tasks (maybe her primary goal) is to break the spell, and restore her parents back to normal. To achieve that goal – which is an awesomely demanding quest for any child, and gives the film such emotional power – Chihiro also has to face many other obstacles, including looking for work and finding a place to stay.

For a while, Chihiro doesn't accept that her mom and dad have been turned into pigs right before her eyes, even though they sit at the same place at the counter in the restaurant, where she left them, and they wear the same clothes. She steps back in horror, and goes looking for her parents elsewhere in the theme park.[64]

---

[62] Chihiro's dad tells her not to be afraid a number of times, such as when they enter the tunnel. Both Chihiro and her father are right: Chihiro is right to be cautious, but her father is also correct to say there is nothing to be scared of. Not really. Because although she is often afraid, Chihiro matches each obstacle and set-back.

[63] As Miyazaki put it, Chihiro can't become the heroine if her parents are hanging around (TP, 217).

[64] As Andrew Osmond noted, it takes something as horrific as this to shake Chihiro out of her passivity: 'In the harsh way of fairy tales, Chihiro's terrifying experience brings her to life' (2008, 63).

This whole sequence is an outstanding example of animation and drama, with every stage in Chihiro's response emotionally convincing – the way she panics and runs, dodging the black blob-men, the way she hurtles down the steps and ends up in a sea, the way she watches in fascination and fear at the illuminated town on the far bank, and the steam ship (and music) floating towards her. And her astonishment when she encounters Haku on the bridge, and finally the way Chihiro sits huddled by a wall, clutching her knees.

The differences between children and parents is a key theme in *Spirited Away*, embodied not only between Chihiro and her parents, but between Chihiro and the parental surrogates, such as the 'bad' and 'good' mothers, Yubaba and Zeniba, and figures such as Kamaji and older sister figure Lin.

The conflicts between youth and age are also manifested in the explorations of the present and the past: in *Spirited Away*, comparisons are offered throughout between tradition, folklore, ritual and the numerous elements of the past, and the contemporary world, with its credit cards, cars, abandoned theme parks and modern ways. Although *Spirited Away* is obviously nostalgic for the past and its values and traditions,[65] which it beautifully and sensationally evokes, it is also critical of them. Some of the old gods for example, such as No Face, are as greedy, insensitive, childish and darkly ambiguous as people in the contemporary world.

FLIGHT.

No aircraft or pilots in *Spirited Away*, but there is some flying – well, quite a bit. Is there is a Hayao Miyazaki film *without* flying? The answer is: no. Yubaba becomes a portly flying bird and hovers over the spirit world; Haku is a white Chinese dragon, who flies in a number of scenes (Haku also grabs Chihiro on the bridge and flies with her); and the River God is also a dragon. And other characters float or fly (and there's a running gag on flight when the fly (Yubaba's transformed bird) carries Boh (the baby transformed into a mouse).

PHYSICAL ACTING.

A marvellous example of modest but effective animation occurs in the scene where Chihiro creeps down the stairs leading down the outside of the bathhouse, from the bridge down to the boiler room (there is wind noise in this scene,

---

[65] Miyazaki recalled that some audiences in Japan wept when they saw *Spirited Away*, because it evoked a world and a landscape now vanished, from their childhoods.

emphasizing Chihiro's precarious position, and her fear). The film moves in very close, to show Chihiro extending those skinny legs slowly and gingerly. This is evocatively observed animation, absolutely convincing from a staging and action point-of-view.[66]

Spirited Away is particularly impressive in the physical acting[67] that Chihiro does throughout the film – her clumsiness, or her expressions of fear and the way she clutches her Tee shirt, or the running gag of the girl falling on her face with her butt or legs stuck in the air (she falls over a lot), or the way she creeps along walls or around doors.[68] There is some brilliant silent movie acting here – *Spirited Away* plays wonderfully without dialogue, because the animation is so extraordinarily expressive.

The scene where Chihiro dances about as she tries to stamp on the wriggling black bug that escapes from Haku's mouth is delightful, with plenty of humour (the soot sprites head it off, for instance, and there's a short ritual between Kamaji and Chihiro, to dissipate the effect of touching the worm: Chihiro makes a square with her fingers and Kamaji cuts it with his hand, saying cut! ('kitta!'). It's terrific, too, when the mouse and a sprite re-enact the rite).

STYLE.

Such rich colours – pinks, reds, oranges, pale blues, lilacs in the theme park (for an abandoned theme park, it looks amazing). The dominant colour theme for *Spirited Away* is red, and the filmmakers employed pure red paint to achieve a really dense red. Red is everywhere in *Spirited Away* – from the opening shot onwards. Gold was another hue of the movie, achieved by different yellows, adding highlights, and sometimes taking down the surrounding colours to make the gold stand out even more, as Yoji Takeshige, the art director, explained.

I've mentioned colour a lot in Hayao Miyazaki's cinema and in *Spirited Away* (it's one of a number of key areas where Japanese animation goes far, far beyond Western animation), but look at the stupendous use of *lighting*: *Spirited Away* is one of those movies that celebrates *light* all its manifestat-

---

[66] My son Jake used to be like that when we crossed wooden bridges with the slats showing a river or a road below; yeah, I'm still a little like that on a shaky wooden pier over the sea.
[67] In the stairs sequence, some of the animation was by Shinya Ohira.
[68] In the Stink God sequence, 'she trips, stumbles, bangs her head umpteen times', and is ridiculed, as Andrew Osmond pointed out (2008, 19). Yet she struggles through.

ions;[69] it's a cinematographer's dream film (Atsushi Okui was DP, and has been on most of Ghibli's movies). There is firelight, moonlight, candlelight, torchlight, dawn, dusk, night, etc.

The manipulation of viewpoint in *Spirited Away* is simply astonishing. This is the journey of a ten year-old girl, and throughout *Spirited Away* the camera angles and viewpoints emphasize that, in ways that one would expect: such as a low angle, Orson Wellesian tracking shot behind Mr Ogino, when Chihiro and her folks enter the tunnel. But they also modulate it in numerous ways, sometimes adding more objective views of Chihiro, as well as looks into camera, and very rapidly moving subjective shots when Chihiro is with Haku, or when she hurtles down the exterior staircase.

THE OCEAN.

The way that the bathhouse turns from being sited over a valley to something like an island, over an ocean, is enchanting (notice how the filmmakers often employ camera angles which emphasize the situation of the bathhouse over the water, rather than ones which link the bathhouse with the land). It's as if Hayao Miyazaki couldn't resist including the ocean – the sea (and rivers and lakes and streams and pools) – is one of the recurring motifs in Miyazaki's cinema. In *Ponyo*, the flood returns, and it's even more spectacular.

The ocean becomes instrumental in the later sequences in *Spirited Away*, such as the extraordinary, unforgettable train ride to Zeniba's house, and the train runs over tracks buried under a foot or so of clear water. Or the scene where Lin and Sen look at the moonlight over the water on the balcony outside their rooms, eating. Or the scene where Sen encounters Haku in his white dragon form.

The breeze is again a magical force in *Spirited Away* – it occurs first when Chihiro and her parents stand before the tunnel entrance (actually, there was another wind moment, in the car, when Chihiro's mom opens the window). It recurs again, at the other end of the entrance building, hinting at unseen powers (like the shrines beside the road, and the squat statue at the tunnel entrance).

---

69 Other movies of light might include *Persona*, *Sunrise*, *Close Encounters of the Third Kind*, *Citizen Kane*, *The Magnificent Ambersons*, *Days of Heaven*, *The Conformist* and *Women In Love*.

MAGIC AND NAMES.

The notion of the magical power of names is of course common in fairy tales, as is a hero having to use another name temporarily. I wonder if some of the inspiration for this in *Spirited Away* derives from the *Earthsea* fantasy novels of Ursula Le Guin. In Le Guin's peerless books, naming is the fundamental source of magic – to know the true name of a thing is to have power over it. Thus magic in the Earthsea world is about knowing true names, in an archaic language (the language dragons speak). When you utter the true name, you hold the essence of the thing. When the letters of Chihiro's name float up into Yubaba's hand, that describes the effect of having power over something, literally grasping it and controlling it.

The title in Japanese of *Spirited Away – Sen to Chihiro no Kami-kakushi* – means *Sen and the Spiriting Away of Chihiro,* thus emphasizing names, and the relationship of magic to naming.

In *Spirited Away,* it pays off *twice* – not only in Chihiro reclaiming her name, but also in Chihiro remembering Haku's true name. At that point, when Chihiro tells Haku his true name, he dissolves from being a flying dragon to being a youth again (though luckily he is still able to fly). There's a backstory to the (love) relationship of Chihiro and Haku which's revealed as the film unfolds, and only pays off towards the end of the movie, when Haku flies into Chihiro's rooms. It involves Chihiro as a child falling in a river, and Haku being revealed as a river god. The movie includes images from that moment, such as in the River God sequence, but doesn't explain them until the full reveal when Chihiro rides Haku in his dragon form (but the images are also very abstract and subjective: there is no long shot, for example, showing Chihiro falling into the river, a shot which would clarify the geography of the river, the bank, the water, and maybe Chihiro's parents nearby).

In the world of *Spirited Away,* Hayao Miyazaki explained, words have power. Chihiro has to be *very* careful about what she says in front of Yubaba. She mustn't say 'I want to go home' or 'no', because the witch would be able to throw her out. But if Chihiro tells Yubaba 'I want to work here', even the witch can't ignore that (H. Miyazaki, 2001).

Having to hold your breath to cross the bridge is a classic dare from childhood, the kind of games that children play. (But it relates to the notion of the bathhouse itself, of cleansing, and that humans have a smell that the creatures pick up on. And it even links to the backstory of Chihiro falling into a river and being saved from drowning). For Jack Zipes, *Spirited Away*, via the symbol of the bathhouse, deals with cleansing – 'cleansing of the soul, cleaning the air, exploring the genuine essence of relationships and work' (2011, 108).

THE STINK GOD SEQUENCE.

The Stink God sequence stand-out sequence is where Chihiro really proves herself (the Stink God that is really a River God).[70] Lin and Chihiro (now called Sen) have been assigned the central bathroom by the foreman, and grudgingly begin cleaning it (naturally it is incredibly filthy, and Chihiro and Lin don't have the right materials for the job). *Spirited Away* is a film where the hero *works*, really *works*, doing physically tough work: Chihiro is shown scrubbing floors, scouring bathrooms, running errands, looking after the customers, etc. Chihiro isn't a fairy tale heroine in the modern style, who sits about doing nothing and worrying about her situation. She only has a break at the end of the day, just like the other workers.

The arrival of the Stink God – another of the blobby, liquiescent and monstrous creatures that are a staple of Hayao Miyazaki's cinema – is a wonderful scene; Yubaba senses its approach from afar; the arrival of the Stink God through the theme park, as lights are switched out and doors shut, might be out of a Clint Eastwood Western when the bad guys arrive in town. The way that everyone clears out of the way, and Yubaba and Chihiro stand stricken by the Stink God's overpowering stench, unable to move, is very amusing (how Chihiro's hair stands on end, as if she's put her fingers in an electric socket, with the reaction also running up her body to her hair. Earlier movies had similar effects, such as with Jiji the cat in *Kiki's Delivery Service*).

Once again, Chihiro proves that she is made of strong stuff – not only does she handle the Stink God on her own, leading it to the big bath, dousing it with water, she also pulls out the thorn in its side[71] (it's not as simple as that, of course: the thorn – actually the handle of a bike – is attached to a cord and the whole bathhouse gathers round to yank out a ton of

---

[70] The River God is *Kawa no Kami*, arriving first in a Stink God or *Okusare-Sama* guise.
[71] There are so many details in this sequence – such as Chihiro not being able to tie a decent knot around the bicycle handle, so Lin helps – Lin is also gutsy.

junk the Stink God's swallowed, beginning with the bicycle).[72] Yubaba flies down to orchestrate the tug o' war brandishing some fans, and everyone in the bathhouse joins in with some cheering and encouragement.

The sequence continues with some remarkable images, such as the Stink God, now revealed as a River God (portrayed as an old, holy man with a mask-like face), rising from water in near-silence, some striking underwater images (including Chihiro caught up in a watery fist, in a bubble of water), and a series of more abstract, magical shots. When it comes to delivering a montage of eye-popping imagery and haunting visual ideas and motifs, Hayao Miyazaki's cinema is up there with the best. And what's so impressive about Miyazaki's films is that these vivid visual effects sequences never feel like visual effects just for the sake of seeing some visual effects. The fx, rather, are integrated into the narrative, and emerge from the story. There is never the feeling that the movie's producers have attended a screening or a story reel presentation and, in between puffs on a big cigar, demanded an action sequence here, or some visual effects there.[73]

The Stink God sequence climaxes with the bathhouse celebrating, and even old Yubaba gives Chihiro a big hug and congratulates her on doing so well. *Saké* all round, everyone clapping, and the gods themselves dancing. This is Chihiro's first big task, and she passes it with flying colours.

The shot of Chihiro's co-workers gathered around her and praising her is very important – they have finally recognized her. But the angle looking up at the balcony high above, where the gods are rejoicing (with the Raddish God prominent, waving his arms), is incredibly significant: here is ten year-old Chihiro, a regular, unremarkable Japanese kid, who is now being applauded by gods! She has certainly come a long way. (It's as if everything that Chihiro encounters in *Spirited Away* is created specially *for her* – every obstacle, every life lesson, as with Alice in *Alice's Adventures In Wonderland*. It's her dream, and has some aspects of a dream at the end. But Chihiro – and the audience – *don't* want to think of this whole movie as merely a dream!).

---

[72] The ecological concerns in Miyazaki's cinema are to the fore again: Haku mentions that his river has disappeared, and the River God is choked with trash. A bike was found when Miyazaki was involved in cleaning a river.
[73] In short, Hayao Miyazaki's movies don't let the visual effects or effects for effects' sake, drive the story or drive the film. And that, unfortunately, is the case with some Hollywood films, particularly the blockbusters and the Summer and Christmas movies.

And yet, no matter how spectacular and incredible the Stink God episode is, it isn't an all-out success for Chihiro, because she still hasn't rescued her parents. Note too the shot of No-Face, an ominous presence in the background of the merry-making – the gold washed by the mud is his doing, of course.

For helping the River Spirit, Chihiro is rewarded with a small lump of medicine (or emetic).[74] This is not for use on humans (Chihiro tries a bite when she's on the balcony with Lin, and covers up the bad taste by gobbling her food). But the medicine pays off twice – Chihiro uses it on Haku, and on No Face when he/ she/ it is at the height of his/ her/ its rampage: it forces No Face to start vomiting (weakening the creature), so that the creatures he/ she/ it has swallowed tumble out.[75]

VISITING THE PIGS.

Chihiro weeps in bed – all the other (young) women are asleep on the floor of the room (all with colourfully patterned eiderdowns), while Chihiro lies awake and crying. The modest but emotive scene has someone entering the room unseen and unheard by anyone else. The point-of-view stays with poor, little Chihiro, hugged up in her bed (it could be anyone – or any*thing* in the crazy fantasy world that Chihiro has landed herself in). The legs approaching and the offscreen voice identify the person as Haku, who offers to take Chihiro to see her parents in the following scene, at dawn.

The next scene shows Chihiro now moving through the deserted bathhouse in the early morning with calm confidence: instead of the fearful creeping down the external wooden staircase, she simply walks up it. Instead of cowering along walls and slinking around corners, she simply steps quietly down the stairs and along the corridors of the bathhouse. After facing up to a giant Stink God and dealing with that, there is nothing now in the bathhouse to be afraid of.

To emphasize in another way that Chihiro is moving into new emotional states, the movie showers her with flowers.

---

[74] For the scene where Chihiro feeds Haku in his dragon the medicine, Miyazaki told his animators to visit a vet and see how a dog would react (this was filmed for the 'making of' documentary).

[75] This is another of numerous inspired action scenes in *Spirited Away*, beginning in a spectacular hall filled with heaps of half-eaten food and painted demons on the walls. Chihiro, like the clever, resourceful girls in fairy tales, leads No Face down the stairs, tiring him out, and forcing him to slow down and spew out his victims. Lin, who's handily organized a circular, wooden tub to row Chihiro out to the railroad track, is still wary of No Face, but Chihiro knows he is now powerless (he's only dangerous when he's inside the bathhouse, she tells Lin). It's also a wonderful touch when Lin warns No Face – when Chihiro can't hear her – that if any harm comes to Chihiro, he will have to pay for it.

Not literally – instead, it has heaps of multi-coloured flowers in the foreground of the shots where Haku takes Chihiro from the bridge where they meet through vegetation to the farm where the pigs are kept (via a travelling shot between banks of yellow and lilac flowers, presumably enhanced with computers). The flowers are so bright and colourful (recalling the Symbolist art of Odilon Redon or Vincent van Gogh), they indicate an ecstatic state. They hint that even if Chihiro isn't quite ready yet to accept her new life at the bathhouse, amongst new friends like Haku and Lin, she is going to be looked after, and all is going to be well.

Another filmmaker might have put this montage of yellows, oranges, blues and reds and Summery, flowery images towards either the beginning of the story (to show where Chihiro is coming from, a tranquil and colourful world), or at the end of the narrative (to show where she ends up, in a paradise of flowers, like a wedding or a celebration). But placing the flowers in the *middle* of the story acts like a foreshadowing of things to come, but also like the film is embracing Chihiro at this point, like a hug from the picture itself, to reassure her that things are going to turn out well.

Another word for it is genius filmmaking.

This sequence is all about Chihiro dealing with her parents and their transformed state: it's moving the way that Chihiro tells her parents that she will save them – but it's done by having Chihiro yell at them in panic, as if she can't believe what she's saying, so she has to blurt it out, then run off. The roles have been reversed, and it's too much for Chihiro to take in, and too much for her to deal with.

Haku sensitively acknowledges this in the following scene, where, acting like an older brother, he crouches down beside Chihiro (next to more flowers), and offers her some food, which he says he has put a spell on, to give her energy. The spell is actually a cathartic one, designed to release Chihiro's repressed emotions about her parents and her situation: as she eats the bread, over-large grey tears spring from her eyes, like something out of *Alice's Adventures In Wonderland*.[76] She weeps (this was animated by Hayao Miyazaki himself).

This is strikingly emotional material for something that is simply ink and paint animation. Very few animated movies have achieved this kind of subtle and sensitive emotion.

---

[76] Wouldn't it be amazing to see Hayao Miyazaki take on *Alice's Adventures In Wonderland* and *Through the Looking Glass*? Actually, he has: it's this movie, in a way (and others). This is Miyazaki's take on Lewis Carroll.

And note too that this intimate moment between the two young people (significantly outside the realm (and power) of the bathhouse itself), is where Haku explains about the notion of naming, and how Yubaba controls people by stealing their names.[77] And this's also the moment when the earlier relationship of Haku and Chihiro is indicated, when Haku tells Chihiro that he has always known her name, since they met. And when Haku also tells Chihiro that he doesn't know his own name, and has been searching for it for years, it is another point at which Chihiro can help to save Haku – she is going to remember his real name later on in the story.

GIVING WITHOUT RECEIVING.

Chihiro never accepts anything that No Face offers her: she is always courteous with her/ him/ it, and bows to her/ him/ it (she learns that good manners help in an institution like the bathhouse), but she doesn't take his gold, or the herbal water formulas. That's another classic fairy tale device – kindness without reward, giving without expecting something in return. (This new Chihiro would do well meeting the old woman at the well in a fairy tale, the woman's who really a witch or fairy, who tests people to see if they are kind enough to give her some water. But the old Chihiro would've likely scampered away).

No Face's form of exchange is in terms of material objects which she/ he/ it thinks Chihiro wants. And when Lin encourages Chihiro to get some of the gold that No Face's handing out to everybody, Chihiro instead goes to look for Haku. That underlines once again Chihiro's higher level of being, if you like, her higher calling, her more noble nature: while most people in the bathhouse think of nothing else but receiving some gold from No Face (they all hold boxes in anticipation), work being forgotten for the moment, Chihiro is on a mission to find (and help) Haku, her friend. Friendship above gold.

And that is demonstrated dramatically in the big scene where the foreman dances before No Face, with the workers lined up neatly on each side, and Chihiro stumbles into the throng. In her rush to find Haku, she ends up in the middle of the corridor, facing No Face. Her simple refusal of his offer of gold makes public Chihiro's nobility and integrity; but no one else can see it. The workers see a silly human that they resent

---

[77] She magically lifts up the characters (*kanji*) from the contract that Chihiro signs into her palm. Chihiro's name is 'Ogino Chihiro', but is renamed 'Sen', comprising a single *kanji*.

being there, who's stupid enough to refuse gold when it's offered for free.

When Chihiro returns to the pig pen (in a dream), carrying the medicine that the River Spirit gave her, she is confronted by a horde of pigs, and can't tell them apart. A horrific shot pans across the angry, grunting pigs' faces, their little, black eyes staring into the camera (the image's replayed during Chihiro's final test, when she has to choose which pigs are her parents. Hence the dream acts as foreshadowing, but also clues the audience into Chihiro's anxieties; also, it reminds the viewers of Chihiro's central dilemma: to save her parents: that's why she's living through the difficult experiences at the bathhouse).

THE NO FACE SEQUENCE.

The 2001 film places Chihiro on her own with a very simple dramatic move: it has Chihiro wake up in the workers' bedroom after everyone else has left. When she goes out onto the balcony, she sees the chimney already smoking, and the rain's created an ocean below. The tranquillity of the balcony scene contrasts with the noise and chaos of the following scenes in the kitchens and halls, as the entire bathhouse cooks like crazy for No Face.

At this point, the No Face sequence is a fantasy of greed, gluttony and power: No Face (still wearing the ancient, white spirit mask) is now a grotesque, black beast with a giant mouth, hurling bowls of food down its throat. Food for gold: the workers bring along dishes, plates, trays and barrels of grub hoping for gold in exchange. You don't need your Karl Marx or Sigmund Freud *For Dummies* to see what's going on here – this is a material-money-gold-shit and oral-anal fantasy gone crazy. It's the community stuck at one level of experience without being able to move into other levels.

Rice, sides of ham, fish, pancake rolls, mounds of whole chickens, apples, tomatoes, even a pig's head: the bathhouse workers offer No Face everything they've got, completely forgetting themselves (and what they'll eat later on). It's the spend-now-and-don't-worry-about-later economy. They go nuts, yelling at No Face, holding up trays piled high with food. Only Chihiro seems to keep her head in this situation: after meeting Lin on the stairs, who encourages her to join in the fun of begging No Face for gold, she excuses herself, and goes back to the balcony.

Notice how Yubaba is absent from the frenzied No Face

gluttony scenes (at first): she has to be, because she'd sense what was going on. But Yubaba finds it difficult to match the powers of the gods when they're in full flight: the River Spirit and No Face are both powerful gods, and Haku too, in his dragon guise, is a formidable rival.

SAVING HAKU AND THE ACTION CLIMAX.

When Chihiro is up on the balcony, at first bored, leaning her head on her hands on the balustrade, the extraordinary sequence with Haku the dragon unfolds at a lightning pace. It's one of those action scenes involving flight and pursuit that Hayao Miyazaki and Studio Ghibli do so well (this sort of scene is a staple of Japanese *animé*, of course).

The animation is at the upper limits of what is achievable in this sequence, with action so brilliantly presented it is breathtaking. Once again, there are some remarkable details – the dragon-point-of-view shot zooming up the wall of the bathhouse, for example, as Chihiro leans over to watch Haku. The pursuit by thousands of white, paper figures, which slam (with very loud sound fx) into the screen as Chihiro closes it. The deep shadow in the room. And the addition of Haku trailing *a lot* of blood (as with *Princess Mononoke*, the sudden appearance of so much blood in a family, 'PG' animated movie is startling. Presumably this amount of *human* blood would mean a higher classification, but *dragon's* blood's a different matter).[78]

But the clue to this incredible sequence is *Chihiro's reaction*: she doesn't run a mile witnessing a full-grown dragon flailing about in her bedroom, spewing buckets of blood. It's not what happens here so much as how the characters react to it. At the beginning of the 2001 film, such a sight would've freaked Chihiro out (this was a girl spooked by an over-grown statue, for instance).[79] But now she's alarmed, yet full of sympathy for Haku. And she wants to help him. Indeed, so strong is Chihiro's response to Haku's predicament, that she is going to stop at nothing to help him. Her desire now drives the whole of the rest of *Spirited Away*, up until she returns from Zeniba's cottage, to save her parents from eternal pig-life.

In screenwriting manuals, the advice for your hero/ine

---

[78] In Britain, the British Board of Film Classification rated *Spirited Away* 'PG'. Usually Miyazaki's movies are given 'G' ratings (*Princess Mononoke* is by far the bloodiest of Miyazaki's films). Presumably *Spirited Away* was allotted a 'PG' due to the scariness of some of the scenes (such as those with No-Face).
[79] But Japanese audiences would probably have seen the statue as benign (A. Osmond, 2008, 57).

towards the end of a movie is to pile on the obstacles. S/he can't just reach the villain's hide-out like getting on a bus and being delivered to the baddie in one piece, as calm and un-ruffled as a trip to the local mall. No, the hero has to struggle through underwater tunnels, or leap over abysses, or fight twenty ninjas.

In *Spirited Away,* the obstacles that stand in the way of Chihiro's consuming desire to help Haku include running through the chaotic assembly surrounding No Face. Of course Chihiro can't take the elevator, that would be too easy, and she can't simply slip by No Face and the foreman, either, even tho' the bathhouse would no doubt have plenty of back ways and secret passages (a nice touch has the bathhouse workers gathered around in lines, holding cardboard boxes in which they hope to collect the gold No Face's handing out).

The route up to the top floor of the bathhouse now has Chihiro in full action hero mode: the sequence is a mirror of the earlier one in which Chihiro gingerly clambered down the wooden steps one by one. In the second scene where Chihiro clambers outside the building, she is brave, resolved to get to Haku at whatever cost. So she slides down a corrugated iron roof, finding the only way across to a steel ladder that leads upwards is along a pipe. Chihiro's determination here is winning – the way she pulls up her pants and tightens her sleeves, preparing to run along the pipe (which breaks away from the building).[80]

True to scriptwriting manual form, the obstacles are heaped on poor Chihiro relentlessly at this point in *Spirited Away*: not only does she have to climb a ladder hundreds of feet above the sea, she has to avoid Yubaba, who's in her bird form, flying nearby. And then she reaches a locked window, which won't budge, even when Chihiro turns and heaves against it. *Obstacle, obstacle, obstacle* – but here the little, paper figure which stuck to her plays a role, slipping through the gap in the window, and opening it.

Once Chihiro has made it all the way up the outside of the bathhouse, and into Yubaba's apartment at considerable peril, once again it isn't simply a case of rushing over to Haku to save him. The filmmakers keep piling on the set-backs for little Chihiro. She's landed in an elegant bathroom; she hurries down a mirrored corridor (featuring triple reflections), and into baby Boh's spectacular rumpus room (another alternative career for Hayao Miyazaki and his art directors would be

---

[80] The animation wasn't exciting enough for Miyazaki, and he asked for revisions (A. Osmond, 2008, 90).

interior design and decoration).

When Chihiro enters Boh's nursery, she is at the heart of the witch Yubaba's realm, and Yubaba is her chief opponent – it's the witch who has kept Chihiro's ma and pa under a spell. So it's another cliché of scriptwriting to have Yubaba approach at that very moment. Having Chihiro dive into the pile of cushions is a terrific touch – it's exactly the kind of thing a kid might do. So when Yubaba enters the room (clearing up as she goes along – Yubaba never stops being a mother), the suspense intensifies (although the viewer might think that Chihiro would be able to handle Yubaba a little better now, after all she's been through).

Like the masters of suspense such as Alfred Hitchcock or D.W. Griffith, Hayao Miyazaki and his filmmaking team twist up the tension even more when Yubaba starts pulling aside cushions to reveal... a giant baby. That is both unexpected and expected (the baby who lives in that nursery has to be out-size), but it's also a classic reveal (and a slight lessening of suspense), when Chihiro isn't found out yet.

When Yubaba eventually leaves, after pacifying her baby (and turning the room into its nighttime setting), the filmmakers add another two more twists for Chihiro: not only can baby Boh talk at a higher age than expected, he's able to exploit Chihiro in his own way, when he grabs her arm and bends it until Chihiro promises to do what he says. This kid must learn fast – not only does he have a big pair of lungs, he can also manipulate people to do what he wants (of course, he has the best teacher for psychological power games in his mom, Yubaba). But Chihiro is a quick thinker, too, and brandishes her bloody palm at Boh (cleverly exploiting his phobias). It's one of the things that children have to learn fast in order to survive – how to exploit other people's weaknesses.

But even when Chihiro manages to wrest herself free of the giant baby, and rush into Yubaba's office, there is yet another obstacle – the three green heads, which bounce around Haku, and seem to want to push him into the hole that's next to the fireplace. And yet another one – Yubaba's bird screeches into the room, attacking Chihiro as she kneels beside Haku, cradling his head.

And another obstacle, in the form of baby Boh, who stomps across the room, demanding attention. The appearance of Zeniba in Yubaba's top floor apartment at this precise moment is a stunning turn in the story. A touch of pure genius, in terms of storytelling – how she chooses to reveal herself in the midst of this noisy, chaotic scene. One can imagine Zeniba really enjoying herself, seeing how far she will let things go before revealing herself.

And how Zeniba gets there is equally imaginative: she is the single paper cut-out figure that attaches itself to Chihiro's back (the filmmakers play with this paper cut-out, having it slide around Chihiro's head to avoid being seen, pantomime-style. At some points, it seems that Zeniba might be guiding Chihiro, but Chihiro is also learning fast how to move quickly when she needs to).

As soon as Zeniba appears, she takes complete control of the situation – she turns Boh into a mouse; Yubaba's bird into a fly; and the three heads into Boh. While this is entertaining and exciting enough, there are also a few pages of dialogue and exposition peppered through the scene[81] (Zeniba explains being the twin sister of Yubaba, for example). Before the situation can develop further, there's a stunning close to the scene, when Haku recovers enough to crush the slip of paper that represented Zeniba's spirit form, and she splits into two.

The escape from Yubaba's apartment is another of Hayao Miyazaki's eye-popping action sequences, as Haku and Chihiro topple into the hole by the fire, which leads down to the dungeons (of course, where else do trapdoors lead in the villain's stronghold?). It's also a call-back to Miyazaki's first theatrical film as director, *The Castle of Cagliostro,* where trapdoors to dungeons were used not once but three or four times. And when Haku and Chihiro fall close to the bottom of the shaft, there's a group of black spectres, like trapped souls – perhaps the people who've been transformed into slugs and frogs (recalling the victims in many a dungeon, and making a change from the usual skeletons – how many times have we seen skeletons in dungeons? Yes, but that's what *all* humans become, sooner or later).

For plenty of filmmakers, this action sequence would be enough, a rescue and escape, and would not be the place for a flashback. Yet Hayao Miyazaki is quirky enough to insert a flashback right here, right in the midst of a scene of his heroine falling to her doom. The flashback is to the time when Chihiro fell into the River Kohaku, and Haku, in his River God form, saved her.

Spirited Away uses match cuts and rapid dissolves to indicate the continuity between the present day and Chihiro remembering what happened to her as a child. We are in Chihiro's mindscreen now, and one of the signature images of

---

[81] For Andrew Osmond, this dramatic twist and the new characters in the narrative were clumsily rendered, but the scene was certainly unexpected (2008, 93).

Spirited Away – and of Hayao Miyazaki's cinema – occurs here: Chihiro staring into the camera, eyes wide open, her hair blowing in the air but also as if under water. Behind her are green fronds, and in front Haku's turquoise hair on his spine. (The scene with the River God earlier has a similar image which foreshadows this scene – as if the River Gods communicate with each other. And when it leaves the bathhouse, the River God trails across the sky as a dragon, as Haku had done).

THE TRAIN JOURNEY.

The journey to Zeniba's house is one of the most enchanting scenes in all of Hayao Miyazaki's cinema.[82] The filmmakers restore a train journey to its rightful place as a potentially wonderful experience – wondrous, but also mysterious, and also wistful, and even melancholy. The long shots are as beautiful as one could ask for, as the train rolls across the ocean on the railroad tracks underneath water, with skies going slowly into twilight and night. These are exquisite images, worthy of framing and putting on the wall, each one.

But pretty imagery is not the whole picture: the *sound* is mesmerizing, too, with the train rattling along the tracks, and the sound of water swishing. And Joe Hisaishi provides a delicate piano and string piece which enhances the pensive mood. And there are other elements, too: such as the mouse (the baby) and the fly (Yubaba's bird) hopping up and down at the window and, most mysterious of all, the other travellers. These are silent and enigmatic figures, shadowy (and, unusually, in Hayao Miyazaki's cinema, most seem to be black). They are clad in 1930s or 1940s clothes, and have a weary, sad air about them.

Where they are going, when they descend from the train, isn't explained, nor why the station contains what appears to be an entrance to a subway; maybe this part of the fantasy world connects to a metropolis like New York City or Tokyo. There's a whole other story evoked in this sequence – the movie could suddenly sidetrack and follow some of those exhausted, gloomy people. (Needless to say, a formulaic approach to scripting from a major, Western film studio would certainly ditch those characters and images; they come from someplace else, they don't connect to the primary narrative,

---

[82] For some, the journey evoked Kenji Miyazawa's 1934 novella *Night On the Galactic Railway*. In it, the souls of the dead are taken along the river of the Milky Way.

they have only a tenuous thematic link to the main themes, and, crucially, they are not 'explained' by the movie. One can imagine a novice executive piping up a story meeting, 'what's with these sad people from the Thirties?' And the answer is: if you have to ask that question, you won't like the answer!).

For Hayao Miyazaki, the railroad journey was the end of the movie: 'what for me constitutes the end of the film, is the scene in which Chihiro takes the train all by herself. That's where the film ends for me'. The train ride was about the experience of the ride itself, Miyazaki explained, when you take a journey by yourself for the first time, not the landscape through which the train passes.

It's one of those train journeys to the end of the line, where everyone else gets off, and our heroes stay on the train (actually, it's the not the final station). But by the time Chihiro and No Face and the others alight, at Swamp Bottom, it is full night. No surprise that as well as the pools of the swamp, there is a forest here – a witch's house simply *must* be situated in woodland.[83]

These scenes could be excised from the 2001 film without losing any important narrative information (it is what screenwriters call a 'lift') – it is simply a journey from the bathhouse to Zeniba's house in a forest.[84] But what this sequence does, among other things, is to give the audience a breather from the action and rapidity and intensity of some of the previous scenes. A moment of calm and peace after so much action.

It's true that Hayao Miyazaki and his team allow this train ride to last *far longer* than it would in a North American or European animated movie, but that is also the beauty of it: at this point in an American film, and particularly a family adventure film or a fantasy film, no producer or distributor would want the piece to slow down this much, or for this long. But Miyazaki and his team have said (or rather, the *film* has said), no, we're not going to rush here, we are not going to have only one long shot of the train and the sky and the ocean, and a couple of images inside the train, we are going to turn it into a major sequence all on its own. (If there was fight over this sequence, Miyazaki clearly won. But would you go up against Miyazaki – the most successful animator of recent times?!).

---

[83] The hopping lamp may be a tribute to Pixar.
[84] The group of four odd characters travelling to see a witch recalls *The Wizard of Oz* for Andrew Osmond (2008, 100).

LOVE STORY.

Spirited Away is also a love story, but a most unusual one: it involves a spoilt, nervous, modern Japanese girl of ten and a mysterious boy a little older who also happens to be a River God, with the alternate form of a flying, white dragon (and under the influence of two witches). Haku is rightly the person that Chihiro first meets at the abandoned theme park.

In the latter part of the Japanese film, Chihiro now has two quests – apart from the main one of breaking the spell her parents are under, she also wants to save Haku from dying. And she does. As Kamaji explains to Haku when he wakes, only love[85] can break the spell of Zeniba's golden seal,[86] and Zeniba confirms this to Chihiro back in the cottage.

In screenwriting terms, two-thirds in, before the climax begins, the heroine's given another task: to save Haku. This complicates the narrative (a common scripting device for a second act), and is a thematic link to saving the parents (but is not directly linked). This's partly why Hayao Miyazaki says for him the movie's over during the train journey, because Chihiro has moved beyond selfish action and thought, and is putting others first.

There is no kiss for Chihiro and Haku (because their love is forbidden in Japanese folklore),[87] but there is a sequence of ecstasy – and, in true form in a Hayao Miyazaki movie, the ecstasy of love is represented by flight. It occurs when Chihiro leaves Zeniba's cottage on Haku's back: the moment of love is also the moment of the breaking of the spell, when Chihiro remembers what happened to her as a child, when she fell into the River Kohaku to fetch her shoe. (The flashback, narrated by Chihiro, is seamlessly integrated into the film, as Chihiro and Haku fly at night above rivers and trees below).[88]

When Chihiro tells Haku his true name – Nigihayami Kohaku Nushi – the spell of naming is broken, and Haku returns to his boy form. As Chihiro and Haku plunge to earth together, they hold onto each other like skydivers, hand in hand. Chihiro is crying (but, in a detailed touch, her tears form around the top of her eyes, not the sides, because they are falling through the air). They press their heads together, the

---

[85] Kamaji uses the Japanese word *ai*, a strong term for their romance.
[86] The seal with the name on it plays into the theme of naming and magic in *Spirited Away*; seals also have an added meaning in Japan.
[87] They are framed in a medium close-up two-shot later, by the stream, the moment when in a conventional movie lovers would kiss. But this is *not* a conventional movie in any sense!
[88] The flashback is portrayed in a highly subjective, abstract fashion, very far away from the conventional form of filmmaking of long shots, establishing shots, and a sequence of images which have a traditional chronology.

closest they come to kissing.

The ending of *Spirited Away* is very under-stated: no action scene, and the transformation of Chihiro's parents back to human form takes place off-screen.[89] The lengthy *dénouement* of Chihiro catching up with her parents, reversing the journey at the start of the movie, isn't dramatically necessary: but it functions to allow the audience to leave the world of *Spirited Away* gently.

The Greek myth of Orpheus and Eurydice is evoked when Haku and Chihiro part: Haku can't cross the river to the human side of the abandoned theme park (recalling the folkloric belief that witches can't cross water). There is a boundary between the realm of the gods and that of humans, and a stream (which becomes an ocean) is as good a boundary line as any. (In *Howl's Moving Castle* the filmmakers place a similar flashback – into childhood – at a similar point in the narrative, and it's a flashback which brings the lovers closer to each other).

It's fitting that Haku should be the last character to be with Chihiro, as he was the first. Haku tells Chihiro to go and don't look back. And she doesn't. There's a moment when she nearly does, just before the tunnel, but then she remembers, and goes on, with her parents. Only in the final scene, re-united with her parents, and on the far side of the tunnel, does Chihiro turn and look back down the tunnel.

And that is rightly a long moment, sustained on Chihiro in close-up, the culminating scene in the movie emotionally: because although an animated movie is only painted ink of plastic cels photographed and speeding through a projector at 24 frames a second, the audience can see that so much emotion is running through Chihiro, as she looks back at all she has experienced, and all the characters she has known.[90]

The reunion between Chihiro and her folks is very understated. No hugs, no joyful tears; instead, her parents admonish her for taking so long, and Chihiro asks if they are all right. As far as they are concerned, nothing has happened. Chihiro is back to reality with a thump – and the movie suggests that it's going to be as difficult as it would have been before. Except now Chihiro has learned a few things, includ-

---

[89] For director Nobuhijo Obayashi, Chihiro's test at the end of *Spirited Away* was to show how much she loved her parents; it wasn't about pigs (in *Kinema Jumpo*, special *Spirited Away* issue, August 15, 2001).

[90] C. Odell and M. Le Blanc note that neither of Chihiro's parents have learnt anything from their experience – they have forgotten everything that happened to them (O, 118). But Chihiro hasn't forgotten. If Chihiro's parents' generation have let her down, the movie suggests that Chihiro will make up for it.

ing one or two skills, which will help her in her life.

The touch of the car being covered with leaves and dusty inside, suggesting that many days have passed (or maybe weeks or even longer), is absolutely right. It's also spot-on that Chihiro's parents don't think any time has passed at all since they last saw Chihiro. Notice how the parents' transformation from pigs to humans takes place off-screen, and now it's the parents who're up ahead, calling to Chihiro to hurry up.

Spirited Away has transcended every limitation of technology and hardware and mechanisms to become a living, breathing thing. Critics said that no one would sit still for a full-length animated movie when Walt Disney produced his 'folly' in Hollywood in 1937 (*Snow White and the Seven Dwarfs*), and *Spirited Away* proves that, yes, they will, and an animated picture can be every bit as emotional and cathartic as a live-action movie.

12

HOWL'S MOVING CASTLE

Hayao Miyazaki wasn't due to direct *Howl's Moving Castle* (2004), but took over the film from another director (Mamoru Hosoda), when he left the project.[91] It was based on *Howl's Moving Castle*, a 1986 book by British author Diane Wynne-Jones (1934-2011).[92] Wynne-Jones wrote further entries about Howl and the other characters (such as *Castle In the Air*, 1991).[93] Wynne-Jones was delighted with Studio Ghibli's interpretation of her book (who wouldn't be – you'd have to be a really grumpy, stupid author not to be wowed by this film). Yes, Wynne-Jones remarked that aspects of her book had been altered by Hayao Miyazaki and Studio Ghibli, and there were some additions to it.[94] But Wynne-Jones welcomed them, drawing attention to the hat shop, for instance. The shooting star sequence was particularly impressive for Wynne-Jones, as was the Castle itself.

Howl's Moving Castle was massively successful at the Japanese box office, with a gross of $190 million ($14.6m on its opening weekend, a new record high, with 1.1m tickets sold).[95] That year in Japan, *Harry Potter and the Prisoner of Azkaban* grossed $121 million, *The Return of the King* $94m, *Crying Out Love* $72m and the first *Spider-man* sequel $59m. That gives you some idea of just how popular Miyazaki's movies are in Japan, because the two fantasy franchises based on British authors, the *Harry Potter* and the *Lord of the Rings* franchises, have topped the global box office every year they are released.

---

[91] There was also a 6-month closure for Ghibli, following *The Cat Returns*.
[92] *Howl's Moving Castle* is the only film adaptation of Wynne-Jones' fiction so far.
[93] Diane Wynne-Jones' other works include *Dogsbody, The Homeward Bounders, Fire and Hemlock, Hexwood, The Lives of Christopher Chant, The Power of Three, Charmed Life, The Magicians of Caprona, Witch Week* and *Archer's Goon*.
[94] The film had been screened for Wynne-Jones in her home town of Bristol.
[95] 12 million tickets had been sold by mid-January, 2005, with a gross of $90m in 4 weeks. *Howl's Moving Castle* also did very well in Korea, with $18m gross from 3 million viewers by February 10, 2005, from 237 screens. In France, *Howl's Moving Castle* grossed $2.1m on its debut weekend, attracting 345,633 viewers.

The Japanese version of *Howl's Moving Castle* featured the voices of Chieko Baisho[96] (b. 1941, as Sophie), Takuya Kimura (Howl), Akihiro Miwa[97] (Witch of the Waste), Tatsuya Gashûin (Calcifer), and Ryunosuka Kamiki (Markl).[98] The English language version of *Howl's Moving Castle,* prepared by the Walt Disney Studios, included the voices of the wonderful Jean Simmons, Christian Bale, Lauren Bacall, Emily Mortimer, and Billy Crystal. (This was the version that I saw in the cinema in 2005, but, once again, it's the Japanese version that is essential viewing).

The production schedule for *Howl's Moving Castle* was from February, 2003 to August 8, 2004; the movie was released in Japan on November 20, 2004 (for the Christmas season – most of Miyazaki's movies have had Summer vacation releases).[99] According to the BBC, *Howl's Moving Castle* was the only non-English language picture (i.e., non-American) to gross over $100 million in 2004. Critics who raved about *Howl's Moving Castle* included Jonathan Rosenbaum, Kenneth Turan, David Sterritt, David Ansen, Glenn Kenny and Michael Sragow.[100]

Toshio Suzuki, Hayao Miyazaki and Yasuyoshi Tokuma were the producers of *Howl's Moving Castle,* for Dentsu, D-Rights, Buena Vista, Nippon TV, Toho and Tokuma Shoten; animation director was Katsuya Kondou; Akihiro Yamashita, Takeshi Inaumura and Kitao Kosaka were supervising animators; Mitsunori Katama directed the digital animation;[101] sound was by Kazuhiro Hayashi, Kazuhiro Wakabayashi, Nobue Yoshinaga and Shuji Inoue, with sound effects by Toru Noguchi; music was by Joe Hisaishi;[102] art directors were Yozi Takeshige and Noboru Yoshida; Atsushi Okui was DP; Takeshi Seyama was editor; Ryoichi Fukuyama, Nozomu Takahashi and Hiroyuki Watanabe were production managers; and

---

[96] Chieko Baisho is best-known for the *It's Tough Being a Man* series (48 movies btn 1969 and 1995), where she played the hero's sister.

[97] Akihiro Miwa, a Gothic Lolita and Visual Kei fashion icon, was the voice of Moro in *Mononoke* and Floy in *Harmageddon.*

[98] The king was played by Akio Otsuka from *Ghost In the Shell,* who had been Curtis in *Porco Rosso.*

[99] *Howl's Moving Castle* was released in 450 cinemas in Japan, the widest distribution for a Japanese movie.

[100] But *Howl* also attracted more negative reviews than any of Miyazaki's recent productions. The critical backlash against Miyazaki, at least overseas, seems to have increased with *Howl's Moving Castle.*

[101] Digital animation in *Howl's Moving Castle* includes the usual functions of 3-D rendering, ink and paint, compositing and layering, morphing, ray tracing, particle animation, texture mapping, and some visual effects.

[102] Youmi Kimura composed the theme song 'Sekai no Yakusoku'. The orchestra was the New Japan Philharmonic.

Michiyo Yasuda was colour designer.[103] There is also a *manga* of *Howl*.[104]

CHARACTERS.

Howl's Moving Castle features a collection of misfit characters, each one wholly individual and exquisitely realized: Howl, the youth, wizard and shape-changer (he becomes a giant feathery bird); Sophie, the young hat-maker and heroine who's turned into an old woman; the Witch of the Waste (who becomes a frail, old woman when the spell is lifted); Markl, Howl's boy assistant, about eight years-old with a shock of spikey, orangey hair;[105] a scarecrow, Turnip-head (*Kabu*), who's really a prince from a neighbouring kingdom; Calcifer, the magical fire demon who lives in the stove in the Moving Castle; Heen, a dog, Suliman's spy; and Madame Suliman, the powerful sorceress of the king.[106]

Having Sophie under a spell from the Witch of the Waste allowed Hayao Miyazaki and his team to depict both the young woman or *shojo* character Miyazaki favoured, and also the tough, old women he liked to portray. In fact, Miyazaki and the filmmakers played with switching back and forth between the young and the old Sophie (she becomes the young Sophie at night, when she's asleep, in a scene where Howl looks in on her). And in the second half of the film, as she is gradually falling in love with Howl, or when she's in the secret meadows, she is far less the old woman, but a middle-aged Sophie [107] (though still with grey hair, which she retains at the end of the narrative).[108]

In 2005, Miyazaki remarked:

---

[103] Other companies were involved in producing the visuals in *Howl's Moving Castle:* T2 Studio, Trace Studio M, Liberty Ship, Mad House, Nakamura, Production I.G., Sakura Create, Studio Cockpit, Studio Takuranka, Anime Torotoro, Dogakobo, Oh Production, and Gonzo Digitmation.

[104] The *manga* (published by Viz Media) is not your usual *manga*: it's full colour throughout, and comprises images from the movie (reframed and altered). Like the other *manga* of Ghibli's movies, it looks like a tie-in photobook, but re-arranged into the *manga* format (they're called *animanga* or *animekomikkusu* or 'film comics'). Reading it, you're struck by just how sunny and warm the imagery in *Howl's Moving Castle* is.

[105] In Diana Wynne-Jones' book, Markl is 15 years-old.

[106] In the book, Suliman is not a nasty piece of work controlling a kingdom from behind the throne.

[107] C. Odell and M. Le Blanc suggest that 'spiritually, her low self-esteem may be just as much to blame for her condition' as the curse from the Witch of the Waste (O, 128).

[108] Pixar's John Lasseter said he'd tried to work out what was the logic for the differences in Sophie's appearance, and concluded that it was do with her spirit or love of life, or her love for Howl. It is *intuitive*, like so many of Hayao Miyazaki's narrative ideas.

Is someone different at age 18 or 60? I believe one stays the same. A 90 years-old woman once said to me that she felt the same as when she was 18. So an 18 year-old young woman is struck by a spell and changes into an old lady. I didn't want a film where the key to happiness would be to break the spell and get youth back. In other words, what means breaking the spell? It's not only to rejuvenate. Being young is not panacea. So what is? How can this heroine be happy? I wondered about this very seriously, and this film is the result of my thinking.

Sophie changes within scenes, and within the same shot, from old to young, or vice versa. For example, when Howl moves the Castle to Sophie's home-town, Sophie, now emotional,[109] grows younger, until she's her original age, but with grey hair.[110] The different visual indicators of age and youth allow the filmmakers to present Sophie as different ages *simultaneously*. Sometimes she might look very old, but she is nimble and quick, like a girl; other times, though she looks youthful, she moves like an old woman.

In the scene where Howl gifts Sophie the pastoral land of his youth, Sophie grows younger as the scene progresses – it becomes close to a love scene, as Sophie tells Howl she wants to help him. But realizing her limits, and her humanity, she becomes old again.

Howl's appearance too changes – not only from being a monstrous bird[111] to a human, but within his humanity. Sometimes he's a dashing youth, with flowing hair, and sometimes appears even younger (such as when he talks about growing up in the house in the mountains, when he shows Sophie his rural world after he's moved the Castle).

One of the fundamental themes in *Howl's Moving Castle* is that everyone is under a spell of one sort or another. Calcifer, the scarecrow, Sophie, and of course Howl are all under spells. The Witch of the Waste, meanwhile, has a spell lifted, and transforms from a powerful, portly sorceress in her late middle-age to a nearly harmless and rather simple-minded old woman. That the enchantments are linked to speaking and expression is classic Miyazaki: Sophie is unable to say what has happened to her – when she does, her mouth seals up, like Chihiro's in *Spirited Away*. And Howl, too, isn't able to give voice to his predicament.

And other characters are not all they seem at first: when

---

[109] When she (inadvertently) confesses her love for Howl to Suliman, she loses years within the shot, becoming close to her usual 18 year-old self.
[110] Some people – like Howl – can see thru Sophie's transformation.
[111] Sometimes Howl is a nasty-looking creature, not only a giant bird.

Sophie is encouraged to visit the palace on her own, Howl says he'll go with her in disguise. When the cute, short-legged, furry dog Heen appears (a classic piece of Miyazakian animation and design), Sophie thinks this must be Howl in disguise. But it isn't. Similarly, the young, blond boys who assist Suliman at the palace may be Howl, but they are not. When Howl lands in a craft and appears as the king, his disguise is soon rumbled by Suliman (the real king appears, but soon hurries off in an excited mood). Suliman, who is Howl's *sensei*, said she knew it was him.

Markl's forerunners include Pazu in *Laputa: Castle In the Sky* and Tombo in *Kiki's Delivery Service:* young, enthusiastic, energetic, practical, and relatively innocent. As Howl's assistant, Markl is an appealing character, an intermediary between Sophie and Howl (he also provides plenty of exposition for the audience in the first scenes in the Moving Castle, because Howl isn't the kind of character to sit there and shoot the breeze with Sophie – well, not at first). Markl's disguise as a dwarf with a long, grey beard and a hood and cloak is particularly amusing. The somewhat gruff, cross manner that Markl has towards Sophie at first soon disappears when Sophie rustles up some breakfast (so many of Hayao Miyazaki's characters love their food, and one of the best ways to cheer themselves up is to eat. Well, that works for most of us!).

Calicifer embodies both the Faustian pact that the young Howl made with the fallen spirit, in order to gain magical powers, and Howl's heart in itself. In a Western animation, the relation between Calicifer and Howl's heart would be more emphatically (and simplistically) spelt out; in the Japanese movie, Calicifer is more complex than that. He is a demon intimately and fatally linked to Howl. But it is the power of love, embodied in Sophie, that saves Howl, in the end. Yep, Miyazaki is an old softie at heart.

SOPHIE.

Women are at the centre of *Howl's Moving Castle*: the main character is a woman (despite the 'Howl' in the title): and Sophie gets to play two aspects of women, a young woman, and an old woman (Sophie plays a nurturing, motherly role, too – looking after Markl and Howl and Calcifer and the scarecrow, who form her second family). The chief villain (or opponent), Madame Suliman, is a middle-aged woman, while the other villain, the Witch of the Waste, is first a powerful, older woman, and later a (mainly) mild, old woman. And Howl, too, is a feminized man, a youth with many traditionally 'feminine' characteristics.[112] Secondary characters include Sophie's mother, and sister Lettie. The book was written by a woman.

Sophie is something of a loner or outsider figure – a recurring motif in Hayao Miyazaki's cinema. That is depicted strongly in the opening scenes, which introduce Sophie, before the spell of the Witch of the Waste transforms her into an old woman. She works in a hat shop (next to a railroad with steam trains, of course), but continues to work, alone, when her co-workers have left. Notice how Sophie is shown in a room on her own, working on a hat by the window, while the laughing, chattering young women are in the next room, the main room of the shop. That says plenty: how your main character is first seen in a movie is crucial: the filmmakers put Sophie away from the social group, and she's depicted at work, at the end of the day. And she stays behind to work when the others leave. That makes Sophie's decision to slink away up into the hills when the spell transforms her into an old woman more convincing: she doesn't seem to have close friends to confide in. And before the Witch of the Waste appears, Sophie has returned to the hat store on her own, as if she has nowhere else to go.

There is an intriguing group of scenes with her sister, Lettie, who's also a worker, but who is immensely popular – the total opposite of Sophie, socially: in the scenes with Lettie, everyone is saying hello to her, many of them guys, with hints of flirtation. They clamour around her in the baker's store, the older guys say hello to her outside when she chats to Sophie.

Lettie is also conventionally pretty, an attractive blonde with big, blue eyes, and much closer to her mother in appearance (their mother is very much an older version of Lettie, further suggesting that Sophie is definitely the outsider in the family. There's no mention of a father – maybe he's at war). Lettie expresses a view (that of conventional society) that Sophie should be doing something more with her life, the suggestion being that Sophie may end up a spinster, alone. Lettie's appearance is also I think a satire – Lettie is just *too* blonde and *too* pretty to be taken straight. She is an exaggerated character, to emphasize Sophie's aloneness and friendlessness.[113] Lettie also represents what Sophie isn't, and

---

[112] One of the directors of the English language dub, Pete Docter, remarked that Western cinema didn't really have an equivalent for the kind of feminized character that Howl was.

[113] And Sophie's own mother betrays her later on – an unusual turn, and rare in Miyazaki's cinema.

maybe can't be, and maybe doesn't want to be.

Thus, one of the narrative themes of *Howl's Moving Castle* is finding friendship: even more than the possibility of romance between Sophie and Howl, it's the family of friends that Sophie discovers during the course of the film that's important: Howl, Markl, Calcifer, Turnip-head and the Witch of the Waste. This is such a cliché, of course, but the film pulls it off by never making it obvious, and never underlining it with the kind of sentimental dialogue that some cinema just can't resist including. Because at the beginning of the movie, Sophie doesn't really have friends, apart from her sister Lettie; by the end of *Howl's Moving Castle,* she is very much at the centre of a strange collection of misfits that function as a family. And, as this is definitely a love story, she has also found love.

WAR.

Once again, Hayao Miyazaki and his team tackle the theme of war:[114] in *Howl's Moving Castle,* the images of warfare are incredibly vivid and apocalyptic: giant bombers flying over cities caught in firestorms,[115] very much in the model of Dresden or Hamburg or London or Tokyo or Hiroshima or Nagasaki (Ghibli films such as *Grave of the Fireflies* had depicted similar red-hued conflagrations). So altho' *Howl* seems to be a light-hearted, colourful fantasy adventure aimed at children, it also contains images of the most traumatic and devastating things that humans have done to each other in their entire history: launched all-out bombing assaults. The only step-up from this is the Holocaust.

In the midst of the fires and explosions, Howl flies in his giant bird guise, with images of superhero battles in the air against enormous aircraft and the flying blob-men (the blob-men are grotesque parodies of the military, sporting top hats and tails and maws of nasty teeth. You can see that the filmmakers *loathe* the military: war-mongers are depicted as ridiculous creatures embarked on completely pointless but violently destructive acts). In these scenes, Studio Ghibli's animation is as extraordinary as any in the history of cartoons.

North America's war in Iraq had infuriated Hayao Miyazaki (as it had angered so many artists and thinkers around the world), and he told *Newsweek* (in 2005) that *Howl's Moving Castle* 'is profoundly affected by the war in Iraq' (O,

---

114 But in Wynne-Jones's novel, war is a far less dominant theme.
115 A line of bomb explosions evokes napalm in the Vietnam War.

127).[116] In relating the movie to the Iraq War, the piece automatically becomes critical of the U.S.A. (and a post-9/11 movie), of the U.S.A.'s contemporary politics, and of the troubled relationship between Japan and North America, which has been such a controversial and much-debated issue since the Occupation of the late 1940s. As producer Toshio Suzuki recalled, 'When we were making it, there was the Iraq war. In Japan we were not in a very good economic situation. From young to old, people are not very happy.'[117] For Miyazaki, America is the epicentre of the problems that affect the whole world, with the American lifestyle dominating so much of contemporary life (TP, 396).

In *Howl*, we see a war raging – horrible, senseless conflict in which entire cities burn. The *causes* of the war have been rapidly lost, and the *goals* of the war are also unclear. Howl is compelled to fight, but he doesn't really know why, and never speaks about it. To demonstrate just how pointless the war was, it ends abruptly, with the war-mongers admitting it's silly to fight.

The first two or three reels of *Howl's Moving Castle* depict a country (called Ingary – Ingaria in the 1986 novel) going to war: as Sophie walks through the town,[118] scenes of patriotic fervour are depicted – aircraft trailing flags flying overhead, people cheering and waving flags, and finally a grand procession through the streets of military hardware and marching soldiers. It is all a giant celebration of war-time, and in particular of a society that has not experienced war in its full horror (or has forgotten the horrors).

The affinities of these scenes of jubilation are very much with Europe before the First World War: it could be France, Italy, Germany, Britain, etc. But the real impact of these episodes is felt later, when the dreadnoughts return, limping into port, badly damaged and also bombed by airships. Then the real horror of war is revealed, and it scares the hell out of Sophie.

For Markl, watching the return of the ships and the troops during a shopping spree, war is spectacle, something to wonder at; but for Sophie it is all too real, and all too painful (the scenes of sailors jumping off the ship as it's bombed in the water recall historical moments such as Pearl Harbor). At

---

[116] And Hayao Miyazaki had 'felt some hesitation about the award' (the Oscar) for *Spirited Away*, because of the U.S.A.'s actions overseas.

[117] In S. Darlington, "Japanese Animation Casts Spell Over Venice Fest", *Reuters*, Sept 5, 2004.

[118] The town's modelled on the Edo-Tokyo Architectural Park near Ghibli, also employed as an inspiration in *Spirited Away*.

this point, the war is someplace else – the armed forces go away and then return. But the citizens don't witness the conflict directly.

In the latter part of *Howl's Moving Castle,* the warfare reaches apocalyptic proportions, and comes to the homeland, with aircraft bombing towns into oblivion. These are among the most extreme depictions of devastation in Hayao Miyazaki's cinema, and draw once again on the battles and air-raids of World War Two, not the First World War. In the black night, all is red – the red of fires and explosions. Through these very disturbing, deadly images, Howl flies in his bird-guise.

There are also moving scenes of evacuation, everybody heading out of the towns and cities. It is the imagery depicted so vividly in *Grave of the Fireflies*.

This is fantasy movie-making grounded very much in reality – take away the flying blob-men and the bird-like Howl, and you have the fire-bombing of cities during WW2. There is an *enormous amount* of warfare and war imagery in *Howl's Moving Castle,* yet I'm sure nobody thinks of it as a war movie, or part of the war genre. That's partly because of the context of Hayao Miyazaki's cinema, and of Studio Ghibli's output, but also of the narrative context of the film itself, with its numerous fantasy and fairy tale elements.[119] Also, there are many lighter or light-hearted aspects to *Howl's Moving Castle*, and the disturbing scenes of horrific devastation are rapidly attenuated with the smaller-scale scenes.

Also, Hayao Miyazaki and his filmmakers are careful not to show graphic close-ups of the horror of warfare – where necessary, Miyazaki and his teams at Ghibli have not held back from depicting blood and gore, but it is not appropriate here, partly because of the genre and narrative of the whole movie. On the other hand, one could argue that some selective and carefully-judged close-ups of suffering (but maybe not 'R' rated blood 'n' guts), might've driven home the torment of war. (But part of the point of the war theme in *Howl* is that isn't wholly clear just what the war is about, or who the enemy is, as in the works of Katsuhiro Otomo (such as *Memories* and *The Legend of Mother Sarah*).)

THE LOOK.

The design of Howl's Castle is one of the signature images in Hayao Miyazaki's cinema: a towering, irregular

---

[119] Sophie is linked to Cinderella, to princesses who wait for their prince, and later she plays Beauty to Howl's Beast.

collection of houses, wheels and pulleys and cables, chimneys belching steam, balconies, circular gun turrets, staircases, windows, and doors. Giant legs with bird claws carry the Castle over the landscape (at the end, it becomes a flying machine, of course).[120] Its ancestors include the bath-house in *Spirited Away* and Laputa in *Laputa: Castle In the Sky*.

Everything is battered, well-worn, and lived-in in the Castle. It's classic, steam-punk Victoriana, extravagant but also completely convincing. The Castle is introduced in the opening frames of *Howl*, which reveals the structure looming out of mist and clouds in some windy upland, which might be mountainous Wales or Switzerland.[121] After those haunting images of the walking Castle being glimpsed behind banks of clouds, the narrative shifts to Sophie in the town, at the hat shop (but the Castle is seen by the people in the town, including Sophie at her window).

Much of the action of *Howl's Moving Castle* takes place in the kitchen and entrance hall of the Castle: this beautifully-rendered space[122] includes a stairway, a broad stove (where Calcifer lives in the grate), cupboards, windows, chairs, and a magical door with steps down to it. It's the domestic space of homes throughout history – chairs, a table, and a fire. It's the space where everyone meets, where people come and go. There are scenes in other rooms of Howl's Castle, such as the filthy bathroom[123] and a corridor and stair-way, but the kitchen is the central zone.

The kitchen, and the whole Castle, is another of the cluttered spaces in Hayao Miyazaki's cinema, where bric-a-brac is piled onto every available surface. This is a lived-in place, full of the junk of everyday life (plus more magical objects, like spell books). It's marvellous how Howl and Markl live in such a mess, so that although they have eggs and bacon, Markl settles for bread and cheese for breakfast. These are two guys living together in domestic chaos (but notice, too, how Howl takes over from Sophie cooking the breakfast on Calcifer's fire, when he returns and encounters Sophie in his kitchen).

---

120 Other flying machines in *Howl's Moving Castle* include the 'aero-kayak', reminiscent of the flaptors in *Laputa: Castle In the Sky*.
121 The filmmakers used Alsace as an inspiration; Miyazaki visited Riquewihr and Colmar for *Howl's Moving Castle*. Diane Wynne-Jones looked to the mountains of Wales.
122 Like all of the spaces in Hayao Miyazaki's cinema, you could walk around it and know where everything is.
123 For some reason, the bath and the walls are covered with what looks like splashes of colourful paint – maybe from Howl's hair dyeing experiments.

The way to Howl's inmost being is along tunnels: to reach the adolescent Howl, in the flashback sequence, Sophie has to walk through a tunnel into the past. Meanwhile, when she goes to find Howl in his bedroom, she discovers him along a tunnel lined with toys; it's such a potent image of childhood and the way that Howl crawls into a cocoon of childhood playthings when he returns from his night flights.

The tunnel's embedded with a host of toys – as if Howl is every child who ever lived, and every child who didn't want to grow up. The film emphasizes Howl's selfishness and immaturity many times – a striking instance is when the movie cuts abruptly from Sophie and Markl rushing in from their shopping spree, when Sophie is very frightened by the realities of war (the smashed battleship, the bombs, the leaflets, the enemy bombers), to Howl hurtling from the bathroom complaining about nothing more important than the colour of his hair. (Howl keeps his hair dark after Sophie praises it that colour.)

In one space in the Castle the filmmakers decided to go completely over-the-top: Howl's bedroom. The room's absolutely jammed with magical devices, with mobiles, and clocks, and globes, and eyes, and stars, and statues, and paintings. It's the ultimate antique room or junk room. But it's the *colours* here that are astonishing: vivid reds, blues, greens, yellows, purples, and all rendered with an intense glow, as if lit by ultra-violet light, like a case of crystals in a museum. The effect also recalls the richly decorative of Symbolist painter Gustave Moreau, or the eccentric, visionary artist Richard Dadd, or maybe Gustav Klimt (there is a giant eye which directly evokes the pastel drawings of Odilon Redon, one of my favourite Symbolist artists). In short, there's no other bedroom like this in all of cinema.

Howl's Moving Castle is truly remarkable as a piece of filmmaking, on every level. But at the level of artistry and detail and visual splendour, *Howl's Moving Castle* is up there with *Snow White and the Seven Dwarfs*. It is a film that must be viewed again and again (and preferably on the big screen).

As with the other works of Hayao Miyazaki's mature period (from *Princess Mononoke* onwards), the filmmakers have decided: 'OK, we are going to put EVERYTHING into this movie!' The level of *detail* is absolutely staggering. It always has been, really, in Miyazaki's cinema: his pictures have always delivered far more detail and research and depth than the stories required. Even *The Castle of Cagliostro,* with its roots in television animation (and a far lower budget than the later works), has swathes of detail that aren't necessary to tell the story.

But *Howl's Moving Castle* is *dense*, and dense again. This is *cinema*, not television or 'filmed theatre'. But even with all its super-abundant imagery and colours, *Howl's Moving Castle* never neglects the plot and the characters: it is *always* telling a story, and driving along the plot. And even when you consciously pull yourself away from the characters and the events and the action to marvel at the settings or the visual invention on display, the drama sucks you back in.

MAGIC.

The magical door of Howl's moving Castle is a marvellous device of time/ space shifting: it opens out onto different places, when the door knob is turned: two places in Kingsbury: a modest back street in Porthaven (overlooking the sea), and the square below the palace in Kingsbury (where Howl is known as Wizard Pendragon and Wizard Jenkins).

The two towns represent the majesty and spectacle of the capital city of a country, and the slower, sleepier, more domestic and everyday aspects of a suburban town (for instance, when Sophie and Markl go shopping, they walk out into the back streets of Porthaven, not the grand squares and boulevards of Kingsbury).

The third region (called 'the Wastes') is a hillside (somewhere up in the mountains, where Sophie first encounters Howl's Moving Castle). That's a space of the natural world, of regeneration and contact with primal forces (it's often raining there, or windy, or it's peaceful – as when Sophie sits by the lake). It is high moorland, and later on a mountainscape from the Swiss Alps, complete with a lake and snow-capped peaks. This is the final image in Miyazaki's last movie, *The Wind Rises*.[124]

The fourth realm (symbolized by a black space beyond, and a black segment in the circular door indicator), is Howl's realm, a place of death and war (and magical transformation). Later in the 2004 film, Howl adds another space, a gift for Sophie, after he's moved the Castle: rolling fields of flowers, with a house by a lake from Howl's childhood (and not only hills and fields and flowers, but the mighty cumulus clouds that populate so many of Hayao Miyazaki's pictures, drifting on the wind. It's the third space, 'the Wastes', transformed back into a childhood paradise). Regeneration and rebirth –

---

[124] It's where Miyazaki has a cabin in the Japanese Alps.

but *out of* nature, and *thru* nature, and *embodied by* the natural world. In Miyazaki-san's philosophy, rebirth (peace, calm, nourishment) comes from the natural world, as well as from communities, friends, families and love.

NATURE.

Once again, the natural world plays a huge role in *Howl's Moving Castle* – there are lakes and oceans, fields and mountains, and always the big sky full of clouds. The rain, the wind, the cold, the snow, the sun, the lake – *Howl's Moving Castle* is shot through with the presence of natural elements. The natural world is where characters go when they need space to breathe, to re-charge themselves. Sophie, when she's fed up with Howl's behaviour, goes out into the rain in her rage. At an earlier moment, there's the exquisite scene where Sophie and Markl hang out the washing in the blustery wind, and take out a table and chairs to eat on the grass outside the Castle. Those scenes, and the scene where Sophie sits right next to the wavelets breaking on the lake shore, are simply marvellous. Characters are hanging out the washing! That's all! But it's wonderful!

We are talking about pieces of shiny celluloid being photographed with a movie camera to produce the illusion of movement and life, yet you really can feel that wind blowing on your face, or the smell the rain in a Hayao Miyazaki film. Which's quite an achievement. Miyazaki's movies are far more than simply colourful shapes being animated on flat surfaces then projected at 24 frames per second.

Meanwhile, the sequence in *Howl's Moving Castle* depicting Sophie's climb up into the hills is a *tour-de-force* of special effects animation, as good as any scene in any animated film you care to mention. In it, Hayao Miyazaki, Toshio Suzuki, Katsuya Kondou, Akihiro Yamashita, Takeshi Inaumura, Kitao Kosaka, Yozi Takeshige, Noboru Yoshida and the team deliver extraordinary scenes of a windy mountainscape at sunset, with the breeze ripping at clothes and vegetation, and flakes of snow spinning through the dark air. It is evening and close to sun-down, a favourite moment in Miyazaki's cinema (and filmmakers everywhere – it's the 'magic hour'), when the sun is near the horizon, sending out low shafts of light. It is a stupendous and very exciting setting for Sophie to encounter the Moving Castle, and to climb aboard, a classic piece of storytelliing, placing the encounter when a character is exhausted and over-extended (in consequence, the contrast between the chilly, windy night on the mountain and the quiet, still interior of the kitchen in the Castle is immense. And no wonder that Sophie is soon falling asleep after she's put some more wood on the fire).

The films of Hayao Miyazaki at these times possess a genuine nature mysticism, a feeling for the natural world which expresses authentic spirituality – as authentic as the pantheism in the nature poetry of the European Romantic poets, for instance, or the Buddhist philosophers of the ancient Chinese era. In cinema, this kind of nature mysticism is rare – you can find it in the pictures of Ingmar Bergman, Akira Kurosawa and Andrei Tarkovsky, certainly, but you seldom find it in mainstream, commercial movies.

SHAPE-CHANGING.

Everyone in *Howl's Moving Castle* is in disguise, or has alternative forms which they employ. Identity is definitely fluid in *Howl's Moving Castle,* and it's one of Hayao Miyazaki's recurring themes. When you watch a Miyazaki movie, you have to remember the first time you meet a character that they will likely turn into something else later on. But the *first appearance* of a character of course fixes their identity somewhat for the audience.

A shape-changer, Howl's alter-ego is a giant bird. It is a supremely shamanic transformation, exactly like shamen in archaic times. In this guise, Howl becomes a superhero warrior, fighting off the flying blob-men and the aircraft bombing the towns and cities. It's a form that fits in perfectly with Hayao Miyazaki's sensibilities: flight, an animal-form, movement, and provides plenty of opportunities for action and adventure.

Howl's Moving Castle also depicts the cost of transforming magically: every time Howl returns from his night-time sorties, he seems more exhausted (and is partially see-thru and wraith-like), and takes longer to transform back into a man. (As Calcifer warns him, he might not be able to change back so easily each time).[125]

TEENAGE ANGST.

It's wonderful how *Howl's Moving Castle* depicts Howl's emotional insecurity and anxiety and adolescence – by having him act as a narcissistic and moody teenager.[126] Howl is a

---

[125] Howl's shape-changing and disguises also suggest that Howl is escaping from reality; he is avoiding the Witch of the Waste, for instance. But the disguises also weaken Howl, to the point where he finds it increasingly difficult to transform back to his human form after becoming the giant bird.

[126] Howl is a *bishonen* or 'pretty boy', a character type found in Japanese *animé*.

dandy, he likes to dress well (he sports luxurious jackets with pink and grey lozenge-shapes, and has a necklace and earrings which tinkle prominently on the soundtrack),[127] he takes a bath often,[128] and he likes his hair a certain way. So when he has yet another bath and his hair turns a colour he doesn't like (ginger), he has a tantrum.

The filmmakers portray a teenager having a moody turn in a hilarious but also alarming fashion: Howl slumps in front of the stove, head down and silent, while the room turns into a German Expressionist, *Dr Caligari* nightmare, with demons as black silhouettes floating around the walls, which bend and distort. Meanwhile, Howl's body becomes sticky, green, oozing goo. Calcifer tries to talk Howl out of it.

This is genius filmmaking, because it's a concise but also precise and vivid manifestation of an emotional state. It's inventive, and original, and it also fits the character – an angst-ridden teenager, but also someone magical, who can conjure up dark spirits.

And narratively it's marvellous that Sophie too explodes – Howl's diva-like tantrum is just too much for her, and she storms out, weeping beside the misty lake. But notice how the two young people deal their anger and resentment (they are both teenagers): Sophie goes for a walk outside, and soon her fury boils over, and she is calmed by the beauty and calming energy of the natural world.

Howl, meanwhile, is still lost in his self-induced depression, now oozing green puss. As Sophie reflects, Howl really *is* dramatic. He is a drama queen who values looks and beauty too highly: he is at this moment more emotionally immature than Sophie. Sophie stands back with Markl to admire this preposterous display of moodiness.

In the following scene, Sophie and Markl hilariously drag Howl upstairs to have yet another bath. There's a nice touch of teen embarrassment on the stairs, when Sophie realizes that Howl's towel has fallen off (she leaves it up to Markl to deal with him in the bathroom).

In an interview, Hayao Miyazaki remarked that he didn't have time, really, to show Howl in detail, because the movie was focussing on Sophie. He related how his collaborators said that when they went home their wives wouldn't know what they'd been doing, and didn't really care that much

---

127 Recalling the tinkling earrings of San in *Princess Mononoke*.
128 Howl's love of having baths is a wonderful way of domesticating this supernatural character, bringing the wizard down to the level of a vain teenager. And it's spot-on and so familiar that Calcifer complains about having to heat up water for Howl's baths, just like a parent.

either. So Miyazaki depicted Sophie like that: 'Sophie doesn't have to care about what Howl is trying to do. So I didn't show it'.

ROMANCE.

The potential for romance in *Howl's Moving Castle* has an intriguing slant, because of the two ages that Sophie embodies: as a young woman, she might be won over by Howl's handsome, suave, magical exterior, but as an old woman she might be fed up with his sulks and changeable moods (even though emotionally she is still the young Sophie). As an older woman, Sophie takes on a motherly role – not only in relation to Howl, but to the other figures in the family of misfits in the Castle.

A romantic movie, but there are only a few kisses (as in most *anime*) – oh yes, Sophie kisses Howl, a few times (among the first kisses in Miyazaki's cinema), and also Calcifer, and Turnip-head the prince.

The first time that Sophie encounters Howl is in the back streets of the town, when he saves her from being bothered by two soldiers (she is a *kawaii* girl, a possible pick-up for them). Howl's reasons for doing so are not wholly gallantry: he is something of a dandy and a pin-up figure for women (as well as being feared).

At first, Sophie finds it all a little overwhelming, with the rescue, followed by the flight from the blob-men. It's fantastical adventure material, and it's depicted in a highly romantic fashion. As they fly over the town, they might be dancing at some grand ball – a classic cinematic stand-in for a love scene.

The erotic relationship between Howl and Sophie is suggested from the first moment they meet: notice how the filmmakers use a point-of-view shot of Sophie standing next to Howl, with the camera at Sophie's eye-level, showing Howl right beside her, with his arm in hers. That curious camera angle is deployed again when Howl shifts Sophie aside at the stove, when she's cooking breakfast. The closeness of Howl at this moment is not only erotic – it also indicates that few people get really close to Sophie, because she is something of a loner, and keeps her distance from others (but Howl moves right into her personal space).[129]

Howl is the kind of guy that Sophie probably she thinks she has no hope of having a relationship with; when Lettie is

---

[129] We first see Sophie in a room separate from the other women at the hat store (and after running her errands, she returns to the store alone).

introduced as the pretty woman surrounded by adoring men, it's clear that Sophie has resigned herself to being alone for much of the time. Meanwhile, Sophie is probably the kind of woman that Howl would not normally notice (in her view, and maybe in his too): in his vanity and superficiality, he would probably plump for a much more desirable kind of woman, like Lettie – a woman as a trophy. Yet, he *does* rescue Sophie from the blob-men.

THE FLASHBACK SEQUENCE.

In the last third of *Howl's Moving Castle,* the set-pieces and spectacle mount up, so that the 2004 *animé* is hurtling from one extraordinary piece of animation to the next. Hayao Miyazaki and his team turn in some of the most astonishing scenes in animation history. There are so many to discuss, but let's take one: the flashback sequence which deals with Howl as a boy, and how he came to have magical powers.

This history of Howl's childhood was introduced by Madame Suliman, when she tries to ensnare Howl and Sophie in the palace in Kingsbury. It's as if Suliman were trying to show Howl to Sophie in a negative light. Later, in the fully-fledged flashback sequence, the meaning of those dancing figures becomes clear: they are demons that fall to Earth like shooting stars.

One wonders if Hayao Miyazaki was influenced in the flashback sequence of Howl's childhood by Lord Dunsany's 1916 *The Kith of the Elf-Folk*, a very beautiful fairy tale of a marsh spirit who becomes a woman for a while. The settings of the marshland, with its pools and starlight, and the way that the elves step across the water on the reflections of the stars in *The Kith of the Elf-Folk* is certainly reminiscent of the flashback in *Howl's Moving Castle*.[130]

Sophie enters Howl's memories down a black tunnel, when she's separated from the others when the Castle falls apart. The allusions to *Alice's Adventures In Wonderland* are sated boldly: Sophie cries enormous wet tears that splash everywhere; meanwhile, the dog Heen, like the White Rabbit, shows Sophie the way to Howl: into a tunnel in the side of a gully (thru the Castle's magical door).

Sophie emerges in the house that Howl showed her earlier, when he re-made the Castle – the house is part of a paradisal landscape of flowers and pools, a high upland in the mountains, clearly evoking the lost Eden of Howl's childhood

---

[130] And it would be very in keeping with Miyazaki's way of writing to include an English fairy tale from WW1.

(we were happiest in childhood, Miyazaki thinks). This is Howl's gift to Sophie, and it's the place she returns to when she tries to find out about Howl's background. (A paradisal realm in the past is a recurring motif in Miyazaki's cinema, and also in other Studio Ghibli movies – such as the part of Tokyo that raccoons live in (from *Pon Poko*), or the countryside before the war in *Grave of the Fireflies*).

In the flashback sequence, Hayao Miyazaki and his team are throwing in everything they've got, every visual effect in the box (and Studio Ghibli have as many visual effects and cinematic tricks as any production house or film studio in the history of cinema). There's a remarkable use of the colour black, for example, to isolate Sophie drifting or floating or running in amongst Howl's memories (reminiscent of abstract sequences in *manga*).[131] Meanwhile, the landscape seems to be in continual flux, bending and warping.

The central dramatic element of the flashback is the moment where Sophie spies Howl in the grassland in the distance, taking up one of the fallen star-demons and absorbing it (into his chest). It is the birth of magic, of Howl's magical powers. Everything about the sequence is magical, from the setting, colours and lighting to the heightened drama and unreality of the scene.

The flashback sequence is merely one of a continuous run of mind-boggling scenes in the last reels of *Howl's Moving Castle*. Another truly amazing sequence is the moving-the-Castle scene, where Howl draws magical figures on the floor of the Castle and the ground outside, and shifts the Castle to Sophie's home town, right into the street (next to the railroad) where the hat store is. (Along the way, Howl gentrifies and feminizes the Castle, adding all sorts of homely items that will make it more comfortable – bathrooms, couches, chairs, tables, tiles, curtains, etc).

And the scenes keep coming: the blob-men attacking the Castle; the Castle falling apart and being re-made; the town being bombed; the Castle hurtling along the top of the mountains, and so on.

THE ENDING.

Notice how pro-active Sophie becomes in the later part of the 2004 movie. When she first meets Howl and enters his Castle, Sophie defers to him in most matters. She does complain, heartily, though, from time to time. But Howl is the boss.

---

[131] And in *manga*, flashbacks're indicated with black backgrounds under the panels.

But when Sophie realizes that Howl isn't going to give up fighting in the war, and might be killed, she decides to do something.[132] The film is really about Sophie first and foremost – she is the main character introduced in the first scene, and she remains the spine of the narrative.

So in the last third of *Howl's Moving Castle*, Sophie becomes the chief protagonist – it's Sophie who removes Calcifer, so Suliman and the blob-men can't find them, then orders the fire-demon to take them to Howl. When he leaves to fight, Howl tells Sophie that he now has someone he wants to fight for – very romantic. But actually it's *Sophie* who saves Howl, not Howl saving Sophie: it's Sophie who saves Howl *from himself*.

Because Howl is his own worst enemy. He runs away from confrontations (the Witch of the Waste teases him about it), but it's Sophie who persuades Howl to look at himself and realize where he is going wrong. Sophie, in short is the emotional and social glue that brings this family of peculiar folk together and unites them. Without Sophie, the narrative soon falls apart.

Only one aspect of *Howl's Moving Castle*'s ending strikes a slightly false note to me, and that's the scene where the scarecrow is transformed into a storybook handsome prince. Yes, the scarecrow was under a spell too. It seems a little rushed, and it's played just a little too straight.

But *Howl's Moving Castle* is a fairy tale in every way, so it has to have the scene where the lovers are re-united, where the love of a woman brings a man back to life (and returns him to himself), where everything ends happily ever after. All of the sub-plots are resolved – Madame Suliman calls off the war,[133] the Castle now flies instead of tramps along, and there are happy, summery, sunny images and smiling faces all round.

Did *Howl's Moving Castle* make complete sense? Not really, Hayao Miyazaki admitted. But it was the movie he wanted to make. Miyazaki said in 2005:

> Even if this film is intended for the young public, and must be entertaining, I couldn't be satisfied with reproducing films that had already been made, where you only had to fight off the bad guys. When I am doing a film I always wonder whether what I'm doing is interesting. I

---

[132] Though he detests the war, part of Howl's curse is to participate in it, to appear in a gross bird-form and undertake violent action.

[133] So the conflict is brought to a halt – just like that! Suliman sees what her spy Heen the dog shows her in a crystal ball out of *The Wizard of Oz* – the heroes triumphant.

cut off all that is dull. By way of that, it becomes a film that even my team cannot understand. It's embarrassing.

For Toshio Suzuki, an ingredient of *Howl's Moving Castle* was sending a message to Japan about its on-going recession:

> it is about a young lady of 18 who turns into an old lady of 90. The reason we did this was that Japan is in a long recession. So we have 2 things: older people who fear for their jobs, and younger people who cannot imagine a worthwhile future. These young ones feel and act old. This film is a message to Japan – although I don't know about the rest of the world.

13
PONYO ON THE CLIFF BY THE SEA

INTRODUCTION.
My reaction to seeing *Ponyo On the Cliff By the Sea* for the first time:

> Unbelievable.
> Incredible.
> A work of genius.

And that's still my response. There are images and scenes and ideas in this movie that you have never seen before, realized with such skill and grace and innovation, you simply cannot believe that such filmmaking is possible.

Hayao Miyazaki is a magician, a masterful conjuror, orchestrating this unsurpassed journey into imagination and childhood.

Ponyo On the Cliff By the Sea is a movie you watch in awe. And there are very few films like that (and even fewer films made recently).

The miracle is not that nobody else can make films like Hayao Miyazaki can, it's that Hayao Miyazaki made this movie at all. (Aided by, let's not forget, an outstanding team of talented filmmakers).

Ponyo On the Cliff By the Sea is beyond sublime. Can Hayao Miyazaki do no wrong? Not only has Miyazaki – and Studio Ghibli – never produced a dud, they have never produced anything less than very high quality, hugely entertaining movies. And apart from *The Castle of Cagliostro* – which was Hayao Miyazaki's first important directing job, and a sequel, and a genre outing, and part of an established franchise – every single one of Miyazaki's works can be considered a masterpiece of animation.

And that, folks, is an astounding record. Not even the Walt Disney Studios, *at their height* – the 'golden age', from 1937 to 1942 – can equal that record.

Who is it who said that in a typical movie you're lucky to find one original idea? (John Lasseter, I think). Well, in a Hayao Miyazaki movie, you can find many more than that. And sometimes they are coming at you thick and fast. This man is a genius, without question.

Where to begin with discussing *Ponyo On the Cliff By the Sea*? Oh boy, just go see the movie again! What better advice can you give to someone who likes Hayao Miyazaki's movies and Studio Ghibli's movies?! Go see the movies again!

Ponyo On the Cliff By the Sea (*Gake no ue no Ponyo*, 2008) was written and directed by Hayao Miyazaki. Joe Hisaishi once again wrote the music, Atsushi Okui was DP, Noboru Yoshida was art director, animation supervisor was Katsuya Kondô, key animators were Hiromasa Yonebayashi and Atsuko Tanaka, and Takeshi Seyama and Miyazaki were editors. Eriko Kimura was sound director. Koji Hoshino, Seiji Okuda, Miyazaki, Naoya Fujimaki and Ryoichi Fukuyama were executive producers. Toshio Suzuki was producer. Buena Vista Home Entertainment, D-Rights, Dentsu Inc., Hakuhodo DY Media Partners, Nippon Television Network, Ghibli and Toho were the production partners.

Ponyo On the Cliff By the Sea began pre-production in April, 2006. The budget was ¥3.4 billion ($34m) – making it one of the most expensive animated movies (or any movie) produced in Asia.[134] The budget allowed for the production of 170,000 animation cels (the highest number employed on a Hayao Miyazaki movie up to that point). And every penny of the budget was up there on the screen.[135] *Ponyo On the Cliff By the Sea* was released in Japan on July 19, 2008 (on a record number of screens for a domestic release – 481).

The two lead voices for *Ponyo On the Cliff By the Sea* were: Yuria Nara (b. Dec 21, 1999) as Ponyo and Hiroki Doi (b. Oct 8, 1999) as Sosuke (both actors were 9). The voice cast included: Tomoko Yamaguchi (Lisa), Kazushige Nagashima (Koichi), George Tokoro (Fujimoto) and Yuki Amami (Ponyo's mother, a.k.a. grandmother). The English dub included: Noah Lindsey Cyrus, Matt Damon, Tina Fey, Frankie Jonas, Cloris Leachman, Liam Neeson and Lily Tomlin.

---

[134] Had it been produced in the U.S.A. or Europe, *Ponyo On the Cliff By the Sea* would probably cost at least $120m.
[135] Worldwide gross has been reported at $195 million. In Japan it opened on 481 screens, and 927 theatres in the U.S.A.

CHARACTERS .

The two lead characters in *Ponyo On the Cliff By the Sea* are Sosuke and Ponyo. Sosuke is a five year-old Japanese boy with short, black hair.[136] Sosuke is sensitive, emotional, caring, smart, brave, heroic, proud, stubborn and obedient. And he's a regular kid: he's the way-in to the movie for the audience, their point-of-entry. He is every kid, every boy, everyone who's ever been young, who can remember being young (or maybe who wants to remain young).

Sosuke is a very endearing character – one of his most adorable aspects is when he is his father's boy – putting on a sailor's cap, wearing binoculars, and communicating with his father at sea via morse code and Aldis lamps. (And, later, standing at the door and waving to his mom when she leaves for the senior center, or saluting to the officer on the boat during the flood). So sweet!

Ponyo is a mermaid, a young, fish-like creature with the familiar wide, squarish Hayao Miyazakian face, recalling Mei in *My Neighbor Totoro* and Chihiro in *Spirited Away*. She has a bright, red body (also reminiscent of a dress), when she's a mermaid. But it's Ponyo's personality that comes through so strongly in *Ponyo On the Cliff By the Sea*: she is feisty, rebellious, independent, eccentric, playful, energetic, athletic, shy, tender, curious, determined, stubborn, enthusiastic, and highly individual (a 'cute troublemaker' Miyazaki calls her [TP, 420]).

The roles of the two lead characters interchange throughout the narrative – one leading, one following; one heroic, the other scared; one active, one passive; one bold, one shy; one wild, one cautious. That's classic storytelling, of course, when you've got a couple at the heart of a narrative. (The gender reversals also enhance the switches).

Aside from the two leads, there are two sets of parents. Of the parents, it's the relationships between Ponyo and her father and Sosuke and his mother that are shown prominently on screen. The other two parents crop up later in the picture (and both are at sea – the human father Koichi and the Goddess mother). (A father complex and a mother complex, then, plus an absent mother and an absent father. Most of Miyazaki's *shojo* charas have a father complex; but then, that almost goes with the *shojo* territory in *manga* and *animé*. Or in all art: if there's a young woman in the lead role, you can bet

---

[136] The design of Sosuke was apparently based on Hayao Miyazaki's son Goro. But make no mistake, this young boy is very much a young Miyazaki in many respects. And so is Ponyo!

there's a father complex too!).

Ponyo On the Cliff By the Sea is very much about the relationships between children and parents as well as children themselves: the dramatic symmetry pairs a young boy and his mother and a young girl and her father. And there are two families portrayed in the movie, though it's significant that both families are not depicted united, in the usual manner: Sosuke and Lisa spend much of the movie together, with Sosuke's father only appearing with them at the end. Sosuke's father's presence is enhanced by his absence: he is not where Lisa wants him to be, coming home for supper.

The magical family, meanwhile, is not your average family, though the emotional and social dynamics follow familiar patterns. Ponyo's mom is a Goddess of the Sea, no less, appearing first as a vast spectre swimming amidst tidal waves, giant moons and haunted shipwrecks. Following her extraordinary introduction in the piece, she takes on more human-scale characteristics, and comes across as much friendlier than Ponyo's father. But she remains grand, regal, imposing, and terrifying.[137]

Ponyo's father, Fujimoto, is a sorcerer,[138] and not your typical dad, but his personality is familiar: he's a rather vain, self-absorbed guy, negligent of his child, but also over-protective, over-compensating for his lack of attention. Underneath the scary sorcerer exterior, Fujimoto is also presented as a little ridiculous, and the movie mocks his pretensions and schemes. If his ideas and goals are endorsed by the movie – for instance, the ecological aspects (the toxic wastes of humanity) – the way he goes about putting them into practice is critiqued. His heart might be in the right place, but he needs some lessons in basic life skills.

The audience first sees Fujimoto in his magical guise, as a sorcerer populating the oceans with prehistoric creatures (it's not made clear at this point that Fujimoto is Ponyo's father). He's a wizard with the appearance of a travelling entertainer or clown, or an 18th century, European dandy (the narcissism of the magicians in Miyazaki's cinema is an important element in their personality). The audience doesn't know exactly what Fujimoto is doing, but it's certainly something magical. The viewer also sees Fujimoto acting a little shifty when he reaches into his back pocket for a magical

---

[137] Gran Mamare is what Ponyo will grow up to be, Miyazaki said: 'she is on the side of all life, is fertile, polyandrous, and has countless children' (TP, 423).
[138] An obvious literary ancestor for Fujimoto is Captain Nemo in one of Hayao Miyazaki's favourite books, *20,000 Leagues Under the Sea*. Fujimoto's submarine too has the look of Nemo's *Nautilus*.

device which flashes.

But this presentation of Fujimoto is turned about completely when the movie takes up Lisa's point-of-view, when she's at her car and the sea-sorcerer approaches her across the grass keeping himself and the ground wet with a strange device. Now he comes across as a weirdo that Lisa deftly outruns.

The dreamy prologue establishes Fujimoto and Ponyo, and Ponyo's sisters, and also the relationships between them: Fujimoto checking up on the noise he hears from the side of the submarine, and Ponyo hiding from her father. The key narrative component – Ponyo fleeing her father's domain – is part of an elaborate sequence of animation in which the screen is teaming with 100s of creatures. The sorcerous elements are signalled from the outset, with visual effects, underwater effects, and many layers to this expensive episode.

And there's no need for dialogue, when the score is one of the grandest in all of Hayao Miyazaki's cinema, with trilling choirs enhancing the other-worldly atmosphere. And as if massed choirs aren't enough, there are remarkably intense rainbow and heightened colours – it's a vision of paradise, or heaven, or another realm in which glowing light radiates everything.

LOVE.

Colin Odell and Michelle Le Blanc, in their excellent introduction to Studio Ghibli's movies, miss the point somewhat with *Ponyo On the Cliff By the Sea* in their account of the movie: it is the *emotional relationship* between Sosuke and Ponyo that is at the *core* of *Ponyo On the Cliff By the Sea*. In short, this film is about *love*.

Yes – ♥ – again.

Again love in a Hayao Miyazaki movie. *Princess Mononoke* was a love story. *Howl's Moving Castle* was a love story. *Laputa: Castle In the Sky* was a love story. *Porco Rosso* was a love story. And *Ponyo On the Cliff By the Sea* is a ♥ story. So what if it's between two five year-old kids?

The feelings that power *Ponyo On the Cliff By the Sea* along and fuse it together are depicted early on in the piece. Look at Sosuke's reaction, when he thinks that Ponyo's dead. He weeps. This is a highly sensitive boy, or rather, an emotional boy. In fact, he's consciously 'feminized', and plays often more like one of Hayao Miyazaki's young girl characters, or the traditional *shojo* personality (and, conversely, Ponyo is often the tomboy, a rough-and-tumble young girl who often acts more like a young boy. These are common gender reversals in *animé* and *manga*).

But they both love each other: one of the very first things that Ponyo says is: 'Ponyo loves Sosuke'. And he is right back at her: 'I love you too, Ponyo'.

To repeat: *Ponyo On the Cliff By the Sea* is a love story.

And the movie also has the classic prohibitions of the classic love story (for this re-interpretation of human-beast fables, including mermaid fairy tales): the lovers cannot be together, they are prevented not only by magic and being different creatures, they also have powerful sorcerers to deal with.[139]

And right after Ponyo and Sosuke have confessed their love for each other, they are separated: it's classic storytelling: *intense desire plus separation*. Sosuke carries Ponyo in the plastic bucket down to the sea, to hide amongst the rocks. Fujimoto spies them and sends his watery henchmen to fetch the mermaid back. Sosuke and his mom may have defeated the sorcerer twice, but not this time.

That the children have confessed their love at this particular moment makes this separation even more calamitous – it pays off in every way, resonating throughout the 2008 movie, and enhances the emotion at the heart of the piece. It's as if the confession of love makes the bond between Ponyo and Sosuke magically unbreakable, as in a fairy tale. Once they have said that to each other, we know they have to be re-united, come what may.

TITLES.

Ponyo On the Cliff By the Sea is in the Hayao Miyazaki tradition in having elaborate titles. Here, a children's storybook approach's taken, with sea creatures swimming under waves drawn with child-like, heavy, black, wavy lines. This time, the credit sequence comes after a prologue, in which Fujimoto is seen at work magicking the ocean, and Ponyo escapes from her father's domain. Combined with the prologue, the credits mean that no word is spoken until some 6m 30s into *Ponyo On the Cliff By the Sea* (the first word is 'Sosuke'). And when that credit comes up – 'written and directed by Hayao Miyazaki' – you know you're in for

---

[139] Sosuke is special and 'truly brilliant', Miyazaki insisted, because he accepts Ponyo unconditionally, promising to love her and protect her. 'He is a five year-old prodigy who sticks to his beliefs without wavering' (TP, 424). The total acceptance of Ponyo is the foundation of the entire movie.

something special.

MUSIC.

Joe Hisaishi and his music team[140] have out-done themselves scoring *Ponyo On the Cliff By the Sea*. There are the usual sweeping strings and very romantic piano cues in *Ponyo On the Cliff By the Sea*, as in many of Hisaishi's scores for Hayao Miyazaki's movies, but also choirs, employed with extraordinary effect in the prologue and in the Goddess scenes, and when Hisaishi quotes from Richard Wagner's *Nibelungen* (the music budget for *Ponyo* is sizable). And twinkle-twinkle-little-star xylophones for when Ponyo's asleep on the couch. And a lonesome trumpet for when Sosuke's mom leaves in the car to go to the senior center. A beautiful piece of operatic vocals accompanies the opening credits (how many children's movies open with opera?).

The Wagnerian allusions in *Ponyo On the Cliff By the Sea* are intriguing: Joe Hisaishi quotes from Richard Wagner's *Der Ring des Nibelungen* (1876), and Ponyo's name, at least as far as her father Fujimoto is concerned, is Brunhilde, the name of the Valkyrie in Wagner's Teutonic *Ring* cycle. In Hollywood movies, notably, Wagner's music has often been employed for ironic effect[141] (ever since Ken Russell demolished Wagner in his 1970s movies *Lisztomania* and *Mahler*, forever linking Wagner and Wagnerian culture to Nazism).

Here in *Ponyo On the Cliff By the Sea*, Joe Hisaishi takes up Richard Wagner's *Ride of the Valkyries* largely for comic effect, but there's no mistaking the grandiose elements of that particular piece, which do fit the unbelievable images of Ponyo running atop the dark blue fish-waves. At this point, she is very much Brunhilde the Valkyrie, eager to be re-united with her Siegfried.

Mention should also be made of the sound crew on *Ponyo On the Cliff By the Sea*,[142] who delivered outstanding sounds for the underwater world of the movie – bubbles, whooshes, glides, splashes. And a delightful, comic children's whistle effect for when Ponyo squirts water out of her mouth.

---

140 Musicians included: Naoya Fujimaki, Takaaki Fujioka and Masako Hayashi.
141 *Apocalypse Now* and *The Blues Brothers* are two famous examples. *The Ride of the Valkyries* had also been used previously by D.W. Griffith in *The Birth of a Nation*, when the Klu Klux Klan attack black people, and in Federico Fellini's *8 1/2*. For Ken Russell, Wagner's music had been subverted by the Nazis, who had revealed its right-wing and anti-semitic politics.
142 Eriko Kimura was sound director, and the sound crew included Takeshi Imaizumi, Yumiko Shibusawa and Koji Kasamatsu.

SCALE.

Scale is one of the hallmarks of Hayao Miyazaki's cinema – from the very large (the airships, the flying land of Laputa, the kingdom of Cagliostro, Ponyo's mother), to the very small (Yubaba's bird transformed into an insect, the baby Totoro, Ponyo's sisters). And *Ponyo On the Cliff By the Sea* is no exception, providing numerous possibilities for portraying extreme differences in scale. Ponyo herself is tiny, in her guise as the daughter of Fujimoto: when the 2008 film first introduces Ponyo, the viewer doesn't really know what size she is (and her sisters are miniature versions of herself). Only when she encounters Sosuke, and the viewer sees Sosuke holding the jar in which Ponyo's trapped, is her true size revealed.

But of course throughout the 2008 movie, scales are changing. Ponyo shifts from that tiny mermaid form to being a regular-sized girl of five. And when her mom appears, she is a vast Goddess of the ocean. Similarly, the fish and creatures in the sea range in size from tiny critters to enormous whales and Devonian Age creatures.

TRANSFORMATION.

One of the primary motifs in all of Hayao Miyazaki's cinema is transformation. His characters have at least two aspects, and sometimes more. It's one of the ingredients that I'm sure some Western viewers find confusing. In *Ponyo On the Cliff By the Sea*, the lead character is sometimes depicted as a tiny fish with a baby human face, sometimes as a quasi-girl with chicken arms and legs, and sometimes as a regular (though highly stylized) human girl. (And there are numerous further moments of stylization).

Similarly, Ponyo's mom is both the Goddess of the Ocean and the Moon in her aspect as an enormous deity of tidal waves and rising oceans. But she can also trim down to human scale (though still a stately giantess), when she wants to communicate with humans on their level.

MERMAIDS.

In mythology and legend, the mermaid figure goes back a long way, to the siren in Homer's *Odyssey*, to ancient Greek mythology (including Triton and the neirids), and to bestiaries and Christian theologies who turned mermaids into figures of lust and sin.

In the history of art, mermaids were an opportunity for (usually male) artists to paint female nudes (the long hair of course covers up those bits deemed unsuitable for certain eyes). At this level, mermaids are a supremely masculine fantasy – an erotic, naked woman. But they embody male fears about women and female sexuality, of course, and like the sirens, sphinxes or harpies of Greek mythology, they are also fatal creatures, linked to death.

The mermaid in *Ponyo On the Cliff By the Sea* is a creature of two worlds, two lives: the sea and the land, a fish and a girl, and two different families. That's the fundamental aspect of the mermaid in Studio Ghibli's movie: someone who is half in one world, and half in another. Two possibilities, two fates. And the link between the two is desire, the wish to move from one world to another.

But in this Japanese animated version of the mermaid myth, erotic desire is downplayed. However, there is no doubt that *Ponyo On the Cliff By the Sea* is intended to be a love story, albeit between five year-old children. Indeed, Ponyo is very much a force of nature, she is pure libido, id run wild, a power that her father Fujimoto recognizes that he can't contain. (Ponyo's strong, like her mother, Fujimoto mutters. What he really means is that he can't control her!).

ALLUSIONS.

For the fan of Hayao Miyazaki's cinema, there are numerous allusions to Miyazaki's earlier movies in *Ponyo*. One of the elderly women in the senior center, for instance, has the same appearance as the Witch of the Waste in *Howl's Moving Castle*.[143]

When Ponyo lies on her back on the jellyfish, and covers herself with a clear bubble, that's a reference to the beginning of *Nausicaä of the Valley of the Wind,* when Nausicaä lies atop the *ohmu*. The father of the family with the baby on the boat recalls Mr Kusakabe in *My Neighbor Totoro*.

OCEAN.

Is this Hayao Miyazaki's 'Ocean Film'? Maybe – but he has been here before – the ocean's employed extensively in Miyazaki's cinema. It's part of his deployment of elemental powers – earth, air, wind, rain, water, clouds, fire, etc. But *Ponyo On the Cliff By the Sea* is of course a major, major ocean picture – however, it is thoroughly stylized (as it nearly always is in animation – and I mean over and above the inherent stylization of cel animation – or filmmaking – itself).

---

[143] The suggestion is that if *Howl's Moving Castle* had been set in contemporary Japan, the senior center is the kind of place that the Witch would've wound up.

In short, Hayao Miyazaki and his team have taken their own path in portraying the sea and marine life, very different from how the sea's explored in movies such as *Pinocchio* or *The Little Mermaid* or *Pocahontas* or *Finding Nemo*. However, *Ponyo On the Cliff By the Sea* does follow a common method in depicting the ocean *first* as a beautiful and tranquil place full of mysteries and wonders (only *later*, as in many another movie made on or about the ocean, do the storms and high waves come).

So, the first minutes of *Ponyo On the Cliff By the Sea*, as with *Finding Nemo* or *The Little Mermaid*, offer gorgeous images of shoals of fish, and jellyfish, and big fish. And very soon the movie moves into extreme stylization, with the birth of the new prehistoric creatures taking place against a smooth, yellow-white background.

WOMEN.

Ponyo On the Cliff By the Sea centres around a young boy character, but this is a film about women: three women in particular: Ponyo, her mother, the Goddess of the Sea, and Lisa, Sosuke's mom, and, importantly, the old women in the senior center.

The secondary characters of the old women are differentiated along classic lines: the warm, kindly one, Yoshie, the more reserved companion, Noriko, and the disbelieving, crabby and neurotic one, Toki (the old folk at the senior center are mainly women, and the carers are mainly women too, including in the kitchen, but there is a male driver).

It's crucial to the narrative that Sosuke is shown with these women, that he knows them, and that they know him. It's the age-old trinity again, the three wise crones. And it's classic storytelling, too, that the one who doesn't quite believe Fujimoto (apart from Toki), is Yoshie, and it's she who stands up to Fujimoto, and helps to rescue Sosuke and Ponyo when they return to the senior center towards the end of the picture.

Lisa is a terrific character, I think. One of the many strong, independent women in Hayao Miyazaki's cinema, there's a toughness, an unpredictability, and a vitality to Lisa (and she is young, too: 25). The way she drives her tiny car really fast, for example, gleefully swooping across the road (Lisa's an amazingly aggressive driver – to the point where she slams the vehicle across the dry dock, right in front of a tidal wave). The unbelievable chase sequence in *Ponyo On the Cliff By the Sea*, for instance, when Ponyo rides the fish-waves pursuing Sosuke, occurs largely because Lisa is gunning the motor to get back home (and very fast, too). Here foreshadowing works neatly – because Lisa's been portrayed as a wild driver from the beginning, and there's a car scene where she licks Sosuke's ice cream cone and swerves across the road, enjoying the danger of movement. This sets up Lisa as a driver capable of performing the crazy car chase later.

And, best of all, the marvellous scene where Lisa's preparing dinner, expecting her sea-faring husband to return, and when he signals via the Aldis lamp that he can't, she sends back some great angry rejoinders, which come up on the screen as staccato phrases: JERK, JERK, JERK... BUG OFF BUG OFF BUG OFF! It's brilliant.

Lisa's rage, which suddenly explodes when she's at the sink, is just fantastic, grounding *Ponyo On the Cliff By the Sea* in so-familiar everyday life. We've all seen people like that. But Lisa's anger is directed at the family not being together, as C. Odell and M. Le Blanc point out (137), not because the family or her marriage's falling apart.

You don't often, for instance, see an animated character in this kind of family adventure movie lying on the floor holding a cushion on her tummy, with her feet on the bed. And the lovely touch of the son trying to cheer up his mom on the bed. And when Lisa lifts her head, revealing just an eye, then grabs Sosuke and holds him in a bone-crushing, motherly embrace, rolling about on the bed,[144] it's so sweet and tender – as are her sudden mood-swings from anger into dejection and now into elation and movement. (The shot where Lisa goes around the house and switches on all the lights – seen from the outside – is a perfect expression of her new-found vitality).

MEN.

What about the men? Oh dear – not so good. Sosuke's father Koichi is absent, away at sea, a classic motif in folk and fairy tales, of course. But later on in the 2008 movie, he appears, and is genuinely miffed when he has to work and can't get home as promised. His messages via the signal lamp are heartfelt, it seems.

But he's still absent, though it's Sosuke more than his mother who voices concern that his dad's ship might've been lost at sea during the tsunami. Lisa's pretty sure that all of the ships have ventured far out to sea, where it's calmer. Only later is it shown that all of the ships are actually trapped beneath the tidal wave in a ships' graveyard (though Lisa and

---

[144] What helps to swing her round is Sosuke wondering if Ponyo is crying – he reminds her of caring for someone else.

Sosuke don't know this).

As to Ponyo's father, Fujimoto: the first character introduced in the 2008 movie (feeding magical elixir to the sea creatures, apparently turning them into prehistoric creatures), he is an ambiguous figure. Sometimes the bad father, the negligent father, sometimes the over-protective father, sometimes the jealous father, sometimes the megalomaniac father,[145] Fujimoto is another of Hayao Miyazaki's questers or searchers: he is the classic alchemist-scientist-magician, someone investigating the natural world, but who also wants to change it. At one time a human (so he knows how despicable they can be), Fujimoto is the Faustian magician who wants to transform the Earth and cleanse it of humanity's pollution. (The story of just how Fujimoto transcended his humanity, or possibly mated with the Goddess of the Sea,[146] isn't explained in the movie).

Visually, Fujimoto sports typical elements of the wizards of *animé*: the wild shock of hair, the sunken eyes, the eccentric costume (with plenty of narcissism and dandyism). Fujimoto is Howl in *Howl's Moving Castle* aged up twenty or thirty years. He has the same combination of hunger for power and vulnerability, magical talent and insecurity. While Fujimoto and Howl may be strong wizards, they are also wracked by weaknesses and faults.

ECOLOGY.

There is definitely an ecological element to *Ponyo On the Cliff By the Sea*, as there has been in most of Hayao Miyazaki's cinema: when Fujimoto complains about the filth in the oceans as he chases Lisa and Sosuke in their car, he is voicing concerns about the environment that have been a key element of Miyazaki's – and Studio Ghibli's – movies. That also places some audience sympathy with Fujimoto, because the filmmakers are definitely behind the view that humans pollute the world.

NAMES.

Names are again important in *Ponyo On the Cliff By the Sea*, as in *Spirited Away*. Sosuke gives Ponyo her name, and she accepts it, to the point when her father calls her Brunhilde, she objects: her name is 'Ponyo', she insists. It's her new identity (the first time she speaks is in response to

---

[145] Is Fujimoto as a 'bad father' Miyazaki's response to the public criticism that his son Goro made of him during the production and release of *Tales of Earthsea*?
[146] In his 2006 notes on the movie, Miyazaki states that Fujimoto is only one of the Goddess's husbands (TP, 420).

Sosuke). As Brunhilde she's Fujimoto's feisty daughter, but as Ponyo she's the best friend of a human boy. It's a remnant of the element in Hans Andersen's story, when the mermaid has to give up her voice and her tail to remain on land, but naming's also a recurring theme in Miyazaki's cinema (employed to bitterest effect in *Spirited Away*: when Chihiro surrenders her name to Yubaba she also gives up her identity and her individuality).

VISUAL EFFECTS.

Ponyo On the Cliff By the Sea is among Studio Ghibli's most complex movies in terms of visual effects. Every single effect is here, *and then some*. This being an animated movie set largely in water or by water, it demands the whole arsenal of visual effects that are available in animation. After nine features, you might think that Hayao Miyazaki and his teams of artists would've been running out of ideas. But no, *Ponyo On the Cliff By the Sea* has a range of new ideas and set-pieces that dazzle the viewer. The level of *imagination* on display here is breathtaking.

One could note all of the visual effects in *Ponyo On the Cliff By the Sea* and end up describing every scene and shot in the movie: perhaps the range of effects to note first and foremost are the elemental ones, to do with water, waves, rain, wind, clouds and movement. Once again, when it comes to depicting rain and storms, Hayao Miyazaki is in the Akira Kurosawa class. The rain effects alone are mind-bogglingly complex, like a thousand *Bambi* movies (with its famous rain scene) squeezed into one film.

COLOURS.

As I often state, as a colourist, Hayao Miyazaki has no equal in contemporary cinema. Aided by the amazing Michiyo Yasuda and her colour team, Miyazaki and his production team have contributed another movie so rich in colours you can bathe in them. The palette ranges from the naturalistic to the storybook look to out-and-out fantasy. The bright primaries and complementary hues of the scenes set on land in and around the town[147] and Sosuke's home are particularly striking – as if you're seeing a picture book from the 1960s and 1970s come to life. These clean, washed colours are a fantasy of remembered childhoods: this is how childhood

---

[147] *Ponyo On the Cliff By the Sea* is set in contemporary Japan. The town that influenced the location in *Ponyo On the Cliff By the Sea* was Tomonoura, a tourist spot that Hayao Miyazaki had visited in 2004.

should be, for everyone.

The underwater scenes encourage far greater freedom for coloration – and though the filmmakers might begin with the expected blues and greens, they soon depart from them. *Ponyo On the Cliff By the Sea* delivers what you *expect* from an underwater movie (it would be crazy not to present a host of familiar elements), but also plenty that you didn't expect. In short, Hayao Miyazaki's movies take you to places – and colours, and movements, and gestures, and set-pieces – that you have never seen before. Never.

And I find that especially remarkable – because this is an era in which millions of people have already seen thousands of movies and TV shows and photographs and paintings and sculptures and plays, etc. To come up with something that no one has seen before is really extraordinary.

ANIMATION.

With its 170,000 cels, *Ponyo On the Cliff By the Sea* is a gargantuan task of hard labour, thousands of woman and man hours – so much work to produce something that flows by in a hundred short minutes (for me, *Ponyo On the Cliff By the Sea* could be a thousand times as long). No padding here, no alternative endings,[148] no botched ideas.

It's one of the common platitudes of animation criticism to say that every frame of a movie could be taken out, blown up, and put in a picture frame. With *Ponyo On the Cliff By the Sea* that's true, of course, to the point where the production team have excelled themselves – and that's very difficult on a Hayao Miyazaki movie. How can you possibly top *Princess Mononoke*? Or *Spirited Away*? Well, at times, the crew on *Ponyo On the Cliff By the Sea* have done so.

As animation, *Ponyo On the Cliff By the Sea* is of the very highest quality in every respect. Not a background, not a movement, not a characterization, not a sequence of shots, not a camera move is wasted or incorrect. This is as near to perfection as one can get in animation. *Ponyo On the Cliff By the Sea* is in the same class as *Snow White and the Seven Dwarfs* or *Bambi* or Jan Svankmajer's *Alice* in this respect – a total miracle of animation.

Again, to note every delight of animation work in *Ponyo On the Cliff By the Sea* would be to cover the movie scene by scene again. This is a film to watch again and again – the first times to enjoy the story and characters and the whole experience, but later viewings to marvel at the depth and variety of

---

[148] There can be only one ending.

detail, of movement, of colour.

Ponyo On the Cliff By the Sea is also a movie which revels in the *joy* of filmmaking. Joy?! Over those long, hard months of work?! But, yes: *joy*. Like *Hero* (2002) or *Once Upon a Time In China* (1990) or *Citizen Kane* (1941) or *Duck Soup* (1933), *Ponyo On the Cliff By the Sea* simply bounces off the screen with energy and imagination. If you know anything about the manufacture of an animated movie, you know that the amount of hard labour it requires to produce this effect is immense. It's an ultimate contradiction, and at times many filmmaking teams must think, 'hell, is this amount of work *really* worth it?' After all, some filmmakers, such as Jean-Luc Godard or a Hong Kong action team, can shoot a movie in two weeks, and edit and dub it in two weeks, and create a masterpiece (1962's *Vivre Sa Vie* for instance).

I don't know whether the production team at Studio Ghibli think it's 'worth it', but they must find some gratification in the millions of fans that Ghibli's movies have (they know, working for Ghibli, that they are pretty much guaranteed to have their work seen by millions). I don't know for sure, but I bet that Ghibli receives thousands of letters and emails and postcards and gifts each year from fans who wish to express their thanks and pleasure at Ghibli's movies.

A WORK OF GENIUS.

A brief look at some of the consumer reviews on websites such as Amazon reveal comments such as 'simple' about *Ponyo On the Cliff By the Sea*. Yes, it does appear to be 'simple' in some respects – but it is the simplicity of great art, the simplicity that can only be gained from years of work, the kind of simplicity attainable only if you really know what you're doing.

Because if you look at any part of *Ponyo On the Cliff By the Sea*, you can see it's not 'simple' at all. In fact, it's clearly fiendishly complicated – and not only on an artistic or technical level. But for people following the story, it can appear 'simple'. But even at the narrative level, *Ponyo On the Cliff By the Sea* is not 'simple' at all. Oh, no. This is very sophisticated, very highly refined filmmaking and storytelling.

But it seems simple. And that is great art.

It's like the sculptures of Constantin Brancusi (1876-1957), to use a classic example in the modern era: Brancusi's sleek, shiny forms of seals, birds, babies, fish and figures seem at first to be 'simple' forms. They seem to have always existed. But no, they haven't. And an artist can only attain such radically simplified forms after moving through years of development and compression and drastic reductionism.

Same with Hayao Miyazaki's movies: they have the obviousness, the simplicity, of great art. It's as if his images have always existed. But they haven't. It's as if there have always been Totoros and flying witches and flying pigs and tiny girls running on top of massive, blue fish in the ocean. But there haven't.

And how Hayao Miyazaki can reach this point of such facility and ease is miraculous and mysterious. You can't explain it, and you can't train people to attain it. The achievement in a movie such as *Ponyo On the Cliff By the Sea* is simply staggering. Not only the slog of the sheer amount of hard labour, or the amount of organization it requires to pull off something like this, it's the level of artistry, of beauty, of skill, of imagination.

And, once again, let's not imagine that Hayao Miyazaki has achieved all this on his own! Maybe he would if he could – maybe Miyazaki would draw every single cel and ink and paint every cel and photograph every cel and edit every cel together and compose the music and everything else (I'm sure that Miyazaki could do many of the jobs on a movie – and very few animation directors – or live-action directors – can do that).

But one of the chief reasons that *Ponyo On the Cliff By the Sea* is a work of genius is the team behind this piece: that means, above all, Toshio Suzuki, producer. And it means DP Atsushi Okui, editor Takeshi Seyama, composer Joe Hisaishi and animation supervisors Katsuya Kondô, Hiromasa Yonebayashi and Atsuko Tanaka. And 100s of other people. They are the finest animation team in the world.

EXTRAORDINARY SCENES.

Ponyo On the Cliff By the Sea contains some extraordinary scenes:

- The prologue.
- Koichi, Sosuke's father, signalling with Sosuke and Lisa.
- Ponyo running on top of the giant, blue fish-waves.
- The car and fish chase sequence.
- Ponyo inside her father's elixir chamber in the Coral Tower, finally becoming human.
- Ponyo escaping from her home bubble, aided by her sisters.

- Ponyo and Sosuke having dinner.[149]
- The magical boat journey with Ponyo and Sosuke.
- The appearance of the Goddess of the Sea and the tsunami.

TSUNAMI.

The entire tsunami sequence has to rank among the most astounding pieces of animation in the history of cinema. And it's a *sustained* sequence of brilliance, with one gag rapidly following another, all of them having a narrative logic as well as Hayao Miyazaki's trademark idiosyncrasy and vision. Miyazaki can take a dusty, old cliché and clean it up and make it shine again – and then he can present it to the viewer and persuade them to see it afresh, as if it were new, as if the filmmakers had just discovered that idea.

It's unbelievable.

This might be the finest sequence in Miyazaki-sama's cinema (tho' there is strong competition in every film!). In the tsunami sequence, for instance, there are so many gags and jokes and bits of business and gems of animation, it'd take a long time to discuss them in full. To cite some examples: in the elixir well chamber sequence in the Coral Tower, the beautiful, golden light that infuses everything (foreshadowed in the opening scene, when Fujimoto adds the elixir to the sea creatures). And the way that Ponyo tugs at her newly-grown hair, leaning over to one side then the other. And the way that Ponyo sails out of the chamber standing on top of a fish! (Not sitting, as astride a horse).[150] And the incredible images of Ponyo's tiny sisters turning into immense fish and racing upwards to the surface of the sea.

And here's another remarkable thing about Hayao Miyazaki's cinema: he can top his set-pieces! Miyazaki and his teams can stage a stupendous set-piece, but they can also top it. Compare that to your average Western action-adventure movie, which'll have one great set-piece, and the rest won't come anywhere near it. Everything's thrown into that one set-piece, with nothing left of imagination (*not* budget) for the other set-pieces. But that's OK: one great set-piece is plenty.

But Hayao Miyazaki's movies do much more than that.

---

149 Hayao Miyazaki and his teams have produced this sort of scene many times before – going back to *Panda Go Panda* and earlier, but it works in *Ponyo On the Cliff By the Sea* as if it was the first time the filmmakers had shown a scene of people eating.

150 'I am happy/ I am the storm/ I am the swelling waves', Miyazaki wrote in a note for Joe Hisaishi to describe Ponyo's mood (TP, 425).

For instance, the elixir chamber sequence in *Ponyo On the Cliff By the Sea* is eye-popping and grandiose and super-charged with energy, but the movie tops that with the car chase. And it tops that again with the boat journey. And later with the appearance of the Goddess.

It's because the *quality* of the *ideas* is so high, let alone the *presentation* and the *animation* of those ideas and set-pieces. Western animation is brilliant at presentation and dramatization and rapid action and all the rest, but so often the *ideas* and the *emotions* are thin. So Western cinema makes up for the paucity of imagination and ideas and feelings by being loud and bold. A big movement, a loud bang, things exploding, that's the Western way (in the West's wars as well as its movies).

And often that's the way in Japanese *animé*. But not in Hayao Miyazaki's cinema. Miyazaki's action and set-pieces make sense, have a narrative logic, but don't follow the rules, don't take the predictable path. It's one of the joys of Miyazaki's cinema that it isn't predictable narratively. That helps to keep it fresh, to keep the audience guessing and wondering, so the movie's not running along the same worn-out, old routes every time.

STORY.

Ponyo On the Cliff By the Sea is another of Hayao Miyazaki's movies which doesn't take a expected path. It's quirky. It's intuitive. It bends the rules and hops outside 'em. Very lightly, very joyfully – like a young child running along a beach or a field. Miyazaki's stories will reach the happy ending, but they won't get there the way most movies do. And this narrative eccentricity is apparent, really, from *Nausicaä of the Valley of the Wind* onwards.

I say 'eccentricity', but Hayao Miyazaki's narratives have a poetic logic, but not always the logic of traditional dramaturgy. For instance, Miyazaki's movies do things story-wise which most other filmmakers wouldn't attempt (or even think of). For example, nearly all filmmakers would *not* have Sophie, the heroine of *Howl's Moving Castle,* change her appearance from scene to scene. They'd think the audience would be confused, or maybe think it a continuity error. But it makes *emotional* or *poetic* sense to have those transformations. (Sophie changing back into her young self when she's asleep – though still with grey hair – has a fairy tale, poetic logic to it. But Hayao Miyazaki and his team go much further, and have Sophie changing from scene to scene).

Similarly with Ponyo, the heroine of *Ponyo On the Cliff By the Sea*: nearly all filmmakers would have their mermaid character in two states: mermaid or girl. They wouldn't use an intermediate state, where Ponyo's girl-like, but with chicken arms and legs. But when the movie needs Ponyo to do certain things, it makes complete sense (for instance, when she fails to leap into Lisa's car, and tumbles into the sea, changing from being a girl to the intermediate mermaid character. Or when she magically fixes the electrical generator in Sosuke's home, she momentarily becomes the girl-like mermaid again).

And the scene where Sosuke and Ponyo encounter a family in a boat, and discuss the mother turning food into milk for the baby – well, that scene wouldn't survive many meetings of writers and producers on a big, American animated movie. U.S. cartoons might include fart gags, but not breast milk! Oh no!

Ponyo On the Cliff By the Sea is an intricate story in its details and its plot points and its foreshadowing. For example, there are numerous examples of foreshadowing, in both the dialogue and visually. In the senior center, for instance, the scenes between Sosuke and the three old women look forward to the latter part of the movie: one of the women says that the paper goldfish that Sosuke has made will bring them luck and save them – and Ponyo does. Toki, the irascible, superstitious one, speaks darkly of a tsunami, and a tidal wave duly arrives.

The script for *Ponyo On the Cliff By the Sea* is on the surface a 'simple' story of the little mermaid and her adventures on land with a boy. But it's actually a very intricate web of carefully placed imagery and events, ranging from rhymes in colour to tiny details in the dialogue.

LOVE STORY.

What a stupendous love story *Ponyo On the Cliff By the Sea* is! What a marvellous depiction of two people who love being together. Friends, lovers, brother and sister, it doesn't matter, this is a great love story.

Check out the emotional climax to the car-and-wave chase sequence, perhaps the most mind-bogglingly brilliant scene in all animation history: first, the pay-off of the green, plastic bucket,[151] which Ponyo (as the chicken-limbed girl) fishes out of the sea. She marches out of the foam, then scurries between Lisa's legs, to greet Sosuke.

Everything is genius here – from the music, the framing,

---
[151] Sosuke puts it on the gate post, as a sign for Ponyo.

the flow of action, the sound design and the timing to the tenderly-evoked emotion. The editing is masterful, too – how the film controls the point-of-view, alternating between Sosuke and Ponyo, mixing point-of-view shots with big close-ups.

The encounter between the two five year-old children is played out with giant close-ups, beginning with the force-of-nature hug that Ponyo gives Sosuke, her face pressed right up against his (like his mom hugs him). The way that Ponyo fastens herself to Sosuke, bodily, is just wonderful (now that she's got him, she's not going to let go!).

Then come the series of big close-ups, from one face to another, the classic way of shooting a romantic rencounter – Sosuke's slow recognition, Ponyo's frown when Sosuke doesn't recognize her immediately, the slow-dawning realization. Meanwhile, Joe Hisaishi and the orchestra are contributing one of those slow string cues that pulse in waves (a popular motif in movies of the 1990s and after).

And to top it all, the sudden burst of golden light and rainbow colours when Sosuke finally realizes it's Ponyo come back as a young girl. And come back to *him*, to see *him*. She has literally crossed oceans to be with him. Wow. And Ponyo's cry of triumph – to her fishy sisters – that she's made it, that she's found the boy who loves her, and the way they leap out of the ocean in the golden, rainbow light, it's astonishing.

This is simply spellbinding cinema – so glorious, so exact, so unusual yet so familiar, and so *needed*. We *need* movies like this, we need to know that movies like this can still be produced, today, that not all of great cinema was made years ago, in the 1960s (the European New Wave), or the 1940s-1950s (Hollywood's golden age), or the 1920s (the silent era's heyday).

Yes – *Ponyo On the Cliff By the Sea* is solid, platinum proof that the magic of movies is alive and well, that movies can still have a soul and a heart, that movies can still thrill and enchant, that movies still have the mystery and power to do things to us we thought were buried and forgotten.

The scene where Lisa leaves Sosuke and Ponyo to drive to the senior center in the storm is a slight lapse in the storytelling. We know that the two children have to be separated from her, so they can continue their adventures. Unfortunately, it's also a scene where a parent leaves two five year-old children in a house on their own, at night. Of course, Lisa is being very thoughtful and caring, venturing out to the senior center in difficult driving conditions, but that doesn't take away from the fact that she has momentarily left two very young kids alone.

GODDESS.

As well as depicting the mythology of the mermaid, *Ponyo On the Cliff By the Sea* also portrays a Goddess figure. Rarely in cinema has a Goddess ever been delineated so beautifully and poetically. Hayao Miyazaki and his animation team know their mythology, their Robert Graves, their Sigmund Freud, their Carl Jung. When Ponyo's mother appears, for instance, the movie includes images of a mighty, yellow moon hanging above the ocean. That tells you everything – the links between women, nature, the ocean, tides, the moon, time and *change*.

And when the Goddess passes by, *Ponyo On the Cliff By the Sea* includes some ravishing effects, such as the rainbow colours, the streams of golden fish, the immense scale, and the genius touch of having the Goddess float face-up in the water, but as a reflection, not a solid body (that comes later, when she emerges from the sea). And Joe Hisaishi contributes some suitably awed choral effects (and the sound editors deliver some delicate but imposing whooshes and glittering sounds). It's an astounding entrance of a new character in a movie.

The Goddess of the Ocean is another of Hayao Miyazaki's mutating figures – sometimes she's an enormous reflection, seen end-on; later she's a giant, 3-D figure, swimming in the sea below Fujimoto's boat; over a cut on movement, she becomes a human-scale figure (though still large and majestic).

FRIENDS.

Part of Sosuke's 'feminization' extends to his caring for Ponyo: from the beginning, he is looking after her, placing her in a bucket, replenishing her water, and becoming highly distressed when she seems to be dead.

The nurturing, mothering aspect of Sosuke flourishes again towards the end of the piece, when Ponyo's powers dissipate. Sosuke has to take the lead again when Ponyo's life force seems to be dwindling – first by paddling the boat himself, then by rushing Ponyo to the shore when the boat begins to shrink.

Most scary of all is the scene in the tunnel when Ponyo reverts to her half-girl, half-mermaid form, with the chicken limbs. The horror of the moment of transformation is underlined by the use of subjective point-of-view filmmaking: using close-ups of Sosuke's face or his hand holding Ponyo's, the filmmakers place great emphasis on the soundtrack, with the clatter of the plastic bucket on the ground taking on an ominous tone.

Sosuke's efforts to look after Ponyo become even more frantic at this point, as he rushes her towards the water, hoping to revive her (Ponyo rapidly reverts from the chicken-legged girl to her tiny fish-form). Then follows the exciting chase as Sosuke escapes from Fujimoto's water-wave henchmen, along a wooden fence, culminating in the slow motion dive into Toki (Sosuke goes back to another mother figure – and literally landing on the breast).

At this point, Fujimoto points to the giant moon looming overhead, the cause of the sea rising and the floods. In *Ponyo On the Cliff By the Sea*, it seems as if the whole of the planet is under threat because Ponyo has disrupted the law of things, crossing the border between the magical, underwater world and the human world. Love thus endangers the entire planet.

Yet *Ponyo On the Cliff By the Sea* is not a disaster movie, and the possibility that the world will end is not taken seriously (there are no flashcuts to flooded Tokyo, London, New York, etc). And after Sosuke and Ponyo have reached the sanctuary of Toki, it seems that Fujimoto admits defeat – his magical wave-henchmen take up the group and rush them down to Lisa, the Goddess and the women in the sea below (there's also a moment when Fujimoto magicks a bubble of air around Toki to protect her, and also hands over power to Ponyo's many fish-sisters).

One aspect of relationships and friendships that *Ponyo On the Cliff By the Sea* illustrates brilliantly is the reliance of each partner on the other: thus, when Sosuke seems downhearted, Ponyo is able to take the lead and cheer him up. And when Ponyo's magic and energy seep away into drowsiness, towards the end of the piece, Sosuke has to become assertive and resourceful, in order to help his friend.

When Ponyo's in the ascendant, the movie bounces about with energy – as when Ponyo's running atop the fish-waves, chasing Lisa's car. But when Ponyo's spirit flags into sleep, there's a different dynamic (it's an extreme version of children retreating into sleep in times of stress that was employed in *Totoro*).[152] *Ponyo On the Cliff By the Sea* illustrates gracefully how friends can help each other out, how one can cheer the other up or care for them when things go wrong.

THE ECSTATIC ENDING.

One of the intriguing scenes in *Ponyo* is at the submerged senior center, towards the end of the piece, with the old women now able to walk and run. The movie employs a fairy tale trope that's cropped up in other pictures,[153] where the old become young again. The scene also acts as a finale, theatre-style, bringing together most of the main characters (with the lawn of the senior center the stage on which much of the climactic action takes place. Although it's in a bubble magicked by Fujimoto, towards the end of the movie in a short sequence it seems as everyone is now under water).

The scene withholds pieces of narrative information – such as the conversation between Lisa and the Goddess of the Sea. The film stands back, and watches them from afar, from the point-of-view of the old women. What can they be talking about? Probably their children, Ponyo and Sosuke, who are on their way to the senior center. They are also bound to be discussing what it will mean if or when Ponyo becomes fully human, and if she decides to live with Sosuke and his family.

That the movie stands back from the two mothers and contemplates their discussion makes it all the more mysterious. But one of the delights of Hayao Miyazaki's cinema is that it doesn't feel the need to explain everything, to underline every motive or goal. (Besides, the movie has already discussed the notion of Ponyo becoming a real girl in the scene between her parents on Fujimoto's vessel, so it doesn't need to go over the same ground here).

The scene where Sosuke, holding Ponyo in the green bucket, stands before Ponyo's mother, is delightful and touching – the way that Ponyo, for example, hides in the bucket from her mother, or the moment of pure delight when Sosuke insists that he will always love Ponyo, and the fish darts around his head, and Lisa's hair.

Here the spell reaches its fulfilment, resolving the primary plot, of Ponyo wanting to become human (completing the

---

152 But there's still a calm tenderness to Ponyo in these scenes: she doesn't react much to Sosuke's alarm and distress when he rushes to Lisa's car to find it empty. The way that Ponyo very quietly takes Sosuke's hand and tells him let's go look for Lisa is unexpected and touching. Even in her depleted, somnambulistic state, Ponyo is still a good friend.
153 Such as *Cocoon*, or *The Twilight Zone*.

emotional journey that Ponyo undertook from the very first time we saw her). But the final moment of Ponyo's transformation is delayed for a minute – so that some of the other narrative strands can be tied up first: these include scenes with the two fathers: Fujimoto makes peace with Sosuke (but there's no farewell scene between Ponyo and Fujimoto), and Lisa spots Koichi's ship; they yell and wave at each other.[154]

The moment when Ponyo finally becomes fully human is rightfully an ecstatic scene – she joyfully shoots into the air, now back to her energetic, charismatic self. When Ponyo's like this, she is irresistible.

Sosuke was told to kiss Ponyo in her bubble by Ponyo's mother, when he was back on land. But Ponyo doesn't wait for him, and flies up out of the bucket: the final image of *Ponyo On the Cliff By the Sea* is Ponyo floating down to the surprised Sosuke and kissing him, with a silent movie iris-in on to the couple.

---

[154] And among the final scenes in *Ponyo On the Cliff By the Sea*, there are all sorts of ingredients and gags slipped in under the main story – the old women running up the hill, without needing their wheelchairs, for instance.

14

THE WIND RISES

The next animated feature that Hayao Miyazaki directed after 2008's *Ponyo* was Toho's *The Wind Rises* (*Kaze Tachinu*, 2013). It told the story of the historical figure Jiro Horikoshi, the Japanese aircraft designer of the Zero fighter. It was based on a *manga* by Miyazaki (published in *Model Graphix*, 2009),[155] and a story by Tatsuo Hori ("The Wind Has Risen", 1937). It's not directly a sequel to *Porco Rosso* (which Studio Ghibli producer Toshio Suzuki had talked about as being the follow-up to *Ponyo*), and it's a more serious tale than *Porco Rosso* (or a more solemn approach), but it's still about airplanes in the 1930s, with references to the world wars.

This is a masterpiece of profound beauty. It poignantly embodies the Japanese concept of *mono no aware* – transience/ impermanence.

The first time I saw *The Wind Rises* (*Kaze Tachinu*, 2013), I was in a state of shock afterwards – I couldn't do anything for half-an-hour except sit and stare and weep and absorb this staggeringly beautiful movie.[156] *The Wind Rises* is shocking for plenty of reasons: because the expectation is so high, for a new Hayao Miyazaki movie... because the movie delivers on that expectation, and exceeds it... because it is an extraordinarily exquisite work of art... because it is deeply moving... because it may be Miyazaki's last feature as director...

Ten thousand things strike you about *The Wind Rises*. Aside from the fact that it is an event in world cinema with few equals – a new film from the greatest living animation director, and a new film from the greatest fantasy filmmaker ever, and a new film from the greatest animation studio of recent times – *The Wind Rises* has a fascinating narrative structure. For the first time in Hayao Miyazaki's career as a feature film director, he has taken an individual's life, and shown us snapshots at several ages, from childhood to

---
155 In the *manga*, the characters had animal heads.
156 I was crying before the movie even started!

middle age (a 24-year span). While most of Miyazaki's movies have taken place structurally within a short time (*Laputa, Totoro, Ponyo*), with the characters barely ageing, or within slightly longer periods of perhaps months (*Kiki, Princess Mononoke*), *The Wind Rises* is a long stretch of a person's life (with the inevitable biographical comparisons between Jiro Horikoshi and Miyazaki – of Horikoshi's life and career with Miyazaki's life and career, with a man's life being seen thru his works, with the interweaving of personal and romantic relationships with the work, etc).

PRODUCTION.

The Wind Rises was distributed by Toho, and produced by Dentsu Inc., Hakuhodo DY Media Partners, KDDI, Mitsubishi Corporation, NTV, Studio Ghibli, Buena Vista Home Entertainment (Japan) and Toho.[157] Toshio Suzuki was producer, Ryoichi Fukuyama, Seiji Okuda and Naoya Fujimaki were associate producers, and Koji Hoshino was executive producer. Koji Kasamatsu was sound director, Eriko Kimura was ADR director, editing by Takeshi Seyama, Katsuya Kondô was character designer and key animator, Kitarô Kôsaka was character designer, colour design by Michiyo Yasuda, Atsushi Okui was DP, Youji Takeshige was art director, special effects by Keiko Itokawa, casting was by Takashi Hayashi and Takurou Okada, Suminobu Hamada was music engineer and music mixer, Joe Hisaishi was conductor, music producer and musician, and the orchestra was Yomiuri Nippon Symphony Orchestra.

The cast of *The Wind Rises* included: Hideaki Anno as Jirô Horikoshi, Hidetoshi Nishijima as Kiro Honjô, Miori Takimoto as Nahoko Satomi, Masahiko Nishimura[158] as Kurokawa, Mansai Nomura as Giovanni Battista (Count) Caproni, Jun Kunimura as Hattori, Mirai Shida as Kayo Horikoshi, Shinobu Ôtake as Kurokawa's wife, Stephen Alpert as Hans Castorp, Morio Kazama as Mr Satomi, and Keiko Takeshita as Jiro's mother.[159]

Certainly the selection by Hayao Miyazaki of Hideaki Anno (b. 1960) for the voice of the hero of *The Wind Rises* was

---

157 Among the many companies contributing to *The Wind Rises* were: Anime Torotoro, Khara, Nakamura Production, Studio Takuranke, Telecom Animation Film, Imagica, Wonder City, T2 Studio, Tokyo Metropolitan Art Space, Victor Studio, Digital Circus, Nichion, Toho Studio, Tohokushinsha Film Corporation, Tokyo TV Center, D-Rights, and Hakuhodo DY Media Partners.
158 Nishimura was Koruko in *Princess Mononoke*.
159 The English dub cast included Emily Blunt, Joseph Gordon-Levitt, Jennifer Grey, John Krasinski, Mandy Patinkin, Martin Short, Stanley Tucci, Werner Herzog, William H. Macy, Darren Criss, David Cowgill, and Elijah Wood.

unusual. Though Anno (the director of *Nadia: Secret of Blue Water*, *Neon Genesis Evangelion* and *Gunbuster* among others), has occasionally done cameos in *animé*, he is definitely not a trained voice artist, and he has a rather gruff, unemotive voice and delivery. Yet Miyazaki was sure that Jiro Horikoshi had to be played by Anno (there are personal reasons, too: Anno's company Khara has worked with Studio Ghibli on many recent productions, and the two are friends (going back 30 years). Miyazaki also selects unusual voices for his films. Anno has produced work in the Miyazakian vein, of course (such as *Nadia*), and both are devotees of *mecha*, science, and action-adventure).

The budget of *The Wind Rises* was enormous: $30 million (one of the biggest for a Studio Ghibli production – tho' *Ponyo* had cost ¥3.4 billion/ $34 million). *The Wind Rises* had a very successful release in Japanese theatres, the top grosser of the year (around $134 million). *The Wind Rises* won many awards,[160] and was nominated for an Oscar (the 2013 Oscar was won by *Frozen*. What a joke! Truth is, *no movie exists* which could beat *The Wind Rises* for an award – in any category, in any year).[161]

The plan was to release *The Wind Rises* with *The Tale of Princess Kaguya*, directed by Isao Takahata (Hayao Miyazaki and Takahata had released *Grave of the Fireflies* at the same time as *My Neighbor Totoro*). But Takahata's movie emerged in November, 2013.

The running time is 126 mins in some sources, 130 mins in others. This put *The Wind Rises* alongside *Spirited Away* and *Princess Mononoke* as one of Hayao Miyazaki's longer pictures (126 mins is long for any animated feature).

THE SCRIPT.

Hayao Miyazaki recalled that *The Wind Rises* originated with his *manga*, but he had resisted Toshio Suzuki's requests for it be made into an animated movie (until eventually Suzuki persuaded him).[162] One of Miyazaki's concerns was that *The Wind Rises* would not be suitable for children (which's true – some of this material would probably by-pass a six year-old child hoping for another *Ponyo*. In fact, Miyazaki was keener to

---

[160] Including the Annie Awards, Japan Academy Prize, and critics' awards in Boston, NYC, Chicago, Toronto, Frisco, San Diego, National Board of Review, Satellite Awards, etc.
[161] But maybe politics played a role here, as the movie enshrined a designer of military aircraft involved in WWII. So the Oscar went to the safe option, *Frozen*.
[162] I would imagine that Toshio Suzuki, one of the great animation producers of recent times, can be tenacious (and patient) when necessary.

deliver a *Ponyo* follow-up).163

> When I make a movie I usually think about one or two
> persons very close to me. For *The Wind Rises* it was one
> boy. I can't tell you who, because he himself does not
> know that I made the film for him. But he said he really
> liked it after seeing it. He's fourteen years old.

'All I wanted to do was to make something beautiful', was a quote by Jiro Horikoshi that had inspired Hayao Miyazaki. The script of *The Wind Rises* – by Miyazaki – took up real history as the basic material for the 2013 movie, but it did not stick to the facts. In truth, Miyazaki and co. seem to have regarded the real people and the real events in the period of *The Wind Rises* merely as the starting-points for a story and a script which they constructed themselves, as they wished. (It is *vital* to understand fully that this is *not* history, *not* a documentary).

Indeed, to indicate just how far the filmmakers were going to deviate from real history they inserted an elaborate and over-the-top dream sequence in the first five minutes. The dream announces that *The Wind Rises* is going to venture into private, psychological and emotional territory, that it is not going to take a documentary approach.

The series of dreams in *The Wind Rises* is just one of 100s of elements invented outside of history for the 2013 Japanese animation. For instance, Jiro Horikoshi did not meet his wife Nahoko Satomi like that, she did not die of tuberculosis,164 he had an older brother not a younger sister, they had children, the time scales of Horikoshi's life and the other characters in the film were altered, as were numerous events.

Meanwhile, the characterization of Jiro Horikoshi also draws on the writer Hori Tatsuo. Hayao Miyazaki said the main character was a combination of both of them (and when observers suggested that there was some autobiography in the portrait of Horikoshi, Miyazaki denied that, saying modestly that he wasn't equal to those men. Miyazaki is always modest – but when your movies are giving great pleasure to literally *millions* of people, you must be doing something right!).

The Wind Rises opens in 1916 (when the real Jiro Horikoshi would've been 13). The Kanto Earthquake occurred in 1923 (when Horikoshi was 20). Horikoshi goes to work at the

---
163 Another concern was that it would require a lot of learning among the Ghibli staff, and lots of research.
164 Miyazaki's mother suffered from tuberculosis, and it features in *Totoro*.

Mitsubishi factory in 1927. The Hotel Kusakaru retreat sequence takes place in 1932. The story ends around 1940.

Once again, a Hayao Miyazaki movie *seems* to have a simple A-to-B-to-C narrative structure: we dip into a character's life at the ages of, say, 15 (1918), 20 (the Kanto sequence, of 1923), and the late 1920s (at the Mitsubishi plant). But no, it certainly isn't that simple. For instance, each time the narrative of *The Wind Rises* stops to explore Jiro Horikoshi it also includes wide, historical views of events, stepping away completely from Horikoshi's viewpoint. And some events are narrated in retrospect, back-announced by a character in the present tense. There are flashbacks for other characters, and some flashbacks're narrated from other points-of-view.

One of the most inventive aspects of *The Wind Rises* from a storytelling point-of-view is the series of dream sequences. The dreams become much more than simply telling us how a character is feeling, or what they're thinking about, or what they're afraid of. The dreams are actually interwoven with the main narrative spine of *The Wind Rises* – so that sometimes we are witnessing events as seen in/ thru Jiro Horikoshi's dreamscape. So we are also watching an idealization and a romanticization of the key events in the 2013 movie (meanwhile, let's not forget that much of *The Wind Rises* is self-consciously sentimental and indulgent, and to support that, it contains one of the sweetest scores that Joe Hisaishi has composed for a Hayao Miyazaki picture: achingly emotional string cues, bold, upbeat marches for the early aeroplane trial scenes, and very delicate piano with plenty of reverb added. And this is a movie where characters lie back on the roof of their house looking up at the stars,[165] or sit by a window moodily smoking, while the music plays soft piano or gentle strings. In a movie so full of passion and beauty and mortality, composer Hisaishi is earning every Yen of his fee, providing a deeply moving foundation for the story. In the second half, in the romantic sections, the music is not only enhancing the emotional content, it is producing it).

Part of *The Wind Rises* is structured as a buddy movie, as Jiro Horikoshi and his pal Kiro Honjo spend many scenes together, including travelling to Germany (in 1928) to visit the Junkers aircraft plant, and working together at Mitsubishi. Altho' Horikoshi is something of a loner (and a dreamer, in the Miyazakian mode), the buddy structure enables many issues to be discussed in dialogue and encounters (Horikoshi has to

---

[165] Jiro Horikoshi thinks he can improve his eyesight doing that.

be a team player, too, tho' – when he arrives at Mitsubishi, he is led to his desk by Kurokawa, a desk in an office filled with workers at desks. Very much like an animation studio!).

THE STYLE.

The Wind Rises is depicted in the familiar Hayao Miyazakian style – sweet and sentimental in the main, with the rounded faces, small chins, tiny noses and large eyes of classic *animé*, plus of course the signature, square, Miyazakian face.[166] In terms of character design, nothing much has changed in forty years in Miyazaki's career, from the TV work of the 1970s to 2013's *The Wind Rises* (no need to change something that works so well!).[167] And yet of course there are numerous developments in the visual approach in *The Wind Rises*, compared to the early works.

One of the striking aspects of *The Wind Rises* is so obvious it hardly needs to be stated: it is the first movie with a strong historical element (and context) that Hayao Miyazaki has directed for some time. Previous movies, such as *Ponyo*, *Howl's Moving Castle*, *Spirited Away* and *Princess Mononoke* were essentially fantasies (despite their grounding in history and reality). You have to go back to *Porco Rosso* for a Miyazaki-directed picture with a significant and real, historical context. However, Miyazaki-san has been dealing with real, historical settings in recent movies *as a writer*: 2011's *From Up On Poppy Hill*, for instance (co-written with Keiko Niwa), was set in 1963 in Yokohama and Tokyo.

The Wind Rises recreates Japan of the 1920s and 1930s – which's outside of the immediate experience of the filmmakers (including Hayao Miyazaki). It meant looking at old photographs, learning about social etiquette, about the way people behaved in those days (there is much more deferential behaviour among the characters in *The Wind Rises* than contemporary Japanese movies – much more bowing and politeness, and Jiro Horikoshi always takes off his hat and stands up whenever he meets anybody).

The historical research on screen in *Kaze Tachinu* is state of the art – as one would expect in a movie from Studio Ghibli. As with the *From Up On Poppy Hill*, the background artists (20 are credited) have scoured every possible historical source for information about Japan in the first half of the twentieth century. No doubt a few museums were visited,

---
[166] Character designers working for the maestro know that they're going to have to incorporate the famous Miyazakian face in their designs.
[167] Miyazaki noted that by the age of forty he had already done everything he wanted to do in cinema.

along with the odd trip to some of the sites depicted in the movie. A Ghibli production has the budget for (some) research trips, and Miyazaki-sensei is of course a keen student of history.

You will spot many familiar faces from Hayao Miyazaki's career in amongst the characters in the crowds in *The Wind Rises*.[168] The crowd scenes are masterpieces of animation on their own. They were enough to break an animator's heart, Miyazaki remarked – because every figure has to be animated frame by frame, as individuals.

The Wind Rises is part of a small but significant genre of movies about flight and aircraft,[169] which includes (among Western movies): *The Right Stuff, Top Gun, Always, The Sound Barrier* and *Only Angels Have Wings*.[170] *The Wind Rises* follows the narrative pattern of aeronautical designers and engineers trying out prototypes (and pilots testing them), with all of the usual moments of elation followed by set-backs, cut-backs, hirings and firings.[171]

That *The Wind Rises* fetishes aeroplanes hardly needs to be said – this is a movie (*another* movie!) in which Hayao Miyazaki and his team at Ghibli and assorted animation houses spend an inordinate amount of time eulogizing aircraft of every form, from models and gliders to test planes and giant seaplanes with wings, tails and engines stuffed everywhere.

As well as dream sequences, there are also cinematic transitions from indoor scenes to flying scenes in *The Wind Rises* – where, for instance, Jiro Horikoshi at his desk at Mitsubishi is so involved in his work,[172] he imagines the aircraft he's designing in flight: his desk hovers in the sky, so he can see the test plane fly (and when the plane crumples

---

[168] Such as charas from *Kiki's Delivery Service*, the Mamma Aiuto Boss (from *Porco Rosso*), and *The Castle of Cagliostro*.
[169] Have you seen a movie with more trains and trams in it? And in a movie that's about aeroplanes?! In numerous scenes, Jiro Horikoshi is travelling around Japan (and later the world) on railroads (to the point where the Kanto Earthquake is experienced from a train. And, in a Miyazakian touch, Horikoski prefers to travel on the footplate, outside the carriage, working away with his slide rule). Miyazaki likes ships, too: ships are 'the most basic form of transport for humans', and the word 'airship' contains the idea of a ship that float and can go anywhere (TP, 166).
[170] Meanwhile, Western movies about pilots in combat scenarios include: *The Dam Busters, The Battle of Britain, The Blue Max, Catch-22, Reach For the Sky, Pearl Harbor, Aces High, 633 Squadron* and *Wings*.
[171] *The Wind Rises* includes standard tropes of the flight and air genre such as pushing the speed barrier, planes falling apart, projects being cancelled, rival projects winning out, etc.
[172] Very much like an artist (an animator) at her/ his work table, deep in a trance. This might be a commentary on making animation – animators sitting at a table, imagining they're in flight.

apart and falls, so Horikoski tumbles to Earth, too, his papers flapping in the high wind. The scene transitions back to the Mitsubishi workroom). In another scene, Horikoshi and Honjo imagine the bomber that Honjo has been working on in flight, and they're transported into the heavens, where it soars away from them. *The Wind Rises* is filled with such breathtaking technical moments, achieved with a masterful flair that makes it all look so easy.

The theme song of *The Wind Rises* is Yumi Matsutoya's song 'Hikoki-gumo' (1973).[173] It was suggested by producer Toshio Suzuki. As well as pastiches of Italian folk music, *The Wind Rises* also includes a song sung at the piano by Hans Castorp in the hotel sequence: 'Das gibt's nur einmal' ('It only happens once').[174] It was typical of Hayao Miyazaki to insist that the soundtrack for *The Wind Rises* be mixed in mono – because he dislikes the loud, multi-channel sound of contemporary cinema (so, no, not 7.1, 6.1 or 5.1 surround sound, not stereo surround sound, and not even stereo – but *mono*!).

The sound effects team added human voices to many elements in *The Wind Rises*, including the voice of the earthquake, the bombs in Jiro Horikoshi's dreams, and many of the plane and engine noises.[175]

The quote on a caption card at the start of *The Wind Rises* is taken from a poem by the French Symbolist poet Paul Valéry: 'Le Cimetiere marin', 'The Graveyard By the Sea' (so you can bet French audiences loved Hayao Miyazaki even more for that – if that's possible!). The Valéry quotation – 'Le vent se leve… Il faut tenter de vivre!' – is cited a few times in the movie[176] (most notably inside the series of Jiro Horikoshi's dreams). Meanwhile, the music cue for the credits is Italian (in keeping with the theme of Italian aeroplane design). There is also a quote from Christina Rossetti's poem 'Who Has Seen the Wind?'

THE CHARACTERS.

Jiro Horikoshi (1903, Fujioka - 1982, Tokyo) studied at university in Tokyo and worked at Mitsubishi Internal Combustion Engine Company Ltd. His aircraft designs included the A7M 'Reppu' ('Strong Gale'), the A5M (1936), the A6M 'Zero' (1940) and the J2M 'Raiden' ('Thunderbolt'). The chief

---

[173] It plays over the end titles, which comprise background art from the movie.
[174] Werner Richard Heymann wrote 'Das gibt's nur einmal' for the film *Der Kongreß tanzt*.
[175] A technique developed on the Ghibli shorts.
[176] Caproni often asks the Japanese boy, his nickname for Horikoshi, if the wind is rising.

client was the Imperial Japanese Navy, and Horikoshi did his most celebrated work as a designer for the Japanese military in the run-up to and during WWII.

Giovanni Battista Caproni (1886-1957), the first Count of Taliedo, was an engineer and aircraft designer. From a young age (early twenties), Caproni had his own aeroplane company (and airfield), Società de Agostini e Caproni (later called Società Italiana Caproni), and his factory produced many planes, including bombers, transports and seaplanes. Caproni had his fair share of air disasters – the Caproni Ca. 60 *Noviplano* crashed on its first flight (in 1921), as depicted in *The Wind Rises*, and one of his Ca. 48 airliners crashed in 1919 (everyone on board died, between 14-17 people).

Father figures and advisers are recurring characters in *The Wind Rises*. Some are bossy, little tykes, such as Kurokawa at Mitsubishi, some are inspirational gurus like Giovanni Battista Caproni, and some are ambiguous, trickster figures like Hans Castorp.

The pint-sized tyrant at Mitsubishi, Kurokawa (small, squat, officious, fussy, fearsome), is perhaps another satirical portrait of producer Toshio Suzuki (who was parodied as Piccolo in *Porco Rosso*). His counterpart at Mitsubishi is the chief engineer, Hattori, a softly-spoken veteran who indulges Horikoshi and his ideas (while Kurokawa is perpetually irritated and impatient).

Hans Castorp, an enigmatic, middle-aged German visiting Japan, is a character from *The Magic Mountain* by Thomas Mann, one of the great, European, inter-war novels.[177] Castorp is given a peculiar design for his eyes which marks him out as very different,[178] instead of the near-black eyes of the usual *animé* character (plus the two or three eye-lights that Hayao Miyazaki favours). Castorp performs a number of functions (not least delivering exposition, plus offering the Germanic view of political events). Castorp also represents something threatening, or ambiguous, as well as playful – the lure of the quest for the Ultimate Aircraft Design, perhaps, or the troubling, ambiguous complexity of adult life, or the puzzling relationship between designers (artists) and the military (governments). *The Wind Rises* raises moral issues such as: what is the relation between design (art) and commerce?, between science and war?, between the individual and their society?, between the individual's morality and

---

[177] The novel is cited in the dialogue.
[178] In *animé*, non-Japanese – foreigners – are often grossly caricatured (in *Fullmetal Alchemist*, fr'instance, invading soldiers are given the electric blue eyes of stereotypical Aryans).

ethics and those of the State?, between an individual's politics and nationalism?, and so on.

DREAMLAND.

That Jiro Horikoshi is a dreamer is indicated in the very first scene of *The Wind Rises*: he is depicted as a child asleep, [179] next to his sister Kayo. The camera zooms in slightly, then we cut to Horikoshi's dream – of – what else?! – the total ecstasy of flying. As with *Porco Rosso*,[180] *The Wind Rises* contains more scenes of flight (and skies and clouds) than even the sub-genre of movies about flight, pilots and aircraft. Every few minutes we are up in the heavens again, or watching from the ground (and if Horikoshi is sitting at his work desk, he imagines himself up in the sky with his creations). This is a *movie* that wants to fly just as much as the characters do and the filmmakers do.

The dreams perform multiple functions in *Kaze Tachinu*, and far more functions than the average dream sequence in the average movie (thus, the dream-life of Jiro Horikoshi is vitally important, and is part of what makes him a great aircraft designer).[181] All of Hayao Miyazaki's heroes are dreamers – and *The Wind Rises* suggests that dreaming is a vital element in the life of a person (whether or not they're creative or artistic. Dreams are literally creation. Because we are *all* dreamers – we all conjure amazing stories *every single night*).[182]

The Wind Rises' dream sequences also allow for the fantastical aspects of Hayao Miyazaki's cinema to be expressed, too: in the first dream sequence, Jiro Horikoshi is piloting a plane he's designed (he couldn't be a pilot in real life due to his eyesight),[183] flying under bridges and over villages in an ecstatic portrayal of freedom and release (the sequence is a summary of Miyazaki's many flying scenes, with *Porco Rosso* being quoted many times, including the beat where the plane flies under a bridge. The dream begins with Jiro clambering onto his roof and into his homemade plane, which feat-

---

[179] His home appears to be a traditional (and idealized) middle class house, with the familiar sliding doors (*fusama*), the *tatami* mats, the pretty garden, etc. His clothes are neatly folded at the end of his bed: this is a family where rules are followed.
[180] In fact, the series of dreams in *The Wind Rises* might be from the unmade *Porco Rosso* sequel (they might be the dreams of the young pig-man).
[181] But not a great pilot – Jiro Horikoshi is not Nausicaä, is too short-sighted to fly (the movie depicts the starry sky as blurry dots, while Horikoshi's sister Kayo can see stars and shooting stars).
[182] Indeed, dreaming and sleeping are vital to life: if you don't sleep, you die.
[183] Jiro Horikoshi is thus another of Miyazaki's heroes who wear glasses and have poor eyesight, just like the master himself!

ures the customary Miyazakian feather-shapes at the end of the wings. The dream closes with a frightening vision of a German air raid during WW1, with falling bombs and a German leviathan that's flown right out of *Laputa: Castle In the Sky*. Sadly for Jiro, it's his eyesight that fails him – as soon as he puts his goggles on, his vision blurs/ doubles, and he is an easy target for the enemy). The dream also establishes the movie in a time – the First World War – and a place – Japan.

It's also significant that Jiro Horikoshi is a dreamer who is dreaming in waking life, too: when he's is rescuing Nahoko Satomi and her maid Kinu during the Kanto Earthquake sequence, he looks up to see ash and particles turning into Italian aircraft. Indeed, the sky is filled with flying debris and dust (ominously evoking nuclear fall-out) throughout the Kanto disaster sequence.

Within Jiro Horikoshi's dreams of Count Caproni, the Italian's career also has a rise and fall structure to it, which echoes that of Horikoshi's life, and of the 2013 movie as a whole: we see Caproni introduced as a visionary aeroplane designer first, a man of energy and imagination who inspires the young Horikoshi (we see a close-up of Horikoshi in his sleep crying, 'Yes!' to each of Caproni's commands – it's *yes* to his unconscious, *yes* to the dream life, *yes* to one's higher self). But as the movie visits Caproni at intervals in Horikoshi's dreams, we also see some failures (such as the giant sea-plane[184] – a vessel on a scale that gives Howard Hughes' aeronautical ambitions serious competition).[185] And towards the end of the middle acts of *The Wind Rises*, Caproni announces that he is retiring from the business.

THE ROMANCE PLOT.

The romantic plot of *The Wind Rises* was inspired by "The Wind Has Risen" (1937), by the Japanese writer Tatsuo Hori, which had been one of the inspirations for Hayao Miyazaki's *manga*. In "The Wind Has Risen", Hori wrote of his relationship with his fiancée, Ayako Yano, who died of tuberculosis.[186]

The romance plot in *The Wind Rises* is outrageously clichéd and completely hokey: it's as overly melodramatic as cheap magazine fiction, as TV soap operas, as trashy block-

---

[184] Probably meant to be the Caproni Ca.60 *Noviplano* (1921), a plane designed to carry 100 passengers (which crashed on its maiden flight).
[185] In that sequence, Caproni is watching the take-off from a nearby boat. He's so furious when his latest creation falls to pieces that he yanks the film outta the movie camera next to him, and hurls the camera and tripod into the drink.
[186] But the name Nahoko Satomi was taken from a novel by Tatsuo Hori.

buster novels – a man falls in love with a woman who's dying. But it gives the movie incredible power. Yep, when clichés are used with this heightened level of imagination and energy, the emotion goes through the roof.

This being a Hayao Miyazaki movie, the romantic courtship between Jiro Horikoshi and Nahoko Satomi is of course played out using the motif of flight. Rather than being in a real aircraft (*à la Porco Rosso* or *Kiki's Delivery Service*), the eroticism of flight in *The Wind Rises* is evoked by Horikoshi making model gliders. In the languorous Hotel Kusakaru sequence in the middle acts of *The Wind Rises,* Horikoshi is depicted hurling model planes into the air, and Nahoko is watching, smiling and clapping from up on her balcony. In this eccentric, playful (and indulgent) riff on *Romeo and Juliet*, no character spouts pages of Shakespearean dialogue – it's all done with looks, grins, point-of-view shots, camera movement, colour, timing, and the physical thing that connects Horikoshi and Nahoko – the air itself (the wind of the movie's title). So the sudden gusts of the breeze in the erotic courtship sequence[187] literally embody inspiration and connection.[188]

The pacing is delightfully stately in the Hotel Kusakaru section of *The Wind Rises.* For instance, it comes after the sequence where Jiro Horikoshi has been given a major assignment of aeronautical design (producing the Mitsubishi 1MF10 for the Navy). Only part-way thru the Hotel Kusakaru episode does a flashback reveal that this new project also ended in disaster – we've seen the first part of the plane tests (this explains the vacation – that Horikoshi has been given leave to rest from his work on the new plane prototype. The sequence began with a rail journey in the mountains).

The pace is stately, but of course it is also hurtling along rapidly, because it is describing a courtship, and it's compressing perhaps several weeks into a few minutes. The episode includes some slapstick humour (Jiro Horikoshi falling into bushes as he tries to catch the gliders), and the encounter with the enigmatic Hans Castorp.

But most of all in the Hotel Kusakaru sequence we are looking at masterful filmmaking: this is exquisite storytelling depicting one of the greatest clichés of all literature, all art, all theatre, all anything: two people falling in love. Hence the heightened colouration, the images of grass and dresses

---

[187] When Nahoko Satomi nearly falls, clutching at the model glider from her balcony, her head face down over the ground below, it's a visual rhyme of the scene where she coughs up blood later.

[188] At the end of the movie, Caproni remarks that Nahoko Satomi was as beautiful as the breeze.

blowing in the breeze, and brooks rippling gently in the sunlight filtering thru the trees...

If you wanted to send a capsule into space to show the rest of the universe how beautiful Planet Earth was, you couldn't really do better than sending the collected works of Hayao Miyazaki. Have you ever seen sunny days in the countryside more gloriously rendered?

The Wind Rises is rare in Hayao Miyazaki's cinema for including a sex scene – that is, a love scene that is directly a love scene, rather than a flying scene standing in for a love scene (when Nahoko Satomi, lying in bed, calls to Horikoshi to come to her. He hesitates, because of her illness, but she insists).[189]

One of the most charming and tender scenes in *The Wind Rises* is the wedding sequence. Hayao Miyazaki and his team have decided to play much of the romance plot absolutely straight and wholly clichéd: for instance, this is a movie where characters really do turn to look at a newly-formed rainbow in the sky and exclaim on the beauty of being alive... the filmmakers stage an elaborate reunion scene at a railroad station, with the lovers hurrying towards each thru jostling crowds. This is a cliché upon a cliché (and the filmmakers select exactly the same sort of shots as the cliché), but it works.

The wedding in *The Wind Rises* is one of Hayao Miyazaki's loveliest set-pieces, totally indulgent, yet riveted to the central theme of love and loss in life. There shouldn't be a dry eye in the house during this magnificent evocation of tradition, ceremony and melodrama in 1930s Japan (even Kurokawa chokes up). Again, it is played dead straight and with a remarkable tenderness (note the tiny flakes of snow spinning thru the scene, another of the numerous evocations of the transience of life in *The Wind Rises*).

POLITICS.

Hayao Miyazaki was fully aware of the ethical and moral paradoxes inherent in *The Wind Rises*, in taking on the story of an aircraft designer whose works are used for the military-industrial machine as weapons of war. Miyazaki is a mass of contradictions, as he happily admits: an avowed pacifist who's fascinated by WW2 and weaponry and planes (he acknowledges that being mesmerized by aeroplanes is rather

---

[189] However, this occurs after the wedding ceremony, so, no, this is not sex before marriage!

infantile).[190]

Inevitably, a major work from one of Japan's major artists on a big political issue like Japan and the military between the world wars led to controversy: both the left-wing and the right-wing camps were disappointed with Studio Ghibli's movie (the leftists that the hero of the movie is an aeroplane designer for the Japanese government in the years before WWII, and the rightists for the critique of nationalism and war-mongering. Left-wing critics claimed that *The Wind Rises* doesn't really address Japan's aggressive policies leading up to WWII, and that the filmmakers sidestepped the complexity of the issues). Miyazaki added to the controversy by penning an article which was critical of the current Japanese powers.[191]

The usual excuses are delivered in *The Wind Rises* – that Jiro Horikoshi doesn't have a say in how his designs are used, that he is merely the designer, not the hawks who run the show, that he can't be blamed for colluding in the Japanese war effort (Hayao Miyazaki completely resists compressing issues such as 'blame' down to particular individuals. Throughout the press interviews for *The Wind Rises*, Miyazaki stressed that history and events can't be reduced to 'right' or 'wrong', to ticking a box labelled 'yes' or 'no').

> Jiro Horikoshi must have believed that he had nothing to do with how the Zero came to be used [Miyazaki commented]. Obviously, he bears responsibility for that war as a Japanese citizen, but I don't see why one engineer has to be held responsible for the entire history of the war. In fact, I think it's pointless to raise the issue of Horikoshi's war responsibility at all. (2013)

The Mitsubishi Zero fighter was a symbol of the fascination and the danger of WW2 – and of Japan, as Hayao Miyazaki acknowledged:

> Including myself, a generation of Japanese men who grew up during a certain period have very complex feelings about World War II, and the Zero symbolizes our collective psyche. Japan went to war out of foolish arrogance, caused trouble throughout the entire East Asia, and ultimately brought destruction upon itself.

For Hayao Miyazaki, Japan became too arrogant in the

---
[190] 'I am a bundle of contradictions. The love of weaponry is often a manifestation of infantile traits in an adult' (2013).
[191] Miyazaki said he thought that *The Wind Rises* might be more controversial than it was.

inter-war years, creating all sorts of trouble throughout East Asia. 'Japan will blow up', is a recurring opinion voiced in the 2013 picture – it was doing too much, being too aggressive, reaching too high, and exploiting resources to dangerous levels. (There is of course plenty of 20th century Japanese history that *The Wind Rises* doesn't refer to much – the fascism, the excessive nationalism, the war on China, on the Soviet Union, etc. These issues are alluded to in the dialogue, and of course some of the imagery references the issues obliquely).

HISTORY.

The Wind Rises is a movie with a wide-angle view of Japanese history as well as being the story of an individual struggling to follow their dreams. There are numerous times in *The Wind Rises* when the storytelling shifts away from Jiro Horikoshi and shows crowds coping with the Kanto Earthquake, or hordes of workers migrating to the cities. In this respect, *The Wind Rises* takes up the familiar cinematic structure of history viewed thru the eyes of an individual – *The Wind Rises* is Hayao Miyazaki's *Doctor Zhivago*,[192] or *The Grapes of Wrath*, or *War and Peace*.

It's noteworthy that there are three national cultures explored in *The Wind Rises* – aside from Japan, it's two European nations: Germany and Italy. Both nations were of course aligned politically with Japan in WW2 (so the choice of Germany and Italy was very conscious). Italian design has been held up by Hayao Miyazaki as one of his ideals of 20th century design, and aeronautical design in particular – embodied in *The Wind Rises* in the figure of Giovanni Battista Caproni (*Porco Rosso* of course enshrined Italian plane designers, and the pig-man hero takes a trip to Italy to have his plane put back together – using, of course, Italian design – which just happens to be in the form of a pretty, seventeen year-old girl! A classic Miyazakian fantasy, romantically combining eroticism and design!).

In *The Wind Rises,* the German connections are evoked in numerous ways, not only with the ambiguous German character Hans Castorp, or the trip to Germany, to see the Junkers factory. For instance, Castorp sings the German song 'Das gibt's nur einmal' at the piano in the Hotel Kusakaru and the gathering of *Japanese* people in the dining room sings

---

[192] I found out after writing this that John Lasseter also compared *The Wind Rises* to *Doctor Zhivago*. Miyazaki remarked: 'Actually I thought the same when I was in the production, so it was funny to see [Lasseter] mention the comparison as well' (2014).

along – in *German* (a self-consciously heightened symbolic moment with no basis in reality).[193] Jiro Horikoshi has disturbing dreams of German bombers. Castorp speaks of Japan and Germany blowing up.

Following the visit to Germany, Jiro Horikoshi imagines a Japanese bomber designed along the lines of the German aircraft they were shown at the Junkers factory. But, in a snowbound landscape, after a startling exit from yet another train,[194] the bomber appears out of a low, dark cloud in a blaze of flame (reminiscent of the UFOs in *Close Encounters of the Third Kind*), and crashes. *The Wind Rises* is full of similarly remarkable, visionary, hallucinatory scenes.

THE KANTO EARTHQUAKE.

In the Kanto Earthquake sequence, Hayao Miyazaki includes a topic he had long wanted to put on the screen. He could've had his hero encountering the love of his life Nahoko Satomi anywhere, but placing it during the spectacular and catastrophic earthquake gives the meeting a grandiose and mythical level (enmeshing their romance with the history of modern Japan). The Kanto Earthquake sequence also looks forward to the conflagrations of World War Two.

That Jiro Horikoshi acts selflessly in helping Nahoko Satomi's maid Kinu (her leg's injured), carries her all the way home, and hurries off without leaving even his name let alone any details about himself, is also a cliché of romantic melodrama (Nahoko says she tried to find Horikoshi-san later, and he says he went back to look for her).

Of course the Kanto Earthquake section of *The Wind Rises* is a *tour-de-force* sequence of visual effects animation (I say 'of course' because this is Hayao Miyazaki we are talking about!). It allows for one of Miyazaki's specialties – colossal devastation and horrific spectacle. The air itself is filled with debris and ash, the sky is the colour of swollen bruises, the ground shakes in grumbling after-shocks (everyone looks about in trepidation), buildings shift uncannily from side-to-side, fires erupt all over the place, and smoke billows continually.

The Kanto Earthquake scene is also a portrait of Japan under attack (and there's no layer of fantasy here, as in the scenes of carnage in *Howl's Moving Castle*, say, or *Laputa: Castle In the Sky* – this is meant to be the real, historical

---
193 Japanese people rarely speak other languages.
194 In the train, Count Caproni appears again, sitting beside Jiro Horikoshi in an empty carriage. Caproni urges Horikoshi to leap out of the speeding train into a whirlwind of snow.

Japan. However, in a movie like *Howl*, the layer of fantasy in the war scenes is very thin – there is no question that the bombardments are meant to evoke WWII and the Americans/ Allies bombing Japan, as well as the Iraq War).

With its evocations of living thru catastrophe very reminiscent of WW2 movies (and animations such as *Barefoot Gen* and *Grave of the Fireflies*), you could wring a whole movie out of the earthquake scenario. The Kanto Earthquake sequence also reminds us that there are bigger forces at work in life on this planet than human-made conflicts and suffering. It reminds us too that life is *very* fragile, and that it can end *at any minute* (themes which prefigure the bittersweet romance of the two lovers – especially when one of them is dying).

THE ENDING.

The bitter-and-sweet dichotomy at the heart of *The Wind Rises* is embodied in the way that the two main plots are entwined in the finale – the romantic plot and the life of an airplane designer plot. It occurs in the tests for the Mitsubishi Zero fighter sequence, out on a grass airfield. All of the main charas from this part of the plot of *The Wind Rises* are present (for their curtain call)

, and Jiro Horikoshi, standing slightly apart from the others, experiences something akin to a paranormal feeling that something is amiss. In the middle of the celebrations, as the plane tests have proved successful, Horikoshi senses that the love of his life, Nahoko, has died.

The way that the filmmakers express this moment of tragedy is distinctly European New Wave – very much like a sequence from a movie directed by Michelangelo Antonioni or Jean-Luc Godard: the camera pans left[195] across empty space at the airfield. It keeps going and going, but doesn't alight on anyone or anything, and doesn't have an end-point to the shot. And the sound of the breeze fills the air (with the noise of the Zero's engine diminished).

There is no cut to Nahoko Satomi, no hint of her in the dialogue – the scene is presented as a subjective experience of Jiro Horikoshi's, a moment which, like all moments, passes (all moments pass, don't they?, everything is changing – all the damn time! *Nothing* stays still! Nothing!).

As a scene of life passing, of loss, this is as fine as anything in cinema. Right at the moment of the hero's

---

[195] Directions of movement in cinema often have a symbolic value.; the movement here is to the left, counter-clockwise. However, in Japan that's different again (they read from right to left, for instance).

triumph, the love of his life is taken away. It's another cliché, yes, but it works.

There's a heaven and hell aspect to the final scene of *The Wind Rises*, however: before the sequence shifts to the dreamy, windy, grassy, Miyazakian moorland, there's a tilt down shot from a sky filled with planes like white crosses, the billowing smoke from the Kanto Earthquake, a distant view of a burning city, and a slow pan shot around a graveyard of crashed aircraft (most of them Japanese). There is also a revival of the memorable scene in *Porco Rosso* when the lost aircraft rise into the heavens (when Jiro Horikoshi's Mitsubishi Zero makes one final fly-past, in a squadron). Count Caproni appears, and asks the Japanese boy, as he calls him, if he enjoyed his ten years in the sun. Caproni muses on the vicissitudes of life, while Horikoshi listens.

The Wind Rises ends on a note of bittersweet optimism, with a message clearly delivered by Hayao Miyazaki to his audience: 'Il faut tenter de vivre!'. In the paradisal landscape of a Miyazakian dreamland (lush, green grass blowing in the wind in an upland, a blue sky filled with fluffy, white clouds), the spirit of Nahoko appears (as beautiful and youthful as when Jiro Horikoshi first met her, in a buttercup yellow dress), and, stopping a short distance away, she looks at him and tells him, twice: 'YOU MUST LIVE'.[196] Caproni, standing beside Horikoshi, says the same thing: 'YOU MUST LIVE'.[197]

RECEPTION AND CONTROVERSY.

The reception of *The Wind Rises* in the media emphasized aspects of the movie which were probably taken straight from press releases: that it was Hayao Miyazaki's swansong, that it would be his last movie. Well, Miyazaki-watchers like us know that the master has threatened to retire[198] (or has actually retired) at least twice (prior to *Spirited Away*, for

---

[196] Then her form melts, and rises upward in a movement of transcendence.
[197] The blocking of the scene is intriguing: it's Giovanni Battista Caproni who stands beside Jiro Horikoshi, but Nahoko Satomi approaches him from a distance, and doesn't come too close (there is no reunion of Horikoshi and Nahoko after death, then). But there is a suggestion that this is where Nahoko will be waiting for Horikoshi. The storyboards don't put them together in the same shot (it's played using shot/ counter-shots). But there is a suggestion that this is where Nahoko will be waiting for Horikoshi.
[198] And of course a person with as much energy and ambition as Hayao Miyazaki isn't going to sit around and watch the clouds move across the sky (tho' he probably does that, too!): he was working on 3 more short films for the Ghibli Museum, as well as helping with an exhibition.

instance).[199] But Miyazaki is a born storyteller, and when his interest and imagination is stirred by a particular story, the urge to tell it himself as a director is not far behind (certainly it's likely that Miyazaki-sensei will continue to be involved with screenwriting and planning of movies).

Critically, *The Wind Rises* was lauded throughout the media in the West, with most of the major, Western film critics enthusing about the 2013 Japanese movie,[200] as well as lamenting that this might be the final feature film as director from Hayao Miyazaki. For some (David Ehrlich) it was 'perhaps the greatest animated film ever made'. Nobody could fault it at a technical level, and the only serious criticisms seem to have been about the distorting of history (and real people), and the failure of aspects of the script to deliver on its promises (some of this was due to a recurring blindspot that Western film critics have to Japanese storytelling, where ambiguity is a given).

(For some critics, there wasn't enough denunciation of war by the hero Jiro Horikoshi: Mark Schilling pointed out that *The Wind Rises* does that by having Horikoshi standing in front of the wrecked plane,[201] and the numerous scenes of carnage. That *The Wind Rises* is passionately anti-war is clear from every frame).

The Wind Rises was also criticized for the amount of cigarette smoking it depicted. Yes, like other Miyazaki movies, every time a character stops and sits or stands, they light up ('There's a lot of smoking', Miyazaki admitted).

CONCLUSION.

The overriding atmosphere of melancholy and bittersweetness is impossible to miss in *The Wind Rises*. It's not only the sadness of the romantic melodrama form (for the Jiro Horikoshi-Nahoko Satomi relationship plot), in which one of the characters is declining into illness and then dies. It's not only the weary gloom of a story about an oncoming military conflict. It's not only the ironic bitterness of a person seeing their dreams and designs being used for mass murder. It's the atmosphere of the whole piece.

And yet, *The Wind Rises* is a masterpiece of colour and

---

[199] Miyazaki said that he hadn't planned on retiring before starting the production of *The Wind Rises*, but afterwards he decided he would (he said he could only work 7 hours a day instead of his usual 12). He announced his retirement in Sept, 2013.

[200] Miyazaki was delighted and surprised that audiences in the U.S.A. took to *The Wind Rises* – after all, he pointed out, Japan had fought the U.S.A. in WWII, and the movie was distinctly pro-Japanese.

[201] This is a call-back to the image in *Laputa* of the abandoned robot.

glowing light, to counter the wistful sadness – as if the sight of cherry blossom, or an exquisite purple-pink sky after sundown, makes everything all the more poignant. (This is the Japanese concept of *mono no aware* – transience and impermanence).

The Wind Rises reminds the audience that life is *incredibly*, almost *intolerably beautiful*, almost too beautiful to bear. Hayao Miyazaki is one of the very few filmmakers of recent times, I keep insisting, to express this in a convincing and highly poetic manner (isn't that one of the key messages of the 2013 movie? – that life is astonishing, and *you must live*).

An artist who can take you to the very depths of existence, who can examine what it means to be alive, who has a magical ability to explore beingness itself, is to be treasured.

Oh yeah, these are *big* claims to make of Hayao Miyazaki and his cinema! But Miyazaki *really* does it! He really is in that super-league of *cinéastes* like Akira Kurosawa, F.W. Murnau or Ingmar Bergman, filmmakers who can remind you that each breath you take, *as you are watching the movie*, is precious!

Wow! Now *that* is awesomely profound!

(© Studio Ghibli/ Toho, 2014)

PART THREE: ISAO TAKAHATA ❀ STUDIO GHIBLI

15
✳
THE CINEMA OF ISAO TAKAHATA

Hayao Miyazaki has been profoundly influenced by one of his long-standing collaborators, Isao Takahata (born October 29, 1935, known by the nickname Paku-san), and has also been intimately involved with the films of Takahata. So it makes sense to have a brief look at some of Takahata's work. For some, Takahata's cinema is as accomplished, as lyrical and as important as Miyazaki's output. If you are a fan of Miyazaki's work, I'd recommend looking at anything directed by Takahata.

THE LITTLE NORSE PRINCE

The Little Norse Prince (1968)[1] was Isao Takahata's first feature film as director, with Hayao Miyazaki contributing key animation and scenic designs.[2] A delightful adventure tale employing Arthurian legend and Northern European mythology, and set in Scandinavia, *The Little Norse Prince* also contains 'vivid, openly socialist content', as C. Odell

---

[1] *Taiyo no Oji Hols no Daiboke*, a.k.a. *Horusu: Prince of the Sun*, a.k.a. *The Great Adventure of Hols, Prince of the Sun*, a.k.a. *Little Norse Prince Valiant*.
[2] Hayao Miyazaki fondly recalled meeting at Takahata's house to discuss *The Little Norse Prince* through the night: youthful times, when 'we were all young and over-flowing with ambition and hope' (SP, 192).
Recalling how he got involved with *The Little Norse Prince*, Hayao Miyazaki said he wasn't part of the core production team, but had sat in on some of the meetings, and had shown Paku-san and others his drawings and ideas for the project. So they gave him more to do, but it wasn't an official appointment.

and M. Le Blanc put it (42).[3]

The Little Norse Prince is instantly recognizable as (Western) sword-and-sorcery stuff, but it's approached not only from a Japanese viewpoint but also the unique vision of Takahata and Miyazaki. Miyazaki in particular would mine this approach throughout his film career – looking at Western literature and mythology (and characters and themes) through a Japanese lens, and adding his own idiosyncratic concerns. That magical mix has beguiled audiences around the world.

The Little Norse Prince contains in its enthusiastic, idealistic hero the forerunners of Pazu in *Laputa: Castle In the Sky* and Conan, the boy of the future. But the most fascinating character in *The Little Norse Prince* is definitely Hilda, a distinctly ambiguous figure, embodying both villainess and princess to be rescued.

GRAVE OF THE FIREFLIES

Grave of the Fireflies (*Hotaru no Haka*, 1988) is an absolutely stunning movie, a masterpiece of animation. If you know detractors who say, oh, animation can't handle serious subjects, it's only good for fantasies and fairy tales and children's stuff,[4] show them *Grave of the Fireflies*. It is undoubtedly one of the great war pictures – in this case, a passionate anti-war movie.[5] *Grave of the Fireflies* takes its place with the great war movies, such as *All Quiet On the Western Front*, *Paths of Glory*, *Apocalypse Now* or Andrzej Wajda's *Kanal* trilogy. Roger Ebert was a

---

3 As Patrick Drazen has pointed out, Toei Animation did not promote *The Little Norse Prince* much: it was shown in theatres in Japan for only ten days (2003). So it wasn't the hit the filmmakers hoped for.

4 Indeed, for Helen McCarthy, the fact that *Grave of the Fireflies* is a cartoon, and cartoons're seen as being solely for kids, makes it even more poignant. Cartoons, McCarthy says, are thought of as light, fluffy and safe: 'to see such a story presented in such a form brings home to us even more strongly the pity and shame of a world which is still allowing children to suffer as Seita and Setsuko and hundreds of thousands like them suffered' (1996, 77).

5 The *animé* masterpiece *Barefoot Gen* (Mori Masaki, 1983) is a significant forerunner of *Fireflies*: based on the real experiences of Keiji Nakazawa (most of *Barefoot Gen* (70%) was autobiographical, reckoned the author), it deals with the bombing of Hiroshima from a child's perspective and in parts is almost too much to bear, so traumatic are the events depicted. (There has been a live-action adaption of Nakazawa's memoirs (1977).)

big fan of the film,[6] and it has also been compared with *Schindler's List* (in some respects, it is superior to the 1993 Universal flick, partly because it doesn't stoop to sentimentality). For Ebert, '*Grave of the Fireflies* is an emotional experience so powerful that it forces a rethinking of animation'.[7]

Grave of the Fireflies is filmmaking at the very highest level, and only one or two people in the whole world could have made it, and only one or two studios could have produced it. You have to have a *very* dedicated, patient and skilled team to produce something as good as *Grave of the Fireflies*. This is one of Isao Takahata's masterworks.

Grave of the Fireflies is a film based on the wartime recollections of Akiyuki Nosaka, published in 1967, in particular the fire bombings of Japan by the United States of America in 1945.[8] It is set in Kobe. It is shown in August each year in Japan, as part of the memorials for Hiroshima.

Isao Takahata wrote the script and directed; Sato Ryoichi, Toru Hara and Shinochosha (publishers) were producers; Yoshio Mamiya[9] composed the music; Yoshifumi Kondo was animation director; Nobuo Koyama was supervising animator; Nizo Yamamoto was art director; Michiyo Yasuda once again worked her magic with colour design; editing was by Takeshi Seyama; and sound was by Yasuo Urakami. It was released on April 16, 1988, where it played with *My Neighbor Totoro*.[10]

The whole picture is seen through the eyes of two children, a four year-old girl called Setsuko and a fourteen year-old boy called Seita; the film is not about war so much as the effects of war on civilians, in this case, two children. The voice actors were Tatsumi Tsutomu (Seita) and Shiraishi Ayano (Setsuko).

---

[6] Italian Neo-realist movies, such as those by Vittorio de Sica and Roberto Rossellini, may have influenced *Grave of the Fireflies*, suggested Roger Ebert. Certainly Isao Takahata has name-checked Neo-realism, and also the French New Wave filmmakers.
[7] For Dani Cavallaro, *Grave of the Fireflies* 'puts us in touch with undiluted, inconsolable and consummate woe, which no vague promises of otherworldly rewards could ever sublimate, and which the bucolic beauty of nature amplifies with harrowing irony' (C, 78).
[8] The impetus for the project came from the book's publishers, Shinchosa, who approached Studio Ghibli.
[9] Yoshio Mamiya, a classical composer, has worked with Isao Takahata on *Only Yesterday, Little Norse Prince, Goshu the Cellist* and *Grave of the Fireflies*.
[10] A live-action version was released in Japan in 2005.

Grave of the Fireflies is as far away from the products of the Walt Disney Studios or typical commercial Western animation as one can imagine: there is distressing imagery that one never, ever finds in Disney's output. For instance, the image of the children's mother in hospital, bandaged all over and severely burnt, or the images of corpses (including the mother, with flies buzzing around her head), and cadavers being placed in mass graves. *Grave of the Fireflies* does not hold back from showing the effects of bombings. Even when Seita and Setsuko go to the beach, in an interlude from their difficult life, there is a corpse.

Grave of the Fireflies is *incredibly* emotionally moving, and climaxes with a scene of unbearable pathos, when Seita cremates his little sister Setsuko on a hill. The body is burnt in a wicker basket, on a bed of charcoal, along with the things Setsuko prized in life. As the day moves into twilight, the fireflies appear, and Seita lies on his back, looking up at the sky.[11]

Isao Takahata and his team are master storytellers: the filmmakers insert a scene of some people (including young girls) returning to their home: the war is over. The irony is savage and worthy of William Shakespeare or Thomas Hardy. And the burial occurs on a beautiful, Summer's day.

After this absolutely devastating scene, the film can go no further, and it *has* to finish there, and the viewer can go no further, either: *Grave of the Fireflies* will leave you weeping and wiped out. (A child's burial is a difficult scene to pull off, to hit the right tone, but this is as good as any similar scene I can think of).[12]

Grave of the Fireflies is not all solemn and downbeat, although the general narrative trend is a decline and decay. There are numerous light-hearted moments, and scenes of intense joy, when the laughter of Setsuko and Seita rings out. There are episodes of cinematic poetry to rival the masters of cinema, such as the scene where Seita and Setsuko collect a box full of fireflies (*hotaru*) and they flitter above the heads of the children in the air raid

---

[11] Takahata has said that he was attracted by the idea of a paradise that wouldn't last: it was the momentariness of this heaven that was the whole point.

[12] *Barefoot Gen* had portrayed the death of children and babies in a very graphic manner, and included the cremation of a baby.

shelter.[13] Or the heart-rending montage of Setsuko playing by herself outside the air raid shelter, running back and forth wearing a white sheet, or playing on the swing, or hopscotch. The technique of visually fading a character in and out of the scene to evoke their absence has rarely been achieved to better purpose than here. (The quiet accompaniment of a woman singing on an old-time gramophone heightens the emotional impact).

Visually, *Grave of the Fireflies* is stupendous, with the Studio Ghibli team working at its height. The scenes of apocalyptic devastation, which are a staple of Japanese *animé*, including the films of Hayao Miyazaki, are here given a level of reality which's crushing: this is not some apocalyptic fantasy with an Overfiend or demon or giant robot blowing Tokyo up, it's a firestorm created by North American bombers. (But the fire-storms and atomic explosions that explode in countless Japanese *animé* OVAs and movies are replays of the attacks on Japan in WW2, of course).

You might be mistaken for thinking that *Grave of the Fireflies* is a sober, sepia-tinted movie, but no, it is produced in the fully saturated, colourful Studio Ghibli style. Except that Isao Takahata and his team have also introduced some darker scenes, visually, as well as a stylized red of fire for the ghost sequences. In these, Seita and Setsuko are depicted lit by a glow of red from the fire bombings. At the level of visual effects animation, the red lighting, usually against black, is exquisitely achieved, and the equal of anything in cel animation. (The movie opens with Seita addressing the camera and relating that he's dead – in the opening scenes, he encounters his sister Setsuko (with the symbolic empty tin of candy that they carried around).[14] So the rest of the film is going to depict how these two characters died. First time through, the viewer might not pick up on this narrative point, having not yet been introduced to Setsuko outside of this stylized sequence).

---

13 The folk belief that fireflies are the souls of the dead adds an extra layer of meaning to the scene. Watching fireflies is a traditional Japanese pastime (G. Poitras, 1999, 47).
14 The candy is Sakuma Drops, a familiar brand in Japan, and boy do those boiled sweets do a lot of dramatic work in *Grave of the Fireflies*.

ONLY YESTERDAY

Hayao Miyazaki produced Isao Takahata's movie *Only Yesterday* (*Omoide Poro Poro = Tearful Thoughts*, 1991), adapted from a *manga* by Hotaru Okamoto and Yuko Tone.[15] *Only Yesterday* was set in Tokyo in the contemporary era, with a 27 year-old woman, Taeko, recalling her childhood.[16] The film switched back forth between the present day and the mid-1960s;[17] a nostalgia trip for the audience as well as the filmmakers.[18]

'The moment I ran across the story of *Only Yesterday* I knew instinctively that Paku-san was the only person who could properly turn it into a film', Hayao Miyazaki remarked in 1990; 'The original story had something wonderful about it, but I also knew that the nature of its composition would make it a very difficult project' (SP, 202-3).

The 27 year-old woman was not a character in the original story: she appeared, Hayao Miyazaki said, and began influencing the project (SP, 203), in the manner of fictional characters who start to influence their authors. Or as Miyazaki often puts it: you don't make the film, the film makes you.

Visually, *Only Yesterday* was constructed partially in Studio Ghibli's high key, pastel-hued mode (for the flashback scenes), with the edges of the frame allowed to bleed to white.[19] The present day scenes were portrayed in the regular Studio Ghibli style – at once 'realistic' or 'naturalistic', and stylized. The setting is Yamagata.

Many of the scenes were very modest, concerning family life. There are nagging older sisters, restrained, unresponsive fathers who hide behind newspapers,[20] and scolding mothers. A lengthy argument about maths homework, with Taeko unable to understand how to do

---

[15] The first part was published in 1990, and was aimed at women.
[16] Imai Miki was the voice of the adult Taeko, and Honna Youko the child Taeko. Casting Yanagiba Toshirou as Toshio was unusual: his delivery was idiosyncratic, full of pauses and hesitations.
[17] Some commentators have put the two periods as 1982 and 1966.
[18] Yasuyoshi Tokuma, Yoshio Sasaki and Ritsuo Isobe were producers; Katsu Hoshi wrote the music; Yoshifumi Kondo designed the characters; storyboards were by Yoshiyuki Momose; Kazuo Oga was background designer and art director; Takeshi Seyama was editor; Michiyo Yasuda was colour designer; Kondo, Katsuya Kondo and Yoshiharu Satou were supervising animators.
[19] Takahata and the Ghibli team would take that high key stylization even further with *My Neighbors the Yamadas*.
[20] The scene where Taeko's father slaps her on the face is shocking.

fractions (how do you divide two-thirds of an apple by a quarter? And why would you want to? It's beyond Taeko). Squabbles with a sister about an enamel handbag. A daughter asking her mom to buy some Puma sneakers.

Only Yesterday is unusual in another respect – apart from being modest and small-scale, it doesn't have explosions, car chases, or giant robots: there is a woman at the centre of it. Indeed, this is very much a 'women's film' in many respects: Taeko's family is all women, apart from the father (there's a grandmother, a mother, and two sisters). At school, Taeko hangs out (understandably) with girls. And at the farm, aside from Toshio and one or two other characters, women predominate.

The ending of *Only Yesterday* is stupendous, a work of genius, demonstrating once again that Isao Takahata is in every way the equal of anyone as an animation director. It depicted the farewell of Taeko, as she leaves the safflower farm for Tokyo, by train, then decides to return, in order to be reunited with Toshio. That in itself is a very clichéd kind of ending: it resolves Taeko's journey from searching for herself and her desires, including moving from Tokyo to the countryside, and finding love. The restrained friendship between Taeko and Toshio blossoms in the final scene into romance.

PONPOKO

Hayao Miyazaki produced Isao Takahata's movie *Ponpoko* (*Heisei Tanuki Gasen, Modern-Day Raccoon War Ponpoko*, 1994), an adventure comedy which deserves to be better known.[21] It is a masterpiece of animation. Takahata wrote and directed the movie; the producers were Yasuyoshi Tokuma, Seichiro Ujiie, Ritsuo Isobe and Miyazaki (Miyazaki is also credited as art director). Animation directors were Shinji Otsuka and Konishi Kenichi; Megumi Kagawa and Otsuka were designers; Michiyo Yasuda was colour designer; music was by Joe Hisaishi; Takeshi Seyama was editor; and sound was by Naoko Asanashi.

Ponpoko is about a group of raccoons (*tanuki*,

---

21 *Ponpoko* was being considered for the Oscars – as best foreign film (best animation film didn't exist then).

Japanese raccoon dogs)[22] trying to save their homeland (the Tama Hills) from being swamped by humans and their roads, houses, stores and high-rises.

The music in *Ponpoko* (by Joe Hisaishi and Shang Shang Typhoon) is stunning, with some delightfully light-hearted songs, and some wondrous combinations of music and animation, the equal of anything in the Disney canon. For the (musical) set-pieces alone, *Ponpoko* is the equal of the best of world animation. The Ghibli Studio was really hitting its stride at this time, with the many of the same people working on both Hayao Miyazaki's films and *Ponpoko*.

The comedy in *Ponpoko* is terrific – rapidfire gags, and some really inventive ideas. There's even more of Akira Kurosawa in *Ponpoko* than in Hayao Miyazaki's movies: it's virtually a replay of *The Seven Samurai*, a format that has been used in other movies, of course. Here it's some raccoons trying to stop their world being swamped by humanity. There's even a gung-ho character rather like Toshiro Mifune in *The Seven Samurai*, Gonta, who's all for killing humans.[23]

There are numerous stand-out sequences in *Ponpoko*: the training of the raccoons in shape-shifting, for example, or the scenes where the raccoons spook the construction workers (as part of the 'Spooking War'), or the marvellous arrival of the three ageing, raccoon masters (the Three Masters of Shikoku) dressed as old hippies from the 1960s in outrageous, colourful costumes, a cool car and snazzy sunglasses (the training scenes are just exquisite, employing animation's talent for transformation to its height: a fireball, an enormous toad, a cloud, a dragon, a flying horse).

Without doubt the most incredible sequence in *Ponpoko* is the goblin procession in the Tama Hills suburb at night. Here the animators unleash one of the most startling, imaginative and overwhelming scenes in recent animation, as the raccoons become *yokai* or spirits.[24]

And *Ponpoko* is a film with a big heart: it is another ecological tale, in the manner of Hayao Miyazaki's

---

22 In Japan *tanuki* look like raccoons, come from the Canidae family of mammals, have supernatural powers, and are seen as amusing (G. Poitras, 1999, 133).

23 The *tanuki* don't agree about how to combat the humans. Some want to co-operate with the humans, while others (such as Gonta) favour an all-out attack.

24 There are references to previous Studio Ghibli outings, such as images from *Porco Rosso*, Kiki the witch, and of course Totoro.

Nausicaä of the Valley of the Wind. The story of a bunch of animals fighting for their natural habitat might seem like pure Disney, but there is no saccharine sentiment here: this is fierce stuff. There are images of raccoons killing humans, and scenes of raccoons being run over on roads by trucks.

Hayao Miyazaki's role as producer of *Ponpoko* is a vital one, but he has said that when he and Isao Takahata produce each other's movies, they try to stand back and let the other get on with it. That's tricky in such a labour-intensive industry like animation. Needless to say, there are numerous correspondences between the films of Miyazaki and Takahata. Too many to mention; but it's true to say that Takahata must be one of the biggest influences of all on Miyazaki's cinema. Not least because they have worked together for such a long time, on so many projects, going back to the TV shows of the 1960s. So Takahata and Miyazaki are filmmakers who know animation backwards, and films such as *Ponpoko* or *Only Yesterday* really demonstrate that.

MY NEIGHBORS THE YAMADAS

My Neighbors the Yamadas was Studio Ghibli's main animated release of 1999.[25] It was a remake, based on a popular *manga* about a Japanese family in contemporary Japan. The *yonkoma* (four panel *manga*) began in 1991, and is still running.[26] Isao Takahata helmed the Ghibli movie, and also wrote the script. The producers were Seichirou Ujiie, Takashi Shouji, Michael O. Johnson and Yasuyoshi Tokuma. Akiko Yano provided the music; Naoya Tanaka and Youji Takeshige were the art directors; colour design was by Michiyo Yasuda; Atsushi Okui was DP; Kazuhiro Wakabayashi was recording producer; and Kenichi Konishi was animation director.

My Neighbors the Yamadas was a delightful movie about a family depicted in a stylized, black ink, outline

---

25 *My Neighbors the Yamadas* was a wholly digital movie. It employed around 150,000 digitally produced frames.
26 The original TV *animé Meet the Yamadas* had been directed by Hiroe Mitsunobu in 1980 for Herald and Fuji (102 episodes of 25 minutes each, shown after *Sazae-san*, the longest-running animated show ever). A follow-up TV series appeared in 2001, designed by Hisaichi Ishii and directed by Nobutaka Nishizawa for Toei Animation.

fashion, with pastel-hued painting. Simple backgrounds, minimal layouts, and an approach like a newspaper cartoon told humorous and heartwarming stories of domestic life. The scenes contained many of the usual situations of television sit-coms, depicted in a witty and touching manner. Cooking, cleaning, washing and eating were recurring activities, along with family arguments, fallings-out, and laughter. There's a scene where ma and pa fight over the remote control for the TV which is genius, like a martial arts duel.

Most of all, *My Neighbors the Yamadas* was delivered with a light touch that was absolutely charming. And Isao Takahata's penchant for surreal imagery and fantastical staging was displayed in full effect in some of the scenes which burst out of the house and ranged across the town. Particularly outstanding was the depiction of married life early in the film, a fantasy sequence which employed boats, planes, trains, cars and a variety of other vehicles to portray the struggles of getting through life and marriage. As *Pom Poko* and *My Neighbors the Yamadas* demonstrate, Takahata is a master of animated comedy, shifting effortlessly from unassuming, domestic whimsy to spectacular, large-scale flights of fantasy.

The modesty and small-scale of *My Neighbors the Yamadas* is deceptive: this kind of animated movie is just as tough to achieve as the big spectacles of aerial dog-fights, explosions and chases of action *animé*. *My Neighbors the Yamadas* does a lot more than capture the delicacy and stylization of a *manga*, reproducing the look and feel of something that's drawn and inked beautifully (difficult enough); it also captures the numerous shifts in emotion and psychology among the key players.

THE TALE OF PRINCESS KAGUYA

For animation fans, the news that *animé* legend Isao Takahata would be directing his first feature film since 1999's *My Neighbors the Yamadas* was very exciting. Takahata helmed *The Tale of Princess Kaguya* (2013) from a famous Japanese folktale; he was 78 when it was released.

Princess Kaguya was due to appear in cinemas in

Japan at the same time as *The Wind Rises,* in July, 2013, but it was delayed, and was released in November. Even so, these two films together amounted to total *animé* bliss. Both are masterpieces of extraordinary vision and emotional power. And both films, from director-geniuses[27] in their seventies, address full-on mortality and loss and the transience of life.

The Tale of Princess Kaguya was produced by Buena Vista Home Entertainment, Dentsu Inc., Hakuhodo DY Media Partners, KDDI, Mitsubishi Corporation, Nippon Television Network, Studio Ghibli and Toho (with a budget of $49 million[28] – an *enormous* figure for Asian animation, and Ghibli's biggest budget for a feature production to date). It was distributed by Toho. It grossed about $22.6 million in Japan (disappointing for a big Ghibli movie, and below expectations).

The Tale of Princess Kaguya was produced by Yoshiaki Nishimura, Toshio Suzuki and Seichiro Ujiie. Isao Takahata co-wrote the script with Riko Sakaguchi. Character designer and animation director was Kenichi Konishi;[29] art director was Kazuo Oga;[30] sound director was Naoko Asari; and Keisuke Nakamura was DP.

Among the voice cast were: Aki Asakura (absolutely stunning as the princess), Takeo Chii (also hugely impressive as Okina), Kengo Kora (Sutemaru), Atsuko Takahata (Lady Sagami) and Nobuko Miyamoto (Ouna). The music was by Joe Hisaishi (altho' Shinichiro Ikebe had originally been commissioned to score the movie).[31]

The Tale of Princess Kaguya continued the exploration of a children's storybook approach to animation, which had been a key element in *My Neighbors the Yamadas.* Thus, *The Tale of Princess Kaguya* was strikingly conceived as a lavish pæan to pastel-hued, children's book illustration (in both Western and the Japanese forms), with visuals comprising beautiful watercolours for backgrounds, blocky, exaggerated figures (with their black outlines prominent),[32] and also

---

[27] Few animation houses on Earth can boast two true geniuses like Takahata and Miyazaki among their directors.
[28] It's difficult to see why *The Tale of Princess Kaguya* cost so much, when *Ponyo* and *The Wind Rises,* which were just as complex and intricate, cost much less ($34m and $30m).
[29] Animation director on *Ponpoko* and *Yamadas.*
[30] The art director of *Princess Mononoke* and *My Neighbor Totoro,* among others.
[31] The orchestra was the Tokyo Symphony.
[32] Close to but not quite *chibi* (super-deformed).

animation which leaves the vestiges of brushstrokes and pencil marks in the final product. (In this movie, white is actually the key colour – the white of backgrounds (or the edges of backgrounds) left unpainted).

The result? An utterly charming approach to animation which gloried in being traditional and conventional, but allowing plenty of room for the quirks and eccentricities for which Isao Takahata is well-known. (Some viewers found the highly stylized approach distracting. But, actually, this is simply another form of storytelling, and you soon get into the narrative, so that the technique is just another technique. Traditional cel animation is of course also a highly stylized form of art: it isn't 'natural', it doesn't just 'happen'!).

The Tale of Princess Kaguya is a story of the two worlds of mediæval/ pre-modern Japan – the worlds of peasants (the bamboo cutter and his wife), farming and the countryside and the world of the court, the city, aristocrats, manners and wealth. Princess Kaguya is part of both worlds (as are her parents), and she moves between the two (sometimes the journey between the two is undertaken willingly and demurely, at other times in a fury of motion and despair).

Themes of exile, of feeling out of place, of wishing for some other place, of separation, permeate *Princess Kaguya*, as the princess finds herself increasingly disenchanted with life in the palace. She retreats into herself, into working her loom, or playing her *koto,* or tending her private, fantasy garden (where she recreates the landscape of what she calls her home, the peasant's world, with little miniatures).

The Tale of Princess Kaguya is an extraordinary swansong for a lifetime of movie-making, of indulging in the fantasy and the storytelling of animation (Isao Takahata's career goes back to the early 1960s). It may not be Takahata's last film, but it evokes a bittersweetness, a wistfulness which strikes home.

ILLUSTRATIONS

Illustrations on the following pages are from the movies directed by Isao Takahata, plus some of the works of Studio Ghibli.

(© Toei/ AIP, top. Toho/ Tokyo Movie Shinsha, above)

: COLLECTOR'S SERIES

Grave of the Fireflies

"It belongs on any list of the greatest war films ever made!"
-Roger Ebert,
Chicago Sun-Times

Includes
BONUS DVD
featuring interviews
with **Director**
Isao Takahata
and film Critic
Roger Ebert

(© Toho/ ADV)

(© Tokuma Shoten/ Toho/ Buena Vista)

(© Toho/ Buena Vista)

(© Shochiku/ Buena Vista/ Studio Ghibli)

(© Toho/ Buena Vista)

(© Studio Ghibli/ Nippon/ Toho/ Touchstone)

(© Studio Ghibli/ Toho/ GNDHDDTW, 2010)

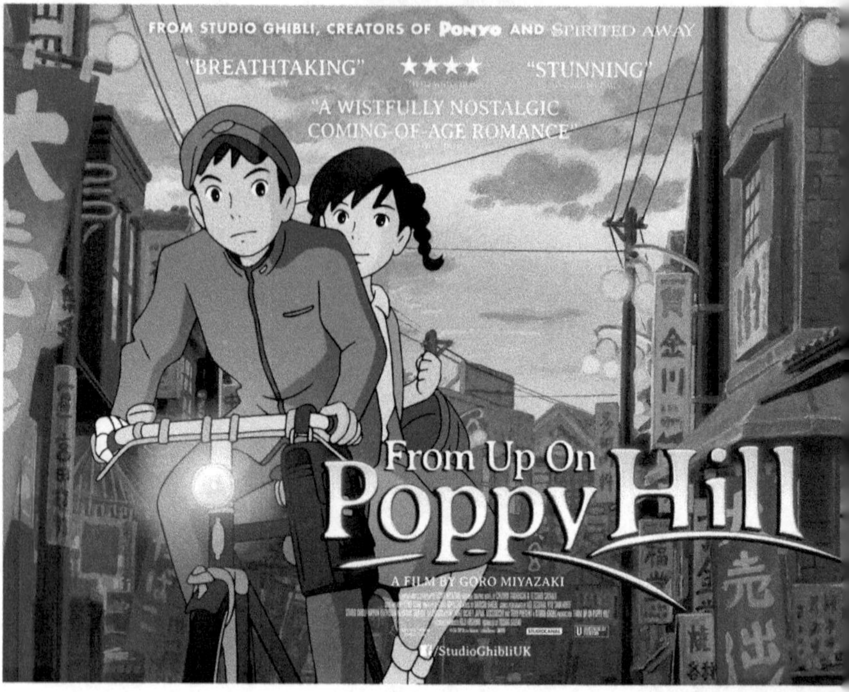

(© Studio Ghibli/ Toho)

16
❖
STUDIO GHIBLI'S OTHER MOVIES

INTRODUCTION TO STUDIO GHIBLI.
As Studio Ghibli and its films feature so strongly in the world of Japanese animation, and in relation to Hayao Miyazaki's movies (after all, Ghibli has been the home of Miyazaki's cinema since the mid-1980s), it makes sense to have a brief look at some of Studio Ghibli's work.[1] Some of the pictures, such as *Only Yesterday* and *Whisper of the Heart,* have significant input from Miyazaki[2] – he was the producer of *Only Yesterday* and the producer and writer and storyboard artist for *Whisper of the Heart,* for instance, and the co-writer of *From Up On Poppy Hill* and *The Borrower Arrietty,* two later Ghibli pictures. Of the 20 Ghibli films, Miyazaki directed 9, and has worked on eight of the 11 he didn't direct (which only leaves three without Miyazaki credits).

The 20 Studio Ghibli feature films are (up to 2014), with Miyazaki's contribution indicated by an asterisk:

> *Laputa: Castle In the Sky*
> *My Neighbor Totoro*
> *Grave of the Fireflies*
> *Kiki's Delivery Service*
> *Only Yesterday* *
> *Porco Rosso*
> *Pon Poko* *
> *Whisper of the Heart* *
> *Princess Mononoke*
> *My Neighbors the Yamadas* *
> *Spirited Away*
> *The Cat Returns* *
> *Howl's Moving Castle*
> *Tales From Earthsea* *

---
1 Other celebrated *anime* houses include Madhouse, Gainax, Pioneer, Tezuka, Production I.G., Sunrise, Toei, Bandai, Studio 4°C, and Clamp.
2 Miyazaki and Studio Ghibli go together, though, as Isao Takahata commented: 'Miya-san is the one who makes Ghibli. So his presence is a huge one'.

Ponyo On the Cliff By the Sea
The Borrower Arrietty *
From Up On Poppy Hill *
The Wind Rises
The Tale of Princess Kaguya
When Marnie Was There

Best known for their movies, Studio Ghibli also produces work for advertizing and television (like all Hollywood studios, and most animation studios). Movies might be what the animation studios are known for, but they have to pay the bills, and commercial work is vital[3] (for Ghibli, merchandizing also plays a key role, bringing in revenue during leaner years between the big hit movies like *Spirited Away* or *Princess Mononoke*). Ghibli produced some TV idents for NTV in 1992 (*Sky-Coloured Seed*), and 5 TV commercials (in 2001), plus others.

Studio Ghibli is among the most successful animation houses in Japan in recent times:[4] although it is one studio among hundreds in Japan, it absorbs a high proportion of ticket sales at the theatre or video and DVD sales, or television viewing figures (35.1% of the audience watched *Princess Mononoke* when it was broadcast on TV in Japan in 1999).[5]

In 1991, Studio Ghibli moved to new premises in Koganei, a suburb in Western Tokyo. Hayao Miyazaki was involved in designing the new studio (down to every detail, and drawing blueprints). The owner of Ghibli, Tokuma Shoten Publishing, paid for the new building (Ghibli had merged with Tokuma in 1997). In March, 2005, Ghibli bought itself out of Tokuma Shoten, becoming an independent company.

The Ghibli Museum was another Studio Ghibli venture: it opened in October, 2001 in Mitaka Inokashira Park in Tokyo. For the Ghibli Museum, Studio Ghibli produced a no. of short animations, which would only be screened at the museum, including *Film Guru Guru* (2001), *Imaginary Flying Machines* (2001), *The Whale Hunt* (2001), *Koro's Big Stroll* (2002), *Mei and the Kittenbus* (2002), *The Day I Bought a Star* (2006), *Looking For a Home* (2006), *Mon Mon the Water Spider* (2006), *A Sumo Wrestler's Tail* (2010), *Mr Dough and the Egg*

---

[3] Making money is always a major consideration in the production of a Ghibli movie: 'obviously, we can't make a film if it's deemed to "never make money"' (TP, 335).
[4] In 2014, Toshio Suzuki said: 'we only did things that we knew worked for certain'.
[5] Mamoru Oshii commented: 'What do other animators think of Ghibli? As far as I know, they basically respect Ghibli. It's half love, and half hate. A general response would be: it's a tremendous place, but I don't want to go there. Because they control you too tightly (at Ghibli).'

Princess (2010) and *Treasure Hunting* (2011). Most were directed by Hayao Miyazaki, and some were written by Miyazaki. *Ghiblies* (2000 and 2002) were short films about an animation studio which were shown on Japanese TV, and with *The Cat Returns* in theatres.

Ghibli Museum is very much Hayao Miyazaki's baby; he contributed to the design, layout, content, displays, etc. For the *Imaginary Flying Machines* show at the museum Miyazaki produced a short movie, which was later shown on Japanese Airlines aircraft.

And so to some of the Studio Ghibli films:

WHISPER OF THE HEART.

Hayao Miyazaki did not direct *Whisper of the Heart* (a.k.a. *If You Listen Carefully/ Mimi o Sumaseba*, 1995), but he did write it – that alone makes it an important project for Miyazaki. As well as scripting *Whisper of the Heart,* Miyazaki was also involved as producer and storyboard artist (and also directed a small section of it). Thus, Miyazaki's input on *Whisper of the Heart* is very considerable, although it was directed by Yoshifumi Kondo; it features numerous Miyazakian elements, including the themes, characters, settings, visuals and motifs.

Whisper of the Heart was based on a *manga* by Aoi Hiragi, who would go on to write *The Cat Returns*, which's a sequel to *Whisper of the Heart* in some respects. It's romance about two teenagers; it's also about creativity (the girl Shizuku is a writer, the boy Seiji makes violins); and it's a growing up or coming-of-age drama.

TALES FROM EARTHSEA.

Hayao Miyazaki had considered adapting the *Earthsea* novels of Ursula Le Guin at one time (and has spoken of being inspired by them). In the end, Studio Ghibli produced a version of *Earthsea* helmed by Miyazaki's son Goro in 2006; Goro Miyazaki has script credit, with Keiko Niwa.[6]

The history of the making of *Tales From Earthsea* and how Hayao Miyazaki's son Goro came to direct it is troubled, and has created some bad feeling in some quarters. Goro Miyazaki says that producer Toshio Suzuki sort of persuaded him to take up the direction (after inviting him to produce

---

[6] I haven't been able to find out much about Keiko Niwa, other than she co-wrote *Earthsea, Arrietty* and *Poppy Hill* for Studio Ghibli.

some storyboards).[7] I would imagine that many of the veteran filmmakers at Ghibli, who had a huge amount of film experience, while Goro had none at all, *really* resented Miyakizaki's son being promoted to the role of film director over their heads.

Hayao Miyazaki has said that he didn't want his son to direct the film. Further, the rift or problematic relationship between Miyazaki father and son has become well-known (and film critics have tried to read it into *Tales From Earthsea* – an unspoken desire of Goro to kill his father, which's depicted in the picture). Miyazaki father and son have had periods when they didn't speak to each other, and the troubled aspects of their personal lives has coloured how some critics have responded to the 2006 movie.

THE BORROWER ARRIETTY.

Studio Ghibli's 2010 animated feature release was an adaption of another British author, Mary Norton, from her 1952 book *The Borrowers*: *The Borrower Arrietty* (a.k.a. *Arrietty* and *The Secret World of Arrietty*). It was directed by first-timer Hiromasa 'Maro' Yonabayashi, an animator on *Howl's Moving Castle, Ponyo,* and *Spirited Away.*

The Borrower Arrietty can be regarded as another Hayao Miyazaki movie – because he co-wrote the script (with Keiko Niwa), and was executive producer (along with Toshio Suzuki). A glimpse at the trailer shows Miyazaki's influence all over it: plants and leaves, for instance, are everywhere (including in Arrietty's bedroom). The movie itself is over-shadowed by Miyazaki to a large degree; but that seems to be inevitable in a Ghibli release.

There are hundreds of Miyazakian ingredients in *Arrietty*, such as: explorations of scale, an emphasis on verticality, densely-decorated interiors, a cat, myriad other animals, etc. And notice how Ghibli's adaption of Mary Norton's book has focussed on the young Arrietty, in line with the rest of their output which consciously foregrounds girls and *shojo* characters. That is a typical Miyazakian departure from the source material, where a classic children's book is transformed into a *shojo* narrative: for instance, it's the father, Pod, who's seen by the convalescing boy, not Arrietty.

---

[7] Goro Miyazaki was working in landscape gardening at the time – and was working on the Ghibli Museum. Goro Miyazaki was collaborating with the long-established animation team at Studio Ghibli, however, so although he was a first-time director, he had immense support from the production team at Ghibli (the animation director, for instance, was Inamura Takeshi, who had worked at Ghibli for years).

FROM UP ON POPPY HILL.

A new movie from the finest animation house in the world promises to be a treat, no matter who writes it, directs it, or buys the saké. Even more so when the greatest living animator co-writes the story! Hayao Miyazaki co-wrote (with Keiko Niwa) Studio Ghibli's 2011 release *From Up On Poppy Hill* (directed by his son, Goro Miyazaki).[8] It was based on a 1980s *shojo* (girls) *manga* by Tetsuro Sayama and Chizuru Takahasi, about an adolescent romance set in 1963 in Yokohama. The voice cast included Masami Nagasawa as Umi Matsuzaki and Junichi Okada as Shun Kazama.[9] The score was by Satoshi Takebe, with Aoi Teshima singing the theme song. Toshio Suzuki was producer.[10]

From Up On Poppy Hill is a *shojo manga*,[11] and the story takes place entirely from the point-of-view of young Umi Matsuzaki (bar a few scenes which step away from her character). Once again, the Ghibli heroine is a conscientious young woman, resourceful, loyal, deferrential, kind and generous. And what a worker! Little Umi goes to school, comes home and cooks for everybody (including a bunch of boarders), and runs the household (there is a cleaner, however).[12] It's not something you see mid-teens doing in Western movies! (Maybe Umi is a little *too* good to be true).

From Up On Poppy Hill is a sweet movie – sweet, sweet, sweet... it's tender, modest, romantic, nostalgic and charming. The romance between Umi and Shun is yet another of the restrained, muted relationships that *shojo manga* and *animé* excels at depicting (nobody can do social restraint and deferrential etiquette like the Japanese!). A courtship where no one emotes beyond a glance, where the lovers barely touch more'n once or twice (instead, they are blushing across their cheeks all the time, or looking down shyly. Which makes Umi's final impassioned outburst and declaration of love, at the end of the Tokyo trip, all the more startling).

---

8 Presumably Miyazaki senior and junior have reconciled a little, if they're working on the same picture; however, when Isao Takahata directed *Only Yesterday*, he and Miyazaki, who was producing, hardly spoke at times!
9 Musically, Satoshi Takebe provides the customary soft, tinkly piano cues for the emotional accents, but much more entertaining are the jazzy cues, and the use of music from the early 1960s.
10 It was made by Dentsu Inc., Hakuhodo DY Media Partners, Kadokawa Shoten, Kodansha, Mitsubishi Corporation, Buena Vista Home Entertainment/ Disney, Nippon Television Network, Studio Ghibli and Toho.
11 The forerunners of *From Up On Poppy Hill* at Ghibli are clearly *Whisper of the Heart*, *Ocean Waves* and *The Cat Returns*.
12 This is a house of women, with only the only guy being Umi's younger brother.

WHEN MARNIE WAS THERE.

Studio Ghibli's 2014 release was *When Marnie Was There* (*Omoide no Marnie,* 2014). It was written by Keiko Niwa,[13] Masashi Ando[14] and Hiromasa Yonebayashi, and directed by Yonebayashi (one of the animation directors at Studio Ghibli, who helmed *Arriety*). It was based on *When Marnie Was There* by Joan G. Robinson. In the cast were: Sara Takatsuki, Kasumi Arimura, Hana Sugisaki, Hitomi Kuroki and Ryoko Moriyama. Yoshiaki Nishimura and Toshio Suzuki produced. The music was by Takatsugu Muramatsu. Toho distributed it; Buena Vista Home Entertainment Japan, Dentsu Inc., Hakuhodo DY Media Partners, KDDI, Mitsubishi Corporation, Nippon Television Network, Studio Ghibli and Toho were the production companies. Released on July 19, 2014 (the traditional release window for a Ghibli movie), *When Marnie Was There* grossed ¥3.63 billion in Japan.

And who is going to follow Hayao Miyazaki? Every so often another Japanese director will be dubbed 'the new Miyazaki' by critics.[15] Truth is, Miyazaki is a one-off film-maker, like Orson Welles or Akira Kurosawa or Sergei Paradjanov, impossible to replicate or follow. Miyazaki is a true original – who else would start full-scale production without even completing the storyboards up to the end of the movie? Who has the stamina and determination to personally check 80,000 key animation drawings, layouts and backgrounds (as well as the drawing skill to re-draw them as required)? Who can work in such a loose, intuitive fashion and yet keep coming up with masterpieces *every single time*? And what individual in animation anywhere in any period of cinema history has produced hit after hit after hit?

Only Hayao Miyazaki.

Arigato Miyazaki-sama.

---

13 Co-writer of *Earthsea, Arrietty* and *Poppy Hill* for Studio Ghibli.
14 One of the supervising animators at Ghibli.
15 At Studio Ghibli, Yoshifumi Kondo was a strong successor, b4 his early death in 1997.

APPENDIX
❖
QUOTES BY HAYAO MIYAZAKI

I'm not going to make movies that tell children, 'You should despair and run away'.

•

Is someone different at age 18 or 60? I believe one stays the same.

•

Don't watch animation! You're surrounded by enough virtual things already.

•

I'm not making a film; instead, it feels like the film is making me.

•

I am an animator. I feel like I'm the manager of an animation cinema factory. I am not an executive. I'm rather like a foreman, like the boss of a team of craftsmen. That is the spirit of how I work.

•

I'm really not good at depicting the bad guys, frankly. They always wind up to be people who are at the core basically good.

•

I can't do a film after having debated it. I am unable to do a film while discussing it with my team. I issue directives. I do not achieve it otherwise.

•

Personally I am very pessimistic. But when, for instance, one of my staff has a baby you can't help but bless them for a good future. Because I can't tell that child, 'Oh, you shouldn't have come into this life.' And yet I know the world is heading in a bad direction. So with those conflicting thoughts in mind, I think about what kind of films I should be making.

•

Modern life is so thin and shallow and fake. I look forward to when developers go bankrupt, Japan gets poorer and wild grasses take over.

•

I never read reviews. I'm not interested. But I value a lot the reactions of the spectators.

•

We live in an age when it is cheaper to buy the rights to movies than to make them.

•

If you watch something for three minutes, you feel like you know everything about it, even what went on backstage, and then you don't feel like watching the rest.

•

When a man is shooting a handgun, it's just like he is shooting because that's his job, and he has no other choice. It's no good. When a girl is shooting a handgun, it's really something.

•

The 21st century is a complex and unforeseeable epoch. Our thinking habits and our values, which until now looked settled, are being challenged.

RESOURCES

WEBSITES

One of the best independent sources on the internet for Hayao Miyazaki information is nausicaa.net. For Miyazaki-related information this is the place to start. It is a well-designed and easy to use website.

Also the Studio Ghibli websites:
onlineghibli.com, ghibli.jp and Ghibliworld.com.

The Disney sites have information on Miyazaki (such as disney.go.com). Buena Vista (Disney's distribution network) distributes Ghibli's movies in many Western territories.

Toei Animation for *Little Norse Prince* and others: corp.toei-anim.co.jp.

Toei is one of the largest animation companies in Japan.

The Lupin III network: lupin-3rd.net. This includes info on the whole Lupin III franchise, as well as *The Castle of Cagliostro*.

And for composer Joe Hisaishi: joehisaishi.com. Hisaishi has composed the scores for most of Miyazaki's movies.

I would also recommend: Anime News Network animenews network.com

It is excellent, and the first stop for any online research on *animé*. Anime News Network has the fullest credits on the web for animation, and each entry is linked, so you can follow your favourite actors, directors, producers and artists, across numerous shows.

Also: Gilles Poitras's site: koyagi.com.
Fred L. Schodt's site: jai2.com.
Otaku News: otakunews.com.
Midnight Eye (for Japanese cinema): midnighteyec.com.
There are fan sites, of course.

BOOKS

Among books in English, the collection of Miyazaki-san's writing, *Starting Point, 1979-1996*, is a must-have. It contains numerous articles and interviews with Miyazaki. This is an indispensable book that should've been published twenty years ago! If you are a Miyazaki fan, you will find much to enjoy in *Starting Point*. It includes his thoughts on his own movies, as well as the ones he reveres. It also gives you an insight into Miyazaki's background, his politics, his philosophies and the influences that helped to form his animation. The follow-up, *Turning-Point*, brings the selection of pieces up-to-date (to 2008).

Helen McCarthy's book *Hayao Miyazaki: Master of Japanese Animation* (1999, revised 2002) is essential reading. It was the first major study of Miyazaki, by one of the experts in *animé* studies. All of McCarthy's books on *manga* and *animé* are first-rate, and worth tracking down. Like Fred Schodt, Gilles Poitras and others, McCarthy knows *manga* and *animé* inside-out.

Dan Cavallaro's *The Animé Art of Hayao Miyazaki* is superb. Cavallaro offers many intriguing ways of approaching Miyazaki. For the illustrations alone this is worth reading. Colin Odell and Michelle Le Blanc's study of Studio Ghibli is useful, taking in Isao Takahata's work as well as that of his key collaborator, Miyazaki.

Andrew Osmond's exploration of *Spirited Away* is about the only study of this movie in book form in English. Osmond's text explores the ways in which the project developed.

The above books are some of the main studies of Hayao Miyazaki: compared to, say, Walt Disney and Alfred Hitchcock, who have stacks of books written about them, there is very, very little on Miyazaki in English.

Books by Frederik Schodt, Helen McCarthy, Trish Ledoux, Patrick Drazen, Fred Patten, Jonathan Clements, Simon Richmond, Antonia Levi, Susan Napier, Jason Thompson and Gilles Poitras are standard works. But apart from those key authors, there is surprisingly little available on *animé* in English.

And most film critics tend to focus on characters, stories, and the biographies of the filmmakers. So many books on *animé* simply tell us the stories. Very few critics grapple with the industrial, social and cultural aspects of *animé* (and even less with theory and philosophy). Which's why critics such as Fred Schodt and Helen McCarthy are so important, because they address issues such as the modes of production, the audience and the market, and social-cultural contexts.

The single most useful book on *animé* is *The Animé*

Encyclopedia (2001/ 2006/ 2015) by Jonathan Clements and Helen McCarthy. If you buy one book on Japanese animation, get this one. *The Animé Encyclopedia* provides entries on pretty much every important *animé* show, OAV and movie to come out of the Japanese animation industry, as well as numerous minor shows and oddities. This is the equivalent of a Leonard Maltin/ *Time Out/ Virgin/ Oxford/ Variety* guide to cinema. Clements and McCarthy are *animé* experts as well as fans (I would also recommend any of Clements' other books, including his entertaining accounts of working in the *animé* business in translation and dubbing, *Schoolgirl Milky Crisis*).

All of Helen McCarthy's books have become standard works: *Anime! A Beginner's Guide To Japanese Animation*, *The Animé Movie Guide*, *The Erotic Animé Movie Guide*, *500 Manga Heroes & Villains* and *500 Essential Anime Movies* (some of these were co-authored with Jonathan Clements). They contain facts, credits and background to *animé* and *manga* which will greatly enhance your studies (and enjoyment) of Japanese comics and cartoons.

Fred Schodt is one of the most valuable commentators on Japanese *animé* and *manga* in the West. His pioneering study of *manga*, *Manga! Manga! The World of Japanese Magazines*, is a marvellous book. Before it, there was virtually nothing. Because of the huge crossover between *manga* and *animé*, many of the chapters on *manga* in Schodt's studies also apply to *animé*. Schodt also offers one of the fullest and most detailed accounts of the history of *manga* and visual art in Japan. (*Manga! Manga!* also includes samples from some famous *manga*, including *Barefoot Gen* and *The Rose of Versailles,* and the illustrations – from the history of Japanese art as well as from *manga* – are stunning).

Fred Schodt's follow-up, *Dreamland Japan: Writings On Modern Manga*, is equally riveting. It includes a huge number of illuminating studies of individual artists and their works (with illustrations), as well as another history of *manga*. *Dreamland Japan* is also probably the finest, most intelligent and best-informed analysis of the *manga* market in both Japan and overseas. As well as Osamu Tezuka, Frederik Schodt also discusses Hayao Miyazaki, the relation of *manga* to *animé*, artistic styles, Japanese publishers, and the big *manga* magazines. It enhances Schodt's books that he has also interviewed many of the chief artists of *manga*, including the 'god of manga' himself, Osamu Tezuka.

Trish Ledoux and Doug Ranney edited an early guide to *animé*, *The Complete Anime Guide*, that is now a standard work. It is packed with fascinating snippets, as well as hard information, credits, etc. The companion volume, *Anime Interviews*, culled from *Animerica* magazine, is wonderful, featuring many of the key practitioners in animation (such as

Masamune Shirow, Shoji Kawamori, Mamoru Oshii, Leiji Matsumoto, Rumiko Takahashi and Hayao Miyazaki).

Gilles Poitras has produced a number of works on *animé*, including *The Animé Companion* and *Animé Essentials*. Poitras offers vital links between Japanese animation and Japanese culture and society. There are objects, gestures, words and customs in *animé* that often surprise or bemuse Western viewers: Poitras' books help to explain them all. You will find yourself recognizing all sorts of elements in *animé* that Poitras includes in his books (which contain many illustrations).

Antonia Levi's *Samurai From Outer Space* is stuffed with information on Japanese society as well as Japanese animation. Clearly written and with an appealing sense of humour, Levi's book is a lesser-known but invaluable work. *Samurai From Outer Space* discusses all of the celebrated *animé* shows that've made the leap across the Pacific to the Western world. Published in 1996, you wish that Levi (like many other authors whose books came out in the 1990s), was able to update them. Many great shows have been released since 1996!

Simon Richmond's *The Rough Guide To Anime* is a superb general introduction to the wild world of *animé*. Like other *Rough Guides*, it selects fifty must-see TV shows and movies, plus providing discussions of related topics like *manga*, adaptions of *animé*, and a history of animation.

Jason Yadao's *The Rough Guide To Manga* is a companion guide to the *Rough Guide To Animé*. It has the same format and is a terrific general introduction to Japanese comics. Yadao's enthusiasm is infectious: you will want to hunt out many of his recommendations. Both *Rough Guides* were published in the 2000s, so they're able to include recent classics like *Fullmetal Alchemist*, *Cowboy Bebop*, *Love Hina* and the masterpieces of Satoshi Kon.

Manga: The Complete Guide (Jason Thompson and others) is another illuminating book, packed with short reviews and longer pieces on topics like games, sci-fi, martial arts, sport, religion, crime, *mecha*, *shojo*, and *yaoi*.

Zettai! Anime Classics is another of those books that looks at 100 classic movies: Brian Camp and Julie Davis spend more time, however, on each of the familiar masterpieces of Japanese animation, exploring the films, OAVs and TV shows in much more detail than the usual single paragraph review.

Manga Impact! from Phaidon is an entertaining survey of Japanese animation, with a format focussing on characters and personnel. *Manga Impact!* has short text entries, but features numerous, wonderful illustrations in colour.

Susan Napier's *Anime: From Akira To Princess Mononoke* is much more theoretical, and somewhat dry. (If you are familiar with the theoretical approaches to Western animation (see the studies noted below), you will find nothing new in Western authors exploring Japanese animation from a theoretical or philosophical point-of-view).

On animation in general, I would recommend the following studies: P. Wells' *Understanding Animation*; E. Smoodin's *Animating Culture: Hollywood Cartoons From the Sound Era*; Leonard Maltin's *Of Mice and Magic: A History of American Animated Cartoons*; James Clarke's *Animated Films; From Mouse To Mermaid: The Politics of Film, Gender and Culture* (edited by E. Bell *et al*); *Animation Art* (edited by J. Beck); and *Reading the Rabbit: Explorations in Warner Bros. Animation* (edited by K. Sandler).

For information on Walt Disney, the standard works include: Leonard Maltin's *The Disney Films*; Richard Schickel's *The Disney Version: The Life, Times, Art, and Commerce of Walt Disney*; R. Grover's *The Disney Touch;* Project on Disney's *Inside the Mouse: Work and Play at Disney World*; *Disney Discourse: Producing the Magic Kingdom* (edited by E. Smoodin); and *Walt Disney: A Guide to References and Resources* (edited by E. Leebron *et al*).

For a study of cinema, there is one book that towers above *every other book* on film (even tho' the competition is fierce!): David A. Cook's *A History of Narrative Film*. If you want one book that covers everything, this is it.

David Bordwell and Kristin Thompson have written many meticulously researched and beautifully crafted books on cinema: *Film Art: An Introduction*, *Narration In the Fiction Film*, *Film History: An Introduction*, *The Classical Hollywood Cinema: Film Style and Mode of Production to 1960* and *Storytelling In the New Hollywood*. Anything by Bordwell and/or Thompson is excellent.

I would also recommend Bruce Kawin's *How Movies Work*, Gerald Mast's *Film Theory and Criticism: Introductory Readings*, and Mast & Kawin's *A Short History of the Movies*.

David Cook, David Bordwell, Kristin Thompson, Gerald Mast and Bruce Kawin will give you all you could need for an in-depth study of cinema. Read their books: it's the equivalent of a degree or PhD in cinema!

AVAILABILITY

All of Hayao Miyazaki's films (and those of Studio Ghibli) are available for Western viewers on video and DVD (and, more recently, Blu-ray). They usually have the original Japanese language soundtrack, plus subtitles, and an English language dub.

The distributors of the movies of Hayao Miyazaki in Japan are: Toei Company. Tokuma Shoten. Toho.

In the U.S.A.: Buena Vista Home Video. Touchstone. Walt Disney Pictures. Miramax Films.

DIFFERENT VERSIONS

For Western viewers, the films of Hayao Miyazaki (and Studio Ghibli) are available in two main versions: the Japanese original version (usually with subtitles), and the dubbed versions.

Hayao Miyazaki's movies have been given very high profile, English language dubs, by some of the best technical people in the business (sound mixes at Skywalker Sound, for instance), and starry voice casts.

However, despite the laudable efforts of the Walt Disney corporation, in terms of the quality of filmmaking, and the significance of Hayao Miyazaki as a filmmaker, the original language versions are always the ones to go for. Why? Because Miyazaki himself has overseen or approved of the voice casts and mixes (as well as the dialogue). And Miyazaki doesn't speak English.

Think of it in the opposite direction: a film by Orson Welles or Alfred Hitchcock that was dubbed into Japanese, even by the best technical staff and the best actors in the Japanese film business, could not be regarded as conforming completely to the filmmakers' vision (unless Welles or Hitch could speak or understand Japanese and were present at the ADR and sound mixing and editing sessions). I also object to dubbing on social, cultural, political and ideological grounds.

It is also the case that Hayao Miyazaki is such a dynamically visual storyteller, dialogue, though important, is only one of numerous devices that Miyazaki and his teams employ. Unlike some movies, you really don't need to have the dialogue translated, via subtitles or dubbing, to know what's going on.

FILMOGRAPHY

A filmography of the chief theatrical movies directed by Hayao Miyazaki.

THE CASTLE OF CAGLIOSTRO

The Castle of Cagliostro (*Lupin III: Cagliostro no Shiro,* 1979).
Monkey Punch/ Tokyo Movie Shinsha. 100m.
Japanese release: December 15, 1979. U.S.A. release: Sept, 1980/ April, 1991.

CREW
Written and Directed by Hayao Miyazaki
Co-writer: Haruya Yamazaki
Screenplay: Yasuo Otsuka
Original Story: Hayao Miyazaki
Original Concept: Maurice Leblanc
Original Creator: Monkey Punch
Executive Producer: Yutaka Fujioka
Producer: Tetsuo Katayama
Distributor: Ghibli Museum Library and Toho
Production: Studio Telecom and Tokyo Movie Shinsha
Music: Yuji Ohno
Character Design: Hayao Miyazaki and Yasuo Otsuka
Art Director: Shichiro Kobayashi
Animation Director: Yasuo Otsuka
Director of Photography: Hirokata Takahashi
Color Design: Hiroko Kondo
Film Editing: Masatoshi Tsurubuchi

CAST
Yasuo Yamada – Lupin
Eiko Masuyama – Fujiko Mine
Kiboshi Kobayashi – Daisuke Jogen
Makio Inoue – Goemon
Goro Naya – Inspector Zenigata
Sumi Shimamoto – Clarisse
Taro Ishid – Count Cagliostro

NAUSICAÄ OF THE VALLEY OF THE WIND

Nausicaä of the Valley of the Wind (*Kaze no Tani no Nausicaä,* 1984).
Nibariki/ Tokuma Shoten/ Hakuhodo. 116m.
Japanese release: March 11, 1984. U.S.A. release: June, 1985.

CREW
Written and Directed by Hayao Miyazaki
Co-writer: Kazunori Ito
Production: Tokuma Shoten and Topcraft
Executive Producers: Yasuyoshi Tokuma, Toru Hara (Topcraft) and Michio Kondo
Producer: Isao Takahata
Distributor: Toei Kabushiki Kaisha
Music: Joe Hisaishi
Supervising Animator: Kazuo Komatsubara
Art Director: Mitsauki Nakamura
Character Design: Hayao Miyazaki and Kazuo Komatsubara
Colour Designers: Michiyo Yasuda and Fukuo Suzuki
Sound: Shigeharu Shiba and Kazutoshi Satou
Editing: Naoki Kaneko, Tomoko Kida and Shôji Sakaii
Backgrounds: Mutsuo Koseki

CAST
Sumi Shimamoto – Nausicaä
Gorou Naya – Yupa
Yoshiko Sakakibara – Kushana
Hisako Kyoda – Obaba
Mahito Tsujimura – Jihil
Youji Matsuda – Asbel
Iemasa Kayumi – Kurotawa
Ichirou Nagai – Mito
Kohei Miyauchi – Goru
Mina Tominaga – Rastel
Akiko Tsuboi – Rastel's mother

LAPUTA: CASTLE IN THE SKY

Laputa: Castle In the Sky (*Tenku no Shiro Laputa*, 1986).
Nibariki/ Tokuma Shoten. 124m.
Japanese release: August 2, 1986. U.S.A. release: July, 1987/ April 1, 1989.

CREW
Written and Directed by Hayao Miyazaki
Production: Studio Ghibli and Tokuma Shoten
Distributor: Toei Kabushiki Kaisha
Producer: Isao Takahata
Executive Producer: Yasuysoshi Tokuma
Music: Joe Hisaishi
Art Directors: Toshio Nazaki and Nizo Yamamoto
Character Designers: Hayao Miyazaki and Tsukasa Tannai
Animation Director: Tsukasa Tannai
Animation Supervisor: Tsukasa Niwauchi
Head Key Animator: Yoshinori Kanada
Sound Director: Shigeharu Shiba
Colour Designer: Michiyo Yasuda
DP: Hirokata Takahashi
Editing: Yoshihiro Kasahara, Takeshi Seyama and Miyazaki
Sound Effects and Editing: Kazutoshi Satou
Visual Effects: Gô Abe

CAST
Mayumi Tanaka – Pazu
Keiko Yokozawa – Sheeta
Nou Terada – Dola
Kotoe Hatsui – Uncle Pom

Fujio Tokita – General
Ichiro Nagai – Mentor
Hiroshi Ito – Okami
Machiko Washio – Shalulu
Takumi Kamiyama – Lui

MY NEIGHBOR TOTORO

My Neighbor Totoro (*Tonari no Totoro*, 1988).
Nibariki/ Tokuma Shoten. 86m.
Japanese release: April 16, 1988. U.S.A. release: May 7, 1993.

CREW
Written and Directed by Hayao Miyazaki
Production: Tokuma Shoten, Nibariki and Studio Ghibli
Producers: Yasuyoshi Tokuma and Toru Hara
Music: Joe Hisaishi
Art Director: Kazuo Oga
Character Design: Yoshiharu Sato
Supervising Animator: Yoshiharu Sato
Colour Designer: Nobuko Mizuta
Sound: Shigeharu Shiba and Kazutoshi Satou
Editing: Takeshi Seyama
DP: Hisao Shirai

CAST
Noriko Hidaka – Satsuki
Chika Sakamoto – Mei
Shigesato Itoi – Mr Kusakabe
Sumi Shimamoto – Mrs Kusakabe
Yūko Maruyama – Kanta
Hitoshi Takagi – Totoro

KIKI'S DELIVERY SERVICE

Kiki's Delivery Service (*Majo no Takkyubin*, 1989).
Nibariki/ Tokuma Shoten. 102m.
Japanese release: July 29, 1989. U.S.A. release: May 23, 1998 (video).

CREW
Written and Directed by Hayao Miyazaki
Co-writer: Nobuyuki Isshiki
Original Creator: Eiko Kadono
Producers: Yasuyoshi Tokuma, Toru Hara, Mikihiko Ysuzuki, Morihisa Takagi and Hayao Miyazaki
Production: Studio Ghibli
Production Committee: NTV, Tokuma Shoten, Yamato Transport
Music: Joe Hisaishi
Animation Directors: Shinji Otsuka, Katsuya Kondo and Yoshifumi Kondo
Character Design: Katsuya Kondo
Colour Designers: Michiyo Yasuda and Yuriko Katayama
Production Designer: Hinoshi Ono
Production Manager: Eiko Tanaka
DP: Shigeo Sugimura
Editing: Takeshi Seyama
Sound: Naoko Asari, Kazutoshi Satou and Shuji Inoue

CAST
Minami Takayama – Kiki and Ursula
Rei Sakuma – Jiji
Mieko Nobuzawa – Kiki's mom
Kouichi Miura – Mr Okino, Kiki's dad
Keiko Toda – Mrs Osono
Kappei Yamaguchi – Tombo
Jaruko Kato – Madame
Hiroko Seki – Bertha
Keiko Kagimoto – Birthday Girl

PORCO ROSSO

Porco Rosso (*Kurenai no Buta*, 1992).
Nibariki/ TNNG. 93m.
Japanese release: July 20, 1992. U.S.A. release: October 9, 2003.

CREW
Written and Directed by Hayao Miyazaki
Production: Tokuma Shoten, Japan Airlines, Nippon Television Network and Studio Ghibli
Producer: Toshio Suzuki
Executive Producers: Yasuyoshi Tokuma, Sokai Tokuma, Matsuo Toshimitsu and Yoshio Sasaki
Distributor: Buena Vista Home Entertainment and Toho
Supervising Animators: Megumi Kagawa and Toshio Kawaguchi
Art Director: Yoshitsu Hisamura
Production Designer: Katsu Hisamura
Character Design: Toshio Kawaguchi
Colour Designer: Michiyo Yasuda
DP: Atsushi Okui
Sound: Naoko Asari and Makoto Sumiya
Music: Joe Hisaishi
Editing: Takeshi Seyama, Katsu Hisamura and Hayao Miyazaki

CAST
Shuichiro Moriyama – Porco
Akemi Okamura – Fio
Tokiko Kato – Gina
Tsunehiko Kamijô – Aiuto Gang Boss
Akio Otsuka – Curtis
Sanshi Katsura – Piccolo

PRINCESS MONONOKE

Princess Mononoke (*Mononoke Hime*, 1997).
Nibariki/ TNDG/ Toho. 133m.
Japanese release: July 12, 1997. U.S.A. release: October 7, 1999.

CREW
Written and Directed by Hayao Miyazaki
Chief Executive Producer: Yasuyoshi Tokuma
Executive Producer: Yutaka Narita and Seiichiro Ujiie
Producer: Toshio Suzuki
Associate Producer: Seiji Okuda
Assistant Producer: Takahiro Yonezawa
Music, Music Arranger and Piano Solos: Joe Hisaishi
Cinematography: Atsushi Okui
Editing: Hayao Miyazaki and Takeshi Seyama

Art Direction: Satoshi Kuroda, Kazuo Oga, Yôji Takeshige, Naoya Tanaka and Nizou Yamamoto
Sound Effects: Muchihiro Ito
Sound: Kazuhiro Wakabayashi
Supervising Animators: Masashi Ando, Yoshifumi Kondo and Kitaro Kosaka
Color Designer: Michiyo Yasuda
Music Production: Kazumi Inaki

CAST
Yôji Matsuda – Ashitaka
Yuriko Ishida – San
Yûko Tanaka – Eboshi-gozen
Kaoru Kobayashi – Jiko-bô
Masahiko Nishimura – Kouroku
Tsunehiko Kamijô – Gonza
Sumi Shimamoto – Toki
Tetsu Watanabe – Yama-inu
Mitsuru Satô – Tatari-gami
Akira Nagoya – Usi-kai
Akihiro Miwa – Moro-no-kimi
Mitsuko Mori – Hii-sama
Hisaya Morishige – Okkoto-nusi

SPIRITED AWAY

Spirited Away (*Sen to Chihiro no Kamikakushi*, 2001).
Toho. 125m.
Japanese release: July 20, 2001. U.S.A. release: September 20, 2002.

CREW
Written and Directed by Hayao Miyazaki
Executive Producers: Yasuyoshi Tokuma, John Lasseter
Producers: Toshio Suzuki, Donald W. Ernst
Associate Producer: Lori Korngiebel
Music: Joe Hisaishi
DP: Atsushi Okui
Editing: Takeshi Seyama
Production Design: Norobu Yoshida
Art Direction: Yôji Takeshige
Animation Director: Masashi Ando
Colour Designer: Michiyo Yasuda
Sound Production: Kazumi Inaki, Tamaki Kojo
Sound Effects: Michihiro Ito, Toru Noguchi
Casting Coordinators: Keiko Yagi and Naomi Yasu

CAST
Rumi Hîragi – Chihiro/ Sen
Miyu Irino – Haku
Mari Natsuki – Yubaba/ Zeniba
Takashi Naitô – Chihiro's father
Yasuko Sawaguchi – Chihiro's mother
Tatsuya Gashûin – Aogaeru, Assistant Manager
Ryûnosuke Kamiki – Bô
Yumi Tamai – Rin
Yô Ôizumi – Bandai-gaeru
Koba Hayashi – River God
Tsunehiko Kamijô – Chichiyaku
Takehiko Ono – Aniyaku, foreman
Bunta Sugawara – Kamajî

HOWL'S MOVING CASTLE

Howl's Moving Castle (*Howl no Ugoku Shiro*, 2004).
Toho. 119m.
Japanese release: November 20, 2004. U.S.A. release: June 6, 2005.

CREW
Written and Directed by Hayao Miyazaki
Original Novel: Diana Wynne-Jones
Production: Howl's Moving Castle Production Committee and Studio Ghibli
Production Committee: Buena Vista Home Entertainment, D-Rights, Dentsu Inc., NTV, Toho, Tokuma Shoten
Distributor: Toho
Producers: Toshio Suzuki, Hayao Miyazaki and Yasuyoshi Tokuma
Animation Director: Katsuya Kondo
Supervising Animators: Akihiro Yamashita, Takeshi Inaumura and Kitao Kosaka
Character Design: Akihiko Yamashita
Digital Animation: Mitsunori Katama
Music: Joe Hisaishi
Sound: Kazuhiro Hayashi, Kazuhiro Wakabayashi, Nobue Yoshinaga and Shuji Inoue
Sound Effects: Toru Noguchi
Art Directors: Yoji Takeshige and Noboru Yoshida
DP: Atsushi Okui
Editing: Takeshi Seyama
Production Managers: Ryoichi Fukuyama, Nozomu Takahashi and Hiroyuki Watanabe
Colour Design: Michiyo Yasuda
Casting: Ayumi Sati, Motohiro Hatanaka, Naomi Yasu

CAST
Chieko Baisho – Sophie
Takuya Kimura – Howl
Akihiro Mirva – Witch
Tatsuya Gashûin – Calcifer
Ryunosuka Kamiki – Markl
Akio Otsuka – King of Ingary
Haruko Kato – Madam Suliman
Daijiro Harada – Heen
Yo Oizumi – Prince

PONYO ON THE CLIFF BY THE SEA

Ponyo On the Cliff By the Sea (*Gake no ue no Ponyo*, 2008).
Toho. 101m.
Japanese release: July 19, 2008. U.S.A. release: June 6, 2009.

CREW
Written and directed by Hayao Miyazaki
Executive producers: Koji Hoshino, Seiji Okuda, Miyazaki, Naoya Fujimaki and Ryoichi Fukuyama
Producer: Toshio Suzuki
Distributor: Toho
Production: Studio Ghibli
Production: 'Ponyo on the Cliff' Production Committee
Production Committee: Buena Vista Home Entertainment, D-Rights, Dentsu Inc., Hakuhodo DY Media Partners, NTV and Toho
Music: Joe Hisaishi
DP: Atsushi Okui

Art Director: Noboru Yoshida
Animation Supervisor & Character Design: Katsuya Kondo
Key Animators: Hiromasa Yonebayashi and Atsuko Tanaka
Editing: Takeshi Seyama and Miyazaki
Sound Director: Eriko Kimura

CAST
Yuria Nara – Ponyo
Hiroki Doi – Sosuke
Tomoko Yamaguchi – Lisa
Kazushige Nagashima – Koichi
George Tokoro – Fujimoto
Yuki Amami – Ponyo's mother, a.k.a. grandmother
Kazuko Yoshiyuki - Toki
Emi Hiraoka - Kumiko
Tomoko Naraoka - Yoshie
Akiko Takeguchi - Noriko

THE WIND RISES

The Wind Rises (*Kaze Tachinu,* 2013).
Toho. 126m.
Japanese release: July 20, 2013. U.S.A. release: February 21, 2014.

CREW
Written and Directed by Hayao Miyazaki
Executive producer: Koji Hoshino
Producer: Toshio Suzuki
Associate Producers: Ryoichi Fukuyama, Seiji Okuda and Naoya Fujimaki
Production: Buena Vista Home Entertainment, Dentsu Inc., Hakuhodo DY Media Partners, KDDI, Mitsubishi Corporation, NTV, Studio Ghibli, Toho
Distributor: Toho
Music and Music Director: Joe Hisaishi
Character Design, Key Animator and Animation Director: Kitaro Kousaka
Art Director: Yoji Takeshige
Character Designer: Katsuya Kondo
Director of Photography: Atsushi Okui
Editing: Takeshi Seyama
Audio Director: Koji Kasamatsu
Color Design: Michiyo Yasuda
ADR Director: Eriko Kimura
Special Effects: Keiko Itokawa
Casting: Takashi Hayashi and Takurou Okada

CAST
Hideaki Anno – Jiro Horikoshi
Miori Takimoto – Nahoko Satomi
Hidetoshi Nishijima – Kiro Honjo
Jun Kunimura – Hattori
Keiko Takeshita – Jiro's Mother
Mansai Nomura – Giovanni Battista Caproni
Masahiko Nishimura – Kurokawa
Mirai Shida – Kayo Horikoshi
Morio Kazama – Mr Satomi
Shinobu Otake – Kurokawa's Wife
Stephen Alpert – Hans Castorp

OTHER CREDITS

Hayao Miyazaki has many credits in animation – including as storyboard artist; animator; in-between animator; concept; script; song lyrics; and planning. (For a full list, see the Anime News Network).

The following credits are for direction and script.

DIRECTOR

Lupin III (1971 and 1980)
Future Boy Conan (Conan, the Boy in Future, 1978; inc. movie)
Sherlock Holmes (Great Detective Holmes, 1981; inc. movie)
On Your Mark (1995)
Film Guru Guru (2001)
Whale Hunt (2001)
Koro's Big Day Out (2002)
Imaginary Flying Machines (2002)
Mei and the Kitten Bus (2002)
The Day I Bought a Star (The Day I Harvested a Planet, 2006)
House Hunting (Looking For a Home, 2006)
Mon Mon the Water Spider (2006)
Mr Dough and the Egg Princess (2010)
Treasure Hunting (2011)

SCRIPTS

Panda! Go, Panda! (1972)
Panda! Go, Panda!: Rainy Day Circus (1973)
Whisper of the Heart (1995)
Secret World of Arrietty (The Borrower Arrietty, 2010)
A Sumo Wrestler's Tail (2010)
From Up On Poppy Hill (2011)

BIBLIOGRAPHY

HAYAO MIYAZAKI

"Interview With Hayao Miyazaki ", *A-Club*, 19, June, 1987
The Art of Kiki's Delivery Service, Tokuma, Tokyo, 1989
"Hayao Miyazaki Interview", *Comic Box*, Oct, 1989
"Money Can't Buy Creativity", *Pacific Friend*, 18, 9, Jan, 1991
Nani ga eigaka, with Akira Kurosawa, Tokuma Shoten, 1993
"Now, After *Nausicäa* Has Finished", *YOM* special, June, 1994
Hayao Miyazaki's Daydream Note, Japan, 1997
Points of Departure, 1979-1996, Tokuma Shoten, Tokyo, 1997
"A Modest Proposal", *Manga Max*, 15, February, 2000
"The Purpose of the Film", *Spirited Away*, 2001
Tenku no Shiro Rapyuta, Tokuma Shoten, Japan, 2004
Tonari no Totoro, Tokuma Shoten, Japan, 2004
Shuna no Tabi, Tokuma Shoten, Japan, 2008
Starting Point, 1979-1996, tr. B. Cary & F. Schodt, Viz Media/ Shogakukan, San Francisco, CA, 2009
Interview, in H. Ota, *Chinese Asahi Asia Antenna*, Aug, 2013
Interview, in A. Thomspon, *Thompson On Hollywood*, Feb, 2014
Interview, in R. Collin, *Daily Telegraph*, May 9, 2014
Turning Point, 1997-2008, tr. B. Cary & F. Schodt, Viz Media/ Shogakukan, San Francisco, CA, 2014

HAYAO MIYAZAKI: *MANGA* WORKS

Puss In Boots, 1969
People of the Desert, 1969-1970
Animal Treasure Island, 1972
Nausicäa of the Valley of Wind, 1982-1994 (English version: *Nausicäa of the Valley of the Wind*, tr. D. Lewis & T. Smith, VIZ Media, San Francisco, CA, 2004)
To My Sister, 1982
The Journey of Shuna, 1983
The Age of the Flying Boat, 1990
Daydream Data Notes, 1992
The Return of Hans, 1994
Dining In the Air, 1994
Tigers Covered With Mud, 1998-1999
A Trip To Tynemouth, 2006
The Wind Rises, 2009

OTHERS

G. Adams, ed. *The Cambridge Guide To Children's Books In English*, Cambridge University Press, Cambridge, 2003
S. Adilman. "*Spirited Away* Gets Extra Word", Animation Cafe, 2002

M. Ando. Interview, *Spirited Away*, 2001

S. Ando. "Regaining continuity with the past: *Spirited Away* and *Alice's Adventures in Wonderland*", *Bookbird: A Journal of International Children's Literature*, 46, 1, 2008

The Art of Spirited Away, VIZ Media, 2002

B. Babington *Biblical Epic and Sacred Narrative In the Holly-wood,* Manchester University Press, Manchester, 1993

R. Bator, ed. *Signposts To Criticism of Children's Literature,* American Library Association, Chicago, 1983

J. Beck, ed. *Animation Art*, Flame Tree Publishing, London, 2004

E. Bell *et al*, eds. *From Mouse To Mermaid: The Politics of Film, Gender and Culture*, Indiana University Press, Bloomington, IN, 1995

A. Benciveni. *Miyazaki: Il Dio Dell Animé*, La Mani, Genoa, 2003

I. Bergman. *Bergman On Bergman, Interviews with Ingmar Bergman*, eds. S. Björkman, *et al*, tr. P. B. Austin, Touchstone, New York, NY, 1986

—. *The Magic Lantern: An Autobiography*, London, 1988

S. Bigelow. "Technologies of perception: Miyazaki in theory and practice", *Animation: An Interdisciplinary Journal*, 4, 1, 2009

J. Bittner. *Approaches To the Fiction of Ursula K. Le Guin*, UMI Research Press, Ann Arbor, MI, 1984

D. Bordwell & K. Thompson. *Film Art: An Introduction*, McGraw-Hill Publishing Company, New York, NY, 1979

—. *Narration In the Fiction Film*, Routledge, London, 1988

—. *The Way Hollywood Tells It*, University of California Press, Berkeley, CA, 2006

J. Bower, ed. *The Cinema of Japan and Korea*, Wallflower Press, London, 2004

J. Boyd & T. Nishimura. "Shinto perspectives in Miyazaki's anime film *Spirited Away*", *Journal of Religion and Film*, 8, 2, 2004

M. Broderick. "Spirited Away by Miyazaki's fantasy", *Inter-sections: Gender, History & Culture in the Asian Context*, 9, 2003

P. Brophy, ed. *Kaboom! Explosive Animation From America and Japan*, Museum of Contemporary Art, Sydney, 1994

—. *100 Anime*, British Film Institute, London, 2005

—. ed. *Tezuka*, National Gallery of Victoria, 2006

J. Brosnan. *Future Tense: The Cinema of Science Fiction*, St Martin's Press, New York, NY, 1978

—. *Primal Screen: A History of Science Fiction Film*, Orbit, London, 1991

S. Bukatman. *Terminal Identity: The Virtual Subject In Post-modern Science Fiction*, Duke University Press, Durham, NC, 1993

E. Byrne & M. McQuillan, eds. *Deconstructing Disney*, Pluto Press, London, 1999

B. Camp & J. Davis. *Anime Classics*, Stone Bridge Press, CA, 2007

H. Carpenter. *J.R.R. Tolkien: A Biography*, Allen & Unwin, London, 1977

—. & M. Prichard. *The Oxford Companion To Children's Literature*, Oxford University Press, Oxford, 1984/ 1999

L. Carroll. *Alice's Adventures In Wonderland*, Puffin, London, 1962

D. Cavallaro. *The Animé Art of Hayao Miyazaki*, McFarland, Jefferson, NC, 2006

C. Chatrian & G. Paganelli, *Manga Impact!*, Phaidon, London, 2010

D. Chute. "Organic Machine: The World of Hayao Miyazaki", *Film Comment*, 34, 6, 1998

J. Clarke. *Animated Films*, Virgin, London, 2007

J. Clements & H. McCarthy. *The Animé Encyclopedia*, Stone Bridge Press, Berkeley, CA, 2001/ 2006/ 2015

—. *Schoolgirl Milky Crisis,* Titan Books, London, 2009

Comic Box, Nausicaä special, vol. 98, Oct, 1995

D.A. Cook. *A History of Narrative Film*, W.W. Norton, New York, NY, 1981, 1990, 1996

J.C. Cooper: *Fairy Tales: Allegories of the Inner Life*, Aquarian Press, 1983

R. Denison. "Disembodied stars and the cultural meanings of *Princess Mononoke*'s soundscape", *Scope: An Online Journal of Film Studies*, 3, 2005

—. "Star-spangled Ghibli: Star Voices in the American versions of Hayao Miyazaki's films", *Animation: An International Journal*, 3, 2, 2008

—. 'Global markets for Japanese film: Miyazaki Hayao's *Spirited Away* (2001)", in

A. Phillips, 2007
J. Donald, ed. *Fantasy and the Cinema*, British Film Institute, London, 1989
P. Drazen. *Animé Explosion*, Stone Bridge Press, Berkeley, CA, 2003
—. "Sex and the single pig: Desire and flight in *Porco Rosso*", *Mechademia: Annual Forum For Anime, Manga, and the Fan Arts*, 2, 2007
K. Eisner. "Kiki Delivers the Goods", *Variety*, July 17, 1998
M. Eisner with T. Schwartz. *Work In Progress*, Penguin, London, 1999
Mircea Eliade. *Patterns In Comparative Religion*, Sheed & Ward, 1958
—. *Shamanism: Archaic Techniques of Ecstasy*, Princeton University Press, Princeton, NJ, 1972
—. *A History of Religious Ideas*, I, Collins, London, 1979
—. *Ordeal by Labyrinth*, University of Chicago Press, Chicago, IL, 1984
—. *Symbolism, the Sacred and the Arts*, Crossroad, New York, NY, 1985
M. Eliot. *Walt Disney: Hollywood's Dark Prince: A Biography*, Andre Deutsch, London, 1994
K. Elwood. "A comparative analysis of requests in *Majo no Takkyubin* and *Kiki's Delivery Service*", *The Cultural Review*, 22, 2003
D. Fingeroth. *The Rough Guide To Graphic Novels*, Rough Guides, 2008
M.-L. von Franz: *An Introduction To the Interpretation of Fairy Tales*, Spring Publications, New York, 1970
F. Freiberg. "Tombstone For Fireflies", *Sense of Cinema*, 14, 2001
—. "Miyazaki's heroines", *Sense of Cinema*, 40, 2006
S. Fritz. "Miyazaki Came To America To Talk", Animation Cafe, 1999
L. Goldberg *et al*, eds. *Science Fiction Filmmaking In the 1980s*, McFarland, Jefferson, 1995
J. Goodwin, ed. *Perspectives On Akira Kurosawa*, G.K. Hall, Boston, MA, 1994
D. Gordon. 'Studio Ghibli: Animated magic', *Hackwriters*, 2006
J. Goulding. "Crossroads of experience: Miyazaki Hayao's global/ local nexus", *Asian Cinema*, 17, 2, 2006
P. Gravett. *Manga*, L. King, London, 2004
—. ed. *1001 Comics You Must Read Before You Die*, Cassell, London, 2011
R. Grover. *The Disney Touch*, Business One Irwin, Homewood, Illinois, 1991
P. Hardy, ed. *The Aurum Encyclopedia of Science Fiction*, Aurum, London, 1991
V. Haviland, ed. *Children and Literature: Views and Reviews*, Scott, Foresman, Glenview, IL, 1973
T. Hagiwara. "Globalism and localism in Hayao Miyazaki's anime", *International Journal of the Humanities*, 3, 9, 2005
P. Hunt: *An Introduction To Children's Literature*, Oxford University Press, 1994
—. ed. *Children's Literature: The Development of Criticism*, Routledge, 1990
J. Hunter. *Eros In Hell: Sex, Blood and Madness In Japanese Cinema*, Creation Books, London, 1998
S. Inaga. "Miyazaki Hayao's epic comic series: *Nausicaa of the Valley of the Wind*", *Japan Review*, 11, 1999
R. Johnson. "Kawaii and kirei: Navigating the identities of women in *Laputa: Castle in the Sky* by Hayao Miyazaki and *Ghost in the Shell* by Mamoru Oshii", *Rhizomes: Cultural Studies in Emerging Knowledge*, 14, 2007
S.S. Jones. *The Fairy Tale: The Magic Mirror of Imagination*, Twayne, New York, NY, 1995
B.F. Kawin. *How Movies Work*, Macmillan, New York, NY, 1987
R. Keith. *Japanamerica*, Palgrave Macmillan, London, 2007
M. Kimmich. "Animating the fantastic: Hayao Miyazaki's adaptation of Diana Wynne-Jones's *Howl's Moving Castle*", in L. Strayner & J. Keller, eds., *Fantasy Fiction Into Films*, McFarland, Jefferson, NC, 2007
Sharon Kinsella. *Adult Manga*, University of Hawaii Press, Honolulu, 2002
U.C. Knoepflmacher. *Ventures Into Childhood: Victorian Fairy Tales and Femininity*, University of Chicago Press, Chicago, IL, 1998
C.H. Kraemer. "Between the worlds: Liminality and sacrifice in *Princess Mononoke*", *Journal of Religion and Film*, 8, 1, 2004
J. Kristeva. *Black Sun: Depression and Melancholy*, tr. L.S. Roudiez, Columbia University Press, New York, 1989
—. "A Question of Subjectivity: an interview" [with Susan Sellers], *Women's*

Review, 12, 1986, in Philip Rice & Patricia Waugh, eds. *Modern Literary Theory: A Reader*, Arnold, London, 1992
A. Kuhn, ed. *Alien Zone: Cultural Theory and Contemporary Science Fiction*, Verso, London, 1990
—. ed. *Alien Zone 2*, Verso, London, 1999
A. Kurosawa. *Something Like an Autobiography*, Vintage, New York, N.Y., 1983
M. Lane. "*Princess Mononoke*", *Triumph of the Past*, 2003
—. "White moments and Miyazaki's *Kiki*", *Triumph of the Past*, 2004
C. Lanier. "Spirited Away To the Working World", mag.awn.com, 2002
T. Ledoux & D. Ranney. *The Complete Animé Guide*, Tiger Mountain Press, Washington, DC, 1997
—. ed. *Anime Interviews*, Cadence Books, San Francisco, CA, 1997
T. Lehmann. *Manga: Masters of the Art*, HarperCollins, London, 2005
U. Le Guin. *The Earthsea Trilogy*, Penguin, 1979
—. *Tehanu*, Penguin, 1992
—. *The Other Wind*, Orion, London, 2001
—. *Tales From Earthsea*, Orion, London, 2001
A. Levi. *Samurai From Outer Space: Understanding Japanese Animation*, Open Court, Chicago, IL, 1996
D. Loy & L. Goodhew, L. (2004). "The Dharma of nonviolence - Hayao Miyazaki's *Nausicaa of the Valley of the Winds* and *Princess Mononoke*", in *The Dharma of Dragons and Daemons: Buddhist Themes in Modern Fantasy*, Wisdom Publications, Somerville, MA, 2004
M. Lüthi: *Once Upon a Time: On the Nature of Fairy Tales*, Indiana University Press, Bloomington, 1976
—. *The Fairy Tale as Art Form and Portrait of Man*, tr. John Erickson, University of Indiana Press, Bloomington, 1985
P. Macias. *The Japanese Cult Film Companion*, Cadence Books, San Francisco, CA, 2001
—. & T. Machiyama. *Cruising the Anime City*, Stonebridge Press, CA, 2004
M. MacWilliams, ed. *Japanese Visual Culture: Explorations In the World of Manga and Anime,* M.E. Sharpe, Armonk, NY, 2008
L. Maltin. *Of Mice and Magic: A History of American Animated Cartoons*, New American Library, New York, NY, 1987
—. *The Disney Films*, 3rd ed., Hyperion, New York, NY, 1995
C. Manlove. *Modern Fantasy*, Cambridge University Press, Cambridge, 1975
—. *From Alice To Harry Potter: Children's Fantasy In England: Children's Fantasy In England*, Cybereditions Corporation, 2003
A. Masano & J. Wiedermann, eds. *Manga Design*, Taschen, 2004
G. Mast *et al*, eds. *Film Theory and Criticism: Introductory Readings*, Oxford University Press, New York, NY, 1992a
—. & B Kawin, *A Short History of the Movies*, Macmillan, New York, NY, 1992b
K. Matthew. "Logic and narrative in *Spirited Away*", *Screen Education*, 43, 2006
K. Mayumi *et al.* "The ecological and consumption themes of the films of Hayao Miyazaki", *Ecological Economics*, 54, 1, 2005
H. McCarthy. *Anime! A Beginner's Guide To Japanese Anima-tion*, Titan, 1993
—. *The Animé Movie Guide*, Titan Books, London, 1996
—. & J. Clements. *The Erotic Animé Movie Guide*, Titan Books, London, 1998
—. "The House That Hayao Built", *Manga Max*, Apl 5, 1999
—. *Hayao Miyazaki: Master of Japanese Animation*, Stone Bridge Press, Berkeley, CA, 2002
—. *500 Manga Heroes & Villains*, Barron's, Hauppauge, New York, 2006
—. *500 Essential Anime Movies*, Collins Design, New York, NY, 2008
S. McCloud. *Understanding Comics*, Harper, London, 1994
—. *Reinventing Comics,* Harper, London, 2000
—. *Making Comics*, Harper, London, 2006
K. McDonald. "Animation seminal and influential: Hayao Miyazaki's *My Neighbor Totoro*", in *Reading a Japanese Film: Cinema in Context*, University of Hawaii Press, Honolulu, 2005
K. Moist & M. Barthalow. "When pigs fly: Anime, auteurism, and Miyazaki's *Porco Rosso*", *Animation: An Inter-disciplinary Journal*, 2, 1, 2007

T. Momma. "Miyazaki Hayao and Japanese animation", *Journal of Japanese Trade and Industry*, 2002

J. Morgan. "Flying with Miyazaki: Flight as a metaphor for power in *Spirited Away*", *Animatrix Magazine*, 12, 2003

A. Morton. *The Complete Directory To Science Fiction, Fantasy and Horror Television Series*, Other Worlds, 1997

S. Napier. "*Mononoke hime*: A Japanese phenomenon goes global", *Persimmon: Asian Literature, Arts, and Culture*, 1, 2000

—. *Anime: From Akira To Princess Mononoke*, Palgrave, New York, 2001

—. "Matter out of place: Carnival, containment, and cultural recovery in Miyazaki's *Spirited Away*", *The Journal of Asian Studies*, 32, 2, 2006

—. "Interviewing Hayao Miyazaki", *Huffington Post*, Jan, 2014

S. Neale & M. Smith, eds. *Contemporary Hollywood Cinema*, Routledge, London, 1998

E. Niskanen. "Untouched nature: Mediated animals in Japanese anime", *Wider Screen*, 2007

P. Nodelman: *Words About Pictures: The Narrative Art of Children's Picture Books*, University of Georgia Press, Athens, GA, 1988

C. Odell & M. Le Blanc. *Studio Ghibli: The Films of Hayao Miyazaki and Isao Takahata*, Kamera Books, London, 2009

R. Okuhara. "Walking along with nature: A psychological interpretation of *My Neighbor Totoro*", *The Looking Glass: An On-Line Children's Literature Journal*, 10, 2, 2006

I. & P. Opie: *The Classic Fairy Tales*, Paladin, 1980

T. Oshiguchi. "The Whimsy and Wonder of Hayao Miyazaki', *Animerica*, 1, 5 & 6, July, 1993

A. Osmond. "*Nausicaä* and the Fantasy of Hayao Miyazaki", *SF Journal Foundation*, 73, Spring, 1998

—. "Hayao Miyazaki", *Cinescape*, 72, 1999

—. "Will the Real Joe Hisaishi Please Stand Up?", *Animation World Magazine*, 5.01, April, 2000

—. "The Animerica Interview: Hayao Miyazaki", *Animerica*, 10, 12, Dec, 2002

— *Spirited Away*, British Film Institute, London, 2003a

—. "Gods and Monsters", *Sight & Sound*, Sept, 2003b

—. "Castles in the Sky", *Sight and Sound*, 15, 10, 2005

C. Ota. "Liminal gazes and allegorical quests: Anime of Hayao Miyazaki", in *The Relay of Gazes: Representations of Culture in the Japanese Televisual and Cinematic Experience*, Rowman & Littlefield, Lanham, MD, 2007

E. Otsuka *et al. Emu no Sedai: Bokura To Miyazaki-kun*, Ota Shuppan, Tokyo, 1989

F. Patten. *Watching Anime, Reading Manga*, Stone Bridge Press, CA, 2004

D. Peary & G. Peary, eds. *The American Animated Cartoon*, Dutton, New York, NY, 1980

A. Phillips & J. Stringer, eds. *Japanese Cinema: Texts and Contexts*, Routledge, London, 2007

C. Platt. *Dreammakers: Science Fiction and Fantasy Writers At Work*, Xanadu, 1987

G. Poitras. *The Animé Companion*, Stone Bridge Press, Berk-eley, CA, 1999

—. *Animé Essentials*, Stone Bridge Press, Berkeley, CA, 2001

M. Prunes. "Having it both ways: Making children's films an adult matter in Miyazaki's *My Neighbor Totoro*", *Asian Cinema*, 14,1, 2003

M. Punch. *Lupin III*, vol. 13, Tokyopop, Los Angeles, CA, 2004

K. Quigley. *Comics Underground Japan*, Blast Books, New Yorkı, NY, 1996

E. Rabkin & G. Slusser, eds. *Shadows of the Magic Lamp: Fantasy and Science Fiction In Film*, Southern Illinois University Press, Carbondale, IL, 1985

T. Reider. "*Spirited Away*", *Film Criticism*, 29, 3, Mch, 2005

D. Richie. *The Films of Akira Kurosawa*, University of Cali-fornia Press, Berkeley, CA, 1965

S. Richmond. *The Rough Guide To Anime*, Rough Guides, 2009

C. Rowthorn. *Japan*, Lonely Planet, 2007

B. Ruh. *Stray Dog of Anime*, Macmillan, 2004

K. Sandler. *Reading the Rabbit: Explorations In Warner Bros. Animation*, Rutgers University Press, Brunswick, NJ, 1998
R. Schickel. *The Disney Version: The Life, Times, Art, and Commerce of Walt Disney*, Pavilion, London, 1986
M. Schilling. "The Red Pig Flies To the Rescue", *Japan Times*, July 28, 1992
—. "Miyazaki Hayao and Studio Ghibli", *Japan Quarterly*, 44, 1, 1997
—. *Contemporary Japanese Film*, Weatherhill, New York, NY, 1999
—. "Majesty of 2-D", *Japan Times*, Nov 24, 2004
F. Schodt. *Inside the Robot Kingdom: Japan, Mechatronics and the Coming Robotopia*, Kodansha, Tokyo, 1988
—. *Manga! Manga! The World of Japanese Magazines*, Kodansha International, London, 1997
—. *Dreamland Japan: Writings On Modern Manga*, Stone Bridge Press, Berkeley, CA, 2002
—. *The Astro Boy Essays*, Stone Bridge Press, CA, 2007
J. Seward, ed. *Japanese Eroticism: A Language Guide To Current Comics*, Yugen Press, Houston, TX, 1993
T. Shippey. *J.R.R. Tolkien: Author of the Century*, Harper-Collins, London, 2000
C. Shiratori, ed. *Secret Comics Japan*, Cadence Books, San Francisco, CA, 2000
G. Slusser. *The Farthest Shore of Ursula K. Le Guin*, Borgo Press, San Bernardino, CA, 1976
E. Smoodin. *Animating Culture: Hollywood Cartoons From the Sound Era*, Roundhouse, 1993
—. ed. *Disney Discourse: Producing the Magic Kingdom*, Routledge, London, 1994
V. Sobchack. *Screening Space: The American Science Fiction Film*, Ungar, New York, NY, 1987/ 1993
Spirited Away Roman Album, Tokuma Shoten, Tokyo, 2001
A. Stibbe. "Zen and the art of environmental education in the Japanese animated film *Tonari no Totoro*", *Journal For the Study of Religion, Nature and Culture*, 1, 4 2007
M. Stokrocki & M. Delahunt. "Empowering elementary students' ecological thinking through discussing the animé *Nausicaa* and constructing super bugs", *Journal for Learning Through the Arts*, 4, 1, 2008
Rosemary Sutcliffe. *The Mark of the Horse Lord*, 1965
A. Suzuki. "A nightmare of capitalist Japan: *Spirited Away*", *Jump Cut*, 51, 2009
T. Suzuki. *Work As Entertainment*, Iwanami Shoten
—. *The Ghibli Philosophy*, Iwanami Shoten
I. Takahata. "Interview", *Grave of the Fireflies*, DVD, 2004
—. "The Fireworks of Eros", in H. Miyazaki, 2009
M. Tatar. *The Hard Facts of the Grimms' Fairy Tales*, Princeton University Press, Princeton, NJ, 1987
—. *Off With Their Heads: Fairy Tales and the Culture of Child-hood*, Princeton University Press, Princeton, NJ, 1992
S. Thill. "The wizard of awe: Hayao Miyazaki's *Spirited Away*", *Bright Lights Film Journal*, 38, 2002
J. Thomas: *Inside the Wolf's Belly: Aspects of the Fairy Tale*, Sheffield Academic Press, 1989
J.B. Thomas. "Shukyo asobi and Miyazaki Hayao's anime", *Nova Religio: The Journal of Alternative and Emergent Religions*, 10, 3, 2007
J. Thompson. *Manga: The Complete Guide*, Del Rey, New York, NY, 2007
K. Thompson & D. Bordwell. *Film History: An Introduction*, McGraw-Hill, New York, NY, 1994
—. *Storytelling In the New Hollywood*, Harvard University Press, Cambridge, MA, 1999
J.R.R. Tolkien. *The Letters of J.R.R. Tolkien*, ed. H. Carpenter & C. Tolkien, Allen & Unwin, London, 1981/ 1999
—. *The Monster and the Critics and Other Essays*, ed. C. Tolkien, Allen & Unwin, London, 1983
J. Tucker. "Anime and historical inversion in Miyazaki Hayao's *Spirited Away*", *Japan Studies Review*, 7, 2003

V. Watson, ed. *The Cambridge Guide To Children's Books in English*, Cambridge University Press, Cambridge, 2001

P. Wells. *Understanding Animation*, Routledge, London, 1998

M. West, ed. *The Japanification of Children's Popular Culture: From Godzilla to Miyazaki*, Scarecrow Press, Lanham, 2009

J. Whalley & T.R. Chester: *A History of Children's Book Illumi-nation*, John Murray, 1988

C. Winstanley, ed. *SFX Collection: Animé Special*, Future Publishing, London

I. Wojcik-Andrews, ed. *The Lion and the Unicorn, Children's Films* issue, 20, 1, June, 1996

C. Wood. "The European fantasy space and identity con-struction in *Porco Rosso*", *Post Script: Essays in Film and the Humanities*, 28, 2, 2009

L. Wright & J. Clode. "The animated worlds of Hayao Miyazaki: Filmic representations of Shinto", *Metro: Australia's Film & Media Magazine*, 143, 2005

—. "Forest spirits, giant insects and world trees: The nature vision of Hayao Miyazaki", *Journal of Religion and Popular Culture*, 2005

—. "Wonderment and awe - the way of the kami", *Refractory: A Journal of Entertainment Media*, 5, 2004

J. Yadao. *The Rough Guide To Manga*, Rough Guides, 2008

M. Yokota. "A psychological meaning of creatures in Hayao Miyazaki's feature animations", *Japanese Journal of Animation Studies*, 1, 1A, 1999

S. Yoshioka. "Heart of Japaneseness: History and Nostalgia in Hayao Miyazaki's *Spirited Away*", in M. MacWilliams, 2008

J. Zipes. *Breaking the Spell: Radical Theories of Folk and Fairy Tales*, Heinemann, London, 1978

—. *Fairy Tales and the Art of Subversion: The Classical Genre for Children and the Process of Civilization*, Heinemann, London, 1983

—. *Don't Bet On the Prince: Contemporary Feminist Fairy Tales In North America and England*, Methuen, New York, NY, 1986

—. *The Brothers Grimm: From Enchanted Forests To the Modern World*, Routledge, New York, NY, 1989

—. ed. *The Oxford Companion To Fairy Tales*, Oxford University Press, 2002a

—. *Breaking the Spell: Radical Theories of Folk and Fairy Tales*, University of Kentucky Press, Lexington, 2002b

—. *Sticks and Stones: The Troublesome Success of Children's Literature from Slovenly Peter To Harry Potter*, Routledge, London, 2002c

—. *The Enchanted Screen: The Unknown History of Fairy-tale Films*, Routledge, New York, NY, 2011

—. *The Irresistible Fairy Tale*, Princeton University Press, Princeton, NJ, 2012

Jeremy Robinson has written many critical studies, including *Hayao Miyazaki, Walerian Borowczyk, Arthur Rimbaud,* and *The Sacred Cinema of Andrei Tarkovsky,* plus literary monographs on: William Shakespeare; Samuel Beckett; Thomas Hardy; André Gide; Robert Graves; and John Cowper Powys.

It's amazing for me to see my work treated with such passion and respect. There is nothing resembling it in the U.S. in relation to my work.
Andrea Dworkin (on *Andrea Dworkin*)

This model monograph – it is an exemplary job, and I'm very proud that he has accorded me a couple of mentions... The subject matter of his book is beautifully organised and dead on beam.
Lawrence Durrell (on *The Light Eternal: A Study of J.M.W. Turner*)

Jeremy Robinson's poetry is certainly jammed with ideas, and I find it very interesting for that reason. It's certainly a strong imprint of his personality.
Colin Wilson

Sex-Magic-Poetry-Cornwall is a very rich essay... It is a very good piece... vastly stimulating and insightful.
Peter Redgrove

ARTS, PAINTING, SCULPTURE

web: www.crmoon.com • e-mail: cresmopub@yahoo.co.uk

The Art of Andy Goldsworthy
Andy Goldsworthy: Touching Nature
Andy Goldsworthy in Close-Up
Andy Goldsworthy: Pocket Guide
Andy Goldsworthy In America
Land Art: A Complete Guide
The Art of Richard Long
Richard Long: Pocket Guide
Land Art In Great Britain
Land Art in Close-Up
Land Art In the U.S.A.
Land Art: Pocket Guide
Installation Art in Close-Up
Minimal Art and Artists In the 1960s and After
Colourfield Painting
Land Art DVD, TV documentary
Andy Goldsworthy DVD, TV documentary
The Erotic Object: Sexuality in Sculpture From Prehistory to the Present Day
Sex in Art: Pornography and Pleasure in Painting and Sculpture
Postwar Art
Sacred Gardens: The Garden in Myth, Religion and Art
Glorification: Religious Abstraction in Renaissance and 20th Century Art
Early Netherlandish Painting
Jasper Johns
Brice MardenLeonardo da Vinci
Piero della Francesca
Giovanni Bellini
Fra Angelico: Art and Religion in the Renaissance
Mark Rothko: The Art of Transcendence
Frank Stella: American Abstract Artist
Alison Wilding: The Embrace of Sculpture
Vincent van Gogh: Visionary Landscapes
Eric Gill: Nuptials of God
Constantin Brancusi: Sculpting the Essence of Things
Max Beckmann
Gustave Moreau
Caravaggio
Egon Schiele: Sex and Death In Purple Stockings
Delizioso Fotografico Fervore: Works In Process 1
Sacro Cuore: Works In Process 2
The Light Eternal: J.M.W. Turner
The Madonna Glorified: Karen Arthurs

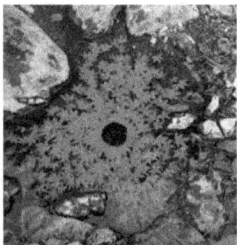

LITERATURE

J.R.R. Tolkien: The Books, The Films, The Whole Cultural Phenomenon
J.R.R. Tolkien: Pocket Guide
Beauties, Beasts and Enchantment: Classic French Fairy Tales
Tolkien's Heroic Quest
Brothers Grimm: German Popular Stories
Sexing Hardy: Thomas Hardy and Feminism
Thomas Hardy's *Tess of the d'Urbervilles*
Thomas Hardy's *Jude the Obscure*
Thomas Hardy: The Tragic Novels
Love and Tragedy: Thomas Hardy
The Poetry of Landscape in Hardy
Wessex Revisited: Thomas Hardy and John Cowper Powys
Wolfgang Iser: Essays and Interviews
Petrarch, Dante and the Troubadours
Maurice Sendak and the Art of Children's Book Illustration
Andrea Dworkin
Cixous, Irigaray, Kristeva: The *Jouissance* of French Feminism
Julia Kristeva: Art, Love, Melancholy, Philosophy, Semiotics and Psychoanalysis
Hélene Cixous I Love You: The *Jouissance* of Writing
Luce Irigaray: Lips, Kissing, and the Politics of Sexual Difference
Peter Redgrove: Here Comes the Flood
Peter Redgrove: Sex-Magic-Poetry-Cornwall
Lawrence Durrell: Between Love and Death, East and West
Love, Culture & Poetry: Lawrence Durrell
Cavafy: Anatomy of a Soul
German Romantic Poetry: Goethe, Novalis, Heine, Hölderlin
Novalis: *Hymns To the Night*
Feminism and Shakespeare
Shakespeare: *The Sonnets*
Shakespeare: Love, Poetry & Magic
The Passion of D.H. Lawrence
D.H. Lawrence: Symbolic Landscapes
D.H. Lawrence: Infinite Sensual Violence
The Ecstasies of John Cowper Powys
Sensualism and Mythology: The Wessex Novels of John Cowper Powys
Amorous Life: John Cowper Powys (H.W. Fawkner)
Postmodern Powys: New Essays on John Cowper Powys (Joe Boulter)
Rethinking Powys: Critical Essays on John Cowper Powys
Paul Bowles & Bernardo Bertolucci
Rainer Maria Rilke
Joseph Conrad: *Heart of Darkness*
In the Dim Void: Samuel Beckett
Samuel Beckett Goes into the Silence
André Gide: Fiction and Fervour
Jackie Collins and the Blockbuster Novel
Blinded By Her Light: The Love-Poetry of Robert Graves

MEDIA, CINEMA, FEMINISM and CULTURAL STUDIES

J.R.R. Tolkien: The Books, The Films, The Whole Cultural Phenomenon
J.R.R. Tolkien: Pocket Guide
The *Lord of the Rings* Movies: Pocket Guide
The Ghost Dance: The Origins of Religion
The Cinema of Hayao Miyazaki
Hayao Miyazaki: *Princess Mononoke*: Pocket Movie Guide
Hayao Miyazaki: *Spirited Away*: Pocket Movie Guide
The Peyote Cult
HomeGround: The Kate Bush Anthology
Tim Burton : Hallowe'en For Hollywood
Ken Russell
Cixous, Irigaray, Kristeva: The *Jouissance* of French Feminism
Julia Kristeva: Art, Love, Melancholy, Philosophy, Semiotics and Psychoanalysis
Luce Irigaray: Lips, Kissing, and the Politics of Sexual Difference
Hélene Cixous I Love You: The *Jouissance* of Writing
Andrea Dworkin
'Cosmo Woman': The World of Women's Magazines
Women in Pop Music
Discovering the Goddess (Geoffrey Ashe)
The Poetry of Cinema
The Sacred Cinema of Andrei Tarkovsky
Andrei Tarkovsky: Pocket Guide
Andrei Tarkovsky: *Mirror*: Pocket Movie Guide
Walerian Borowczyk: Cinema of Erotic Dreams
Jean-Luc Godard: The Passion of Cinema
Jean-Luc Godard: Pocket Guide
John Hughes and Eighties Cinema
Ferris Buller's Day Off: Pocket Movie Guide
The Cinema of Richard Linklater
Liv Tyler: Star In Ascendance
Blade Runner and the Films of Philip K. Dick
Paul Bowles and Bernardo Bertolucci
Media Hell: Radio, TV and the Press
Detonation Britain: Nuclear War in the UK
Feminism and Shakespeare
Wild Zones: Pornography, Art and Feminism
Sex in Art: Pornography and Pleasure in Painting and Sculpture
Sexing Hardy: Thomas Hardy and Feminism

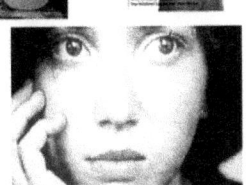

The Light Eternal is a model monograph, an exemplary job. The subject matter of the book is beautifully organised and dead on beam. (Lawrence Durrell)
It is amazing for me to see my work treated with such passion and respect. (Andrea Dworkin)
Sex-Magic-Poetry-Cornwall is a very rich essay... It is like a brightly-lighted box. (Peter Redgrove)

CRESCENT MOON PUBLISHING P.O. Box 1312, Maidstone, Kent, ME14 5XU, Great Britain
0044-1622-729593   cresmopub@yahoo.co.uk   www.crmoon.com

www.ingramcontent.com/pod-product-compliance
Lightning Source LLC
Chambersburg PA
CBHW071656170426
43195CB00039B/2205